*To my mother, who would have taken issue with much of what
I've written, but nonetheless would have been proud of me. I hope
the future includes virtues that transcend partisanship.*

SUBORDINATING AMERICAN DEMOCRACY

EXPLORING THE FUNCTIONALITY OF
"DYSFUNCTIONAL" HYPERPARTISANSHIP

Robert L. Foster

GLENWOOD LANDING, NEW YORK

BEAUTIFUL HYBRID
PUBLICATIONS

Contents

List of Illustrations

Without change, something sleeps inside us, and seldom awakens. The sleeper must awaken.

—FRANK HERBERT, *Dune*

Preface

I was certain of my thesis. It was all about money, until it wasn't. Transformations ensued. Natural consequences of transposing abstract representations within the brain to formal written language, I supposed.

It was more than that. My thesis changed. Articulating arguments revealed flaws, but also illuminated alternative analytical frameworks, leading to promising lines of reasoning.

But it was much more than that. The most relevant transformations concerned the dynamic relationship between my comprehension of the subject matter and *me*. The more I struggled to grasp the essence of hyperpartisanship, the more conscious I became of my personal connection. I was implicated. I caught glimpses of my culpability.

Initially, I analyzed the phenomenon distinct from myself like a dispassionate scientist dissecting a chrysalis. But the process proved such distinctions insincere. I'm integrated with the subject matter. My self-awareness evolved with my appreciation of hyperpartisanship. Eventually, I understood that to adequately answer the question of how *we* got here, I had to examine how *I* got here. Why in hell am I interested enough in hyperpartisanship to author a book about it?

Activist

I worked for a nonpartisan, not-for-profit, New York State environmental advocacy organization from 1992 to 2004. We did grassroots organizing, media outreach, worked with various community groups, and lobbied at the local, state, and federal levels. At various times, I performed each of those duties.

For media outreach, I would send press releases to every outlet in New York State, but my follow-up calls were to environmental reporters at the *New York Times*, local papers, local cable news, local TV network reporters, and local NPR correspondents. I never called CNN, Fox News, or MSNBC. I was aware of them, but since they were not outreach targets, I didn't pay them much attention. At that time, strictly electronic outlets—if they even existed—weren't targeted.

Most of the lobbying was in Albany, New York, where I lived from 1999 to 2008. I also flew to Washington, D.C., several times a year to meet with federal representatives from New York, sometimes by myself and sometimes as part of coalitions including other environmental organizations.

I was in the game. I met with insiders from all sides who understood it for what it was and laid bare its works to enhance efficacy. I was a sponge.

It was also a time of political correctness and a fair amount of sanctimony. I attended annual conferences convened by grassroots not-for-profits from around the country. Most were environmental, but organizations advocating on issues such as single-payer health care also participated. All represented themselves as nonpartisan.

Portent

At one of these conferences in the mid-1990s, a Democratic pollster addressed the congregation. She spoke to us as if we were all on the same team. Assuming support is a time-honored sales tactic. Although I was a registered Democrat, attendees included Republicans. I wondered how they felt. No equivalent Republican spoke. At that time, moderate or "Green" Republicans existed, not only at that conference and in the general population, but in Congress as well.

She spoke of how well environmental issues polled. This was before climate change consumed the entire environmental platter. An overwhelming majority of Americans supported cleaner air, cleaner water, and the like. Issues such as single-payer health care did not poll nearly as well.

Imagine we were all on the same team. This was the pitch. We were being worked, and I didn't like it. I felt manipulated. It was an aggressive courting mixed with subtle notes of partisan indoctrination. Being an environmentalist wasn't good enough. We were being asked to adopt the entire progressive portfolio, and we had to be in it together . . . as Democrats.

Let's take a more clinical approach. Environmental issues garnered support that transcended partisan delineation. Democrats *and* Republicans supported policies to protect air, water, and land. Other issues within the progressive portfolio didn't enjoy such popularity. Democrats achieving exclusive dominion over environmental issues would be quite the coup.

But victory delivers collateral consequences, exclusivity is divisive, and relationships are dynamic. In the grand scheme, it was "too clever by half."

Partisan Politics versus Nonpartisan Issue Advocacy

While this anecdote raises questions, its immediate significance is a data point in the continuum of my experiences inciting me to contemplate the relationship between partisan politics and nonpartisan issue advocacy. I think of it now, and describe it later, as subordinating environmental issues to partisan electoral strategy. At the time, it just rubbed me the wrong way.

It's also significant because it occurred approximately thirty years ago as I write this sentence. It was before W., before Obama, and long before Trump.

Construction Worker

In 2004, I changed course and took a laborer job for a general contractor to pay rent. I was the lowest-ranking person. I lugged materials to skilled workers for their constructions.

During my first month, I used a sledgehammer to deconstruct a brick wall. As I aggressively pushed a wheelbarrow full of bricks across the job site to a scrap pile, the wheelbarrow abruptly stuck in a rut, and a handle jabbed my ribcage. I labored in pain for months without missing a day.

Although my experiences on the job inspire me to imagine constructing a dream house from foundation to finish, the takeaway is humility. I'll explore the relevance of humility deeper in.

In autumn 2007, I found myself crouched in a four-foot-high basement/ crawlspace as my boss tried to pass me a wire through an alleged hole in the floor above me. He blew a gasket, as he was prone to do, at his failed attempts—or rather at my failure to perceive my end of the wire. I was too old for this shit. At day's end, I told him so. I agreed to stay on until he found a replacement, but in January 2008, I was unemployed.

Bystander

It's tempting to write off the next chapter of my life as inconsequential, and before authoring this book, I would have. But what in isolation seems unremarkable proves most relevant when contextualized in retrospect. I discovered national cable news. For the first time, I regularly watched CNN, Fox News, and MSNBC.

Initially, I may have been compensating for being out of the game. I watched from the sidelines with the yearning of a has-been. It was addictive. Among the intoxicants getting me through the day was partisan "news" programming. Writing this book has led me to understand it as addiction, and examining the underpinnings of that addiction is essential to understanding hyperpartisanship.

Also, around this time, I became aware of presidential candidate Barack Obama. His message of unity resonated. He seemed less partisan than other candidates. He became my candidate.

I volunteered to go door-to-door in Rutland for the Vermont primary. I submitted my résumé for a paid position with his campaign. Lessons in humility in the form of rejection present with a frequency that suggests immunity from the law of diminishing returns.

Before moving to the next chapter, I call attention to an apparent paradox: while my addiction to cable news was clearly a function of my partisanship, candidate Obama appealed to my nonpartisan disposition. My proclivities aren't pure; I'm a hybrid. I'm not troubled by this.

I didn't intend to reveal my partisan inclinations. I was concerned I would turn off potential readers whose established politics were discordant with my own.

But as I said, I'm integrated with the subject matter. So, for purely scholarly reasons, I describe my variety of nonpartisanship thus:

I revile both parties. While my revulsion for one party might be slightly deeper than my revulsion for the other, my revulsion for the two-party system, for the concept of political parties, and for hyperpartisanship is deeper than my revulsion for any single party.

Law Student

After abundant opportunities to reinforce humility by failing to secure desired employment, I concluded my résumé needed a makeover. I started law school in August 2013 and graduated in May 2016. Here, I consider a material concept and relevant project from that experience.

The material concept concerns substance versus process. When I began law school, I was all about substance. I wanted to know substantive law. I hated my first semester of civil procedure. I couldn't have cared less about submission timelines for responses to complaints. I was interested in constitutional law.

I came to realize constitutional law is procedure. Ultimately, the degree of fidelity to constitutionally guaranteed procedures appraises our democracy.

As part of Law Review, we wrote and submitted our own articles, and the one considered best would be published. It was my first attempt at formalizing the topic that would evolve into this work. My "Topic Statement" was: *The Relationship between Unlimited Political Spending, Hyper-Partisanship and Congressional Dysfunction*. I titled my first draft *Hyper-Partisan Incentives within the Political Industrial Complex*. It was all about money.

Even narrowing the topic to legalities surrounding political spending proved too unwieldy for a thirty-page article. Another lesson in humility learned. I also began to understand that the legal aspects of hyperpartisanship weren't what interested me most. Something else was going on. It was personal.

Repurpose

My father passed away in 2009, and my mother passed shortly after I graduated law school. During the following year, I stayed in the home that had been in my mother's family since the early twentieth century to prepare it for sale and settle the estate. My father was a hoarder, and sorting accumulated stuff into appropriate categories of finality was a job. Some I kept and distributed to family; some was sold; some was donated; and some was recycled. The biggest portion ended in a dumpster.

I spent my days sorting, cleaning, and dealing with estate logistics. It was mostly routine, but occasionally I would come across a box of old clothes with a tee shirt I had worn as a teenager that my father had saved. The flood of memories coupled with a psychology of acceptance would temporarily bring my world to a standstill.

I spent my evenings in a miasma of intoxicants including national cable news. I gained fifty pounds in a year. A look in the mirror and vanity precipitated sobriety.

In that eclectic brew of settling the past and considering the future while circumventing impediments of my own making, the idea of turning my law review topic into a book first occurred to me. I had dreamed of writing a book since I was an undergraduate. If not now, when?

Author

I opened a file and made bullet points of my brilliant ideas. I branded my cable news addiction as research. I had a long way to go.

I struggled for years and gave up several times. Perhaps an unconscious defense mechanism segregated thematic content from personal evolution. Not until I appreciated how fully integrated I was with hyperpartisanship did barriers to accomplishing my task dissipate. However, that awareness didn't emerge through introspection.

I considered how our politics became polarized to the point of dysfunction. I could rewrite that sentence to read: I wondered how our politics *evolved* to the point of dysfunction. Yet more than a year's worth of bullet points accumulated before any form of the word "evolution" occurred to me. When it finally did, it was like a lightning bolt. Consciousness of the concept of evolution juxtaposed with hyperpartisanship reordered the subject matter in my mind.

It's strange how I could contemplate the gradual development of a phenomenon without realizing I was examining an evolutionary process. Stranger still that I could contemplate the process of evolution without epiphany, and yet when the word defined by the process in which I was entangled broke the surface of my consciousness, I evolved. An intricate set of tumblers within a complex lock and safe fell into place to reveal an auspicious analytical framework.

Evolution and ecology occupy two sides of the same coin. The interconnectedness of our ecology fashions selective pressures provoking adaptation.

In contemplation of interconnectivity, I came to appreciate hyperpartisanship as a highly adaptive phenomenon that transcends politics, and I'm a relevant part of the ecosystem that enables it to bloom to the point where it menaces our democratic republic. This book results from an examination of my relationship to American politics and its instrumentalities, such as national cable news.

My partisan inclinations are hybrid. My perspective is bifurcated. I've played the game and watched from the sidelines. Reconciling or integrating those unique vantages provided the creative impetus for this endeavor.

So, I begin anew, with less certainty but greater clarity.

Introduction

Are combatants joined in battle competent to analyze the cause and perpetuation of their conflict? Imagine two cold warriors locked in a death match—something out of James Bond. Hit pause, and ask, "Why do you fight?" "Because your hatred for one another runs so deep?" "Because your faith in the cause is authentic?" "Because love for your side is all-consuming?" "Because it's your job?"

If one were silly or brave enough to ask a mercenary how to end a war he was being paid to wage and he was inclined toward candor, his answer could be quite simple: "Stop paying me."

Premise

We are in *hyperpartisan* times. Most people accept the premise. Nevertheless, I will briefly explain and provide a rationale for it.

Resistance to the premise is predicated on the statement: "We've always been divided." This is exactly right—and completely misses the point.

Hyperpartisanship is not political or partisan division. Hyperpartisanship concerns the impacts of our partisan affiliations or divisions. Without being exhaustive, and for the sole purpose of lending credence to the premise, I briefly examine two aspects of hyperpartisanship.

First, it concerns the process, not the substance, of our disagreements. As the resistance properly noted, we've always been divided, and I expect that trend to continue. Hyperpartisanship corrupts the process of either managing or resolving disagreement.

Freedom and democracy *necessitate* substantive disagreement. Progressive dialectics require contradiction. Unanimity of thought, vision, ideals, and aspirations terminates the dialectic.

Hyperpartisanship subverts dialogue or process, rendering our diversity impotent at best. Hyperpartisanship interferes with our ability to understand our differences as assets, thereby undermining the utility of diversity.

Second, hyperpartisanship both disturbs and results from the disturbance or imbalance in the dynamic relationship between individuals and their partisan or ideological affiliations. There's always some give-and-take in such relationships. Groups reflect their membership, and to a certain extent individuals take on group attributes. But in a hyperpartisan environment, partisan affiliations determine individual attributes to a greater extent. The dynamic relationship becomes skewed toward group affiliation and away from individuals. I'll restate in several ways in hope of greater clarity.

It's one thing to allow our opinions to decide which side of the divide we're on. It's another to allow the side of the divide to decide our opinions. The second is hyperpartisanship.

Political division is different from political affiliation predicting traditionally nonpartisan decision-making, such as whether to get vaccinated.

Developing a personal ideology based on the totality of one's experiences is different from conforming to an ideology to smooth partisan affiliation and operation within partisan systems or structures.

A party platform reflecting the assortment of priorities of party members is distinguishable from party membership determining individual priorities.

Editorial positions may be partisan. Allowing editorial positions to determine which facts media shares with audiences is hyperpartisan.

It's one thing to say we're politically divided. It's another to say we're more likely to conform our identities to the sources and institutions of those divisions. We're allowing our divisions to define us. Actually, "allowing" is not strong enough. If we add a pinch of sanctimony, we are *choosing* to be defined by our divisions. It's trendy.

Hyperpartisanship perverts self-determination. Self-determination is fundamental to a free and democratic society. Perverting self-determination through hyperpartisanship diminishes democracy's functionality. This is "dysfunctional" hyperpartisanship.

So, the question of whether we're more divided isn't particularly relevant. The impacts of our political disagreements have mutated into a malignancy. These are *hyperpartisan* times.

Supporting Data

While the premise derives from my experiences and observations, there is supporting data. Quantifying political polarity is conceptually challenging, yet distinct methodologies have been employed to do just that. Here, I summarize results from two *Values Surveys* by Pew Research Center as well as research tracking "crossovers" from Fair Vote.

According to Pew, value differences in Americans now correlate more strongly with party affiliation than gender, age, ethnicity, religion, or economic class, which is in striking contrast to results from earlier surveys.[1] Partisan division on policy issues is increasing. The influence of moderates has diminished in both parties. The Republican Party is becoming more dominated by conservatives and the Democratic Party by liberals.

A crossover representative is a congressional member whose district favors the opposing party, and a crossover vote occurs when a representative votes against the majority of their party. According to the organization Fair Vote, both crossover voting and representation has diminished precipitously.[2] In addition, competitive districts—districts where voter registrations are more balanced among parties—tend to produce moderates. Non-competitive districts—districts dominated by one party—tend to produce more extreme partisans. In other words, integration leads to moderation and segregation to extremes in representation.

Finally, both Pew and Fair Vote indicate that hyperpartisanship evolved most precipitously during the last decade of the twentieth century and the first decade of the twenty-first century.

While we've always been divided, aspects of our divisions recently changed.

---

1 Pew research is summarized from two of its *Values Surveys*. "In a Politically Polarized Era, Sharp Divides in Both Partisan Coalitions," Pew Research Ctr. December 17, 2019, https://www.pewresearch.org/politics/2019/12/17/in-a-politically-polarized-era-sharp -divides-in-both-partisan-coalitions/, and "Partisan Polarization Surges in Bush, Obama Years," Pew Research Ctr. June 4, 2012, https://www.people-press. org/2012/06/04/partisan-polarization-surges-in-bush-obama-years/.

2 "The Polarization Crisis in Congress: The Decline of Crossover Representatives and Crossover Voting in the U.S. House," 1-7 Fair Vote, Nov. 2013, https://fairvote.app.box. com/v/mp14-crossover-voting.

We're calling it hyperpartisanship. We are in hyperpartisan times. The question is: Why?

Issue

How is "dysfunctional" hyperpartisanship sustained?

Thesis

An entrenched and burgeoning dysfunctionality is antithetical to the concept of America. When a phenomenon perpetuates in America, it's proper to ask: Who profits from its maintenance? The short answer: Professional Partisans (PPs) do. In other words, from the financial perspective of PPs, there's no dysfunction.

Analytical Framework

However, political and social systems are like ecosystems in that isolating a single phenomenon from the complex web of relationships diminishes understanding. Moreover, within any system, environmental factors continuously change, ceaselessly modifying the web, resulting in perpetual evolution. Consequently, ecology combined with evolutionary theory provides a suitable framework for investigating hyperpartisanship.

Methodology

This book identifies and examines environmental factors relevant to evolving hyperpartisanship and illustrates our societal web to highlight threads supporting and perpetuating "dysfunctional" hyperpartisanship. I delineate relationships between supporting threads to conceive a web of hyperpartisanship within our society.

I explore hyperpartisanship in a manner that consciously resists incorporation into partisan warfare. This work disdains the names-and-dates approach to avoid triggering an escalating cycle of finger-pointing.

For example, candidate and President Bill Clinton seized the political center in the early to mid-1990s. Republicans under the leadership of Newt Gingrich renounced the center and moved to the right. Presently, both parties are moving from the center toward the extremes.

This anecdote raises at least three relevant points. First, it opens the door for partisanship. The narrative can be skewed to advantage either party, which means blaming the other for destructive trends.

Second, America does better when politicians and parties compete for the center. Consider it another premise for this work. I substantiate the premise with: At least when parties compete for the center, there's meaningful engagement. When each party caters to its extremes, they're not even participating in the same conversation.

Third, this book examines societal changes that allow both parties to migrate from the center. "They did it, so we had to" doesn't make sense. Imagine the political landscape as an ecosystem. Just because elephants stop grazing in the center doesn't mean donkeys must follow suit. Grazing lands must have changed, precipitating both herds to adapt foraging behavior.

Dysfunctional versus Functional

Initially, I considered hyperpartisanship exclusively dysfunctional in contravention of evolutionary theory. Evolution and persistence of exclusively dysfunctional phenomena doesn't make sense. Thriving phenomena must function within the ecosystem.

Hyperpartisanship manifests as dysfunctional within the political system. Actually, that's not quite right. Hyperpartisanship undermines legislative and policymaking processes contained within a broader political system that includes political parties and electoral politics.

Also, political systems integrate with society through the entertainment industry or media, as well as through cultural systems including secular and nonsecular institutions such as schools and churches to constitute the hyperpartisan web.

In addition, the fundamental unit of democracy and all its institutions and systems is *Homo sapiens*. The relevant ecosystem is peopled.

Insight into thriving phenomena must come from understanding function. Understand function by looking beyond systems where hyperpartisanship causes dysfunction. Do not mistake functional for desirable. I don't endorse hyperpartisanship.

Another Premise or Hypothesized Rule

If a persistent phenomenon *persistently* prevents a subsystem from functioning properly, then that subsystem is inferior or subordinate to the subsystem(s) where that same phenomenon supports function. In other words, legislative or policymaking processes where hyperpartisanship prevents proper functioning must be subordinate to system(s) where hyperpartisanship proves functional.

Methodology Redux

I trace the filaments of the hyperpartisan web to uncover rules describing subsumed relationships.

Purpose

I aspire to discover *abstract* rules relevant to hyperpartisanship's evolution and perpetuation. However, my purpose in articulating a rule is not to make or even suggest a rule, but to suggest there might be one. The suggestion stimulates a conceptual approach conducive to discovering relationships between components and systems ensnared by the hyperpartisan web.

I imagine the subject matter within layered systems. Within the universe are galaxies, and within the Milky Way is our solar system. On Earth, ecological, economic, political, and cultural systems interact in a complex network. Within each system, interacting subsystems add complexity. Suggesting a rule can challenge conventional conceptual frameworks and provide opportunities for discovery.

Abstractions

Abstractions are less likely to trigger partisanship or precipitate bellicosity. For example, the first iteration of the hypothesized rule above concerning dysfunctionalities within a subordinate subsystem is abstract. Regardless of your partisan inclinations, the proposed rule probably didn't set you off.

In addition to being emotionally nonthreatening, abstractions are difficult to leverage for partisan advantage. For a partisan warrior (PW) or PP,[3] abstract rules like the one above are useless. There is little danger abstract rules will be incorporated into partisan warfare.

Although the text is replete with specific examples from recent history relevant to hyperpartisanship, my takeaways tend to be abstract and transcend partisanship. I deliberately resist easily weaponized examinations or analyses. I don't want the exploration of partisan warfare weaponized for partisan advantage. Whether or not I'm successful is to be determined.

Thesis Revised

It's not just money. Although expert consensus presumes that partisanship is financially incentivized, the hyperpartisan web is extensive and supported by institutional and systemic structuring, cultural trends including partisan segregation or tribalism, and human psychology. In other words, partisanship is financially, psychologically, and culturally incentivized.

Aspirations

Personal success aside, I imagine modifying our ecosystem. I'm suggesting an alternative methodology for approaching the subject matter. Combatants joined in battle are fundamentally conflicted as to the cause and perpetuation of their conflict. It's reasonable to be concerned that mercenaries might prefer analytical frameworks destined to perpetuate conflicts from which they profit.

The "how" and "who" inexorably connect. Changing protagonists changes the manner of public discussions. But the manner and identity of the protagonists are part of a complex ecosystem that financially incentivizes conflict and ultimately depends upon people for sustenance.

---

3 PWs are intensely partisan legislators or government officials, whereas PPs work in the private sector.

This work explores complex relationships between protagonists of public discourse, systems, institutions, and economics supporting discourse skewed toward partisanship, and a hyperpartisan culture ultimately composed of citizens of our republic.

Although I don't reject dispositive conclusions out of hand, I primarily wish to affect the approach for examining and discussing the subject. I'm theorizing about a sociological phenomenon that implicates politics, and I'm using an ecological and evolutionary framework to do so.

I am consistently exasperated with authoritative figures treating the electorate like children. Self-fulfilling prophecy afflicts the strategy. Children want definitive answers to every question, and adults should understand that's impossible. I prefer to frame inquiries to inspire ceaseless participation in the examination rather than provide answers destined to arrive at specific ideological termini.

For democracy to endure, we all must do some of the work. Some of that work involves scrutiny. The most fundamental right, *and responsibility*, in a free and democratic society is thinking for ourselves. Subbing out our citizenship to professionals who profit from our division, organize us into factions, steer us toward blaming other factions, and who are employed by a system that financially incentivizes partisanship, inevitably generates "dysfunctional" hyperpartisanship.

Democracy is self-government. Governing ourselves requires self-awareness, self-control, and performing essentials of citizenship ourselves.

Evolutions

Biological evolution as described by Darwin provides this work's analytical framework and relevant psychological predispositions of the fundamental units of democracy. I stipulate that human behavior is shaped in part by biologically inherited psychology, and objections to evolutionary psychology are ideological and unscientific.[4] That it's possible to mitigate impacts of inherited

4 "Evolutionary Psychology," *Psychology Today*, accessed Oct. 22, 2023, https://www. psychologytoday.com/us/basics/ evolutionary-psychology.

psychology through learning and awareness is premise. Simply surrendering to primitive or tribal psychology without inspection contributes to hyperpartisanship, i.e., the subject matter implicates different types of evolution.

We can't evolve fast enough biologically to solve the problem.[5] On the other hand, cultural evolution, as well as personal growth, can provide contemporary remedy. Context distinguishes the types of evolution to which I refer.

Web of Hyperpartisanship

I start by graphically depicting the hyperpartisan web. In one sense, the illustration is more exact than the prose that follows, because major components can be taken in at once. Discrete web elements actuate concurrently. In addition, individual constituents contribute to a dynamic network whose continuous interactions produce the phenomenon we are investigating.

Many of the nodes represent ideas bandied about in the media, such as financial incentivization. The text fleshes out skeletal popular discussions while providing connective tissue. Although we explore relationships embedded within the hyperpartisan web in a linear fashion as prose demands, the web itself runs continuously and simultaneously.

Part I

Part I dissects financial incentivization by exploring dynamic relationships between hyperpartisanship and our institutions and systems. It begins with a brief discussion of natural selection, which, along with the web illustration, provides the template for exploration.

I go on to identify factors within our society, such as media fragmentation and industrial political spending, that have recently evolved to radically alter the ecosystem to favor rapid growth of hyperpartisanship.

5 "Lasting evolutionary change takes about one million years," Oregon State University, Aug. 22, 2011, https://today.oregonstate.edu/archives/2011/aug/lasting-evolutionary-change-takes-about-one-million-years. The rate of biological evolution isn't certain but varies according to circumstance and species. It may take upwards of one million years for evolutionary change to persist in complex organisms, such as humans, and for changes to persist, underlying causes must also persist and be widespread.

Marketing Partisanship

Next, I recognize a partisanship industry (PI), and I delineate its campaign and entertainment subsectors. Through the concept of marketing, I explore dynamic relationships between PI and instrumentalities of our democratic republic, including political parties, the primary system, politicians, and the electorate. This examination exposes the nuts and bolts of financial incentivization.

PI's entertainment subsector comprises media that provides partisan content for profit. While experts in this subsector comfortably assert that partisanship is financially incentivized, descriptions and details of the method have been lacking. In scrutinizing partisan media's relationship to the issue of hyperpartisanship, I reveal a fundamental conflict that explains both a reticence and inability to effectively deal with the topic. I illustrate the futility of self-policing by a free press in a hyperpartisan environment, as well as the illusion of balance allegedly provided by news outlets on opposite sides of the political spectrum.

The Relationship between Hyperpartisan Media and Issue Advocacy

Contemplating the relationship between partisan politics and nonpartisan advocacy fundamentally motivates my consideration of hyperpartisanship. By using broad benchmarks for success, I undermine the notion that hyperpartisan media (HM) outlets improve prospects for progress on issues of popular interest to their respective constituencies. In other words, "advocacy journalism"[6] doesn't work, apart from seducing the like-minded into subscribing.

Using my experience as an audience member, I explore the relationship between audiences and partisan programming. Awareness of the addictive qualities of identity validation and righteousness affirmation is essential to mitigate harmful impacts of advocacy conducted under the banner of journalism. As such, I treat *echo chambers* (ECs) not as a political problem, but as a personal challenge of addiction with political and social consequences.

---

6 "genre of journalism that combines reporting with point of view." Ingrid Bachmann Cáceres, "Advocacy Journalism," Oxford Research Encyclopedias, June 25, 2019, https://oxfordre.com/communication/display/10.1093/acrefore/9780190228613.001.0001/acrefore-9780190228613-e-776.

Feedback Loops

Interspersed throughout, I discuss relevant evolutionary and ecological concepts that both transcend and implicate hyperpartisanship. The relationship between media and society involves *feedback loops*, which repudiate the notion that media simply reflects social trends. Partisan content nurtures partisanship, and as partisanship intensifies, financial incentive to provide partisan content increases. As increasingly segregated partisan content is provided, more and more people migrate toward partisan fragments, and so on.

Partisan programming features analytical frameworks that prejudice conversations from inception to guarantee polarizing outcomes. Using the red/blue paradigm to evaluate every issue or event reduces some news stories' potential for conveying relevant information and impairs both comprehension and responsiveness to societal challenges.

Conduits of Institutionalized Polarity

Contemplating partisanship without considering political parties is difficult. Yet as I struggled to place them within the hyperpartisan web, enigmatic purposes of political parties resisted arrangement. Definitions prove inadequate to fathom their character or function. I conclude they primarily operate to convey private money to political campaigns to market candidates by emphasizing differences. Marketing the differences between candidates financially incentivizes divergence.

In addition to serving as financial conduits between the private sector and campaigns for public office, parties lend polarizing structure to our differences. Just as hyperpartisanship is not partisan division, polarity is not political disagreement. But channeling our diversity into a two-party system institutionalizes polarity, thereby reducing and exploiting our complexities to finance and generate hostility in a binary system that perpetuates hostility to generate revenue.

As a result, moderates and independents are like flies in the ointment. Within institutionalized polarity, moderation is dysfunctional, and extreme differences are adaptive. In other words, the relationship between extremism and hyperpartisanship is mutualistic.

Extremism

Extremism justifies hyperpartisanship by nullifying common ground and rendering compromise silly. Conversely, segregated hyperpartisan platforms provide nurturing environments for extremism to develop.

Beyond delineating this reciprocal relationship, I dissect extremism in terms of psychological motivation and its relationship to issue advocacy. I repudiate the philosophy of balance and argue instead that lefty and righty extremism sustain one another to support a system profiting from extremism. I conclude that while democratic institutions hold, even barely, PI incorporates extremist, radical ambition into partisan warfare for its enrichment. Fear of opposition extremism loosens donor purse strings to the financial benefit of the campaign subsector while the entertainment subsector profits from provocative content.

Hyperpartisan Campaigns and Primaries

I go on to illustrate how presidential campaigns and primaries function to enrich PI rather than promote the most qualified candidates for public office. I suggest a more democratic and less fragmenting alternative to the primary system. I argue for an open tournament to diminish party control over political processes, thereby reducing systemic polarization. I demonstrate how the alternative would devalue ideological differences and elevate competence and character as determinative voting criteria.

Politicians

As to candidates for public office, I challenge readers to exercise their empathy muscles to understand politicians, precisely because they are unsympathetic characters. I counsel empathy not as an apologist for political corruption, but as a citizen activist who considers understanding to be a restraint on partisanship and essential to effective advocacy.

I discuss the drawbacks of evaluating politicians by relying on national HM. In such an environment, conforming to a particular ideology trumps competence, and partisan affiliation substitutes for character. I conclude that practicing citizenship, instead of subbing the work out to professionals, engages the electorate at a level that makes insight into character more likely, which in turn enhances functionality while reducing partisanship.

Financially Incentivized Subordination

Part I summits with "The Eternal Game." I use a sports metaphor to illustrate PI dominance over policymaking. I parse "functionality" by demonstrating the role hyperpartisanship plays within dominant and subordinate systems. I flesh out the process whereby political spending ultimately finances hyperpartisanship to benefit the dominant system. I use examples such as the impeachment of President Trump to show how partisan financial pursuits and electoral schemes subordinate democracy.

Next, I identify ancillary beneficiaries to a hyperpartisan environment. I explain how taking advantage of either functional or dysfunctional aspects of hyperpartisanship is possible. Our enemies, both foreign and domestic, tend to benefit from our hyperpartisan dysfunctionalities. Entrenched power may also profit, as legislative stagnation protects bottom lines from inconvenient regulation. However, non-PI corporations can make use of identity by marketing to specific partisan or ideological demographics, thereby utilizing hyperpartisan functionality. I also resolve an apparent paradox by showing how both entrenched power and alleged revolutionaries profit from the same phenomenon.

Exceptionally Self-Destructive

Before concluding Part I, I reflect upon American exceptionalism. I use the COVID pandemic to illustrate the relationship between hyperpartisanship and our persistence. As a highly adaptive phenomenon, hyperpartisanship outperformed crisis management. Even patriotic propaganda took a back seat to partisan advantage. This should have been a wakeup call. Hyperpartisanship is more than faddish fare for politicos. It undermines crisis management.

Therefore, we must pursue remedy. But what can remedy an ailment of human inclination and industrial profitability whose adaptive nature expedites permeating society surreptitiously?

We must evolve. Awareness can mitigate destructive individual proclivities. Consumer activism and profitability-diminishing policy can moderate environmental factors.

Defunding PI

Part I concludes with an examination of constitutional amendments designed to disincentivize partisanship. Universal understanding that a free press is essential to democracy, coupled with First Amendment proscriptions, confers practical regulatory immunity on PI's entertainment subsector. On the other hand, through policy change, opportunities exist to reduce corrosive machinations of the campaign subsector as well as the institutionalized polarity that results from traditional political structures and electoral logistics.

Using the formal structure of constitutional amendment, I argue that proposals conceived to enhance fair representation also work to reduce partisanship. Through a "mock Congressional Record," I debate imagined colleagues over the amendment's justifications, provisions, and effects.

I deliberately broaden the discussion to explore fundamentals of our democratic republic relating to hyperpartisanship. I conclude that "in order to form a more perfect Union," we must evolve, and evolution is by trial and error. Persistence of the American Experiment requires experimentation.

Part II

Part II examines aspects of human psychology and culture that sustain hyperpartisanship and interfere with constructive evolution within constitutional democracy. Exploration of our predilection for emphasizing differences sets the stage. Recognizing our differences as assets is the challenge of a free, diverse, and democratic society.

Partisan Tribalism

Tribalism, however, interferes with productive use of our differences by relegating diversity to a basis for conflict. While political analysts accept tribalism as premise while offering it as explanation, what it is and how it works to sabotage functionality has been unexpressed.

I initiate the examination by distinguishing modern partisan tribes (PTs) from ancestral tribalism. Disparities between primordial environments in which ancestral tribalism, along with its commensurate psychology, evolved and modern environments of constitutionally democratic nation-states inevitably lead to anachronistic functioning. Awareness that hundreds of millennia disjoint our inherited psychology from contemporary reality mitigates harm.

The tonic is pervasive. Experience modifies our inherited biology. Awareness of our nature is experiential. Awareness is experience that helps shape us. Consciousness can modify our psychology, or at least our behavioral responses to our inclinations.

I scrutinize the structure of present-day PTs not only to distinguish them from prehistoric antecedents but to glean insight into how they sabotage democracy. I conclude that the probability of constitutionally democratic nation-states surviving tribal politics diminishes as tribalism further perverts our culture through tribal journalism, tribal academics, and tribal science. As a result, I advocate for evolving a human culture disdaining tribalism.

Ideological Faith

Then, because partisanship executes with religious zealotry, I examine impacts of religion and faith-based thinking on our politics. I contrast democracy with faith as policymaking procedures. I argue that commingling faith with political ideology undermines democracy by sanctifying intransigence. I show how ideological faith permits political parties to take constituencies for granted.

Beyond these fundamentals, I examine other factors within the hyperpartisan web that evoke religiosity such as purity, judgmentalism, cancellation, and apocalyptic psychology. I conclude that establishment of ideology threatens democracy similarly to establishment of religion, and separating faith-based thinking from democratic processes is even more essential than separating church and state.

Professional Partisans

Next, I take a closer look at PPs. As citizens are fundamental units of democracy, PPs are fundamental to hyperpartisanship. PPs work for PI's entertainment or campaign subsectors to find and create partisan advantage. I explore a smidgen of their tactics that broadly infiltrate the public square to regress civic discourse toward bellicosity and derail functional collaboration.

In contrast to my advocacy for self-awareness, PPs prefer to leverage primitive psychology for tribal opportunism. Partisan segregation creates safe spaces for PPs to indulge negative emotion and coerce outrage toward outgroups. Within congenial ECs, PPs substitute pejorative labeling for rational argument. As a result, public discourse transforms into insular grievance sessions featuring resentment and judgment, and constructive process succumbs to juvenile impatience.

Impropriety of Purity

Finally, I devote an entire chapter to praising hybridization while disparaging the pursuit of ideological purity. I imagine tensions between competing visions, ideals, and aspirations as resources of constitutional democracy. I beseech an understanding of diversity as the utility of a free and democratic society. I show how hybridization frustrates PI's business model. I envision America as a beautiful hybrid.

Democracy Consciousness

I conclude by scrutinizing the eternal vigilance required to sustain liberty within constitutional democracy. Understanding democracy as functionally integrating authority with the governed strengthens our vigilance. The vigilance of self-governance is self-awareness. On the other hand, perceiving government as segregated from us exhausts our vigilance through delusion.

Surrendering to a mindset that segregates us from our citizen colleagues and institutions as well as segregating rights from responsibilities subordinates democracy. Realizing the extent and significance of interdependency enhances democracy and permits greater functional integration. The diligence with which we deliberately evolve this democracy consciousness appraises our vigilance.

Perspective

Fray participants pose no threat to the fray; participation perpetuates the fray. I've been living in the mindset of an outsider to the conflict. I've clinically removed myself from the contest. I am a correspondent in the colosseum observing gladiators—and the crowd to which I also belong.

Warriors probe one another while considering the composition of the terrain they must navigate. The spectators' dreams are invisible to the combatants. Wake up! *They fight for themselves.*

Palate Cleanser

If you can, and I think you can, allow partisan feelings to fade. Partisan notes are insistent. They sing their own songs and interfere with our appreciation of the present composition.

Begin with the pictorial representation of the hyperpartisan web. Identify its nodes. Imagine content subsumed by the threads. Allow its complexities to engross your consciousness, thereby dispelling binary mindset polarity. Web geometry provides a template for effective absorption.

As you allow the ensuing prose to unfold linearly, envision placing its concepts within the pattern. You are its architect.

Abbreviations

Web of Hyperpartisanship

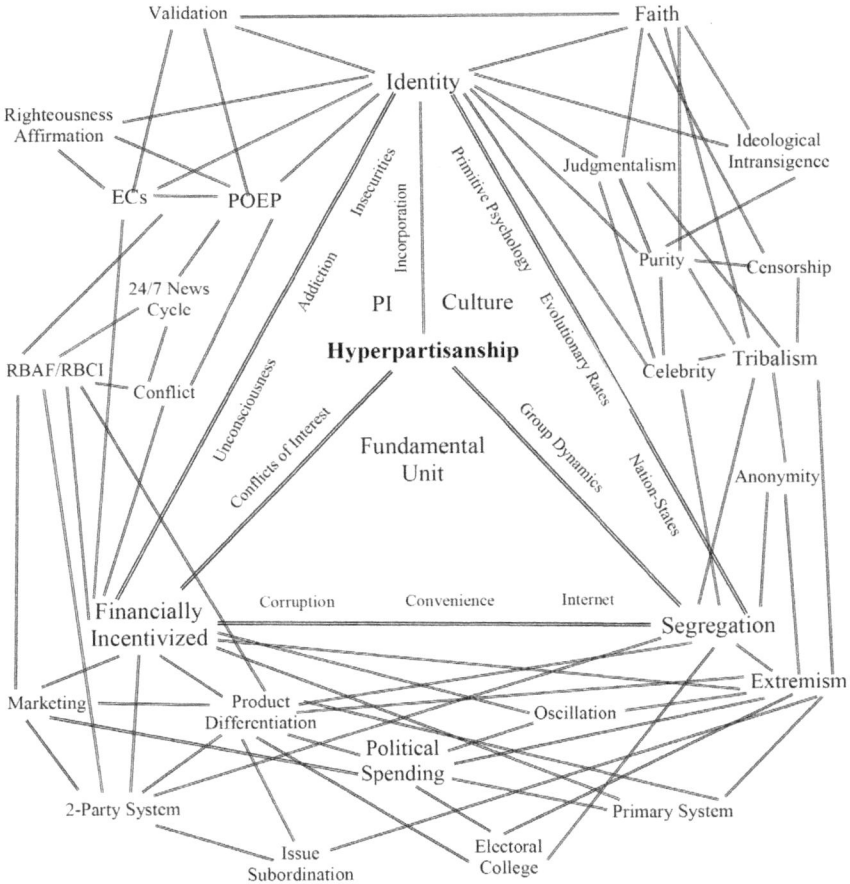

Validation — Faith

Identity

Righteousness
Affirmation

Ideological
Intransigence

ECs — POEP

Insecurities

Judgmentalism

Primitive Psychology

Incorporation

Purity

Censorship

24/7 News
Cycle

Addiction

PI | Culture

Hyperpartisanship

Evolutionary Rates

Celebrity

Tribalism

RBAF/RBCI

Conflict

Unconsciousness

Conflicts of Interest

Fundamental
Unit

Group Dynamics

Nation-States

Anonymity

Corruption   Convenience   Internet

Financially
Incentivized

Segregation

Extremism

Marketing

Product
Differentiation

Oscillation

Political
Spending

2-Party System

Primary System

Issue
Subordination

Electoral
College

Web of Hyperpartisanship

Part I: Institutions and Systems

Part I emphasizes the role institutions and systems play in financially incentivizing hyperpartisanship. However, elements explored in greater detail in Part II, such as human psychological predispositions, are alluded to in advance. All relevant factors naturally operate and intermingle concurrently. This is the nature of evolution and the web.

—1—

Natural Selection

Evolution carries unanticipated consequences.
—THE AUTHOR

Darwin proposed that different species can evolve from common ances-tors through natural selection.[7] Individual organisms of a single species vary genetically, manifesting different traits. Environmental factors such as temperature, amount of sunlight, availability of water and food, intra- and interspecies competition for resources, and types of predators determine the utility of traits. Organisms with traits better suited to their specific environ-ment are more likely to survive, reproduce, and pass their genes to succeeding generations—survival of the fittest.

When organisms of the same species inhabit discrete environments, they experience diverging selective pressures. Traits proving successful or adaptive and selected *for* in one environment may be less adaptive in another environ-ment and selected *against*. For example, what is adaptive in rainforests may be unsuitable for deserts. Given enough time, i.e., enough generations, separated organisms may evolve so differently that they become distinct species.

Similarly, changing environmental conditions within an ecosystem adjust adaptability. Traits that were adaptive may become obsolete, and genetic combinations that were useless or inconsequential may manifest in highly adaptive traits that thrive.

---

7 Regina Bailey, "6 Things You Should Know About Biological Evolution," ThoughtCo., updated Oct. 26, 2019, https://www.thoughtco.com/biological-evolution-373416.

Natural Selection and Non-biologicals

Survival proves viability. For non-living entities and phenomena such as corporations or trends, financial viability is most relevant. Market forces provide selective pressures. Ability to adapt to changing market forces to sustain financial viability determines longevity.

Financial viability is a function of popularity. Will people buy it, use it, watch it, consume it, eat it, work with it, play with it, contribute to it, or fund it? Environmental factors influencing financial viability include economic systems, economy strength, available technology, competition, subsidy, and culture, which includes everything else: societal norms, language, art, food, religion, values, ethnicity, social institutions, etc.

Hyperpartisanship Viability

Partisanship, meaning *prejudicial allegiance or opposition to a political party, faction, group, tribe, person, ideology, or cause,*[8] is a trait predating America and has been a part of our culture, and perhaps our biology, for a long time. Vociferously debating policy has been a part of our national character since inception. The intensity and tenor of our disputes has at times been sufficiently polarizing to threaten persistence. The Civil War is our most notorious instance of debilitating partisanship.

We have been trending toward more intense partisanship, popularly described as "hyper" and "dysfunctional." Some evidence for "dysfunctional" hyperpartisanship is anecdotal and some is based on statistical methodologies. However, as discussed in the introduction, this book accepts the phenomenon as premise. The evolution and status of hyperpartisanship in America implies its financial viability.

---

8 This working definition of partisanship is an amalgamation of multiple sources as well as my own preferences.

2

Introduction to Changing Environmental Factors

M odifying environments amends the adaptiveness of certain traits. Here, I identify factors in our continuously changing environment relevant to hyperpartisanship's viability.

Television

When I was growing up, TV had three networks, three local channels, and public television (PBS). That was more than in most of the country because the New York market was so large. Now, a basic package has dozens of channels, and premium options have hundreds. As viewing options increase, the percentage of the population watching the same programs decreases and audience fragmentation increases.

Fragmentation reduces experiential commonality. With respect to television viewing, we're becoming increasingly segregated. However, the subject matter of this book is narrow—the evolution and perpetuation of hyperpartisanship. From the similarly narrow perspective of a TV watcher, I couldn't be happier. I don't want to go back. We shouldn't go back. But with greater diversity, broader choice, and superior quality provided by contemporary television, fragmentation increases. Evolution carries unanticipated consequences.

Notice I haven't mentioned fragmentation of partisan political programming, which was not present at the genesis of broadcast expansion. Fragmentation seemed benign at first. I don't remember fragmentation being discussed as an issue until more recently, in the context of partisan political content. But it was there, and it was evolving.

Fragmentation matured in a petri dish of the innocuous. You could spend your entire viewing time in movies, sports, travel, cooking, classic TV, nature, music, documentaries, celebrity gossip, etc. Network programming still thrived as well, but you could go your own way, and eventually, we all did.

I'm not saying we'd be better off all watching the *Brady Bunch* on Friday night. But fragmentation was happening, and it began before partisan programming existed. Why is this relevant? I take the ecological view. How we do politics connects to how we do everything else. Phenomena such as fragmentation occur broadly throughout society. Expanded viewing options dividing audiences among more channels became financially practical before programs dominated by partisan content burst on the scene. Apolitical fragmentation smoothed the way for partisan fragmentation.

Ratings-Driven News

The classic 1976 film, *Network*, concerned the economics of TV news.[9] Anxiety about shallow sensationalism resulting from attempts to secure a competitive market share as cable television expanded was its main theme, epitomized by a young network executive's idea to cover a terrorist group to increase ratings. To be repulsively honest, terrorism delivers ratings. Who wasn't watching cable news after 9/11 or the Boston Marathon bombing?

But I doubt the idea that partisan politics would be a ratings winner occurred to anyone involved in production, or for that matter, anyone who saw the movie at that time. It didn't occur to me. The economics of subscription TV make it possible. Under the new and evolving system, you can make a buck with a smaller audience share. Niche and boutique programming are feasible. Financial viability no longer requires securing a ratings plurality or aiming for the political center.

9 *Network*, directed by Sidney Lumet (Metro-Goldwyn-Mayer Studios, Inc., 1976).

Beyond News

Partisan political content has spread. It's growing. It has infiltrated and taken over formats either traditionally nonpartisan or mostly apolitical. Compare opening monologues of current late-night hosts to those who performed decades ago. I'm not saying Johnny Carson never had fun with politics. He did. But most of his opening monologue was apolitical, and his jokes at politicians' expense weren't aggressively partisan. Don't confuse my reminiscences with quaint nostalgia. I'm tracing relevant points in an evolutionary trend:

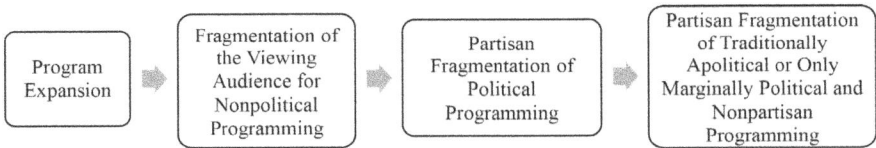

Program Expansion ⇒ Fragmentation of the Viewing Audience for Nonpolitical Programming ⇒ Partisan Fragmentation of Political Programming ⇒ Partisan Fragmentation of Traditionally Apolitical or Only Marginally Political and Nonpartisan Programming

Figure 2.1: Evolution of Partisan TV Fragmentation

The Internet and Social Media

With respect to fragmentation, if expanded TV programming is a water pistol, the internet is a hydrogen bomb without security codes. More than one billion websites populate the internet, and roughly 200 million are active.[10] Now we're talking. Now you can really go your own way.

Fragmentation is fundamental to virtual reality. It wasn't promoted as such. It was supposed to be like a global commons *connecting* people from around the world. And it does, sort of.

But it's not a commons in at least two ways. First, most gatherings aren't in the public square. Private for-profit companies such as Facebook host assemblies. More importantly, while all members of society may access the internet, each of the 200 million individual locations *on its own* is uncharacteristic of society at large. They are idiosyncratic. They're biased.

---

10 "How Many Websites Are There in the World?" siteefy, accessed Aug. 12, 2024, https://siteefy.com/how-many-websites-are-there/.

For marketing or research, the internet is the most powerful tool that has ever existed in the known universe. You can find whatever you're looking for. Better still, what you're looking for finds you. With data mined from internet surfing, algorithms continuously improve their ability to predict your preferences and offer desirable content more accurately. The virtual world adapts to you.

Normally, data mining and marketing algorithms elicit privacy apprehensions. But here, we're concerned with evolutionary trends relevant to hyperpartisanship. *Virtual reality adapts to you.* No compromises needed. No effort to get along required. No need to identify common ground. No need to identify yourself. No need to assimilate. No need to integrate. Civil discourse? Optional. Cultivating qualities essential for diplomacy or legislating is inapposite to internet business.

You can find whatever you're looking for. To use an extreme example, let's say you're a Nazi. But your hometown doesn't have enough Nazis to facilitate the vibrant Nazi discussions you crave. And even if there are, due to societal norms, greatly outnumbered Nazis are a little shy about having open Nazi discussions in public, let alone marches and rallies.

The few there can gather in seclusion and have tiny Nazi discussions. Some eventually realize it's kind of pathetic. Some may go off to college or get a job and develop substantial contacts with non-Nazis. Some may grasp that integrating into society in a satisfying way requires leaving Nazi ways behind.

Enter the internet and link to all the Nazis you want. You can link to Nazis in your town, county, state, country, or around the world. Now you can take part in a genuine Nazi march or rally just like you've dreamed. Who said the internet doesn't connect us?

It doesn't have to be Nazis. It can be Republicans, Democrats, liberals, conservatives, far-right, far-left, socialists, libertarians, or apolitical types—whatever fragment fits you best. By linking to greater numbers within your fragment— because whatever your fragment is, it's larger on the internet than where you live in the real world—you reinforce your connection to that fragment.

Rule: The incentive, ability, and opportunities to defragment or integrate with those outside your fragment diminish as connections within your fragment become more substantial.

The more time you spend connecting within your fragment, the less time you have for connecting across fragments. The more people connect within a particular fragment, the less people connect across fragments. The deeper you dive into your own fragment, the further you segregate from those outside your fragment. Internet "connections" strengthen or solidify fragments rather than sewing them together.

Desire to connect with the like-minded is understandable. It's human nature. But technological advances make extreme indulgence of that desire possible. Extreme indulgence in any desire comes with consequences. The internet is truly egalitarian. It allows unrestricted and democratic access to indulgences in extremity. *Of course* there are consequences.

As the real universe expands, average distance between objects increases. As the virtual universe expands, fragments multiply. As fragments increase, the commonality of human experience shrinks. We become increasingly distant from those outside our fragment.

Virtual reality is both fragmented and fragmenting. The net effect is that factions multiply and intensify, while cordial connections between factions wither.

Fragmentation/Segregation

Recall that when populations of the same species separate into different environments, they can evolve into distinct species, given enough time in isolation from one another. This is known as speciation.[11]

If, after speciation occurs, a male from one population encounters a female from the other, they will no longer be able to produce viable or fertile offspring. This happens for a couple of reasons. First, after the encounter, they may refuse to mate, possibly because they no longer recognize one another as potential mates. Or they do mate, but either a fetus does not develop, or the offspring aren't fertile. The two populations separated for too long. They can no longer "get it on" constructively. The type of genetic interaction needed to

---

11 "Speciation," Dictionary.com, https://www.dictionary.com/browse/speciation. Speciation is the formation of new species as a result of geographic, physiological, anatomical, or behavioral factors that prevent previously interbreeding populations from breeding with each other.

produce viable offspring is no longer possible.

Speciation is an extreme result of biological segregation that takes a long time. For humans, it could take a million years, which is clearly beyond the present scope. But the mechanism is instructive.

Geneticists view genes as information.[12] Genes hold information about our history and ultimately our future. After speciation, genetic information exchange between potential mates is blocked or corrupted. The quintessential consequence of segregation is:

> Separation to an extent that inhibits or distorts communication on a fundamental level.

The individuals become programmed with a distinct set of underlying facts. That can't happen without segregation.

Private Political Spending

Private sector political spending on campaigns is industrial and has risen substantially over the last couple of decades. The total cost of federal elections has risen from $2.9 billion in 1998 to $8.9 billion in 2022 for non-presidential election years, and from just over $5 billion in 2000 to more than $16 billion in 2020 for presidential election years.[13] In addition, billions are spent on state elections.[14]

Political spending data typically prompts apprehensions about fairness and corruption. Through spending, corporations and the well-heeled gain disproportionate access to political processes. Leveraging that access to skew the legal framework in their favor undermines representative democracy.

---

12 "Part 1: Dawn of the Modern Age of Genetics." *The Gene: An Intimate History.* Ken Burns. PBS, April 7, 2020.

13 "Cost of Election," OpenSecrets, accessed July 5, 2023, https://www.opensecrets.org/elections-overview/cost-of-election.

14 Taylor Giorno and Pete Quist, "Total cost of 2022 state and federal elections projected to exceed $16.7 billion," OpenSecrets, Nov. 3, 2022, https://www.opensecrets.org/news/2022/11/total-cost-of-2022-state-and-federal-elections-projected-to-exceed-16-7-billion/.

The current legal framework also implicates anonymity, which relates to corruption and fairness. Who's contributing? Should "dark money" influence democratic elections?

But here, where the money comes from is not of great concern. With hyperpartisanship, *how money is spent* dominates our analysis. Although we'll explore this subject in greater depth in subsequent chapters, in short, money is for distinguishing candidates and politicians in one party from candidates and politicians in the other.

Rule: As the pool of money used to distinguish partisan adversaries increases, financial incentives for polarization and adversarial behavior increase accordingly.

Summary of Relevant Environmental Factors

Partisanship is a trait sustained within human culture predating the United States. It probably predates recorded history. I bet partisanship insinuated itself into human politics during the period when we existed exclusively within extended family units known as tribes.

But human culture and politics cannot be defined entirely by partisanship. Cooperation, imagination, and a desire to improve upon what has been bestowed can fairly be considered features of our character. However, through the lens of media coverage, which is a most popular lens, we bear witness to an age of hyperpartisanship.

During the last several decades of the twentieth century, along with the first decades of the twenty-first, aspects of society radically evolved to fashion an ecosystem favorable to growing partisanship. Through TV programming expansion and internet, media audiences fragmented to an unprecedented extent. The economics of audience fragmentation permitted more narrowly tailored content, including political content custom-made for partisan audiences.

In addition to partisan segregation, private spending, which ultimately finances political polarization, mushroomed. Segregated media outlets deficient of competing theories incubated unbridled partisanship. Disconnected fragments nurture ideas emphasizing our differences. A steadily increasing flow of private political spending fuels partisan expansion and hyperpartisan persistence. A trait sustained throughout our existence rises to preeminence in our politics and begins to infiltrate and corrupt more sectors of society.

The following chapters explore in greater detail the relationship between relevant environmental factors, hyperpartisanship, and mechanisms promoting its perpetuation. I also examine psychological predispositions and cultural trends working in synergy with segregation and political spending to intensify partisanship. Although Part II focuses on innate psychology and culture, keep in mind the visual representation of the web. All factors act concurrently in dynamic relationship with one another. As segregation and political spending nurture partisanship, amplified partisanship becomes an environmental factor changing the ecosystem in which our culture evolves. How our culture *is* evolving affects how our culture *will* evolve.

3

The Partisanship Industry

There is a Partisanship Industry (PI). It's not recognized as such, but it's there. This private sector industry profits from partisan media content and advancing partisan interests.

You won't find it by browsing the Bureau of Labor Statistics. The PI is a mixture of recognized industries. PI includes partisan media as well as political consultants who employ communication outreach in the form of television advertising, social media, email, snail mail, phone banks, and door-to-door canvassing.

PI is undergoing both vertical and lateral expansion. In addition to and partly as a result of increased political spending, which can be considered a form of vertical expansion, partisan content continues to broadly infiltrate media and other sectors of our culture such as academia and science.

Notice I didn't mention politicians or political parties. Relationships between private sector PI and politicians, and especially political parties, are sometimes straightforward, occasionally inscrutable, and at times vexing. I explore these relationships in subsequent chapters.

Marketing Partisanship

The PI is essentially a marketing industry. In its most familiar form, PI uses money spent on campaigns to market candidates. Of $16 billion spent on federal elections in 2020, nearly sixty percent went to media advertising.[15]

15 "Expenditures," OpenSecrets, accessed July 5, 2023, https://www.opensecrets.org/campaign-expenditures?cycle=2020.

Interestingly, the next-largest category of expenditures was fundraising, at over $1.6 billion. It cost $1.6 billion to raise $16 billion. Not bad—only ten percent if the $16 billion resulted entirely from fundraising without any unsolicited donations.

But PI does more than work on campaigns. Its purpose is richer and its reach more pervasive.

PI markets support for, or opposition to, political candidates, politicians, political parties, factions, and ideologies.

In other words, it markets partisanship.

From this description, one might conclude politicians and parties employ the PI. That's true to a certain extent, but the relationship turns out to be more complex and dynamic. Employing PI affects the way politicians and political parties operate. PI incentivizes partisanship. As a result, dominant and subordinate roles normally associated with vendor-client relationships are at best obscured. Exploring symbiosis between PI and our political system is central to our analysis of "dysfunctional" hyperpartisanship.

PI includes two subsectors. Revenue for the *campaign subsector* comes from political spending. This subsector includes people and firms who raise funds, develop strategy, create campaign messages and talking points, produce campaign ads, research opposition, prepare candidates for debates, provide media consultation and communicate with media outlets, coordinate grassroots efforts, and perform any other tasks campaigns require, including administration and logistics such as transportation and housing.

The *entertainment subsector* profits from presenting partisan content in media including TV, internet, print, and movies. This subsector includes corporations providing forums and venues for content as well as people paid to deliver content, including producers, writers, hosts, certain guests, anchors, and analysts.

Product Placement Is Content

There is a noteworthy distinction between subsectors. The campaign subsector must pay for advertising. Firms and people who write and produce ads certainly get paid, but some revenue from political spending buys airtime for commercials. Even if someone working for a campaign appears as a guest on a political show, i.e., as part of the show's content, the campaign pays for the guest's salary, transportation, and accommodations. The campaign pays, at least in part, for the commercial benefit of that guest's appearance. PI's campaign subsector spends for partisan media content.

The entertainment subsector works differently. It gets paid for partisan content. Here is a delightful irony. Revenue for commercial television comes from TV commercials. Duh. Sponsors pay. The beneficiaries of partisan content don't have to.

For example, if a late-night TV host spends his entire opening monologue excoriating the red team to the benefit of the blue team, the blue team doesn't have to pay a dime. Advertisers such as car companies, insurance companies, or soda companies foot the bill.

Normally, when a company integrates product into a show's content, the company must pay. It's called product placement. But here, non-PI corporations pick up the check. It's a beautiful thing.

In general, corporate sponsors don't mind. Corporate calculation is simply paying for advertising commensurate with ratings. As discussed, after broadcast expansion and corresponding viewer fragmentation, economics permit shows featuring partisan content. Enough people tune in to attract sponsors and make the whole thing work.

But comparing the dynamic described above with product placement is insultingly inadequate. Product placement happens when a star drinks a specific brand of beer in a movie. The movie isn't about beer. The beer is just a prop.

With partisan programming, product integration isn't trivial. It's not a prop. It's the show's content. It *is* the show. Product placement becomes content. Advertising as content, like an infomercial with commercials. Part and parcel acceptance by the audience as totally normal. If you don't like it, change the channel. This isn't your fragment. Find your fragment. If you can't find it on TV, go to the internet. The internet has two hundred million "channels." Find your fragment. Fragment.

Product Differentiation

On July 29, 2019, during a health care discussion in a Democratic primary debate hosted by CNN, U.S. Senator Elizabeth Warren (D-MA) chastised one of her opponents by declaring, ". . . we should stop using Republican talking points . . ." First, as an American troubled by hyperpartisanship ravaging democracy, I jumped for joy. I couldn't be happier. The left using Republican talking points or the right using Democratic talking points is worth celebrating. We found common ground. Yay! Don't put it down—grab hold and run with it.

Second, let's briefly examine the hyperpartisan dynamic. "Stop using Republican talking points." This goes beyond party membership. This is a political party, or one of its prominent members, deciding acceptable speech, and speech is progeny of thought. Prominent party leaders comfortably reprimand nonconformist thinking. The message is clear. Tribal membership requires kowtowing to tribal dogma. Unfortunately, some fold under pressure of partisan bullying and conform their identities to prescribed doctrine, thereby perverting democracy; that's hyperpartisanship.

Third, the Senator's assertion is pregnant with issues relevant to hyperpartisanship that will be examined further on, such as the nature of political parties, purity, group identity, indoctrination, and tribal dynamics. Here however, the focus is *product differentiation.*

Creating the perception your product is different and better is a fundamental and universally employed marketing strategy. Marketing products such as colas or detergents with nearly identical ingredients is challenging. That's why advertisers make the big bucks. The best create perceptions of difference and supremacy with transcendent skill. The appearance of great differences between products makes marketing easier.

Built-in constraints limit differentiation for most products. Messing with detergent ingredients to easily distinguish the product runs the risk of rendering the product less effective. Cleaning chemistry controls and provides objectivity. Millions of people use the products. Product efficacy is continuously evaluated.

PI faces no such constraints. There's no need to create a perception of differences. Products really are different. Marketing simply requires emphasizing existing differences. Going one step further, from PI's perspective, why not encourage products to further differentiate themselves? Greater actual differences help marketing. Emphasizing and encouraging differences is financially incentivized. Product differentiation provides a financially sound rationale for polarity. Stop using Republican talking points!

Beyond differentiation, creating a perception of product supremacy is required. What a drag. The good news is physical reality, or any reality for that matter, isn't constraining. There's no way for the public to test products for efficacy. In other words, conditions are ripe for swindlers.

Evolutionary Principles Revisited

I'm not suggesting conspiratorial or nefarious intent or manipulation. Partisan content may or may not reflect the natural inclinations of its producers and participants. In other words, the motives of PI professionals aren't relevant to the analysis. Due to changing environmental factors, more niches are available for PPs, which is another way to consider PI lateral expansion. Cynical opportunists or idealists, true believers, or scoundrels can fill those niches. But in a free and market-driven society like ours, any identifiable profitable niches will be filled. Discerning the inhabitants' motives is unnecessary.

Inferences of contrivance aren't justified. I'm nonjudgmental, although I favor natural selection over intelligent design. Identified profitable niches will be inhabited. Discerning inhabitants' motives is unnecessary deviation. My analysis treats true believer and scoundrel as colleagues.

I use Roger Ailes to make my point. Roger Ailes founded Fox News in 1996 and was its first CEO. Roger Ailes was a partisan conservative most of his life. Although he had an early career in television, including as executive producer for *The Mike Douglas Show*,[16] he began working for the PI campaign subsector in 1967 by prepping then presidential candidate, Richard Nixon, for TV appearances.[17] He went on to work as a media consultant for several

---

16 "Roger Ailes," Wikipedia, https://en.wikipedia.org/wiki/Roger_Ailes.

17 Olivia B. Waxman, "Before Fox News, Roger Ailes Helped Get Richard Nixon Elected," *TIME*, May 18, 2017, https://time.com/4784104/roger-ailes-richard-nixon/.

Republican presidential campaigns.

But Fox News would not have been possible during any of that time. It wasn't until after broadcast-expansion economics had been worked out, allowing substantial audience segregation, that Roger Ailes was able to take advantage of the modified TV landscape to make his news fantasy into television reality and become the entertainment subsector's first king.

Human history is replete with individuals attaining wealth and power through extraordinary ambition or even ruthlessness. But means to end vary according to ecosystem. Marketing partisanship is now a means to that end. Evolution carries unanticipated consequences.

—4—

It's the Chicken *and* the Egg

The concept described here is relevant throughout this book. When I first wrote that sentence, I wanted to say, "the concept described here is always relevant." But I'm afraid of words like "always" and "never." But I really think it's always relevant. I really do.

I'm talking about feedback loops, and in particular, *positive* feedback loops. Feedback occurs when system outputs become future inputs to the same system. Positive feedback tends to amplify and negative feedback tends to dampen.

Counterintuitively, positive feedback makes bad situations worse. For example, global warming melts ice. Ice reflects the sun's energy while bare soil absorbs it. Melting ice bares more soil, which causes greater warming. Greater warming melts more ice, baring more soil, causing greater warming, and so on. Global warming implicates positive feedback. Positive feedback can amplify destructive phenomena until the system self-corrects or burns out.

Evolution and ecology also engage feedback loops. The summation of interactions between organisms and the physical environment within an ecosystem determines both selective pressures influencing the evolution of organisms within the ecosystem and the evolution of the ecosystem itself. Interactions alter the ecosystem, which alters selective pressures within the ecosystem, which alters evolution of organisms and the ecosystem, which affects future interactions, which affects evolution, etc. Relationships are dynamic and involve feedback loops. The ecosystem shapes evolution and evolution changes the ecosystem, which impacts evolution, etc. You can't get away from it, and the more complex the system, the more difficult to predict its outcome in aggregate. Evolution carries unanticipated consequences.

As changing environmental factors such as broadcast expansion and viewer segregation make partisan programming economically feasible, partisan programming occupies an expanding share of the ecosystem. Within any system, environmental factors continuously change and endlessly modify the web, resulting in perpetual evolution.

Partisan Programming Is an Environmental Factor Affecting Societal Evolution

It's part of the landscape. Unlike when I was growing up, today's young adults, teenagers, and children will develop comprehension, opinions, and thought patterns in an environment of ubiquitous partisan content.

This explains the time lag between the evolution and recognition of hyperpartisanship. While relevant environmental factors changed most precipitously in the 1990s, aughts, and first few years of the second decade of the twenty-first century, media discussions often imply hyperpartisanship evolved more recently. This makes sense because those who have experienced segregated hyperpartisan environments for their entire lives are just beginning to reach adulthood.

Vocational aspirations are in the mix. More private political spending means more jobs in PI's campaign subsector. More partisan media content means more jobs in the entertainment subsector. On the other hand, if you're inclined toward a career in journalism driven by facts rather than narrative, you might want to reassess.

You can almost hear a TV pundit ask, "but is segregated partisan content really responsible, or does it simply reflect deep societal divisions?" It's both. It's *always* both. What's happening in society affects what's happening in media, and what's happening in media affects what's happening in society, all the time. It's the chicken *and* the egg. As lines are drawn and divisions deepen, financial incentives for partisan content grow. As more fragmented partisan content is provided, more and more people migrate toward a fragment, and so on. Spiraling and expanding—a positive feedback tornado sucking in more and more. Politics. Entertainment. Science? Academics? Runaway partisanship. Irresistible feedback loop. A seemingly inescapable vicious cycle of partisan escalation.[18]

---

18 See Appendix A for a list of implicated feedback loops.

—5—

Media

So tell me, since it makes no factual difference to you and you can't
prove the question either way, which story do you prefer?
—YANN MARTEL, *Life of Pi*

The seemingly self-evident but unsubstantiated premise for this chapter
is: *The better informed the electorate, the better democracy functions.*

Specifically, I'm referring to accurate information about societal conditions,
how specific policy proposals affect those conditions, how incumbents have
addressed those conditions, and what candidates for public office propose
to do.

Most of us get that information through the media. People who can access
such information more directly are either employed to do so or employ others
to gather it for them. Most of us don't have the time or resources. We watch,
read, and/or listen to the news.

This is not to say media is all about accurate information. In addition to
providing entertainment, and within the entertainment itself too, media
creates and nurtures perceptions about conditions within our society and
how professionals or experts as well as the public feel about those conditions.
Editorializing cultivates perception. Shaping perception isn't exclusive to
editorializing. Choosing which facts to report and the way they're reported
also influences perception.

By and large, cultivated perceptions are self-serving. This doesn't imply
devious intent but implicates natural selection. Over time, media outlets cultivating self-serving perceptions are more likely to be financially viable than
media outlets cultivating either counterproductive or ineffective perceptions.

Promoting self-serving perceptions neither precludes nor requires cynical behavior. It's part of a successful business model.

Interestingly, with segregated viewing audiences, news outlets may promote self-serving perceptions that contradict the self-serving perceptions of competing outlets. What constitutes self-serving depends on the ensnared audience. One audience's trash is another's treasure.

In sum, media provide self-serving mixtures of information, entertainment, and cultivated perceptions. Sometimes these elements are delivered independently, and sometimes they're packaged together.

Single-Point Failure

I watched a PBS documentary about a bridge collapsing. Older bridges had serious design flaws. Corrosion at a single point could collapse the entire bridge. Now engineers design bridges to withstand failure at a single point.

HM reveals a flaw in our constitutional democracy like an outdated bridge susceptible to single-point failure. Independent press is essential to democracy. But unlike the three branches of government, which provide mutual oversight and constraint, the fourth estate is impervious to formal checks and balances.

The Constitution has little to offer. The First Amendment states: "Congress shall make no law . . . abridging the freedom . . . of the press . . ." The regulatory framework is laissez-faire. The reason is tautological. Free press means not restricted or controlled by government censorship. A free press is considered an essential additional check on government overreach beyond separation of powers. But there's no check on the checker—no oversight on the overseer.

Freedom from government interference with respect to content means media is free to cherry-pick facts, present opinion as fact, present stories driven by narrative instead of facts, skew presentations to support narrative, disproportionately report stories supporting narrative, frame stories to emphasize narrative, manipulate human psychological predispositions and emotions to market narrative—you get the idea. What's the narrative? We're right, and they're wrong. Truth and justice belong to us. We're the good guys.

So, what's the answer? Is constructive renovation possible? Is expecting the consistent presentation of relevant information realistic? Even socialists, or at least the ones appearing in media, aren't calling for a government takeover of media, which would abolish independent press.

Therefore, solutions can only come from audiences and the media itself.

Audiences can turn it off. But where do we get our news? For now, because news has been so corrupted by factionalism and a desire to secure ratings, we would be better off as a society if, for a period of time, we stopped consuming partisan content-driven news. Think of it as fasting.

As media currently functions, the negative impacts of its self-serving propensities substantially outweigh its informative value.

Self-Policing

Yeah, that always works. Self-policing is rendered especially impotent by partisan fragmentation. The issue of professional responsibility becomes incorporated into partisan warfare. Media personalities on the left point fingers at conservative media, and media personalities on the right point fingers at liberal media. Segregated audiences are predisposed toward their fragment's narrative. The overall effect is escalation. Partisan fragmentation of media undercuts the utility of self-policing.

The press is *not* free. It's censored by the expectations of audiences, shackled by factionalism, corrupted by fragmentation, and restricted by revenue necessities.

Illusion of Counterbalance

Seesaws or teeter-totters are the most familiar representation of counterbalance. A board rests on a fulcrum with a child seated at each end. I recall enjoying seesaws with friends. Sometimes we would spring up and down, but sometimes we would hang suspended without touching ground in perfect counterbalance.

Connection is essential for counterbalance to function. Children at both ends connect through a single board. Therefore, liberal, or progressive "news" outlets do not counterbalance conservative "news" outlets. Their connectivity is marginal because audiences are too segregated. The board is sawed in half with both children sitting on the ground. Or better still, it's like dozens of children are stacked on the end of one seesaw with dozens of others piled on a different one. It's pointless at best, but really kind of sad and disturbing. It doesn't function as a proper counterbalance. The seesaw is broken.

Counterbalance Philosophy Infiltrates Psychology to Impair Cognition for PI Profit

Conceptually integrating counterbalance into the fundamentals by which we understand society, without rigorous examination, enables hyperpartisanship and extremism. It also contributes to transforming journalism into ideological activism. It seems innocuous. It's a seesaw. But it's not innocuous. Accepting a counterbalance philosophy normalizes HM. Consider it partisan grooming.

The illusion of counterbalance fuels partisan conflict. "Journalism" unbalanced to the right justifies "journalism" unbalanced to the left and vice versa. Lefty news outlets provide content for righty news outlets to disparage and vice versa. The presence of Fox News supports the MSNBC business model, and the presence of MSNBC supports the Fox News business model. They benefit from each other's presence. Righty extremism provides a rationale for lefty extremism and vice versa.

I'm describing a system. Righty and lefty partisanship are interdependent, but categorizing that interdependence as counterbalance is a euphemistic diversion that impedes comprehension. Counterbalance is irrelevant to system functionality. In fact, audience segregation precludes counterbalance. The system depends on conflict.

Those who profit from partisanship on the left depend on the right, and those who profit from partisanship on the right depend on the left. Righty professionals pose no threat to lefty professionals. On the contrary, they vindicate each other's existence. Without each other, both sides would be tilting at windmills. From a financial perspective and borrowing terminology from ecology, their relationship is mutualistic symbiosis or *mutualism*.[19]

---

19 "interactions between organisms of two different species, in which each organism benefits from the interaction in some way." BD Editors, "Mutualism," biology dictionary, April 28, 2017, https://biologydictionary.net/mutualism/.

In the context of war profiteering, including partisan warfare, the concept of balance is problematic and should be reconsidered. Arming both sides with ideological proselytizing media outlets facilitates neither productive dialogue nor peaceful balance. It's not about counterbalance!

Instead of promoting stable accord, the idea of counterbalance perpetuates a discriminatory, lucrative, and destructive cycle. While professionals profit, an illusion lurking in the shadows of our collective psyche excuses the destructive paradigm. Spectators accept its presence without inspection. Its motives and effects slip our consciousness.

The Fundamental Conflict

PPs work for either the entertainment or campaign subsector of the PI, and I devote Chapter 23 to their tactics. For now, it's enough to know they appear in many guises including campaign representative, analyst, pundit, anchor, host, guest, journalist, expert, and so on. They're recognized by spin. Their perspective exposes their natures even when their titles or organizations evince neutrality. They're salaried combatants in the red/blue holy war. They're partisan, and they're getting paid to be partisan. It's their job.

> People who profit from presenting partisan content or get paid to create or ascertain partisan advantage aren't qualified to mediate the national discussion about "dysfunctional" hyperpartisanship because they're conflicted.

The media, including HM, and PPs, loves to call out conflicts of interest. The media considers politicians who receive donations from corporations while legislating to regulate those same corporations conflicted. Local district attorneys who work with local police are considered conflicted when they are responsible for prosecuting those same police accused of crimes.

Conflicts of interest appear to be of great concern, except when discussing hyperpartisanship. I've never heard anyone raise the issue of conflicted interests while discussing hyperpartisanship. The media is content to allow PPs to weigh in and grab leading roles in framing the national discussion. It's like asking mercenaries for a peace plan. It's like asking Brigadier General Jack

D. Ripper how to end the cold war.[20] It doesn't make sense. It offends logic unless you make a living by presenting partisan content or get paid to argue for partisan advantage. Then, the sense is plain. "Dysfunction" is contextual.

Treat It as a Real Issue

The way media treats "dysfunctional" hyperpartisanship is easily distinguishable from other issues. Discussions often start with the impression of sincerity. "It's tearing us up. It's ripping us apart. It's a real problem." Then, invariably, the discussion proceeds in one of two ways. The first one is predictably unhelpful, but the insidious nature of the second is malignant.

The first path is *incorporation*. The issue of "dysfunctional" hyperpartisanship is incorporated into partisan warfare, i.e., it's the other side's fault. While incorporating hyperpartisanship into the partisan war is not without irony, it's not unusual. Contriving antagonistic positions on inherently nonpartisan issues is part of the game. It's integral to professional partisanship.

Although PPs occasionally try incorporation, it's awkward. Hyperpartisanship *as an issue* isn't tailor-made for gaining partisan advantage. It takes two to tango. PPs can have a go at assigning a larger portion of blame to one side, but there's plenty of blame to go around.

"Dysfunctional" hyperpartisanship is acknowledged, but from a partisan perspective, there's not much of a payoff because differentiation isn't clear-cut. There isn't a Republican and Democratic policy position on the issue of hyperpartisanship, in contrast to issues such as health care or climate change. Both sides acknowledge dysfunction and simply lay a larger part of blame on the other side. The opportunity cost of spending resources and media time on an issue that doesn't dramatically differentiate Republicans from Democrats isn't worth it.

The second path, which implicates a positive feedback loop, deserves greater scrutiny. The media treats hyperpartisanship disingenuously.

Discussions between host and guest or panel begin innocently enough,

---

20 *Dr. Strangelove or: How I Learned to Stop Worrying and Love the Bomb,* directed by Stanley Kubrick (Columbia Pictures, 1964).

but wrap-ups are problematic. Invariably, someone will say offhandedly, "hey, there's real division out there." As if to say, "that's who we are." "People fundamentally disagree with one another." "There's nothing we can do about it."

I agree divisions are real. But we don't treat other issues like that. For instance, we don't conclude income inequality discussions with: "Hey, that's just the way it is. There have always been haves and have-nots. That's just who we are." Instead, we treat income inequality as an issue that should and *can* be addressed. Both acknowledging a problem exists and addressing it with a genuine desire to solve it are essential. We need to do a little better on the genuine desire part.

Discussions shouldn't resolve with comments reinforcing the notion that "dysfunctional" hyperpartisanship is unsolvable. Those wrap-ups leave lasting impressions that worm into the collective psyche to disincentivize productive thinking, discussion, and action. That's who we are. There's nothing we can do about it.

Financially Incentivized

> Please get her fired . . . Seriously . . . What the f***? I'm actually
> shocked . . . It needs to stop immediately, like tonight. It's measurably
> hurting the company. The stock price is down. Not a joke.
> —TUCKER CARLSON TWEET, NOV. 12, 2020

We also need to elevate the underlying issues of financial incentives and fragmentation. Most of us have heard TV analysts proclaim partisanship is financially incentivized. I agree. When I've heard that conclusion, assembled experts concur each and every time.

The media analyzing politics unanimously asserts partisanship is financially incentivized. If it's true, it's worth exploring beyond just stating the conclusion. I mean *really* exploring—to the degree that Donald Trump is explored. The subject merits such exploration. It's more fundamental than Donald Trump, more pervasive, and more enduring. Hell, you have 24/7 "news" programming. Go for it.

But there's a slight problem with all that. I call it the fundamental conflict. An honest treatment of the subject matter demands investigation beyond blaming the other team. In other words, it requires analysis not geared for attaining or measuring partisan advantage.

Examining hyperpartisanship requires taking a step back from the conflict. A substantial portion of media isn't cut out for that. They're invested. They're conflicted.

They're also implicated. Financial incentivization of partisanship is not exclusive to political spending, i.e., the PI's campaign subsector. The entertainment subsector, aka the media, feeds at the same trough. In other words, an exhaustive study of the financial incentivization of partisanship by media would require self-examination, real self-examination. Not the type where left-leaning media examines righty media and vice versa. That won't cut it.

There's an added problem. The required examination implicates audiences. Investigating the financial incentivization of partisan content without discussing audience fragmentation is inadequate. The programming model needs audiences segregated according to ideology or partisan bias.

That investigative path leads inexorably to audience introspection. Why am I part of a segregated audience? Why can I only tolerate opinions I agree with? That's a no-no for commercial TV. Copious finger-pointing peppered with tiny morsels of self-examination makes commercial sense. Huge chunks of programming that conclude we're all culpable is a bad idea. If I ran a network depending on advertising revenue, I wouldn't be down with "our audience is part of the problem."

Fragmentation

The actual and virtual segregation of society along partisan lines may be *the* issue of our time. The purpose of this section is not to exhaustively explore fragmentation, but to make the case that the issue is not given its due in media. Here, I briefly outline fragmentation's breadth.

Fragmentation Implicates Marketing

Target audience identification is universally accepted and mostly without inspection. The target audience is a fragment of the entire audience. Fragmentation is inherent to marketing.

While the words "fragment" or "fragmentation" provoke conscious consideration of the subject matter, marketing to target audiences may utilize fragmentation without awareness of broader societal concerns. We're comfortably plugged in. Algorithms permeate the virtual world, finding and connecting consumer fragments with appropriate merchandising and content-providing fragments. I imagine AI as an expediter of financially optimized fragmentation.

Ideology is merchandise marketed for profit. The social utility of an ideology is not necessarily relevant to its marketability. Flashy, provocative, sexy, chic, and convenient, especially convenient, outsells social utility seven days a week and twice on Sunday.

American consumerism, convenience, and ideology make for a salacious *ménage à trois*. "Get your most convenient ideology right here." No assembly required. Just point your finger and blame away. Endorsed by three out of five celebrities. 100 percent post-consumer recycling. No refunds available.

Fragmentation Undermines Accountability

It reduces the incentive, likelihood, and efficacy of self-policing, as mentioned above. When audiences or constituencies segregate along partisan lines, criticizing or holding the other team accountable comes across as gamesmanship and causes escalation. In a frenzied partisan environment, accountability must come from within. But anyone criticizing his own team risks ostracism by fundamentalists. We miss you John McCain.

Fragmentation Exploits Addiction, Has Narcissistic Appeal, and Facilitates Escapism

Flatscreen, flatscreen within the wall, who's the smartest of them all? Whose beliefs are never wrong, and who's been righteous all along? It's you. It's *you*. Your judgment of others is on the ball and your opinions are a clarion call.

What do nicotine, alcohol, gambling, and righteousness affirmation have in common?

Legal + addictive = marketing rapture.

Fragmentation Affects Evolution

No adaptation needed. Just find your place. TV requires the exertion of scrolling and sampling. On the other hand, the virtual world adapts to you. Just do what you do. Eventually your perfect places will be decided for you. The internet learns you. Can't wait for AI. Don't struggle. There's no need. Enjoy.

Fragmentation Is Psychologically, Emotionally, and Intellectually Convenient

It's easier to engage with people who agree with us. Segregation is easy. Integration is demanding work.

Fragmentation Implicates Primitive Inherited Psychology

It's tribal.

Fragmentation Affects Traditionally Nonpartisan Decision-Making

COVID. Those who got news from left-leaning outlets were more likely to get vaccinated than those who watched righty outlets.

Partisan segregation is pervasive, and its effects are not trivial nor adequately understood. Ideologically segregated media isn't up to the task. Imagine analysts regularly appearing on national cable news having a go at a comprehensive examination of ideological segregation. Those venues featuring habitually conscripted "experts" are woefully inadequate. People paid to analyze for partisan advantage aren't qualified to examine hyperpartisanship. Their expertise is a poor fit, and they're conflicted.

A productive exploration of ideological fragmentation requires a combination of economists, psychologists, sociologists, computer and internet specialists, evolutionary biologists, and yes, political analysts. But experts who consistently and enthusiastically take sides in the partisan fray should recuse themselves because they're conflicted.

Societal segregation along ideological lines transcends partisan politics. It affects partisan politics, but heaping blame on the other team doesn't help understanding or deliverance. However, understanding or deliverance cannot be found on the media's bottom line.

Partisan Opinion Entertainment Programming (POEP)

It's just a TV show.

As a kid, playing sports was my favorite activity, and when I couldn't play, I watched sports on TV. I'm not the fanatic I once was, but I still watch sports programming. One show I like is *Pardon the Interruption,* hosted by Tony Kornheiser and Mike Wilbon on ESPN.

One point Tony and Mike repeatedly make is that sporting events such as the Superbowl are TV shows. The Superbowl draws roughly 100 million viewers,[21] and networks take in hundreds of millions in advertising revenue.[22] The actual game is played with some of the finest athletes in the world competing at the highest level, but the Superbowl . . . *is a TV show.*

National Cable News Is a TV Show

Choice is what modern television is all about. You can watch a movie, a baseball game, something educational on PBS, a sitcom, reality TV, or you can watch some POEP. All are valid choices.

With POEP, spin direction and personality are the material distinctions guiding consumer choice. It can't be breadth of coverage, or the particular stories covered. There are more than 300 million Americans, nearly eight billion people in the world, close to 200 countries, dozens of armed conflicts, thousands of bills pending in Congress, fifty states, hundreds of issues, and

---

21 "2020 Super Bowl ratings revealed: Chiefs-49ers ranks as the 11th most-watched show in TV history," CBSsports.com, Feb. 5, 2020, https://www.cbssports.com/nfl/news/2020-super-bowl-ratings-revealed-chiefs-49ers-ranks-as-the-11th-most-watched-show-in-tv-history/.

22 "The Super Bowl is worth billions each year—Here's who makes what," CNBC, Feb. 1, 2019, https://www.cnbc.com/2019/02/01/the-super-bowl-is-worth-billions-each-year--heres-who-makes-what.html.

"eight million stories in the naked city,"[23] but only a few qualify for POEP. Unless there's a crisis, then it's down to one.

Statistically speaking, it's impossible for the limited coverage provided by POEP to be representative of the universe of significant stories. To be fair, that type of representation is impossible for any news outlet. Therefore, there must be a winnowing system.

Extensive study isn't needed to figure out the winnowing system for POEP. The common theme of partisan differentiation is glaring. It's obviously deliberate and not justifiable under the rubric of "news." An hour of nightly network news has more wide-ranging coverage than a week's worth of 24/7 POEP.

So POEP has more time, 24/7, and uses that time to cover fewer stories. But that's OK—right?—because they're doing a deep dive. They dive deeply into fewer stories. They're not supposed to just run through the headlines of the myriad stories relevant to our existence.

But there's a pattern to their deep dives; it's not random, nor should it be. They should dive deeply into the stories that are most relevant to navigating our complex existence. But it's not that either. They dive deeply into stories where ideological and partisan divisions are most striking, thereby emphasizing those divisions.

POEP Presents an Interpretation of Reality Distorted by Proportionality

Consider the feedback loop concept. POEP doesn't simply reflect what's happening. Your nightly network news provides a more accurate reflection.

Not every news story is conveyed most effectively through the lens of partisan analysis. Yet that's the impression cast by POEP, and that impression becomes part of the landscape.

Even when national cable news is in singular crisis mode—think COVID— if there is a partisan angle to measure, it's measured in full.

---

23 *The Naked City*, ABC Television, 1958-1963.

The Seduction of Affirmation

I remember when I was a small child my father gently challenging me with questions about how basic things work. Nothing felt better than to hear him say, "that's right." The warm feeling at my core radiated through my being, and I would beam up at him. He made me feel so smart. What a wonderful feeling.

I was good at school, and I was not shy about answering teachers' questions. My hand would shoot up trying to be first, trying to be best. Answering correctly in front of the entire class felt good too. I was proud.

Sometimes my hand would shoot up without understanding what the teacher was asking. I would blurt out something entirely wrong. Occasionally my answers made so little sense they inspired laughter from my classmates. Then I felt the opposite of good. With crimsoned face and downcast eyes, I would try to disappear while enduring the necessary time for opposite-of-good feeling to dissipate. Live and learn. In addition to knowing beyond any doubt I'm not always right, at some point I gained a modest appreciation for discretion.

Psychotherapist and marriage counselor Mel Schwartz asks couples "if they'd rather be right, or if they'd rather be happy."[24] Although the spoken response is almost always "happy," couples' behaviors toward each other suggest "right" is more compelling.

Finding suitable POEP provides comforting affirmation. I am right. I have all the correct opinions. Don't take my word for it—just listen to the panel of professionals. How glorious to have opinion authorities to call upon with a click to confirm my thinking, like a chorus of sycophants singing, "You are right sir."

It's Addictive

The exploitive nature of television is immortal. All that remains is tailoring content to vulnerable populations. Saturday morning cartoons for children

---

24 Mel Schwartz L.C.S.W., "Why Is It So Important to Be Right?" *Psychology Today*, Mar. 7, 2011, https://www.psychologytoday.com/intl/blog/shift-mind/201103/why-is-it-so-important-be-right.

with accompanying commercials pushing sugar-packed cereals, day-time soaps for lonely and bored spouses, etc. People whose identities inexorably link with partisan affiliation are particularly susceptible to ideological righteousness affirmation. Providing such validation makes good business sense.

Distinguishing Transparency from Entertainment and Publicity

I'm all for transparency, especially concerning political spending. How do political parties and other fundraising entities like political action committees (PACs) and super PACs decide how to distribute all the cash? Precisely who is making those decisions and what are the criteria? I'm a huge fan of more transparency in the political spending arena. I'm eternally interested in knowing if key players benefit from political spending by entities affected by relevant legislation or policy.

However, for negotiating bill provisions or public policy specifics, not so much. "The devil's in the details," you say. That's true. But there's a fine line, and sometimes the line is not so fine, between negotiating in good faith and using media to blow up negotiations either for partisan advantage or self-promotion.

This chapter concerns media and its hyperpartisan impact. Whether shining a large spotlight on policy negotiations between party leaders helps or undermines those efforts isn't relevant to commercial media. What do you call a scoop that blows up a negotiation? It's called a scoop! The banner of transparency is see-through.

Imagine you got in trouble in school, and you're negotiating a resolution with school officials. Or imagine you wish to avoid a lengthy trial and decide to negotiate a settlement. Or imagine you are in marriage counseling with your spouse. How about broadcasting those negotiations on television? Honesty requires admitting live broadcast changes behavior and negotiation dynamics.

Don't get me wrong. Each one of those scenarios would make excellent reality TV. Marriage counseling has been done. I just googled it, but I haven't seen the shows. I don't need to. I've seen reality TV, and I've seen how people behave in those shows. It's unreal, and politicians are people.

Some people avoid cameras. This might seem strange for a politician, but personalities vary even among politicians. The community of politicians is not monolithic. When trapped by cameras or microphones, some people speak lots of words without saying anything. This isn't a bad strategy if you're genuinely concerned with ongoing negotiations and negotiating in good faith. Being secure and not needing the spotlight for self-aggrandizement also helps.

Of course, some people relish the limelight. Most of you have heard the joke about the most dangerous place in the world being between a camera and a certain politician. But using that spotlight for self-aggrandizement is relatively benign. It's nauseating, true, but doesn't necessarily undermine ongoing negotiations.

Conflict versus Accomplishment

Using media to negotiate is cancerous. It's often a ruse to scuttle negotiations. Each team can blame the other for failure and argue that the only path to progress is electing more of us and fewer of them.

This is especially true for public discussions based on characterizations of each side's positions skewed to support partisan narrative. Negotiations based on characterizations allow both sides to truthfully argue the other side's characterizations are wrong or unfair. It's a beautiful thing.

Negotiating in the media works better as a partisan electoral strategy than for finding common ground to advance an issue. I characterize this phenomenon as *issue subordination*, which I explore in greater detail in subsequent chapters.

Even politicians negotiating in good faith who put issue before party can fall prey to the malignancy. A partisan zealot leaks to the press or makes an accusatory public statement. A member of the free press sticks a microphone in the face of the politician negotiating in good faith and with cameras rolling repeats the accusation looking for comment.

In a closed room without cameras, there are many options including ignoring incendiary comments. But when keeping your job requires winning the next election and a national media outlet is recording, the decision-making paradigm can get corrupted. What happens within the brain of a human backed into a corner?

Maybe it decides that finding common ground on the issue isn't so important. After all, compromise is out of fashion. "We've compromised too much already!"

It's hard for me to believe media is not consciously complicit. Media knows broadcasting negotiation details will most likely compromise negotiations. It sets the stage for partisan grandstanding. Using TV to negotiate results in TV programming.

That's not bad for ideologically segregated media outlets. All-out partisan warfare trumps progress on any single issue. That which sabotages progress makes for better TV than progress, and it can all be rationalized as transparency.

Implicit Prejudice

The way anchors and hosts introduce guests or panel members is regularly biased and inappropriate for objective journalism. Sometimes it's explicit. Host or anchor will indicate the next guest is "a friend" of the show or words to that effect. Broad smiles accompany greetings. The message to audiences is unmistakable. "She's one of ours." We agree with what she will say. Her arguments are sound. Allow her to infiltrate your reasoning. Adopting her position is safe.

Sometimes, the host introduces another type of guest. A frown or pursed lips replace a warm smile. Instead of making eye contact, the anchor will appear to look at his notes with furrowed brow. Words like "controversial" replace "friend." The interview will feel more like cross-examination with questions designed to box in the guest—less like questions, more like weapons. Again, the message is unmistakable: "We don't like this guest, and you shouldn't like him either."

The press is free to behave as it sees fit. But I can't pretend I'm not witnessing partisanship. Democracy includes partisan activism. But partisan gamesmanship under the banner of journalism undermines democracy by degrading the institution of the fourth estate. Media incessantly points out that Americans are losing faith in their institutions. Partisan gamesmanship within traditionally nonpartisan institutions contributes to declining faith.

Segregation, Partisanship, and Mediocrity

In a neutral forum with the host on the ball, you'd better have game. It's dynamic. Guests will have to listen carefully to the host and the other guests. Answers will have to be responsive. Falling back on talking points or stringing a bunch of unsubstantiated conclusions together won't cut it. Lack of depth or laziness will be apparent.

Not so with POEP. You just need to be available on the right channel. You can state opinion as fact. You can restate conclusions ad nauseam. Your host, who is also your teammate, passes over shallow arguments and indecipherable sentence construction. The response to the incomprehensible is, "That's OK, we know what you mean." All you need is a constituency and availability.

Media segregation provides soft environments for partisans. Weak arguments are given a free pass. Flawed logic is overlooked. Instead of being weeded out, mediocrity thrives.

24/7 Tit for Tat

The twenty-four-hour rule for responding to incendiary provocation is becoming vestigial. A cooling-off period can be fatal. Media are incessantly looping footage of my opponent sticking it to me into the public psyche. I need to respond now!

The media's role: "He still hasn't responded. He looks weak. He's hiding. This isn't going away. He needs to come out with a statement. The longer he waits, the more we're left to speculate." Hah.

Diplomacy seems silly. There's no legitimate business purpose for the media to facilitate diplomacy between ideological factions or political parties. Light the fuse. Pour gasoline on the fire. That makes sense.

While it's not the media's job to facilitate diplomacy, it's also not the media's job to pour gasoline on the fire. One makes good business sense. One doesn't.

Speak before You Think

The concept transcends political coverage. Sports commentators enthusiastically self-identify as disciples of the philosophy. They gush over athletes who say whatever comes into their heads. Unguarded remarks provide amusing content. Coaches and athletes who are too cautious incur disfavor.

Political commentators are less blatant. Sometimes you'll hear one of them say, "he chooses his words very carefully." Or "he's being very deliberate." Those statements are not complimentary. They imply duplicity. They're meant as red flags: "We need to watch this guy. He's one of those people who chooses his words carefully. You know what *that* means."

Ideas pieced together across neural synapses may consist of images, symbols, metaphors, or other abstractions. Communication requires translating abstractions into written or spoken language. It's difficult even when we take our time, and translations are never perfect.

At least writing includes opportunities to proofread and edit. When speaking extemporaneously, speaking carefully makes sense. Even if you correct yourself on the fly, HM can replay spoken mistakes nonstop without corrections.

From a commercial perspective, scrupulous care is tedious. It interrupts flow. POEP guests spill troves of talking points ad nauseam. Rapid-fire talking points simulate extemporaneous communication and expertise without appearing too careful. It's deceitful. PPs make points without pause because their answers are nonresponsive. They don't advance the dialectic.

It's not conversational. PPs just make their points, which they've made hundreds of times before. There's no spontaneity. It's rote discharge. There's no exploration. There's no discovery. Exploratory dialogue leading to discovery requires responsiveness. It requires participants to listen to one another. When we genuinely listen, scripted talking points prove awkward.

Exploratory dialogue resulting in creative discovery sounds like a ratings winner. But in practice, drawbacks disqualify it. Responsive dialogue requires thoughtfulness. Commercial television can't abide thinking without talking. Also, improvisational dialogue invariably leads to ideas discordant with ordained narratives.

Unconscious Appeal

Sports media explicitly loves unconsciousness. When a basketball player hits several shots in a row at a critical juncture, odds are strong a commentator will say, "she's unconscious." Attributing unconsciousness to an athlete during a performance may be the highest possible compliment. "He's unconscious." Yay!

Former MLB catcher and baseball commentator Tim McCarver used to say about a player mired in a batting slump, "analysis leads to paralysis." I've heard similar wisdom applied to struggling golfers. Overthinking can prolong underperformance, so there's wisdom in pursuing unconsciousness. It seems strange, but for performance, too much consciousness is debilitating.

The guidance isn't as clear for public speaking. Overall, media seems biased toward unconsciousness. This is just another way of saying, "speak before you think." People who speak without deliberation or conscious awareness of the impact of their comments provide rich content. Inappropriate remarks offer media and audiences opportunities to wag fingers, thereby assuming positions superior to the unconscious speaker. "He should have put a little more thought into his comments." This provides an almost adequate segue into partisanship.

The Awareness-Raising Charade

Some deeply into partisan politics want to shout, "you got it all wrong. We want to raise consciousness. That's what we're all about—raising conscious awareness." That sentiment is tactical partisanship.

As stated, this book results in part from self-examination. Here, I examine my relationship with partisan activism operating under the banner of journalism. Becoming consciously aware of my desire to have my opinions affirmed is humbling. I'm not as secure as I pretend to be. I prefer to think of myself as someone who values substance over affirmation, yet I've sought affirmation above substance.

I'm now conscious of this foible. As a result, I'm less susceptible to certain types of manipulation. Or at least if I'm susceptible, I'm more aware while it's happening. Inspecting a compulsion makes it less compelling or mitigates its harm. I have a deeper understanding of my relationship with media, resulting in a less unbalanced relationship. I've gained power through consciousness.

Raising awareness for PPs means something else entirely. First, they're not concerned with raising their own awareness. Why would they? They've already achieved lama-levels of consciousness.

They're not talking about tuned-in audiences either. The awareness-raising performance is presented as such, but it's a play within a play. Audiences are in on it. They've heard this stuff hundreds of times.

Loyalist, segregated audiences aren't being edified. They're being stroked. They're floating weightlessly in a womb of affirmation. "I'm already aware. I can count myself among the highly conscious. Those other people need greater awareness. If only those others were as conscious as me. If everyone were as aware as I am, everyone would agree with me about everything, and the world would be a better place."

The Quicksand of Conflict

People who speak without thinking can be entertaining. They also tend to escalate conflict. In applying for a United Nations job, you wouldn't want to assert that you tend to say whatever comes to mind without considering ramifications or that you like to just throw stuff out there.

Diplomacy clashes with media business. Focusing on commonalities or extending olive branches requires a genuine desire for peace. Media genuinely desires ratings, clicks, and subscriptions. Public policy and political discussions mediated by for-profit media are for-profit discussions. But we're stuck because media provides venues for national dialogue.

Reporters Reporting on Other Reporters' Reporting

This one bothers me without any connection to hyperpartisanship, though it is connected. However, the exacerbating effect on hyperpartisanship is ancillary to and overshadowed by journalistic degradation.

Here, we explore relationships between 24/7 news, journalism, faith in the institution of the free press, and hyperpartisanship. This web part centers on "Faith in the Free Press," however, hyperpartisanship is implicated. To kick off the investigation, I lay out a couple of scenarios based on POEP segments I witnessed. Both situations speak to the role reporters play in 24/7 coverage limited to stories suitable for polarization.

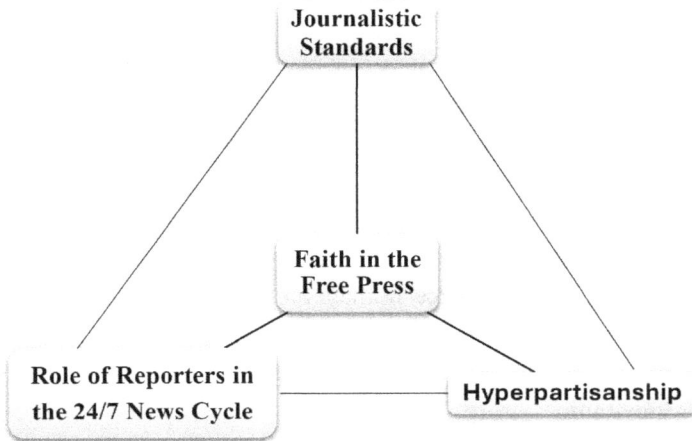

Figure 5.1: Faith in the Press Sub-web

In the first scenario, the anchor introduced a reporter who reported that Axios, based on an anonymous source, had reported on an interaction among staff members in the Trump White House. The anchor cut to a second reporter who reported that the *Washington Post* had also reported that Axios had reported on an interaction in the Trump White House. Neither TV reporter worked for Axios or the *Washington Post.*

First, Axios is the source for the story. Reporting that the *Washington Post* reported that Axios reported the story does not confirm the Axios story. It only shows someone at the *Post* read and decided to report the Axios story. There's no independent confirmation. It's repeating a rumor. More troubling is the national cable news outlet decided to report on the *Post*'s reporting of the Axios reporting. It was clearly to add weight to the rumor. That's sleazy.

The apparently frivolous use of reporters is worth examining. TV reporters reporting on the Axios reporting and the *Post*'s reporting of Axios's reporting were extraneous from a journalism perspective. The anchor could have simply informed his audience of the Axios reporting. Instead, the network employed a reporter to report on the Axios reporting. The reporter was not in studio with the host but was sort of on location. By "on location," I mean somewhere outside in Washington, D.C. I say "sort of" because the reporter was reporting on Axios reporting. That means the TV reporter was reporting what he *read* in Axios. He could have read Axios anywhere.

The network employed a second reporter to report on the *Post*'s reporting of the Axios reporting. So one reporter read Axios, and the other reporter read the *Washington Post*. The two network reporters reported what they read to the host and the host's audience. As to why the network operated in this fashion, we can only guess. Here are my guesses.

My first guess is dramatic effect. Having the anchor simply report the Axios story is bad TV. Cutting to reporters "in the field" is more compelling.

Let's examine from a resource-management perspective. Does a TV network want to employ two reporters to read and report on reporting from two other media outlets? The answer, given the operating paradigm of 24/7 POEP: It's inevitable.

Ideally, every reporter for every media outlet follows their own leads on whatever story they're working on. There are eight million stories in the naked city. There's plenty to go around.

However, stories custom-made for POEP are exceptional. HM chases down reports undermining the opposition or highlighting partisan differences. POEP nurtures stories validating segregated audiences' identities. Round-the-clock coverage geared toward partisan advantage inevitably leads to reporters reporting on other reporters' reporting. When a story perfectly tailored for partisan division is pinpointed, it's all hands on deck for that story. It's POEP gold.

The second scenario relates to the first in that we're dealing with unconfirmed or single-source stories but taken one step further. The next step is the hypothetical analysis or partisan implications of the unconfirmed stories based on anonymous sources. Once again, this consequence of 24/7 coverage focused on partisan advantage or division is inevitable.

It goes like this. The host tells the gist of the unconfirmed story from an anonymous source, which is another way of saying the host repeats a rumor. Then the host turns, usually with some physicality like a turning of the head or torso toward a reporter who may or may not be in the studio to physically turn to, and says something like, "*if the reporting is true*, what does that mean as far as such and such or for so and so?"

Reporter A: "If the reporting is true, then ..."

Host: "Right, if the reporting is true. Reporter B, what do you think, if the reporting is true?"

Reporter B: "If the reporting is true ..."

Host: "Definitely, if the reporting is true. What about you, Reporter C?

Reporter C: "If the reporting is true …"

Host: "No doubt, if the reporting is true. As usual you've all done an incredible job. That was excellent reporting, and we'll have you all back."

Why would a network dedicate time to analyzing hypothetical implications of unconfirmed stories from anonymous sources? Why not wait for facts to be confirmed or refuted? Then reporters, journalists, and analysts can speculate on the implications of nonspeculative facts rather than speculating on rumor. Once again, there are eight million stories in the naked city. There's plenty of concrete material to hash over while waiting for confirmation of partisan rumors.

But then it wouldn't be POEP. For POEP, hypothetical discussions around conjectural implications of rumors based on anonymous sources are better than concrete news, as long as the hypotheticals properly focus on partisan advantage or differentiation. Twenty-four/seven POEP necessitates discussing hypothetical ramifications of unconfirmed rumors from anonymous sources.

Before moving on, I call attention to the phrase, "if the reporting is true." The media prefers this phrase over "if the story is true." So it's not about the story per se, it's about the reporting of the story. It elevates reporting the story over the story itself, thereby elevating the reporter.

Reporters Take Center Stage

I want to briefly examine this before circling back to hyperpartisanship. Reporters are vying for celebrity status. This section identifies factors that might account for this phenomenon, as well as its hyperpartisan implications.

There's a self-serving element that's repulsive. I want to say I don't give a damn about reporters; I only care about the story. But as I've indicated throughout, this book results in part from introspection, especially concerning my relationship with POEP. Is it possible all the chummy, congratulatory pats on the back from anchors or hosts have taken me in? Have I been seduced by the familiarity and ease with which speculation on anonymous rumor is presented as news? Do I unconsciously regard TV journalists the way I regarded rock stars as a teenager?

I don't think so. In fact, this phenomenon helped me kick the POEP habit.

I'll own up to my habit as I owned up to my desire for affirmation. I allowed myself to be stroked by opinion pushers. Kicking back in an intoxicating ether of my own ideas while pasting targets on the cretins to be slain with my superior understanding was excellent escapism. It was good TV.

But a countercurrent rippled beneath my euphoria that, every once in a while, broke the surface to kill my buzz. I can be seduced by affirmation. I love being correct. I admit it. I'm not immune to flattery. However, there's something about alleged journalists stroking each other on TV that makes me want to stick a finger down my throat and purge myself of whatever self-deluding intoxicants I ingested to get me to watch such an obvious perversion of the fourth estate in prime time.

I don't believe I'm alone. Responsibility for the erosion of faith in the institution of the free press rests with the free press. Not the other team's free press. Not red free press or blue free press. Free press is to blame for erosion of faith in free press.

The public knows the difference between TV star and reporter. The essence of celebrity contradicts the essence of journalism. Performers play to the audience. Journalism demands reporting that offends ideologues and fanatics of all stripes.

Many understand what they're consuming is either not journalism or at best a severe degradation. Don't confuse consumption with either endorsement or faith in the institution. Even a junkie knows a casserole from crack.

Back to Hyperpartisanship

Several previous sections speak to the informal nature with which "journalism," especially POEP, is conducted. Having a casual conjecture with "friends of the show" about hypothetical implications of unconfirmed rumors from anonymous sources under the banner of journalism attenuates fact-based reporting while elevating narrative-based reporting to preeminence.

Narrative-based reporting involves zealously chasing down stories supporting an outlet's narrative while emphasizing facts supporting the narrative and ignoring or burying contradicting facts. That's why conducting hypothetical discussions based on unconfirmed rumors from anonymous sources as "if the reporting is true" works so well. There aren't any facts to interfere with narrative. It's not really news. It's story time for one tribe: tribal journalism. Tribes get to tell their stories and pretend it's news, but it's not. It's just a TV show where people tell their team's stories.

Political affiliation or ideology influencing both the way news is reported and the substance of news is hyperpartisanship. It's one thing for media members or outlets to strongly adhere to a party or faction; it's another for that adherence to infiltrate the media's identity to an extent that transforms the way the industry conducts its business and alters the product the industry hawks. Partisanship marketed under the banner of journalism is hyperpartisanship.

Relationship between Media Hyperpartisanship and Faith in the Free Press

Rule: *As media hyperpartisanship increases, faith in the institution of the free press decreases.*

Again, let's not confuse faith with consumption. Lack of faith doesn't imply abstinence. People consume for all sorts of reasons. I confess I slurped POEP due to affirmation-euphoria addiction.

The bottom line requires consumption, not faith. From the financial perspective of commercial media, degradation of faith in free press, at least in the short term, isn't necessarily a degradation of the bottom line. Financially, erosion of faith isn't necessarily dysfunctional. From the short-term financial perspective of commercial media, hyperpartisanship isn't dysfunctional.

Too Clever by Half

For this discussion, step into the shoes of a character I refer to as an issue ideologue. Her persona fuses with a desire for progress on a particular issue or set of issues. She believes progress on the issue or issues can only result from ideology she adheres to and action by the political party she's aligned with. She correctly views the opposition party as obstructionists on issues she cares about.

She finds the coverage by certain media outlets heartening. There's finally primetime, mainstream coverage of her issues. They're not just covering her issues; they're coming from the same place she is. They share her values. Their coverage makes clear the opposition party stands in the way of her progress.

Their coverage bolsters her sense of self while stoking her anger at obstructionists. Not only is the path to victory clear, but the fact that mainstream media illuminates that path in primetime is victory in and of itself.

But here's the cruel twist of too clever by half:

> As media segregates according to ideology and partisan affiliation, its credibility to broader audiences diminishes.

As each outlet's content becomes more narrowly tailored, it begins to feel more like advocacy and less like journalism. The precise quality that bolsters the issue ideologue's faith diminishes the broader public's overall faith in the institution of the free press.

> Advocacy journalism strengthens connections to narrow, ideologically aligned audiences while undermining credibility to broader audiences.

While some viewpoints achieve greater media presence, presentation is less likely to be taken at face value by the public at large because it is more likely to be perceived as advocacy conducted by advocates with a partisan agenda instead of as objective journalism by journalists.

Notice the negative feedback loop. Most feedback loops discussed so far have been of the positive variety. As a reminder, positive feedback tends to amplify, while negative feedback dampens. The phenomenon we're examining here is the effect of partisan media with ideologically segregated audiences on issue advocacy efficacy.

Effect of Hyperpartisan Media on Issue Advocacy

On the one hand, HM is more likely to champion certain issues. But as free press transforms into media for partisan advocacy, public faith in objective journalism decreases. As public faith in the free press for objective journalism decreases, the efficacy of using free press for advocacy also decreases. A logical response to decreased efficacy is to increase advocacy. More advocacy can theoretically counter decreased efficacy. But increasing the volume of advocacy in the free press further reduces faith in objective journalism. So a reduction of faith in a free press dampens the effect of increased presence. Whether HM is a boon or liability for issue advocacy isn't clear. Greater presence, or quantity, is at the expense of credibility, or quality.

I've framed this discussion from the perspective of the issue ideologue. Greater clarity may arise from an alternative perspective. How about officers or board members of commercial media outlets? Issue advocacy efficacy what?

Profitability rather than effective advocacy measures private sector viability. If officers and board members don't act accordingly, they breach fiduciary responsibilities to shareholders. Whether HM with ideologically segregated audiences is a boon or liability for issue advocacy is beside the point. It's about ratings, clicks, and subscriptions. And where is the issue ideologue under this analysis? That one's easy. She's a ratings data point.

Let's try on one more pair of shoes. What about "nonpartisan" not-for-profit organizations advocating issues of public interest whose professional representatives make regular appearances on the POEP circuit? I wonder if not-for-profits believe HM helps or hinders their advocacy.

I don't know the answer, but I'll frame the inquiry through bifurcated analysis. We've explored the two lines to some degree through our issue ideologue and commercial media outlet board of directors.

Actual Progress

First, it makes sense to consider the question in terms of tangible progress on issues. More progress means HM helps advocacy and less progress means hyperpartisanship thwarts advocacy.

Here, I bifurcate the analysis. What is progress? Progress can mean policy change. Government either passes a law, changes regulation, or more fairly or efficiently enforces existing law. Or private sector entities like corporations transform their business. That's progress!

Raising Awareness Is Also Progress

Making more people aware of an issue or fundamental societal problem is progress. The hope is greater awareness will lead to congruent policy or behavioral changes.

Once again, I partition the inquiry. As a reminder, our first line of inquiry is progress on the issue, i.e., actual policy change or awareness-raising. But whose awareness does HM with ideologically segregated audiences raise, and to what effect?

Preaching to the Choir

Awareness-raising to ideologically segregated audiences is preaching to the choir. While some choir members may not have had the opportunity to familiarize themselves with all the hymns, most will have memorized the popular refrains.

However, awareness-raising within HM has at least two other purposes.

Identity Validation

The first is identity validation or stroking the audience. Choir members who memorize the refrain can feel good about being in that number who are aware.

Weaponization

The second purpose is weaponizing awareness-raising for partisan advantage. My team is the aware team. The problem with this country is people on the other team aren't as enlightened. Anyone as aware as I am would agree with me about everything important.

Awareness-raising can lead to positive change. However, using HM to raise awareness is problematic. It doesn't feel honest. It raises the degree of awareness among the already aware, instead of raising the amount of awareness by reaching the previously unaware.

This gets back to faith in free press and too clever by half. HM provides platforms for advocates. But mixing awareness-raising with partisan advocacy undermines cognitive responsiveness. A part of our brain recognizes the duplicity and whispers, "I don't think so."

Now let's explore the second line of inquiry in our attempt to provide a suitable framework for analyzing whether HM is a boon or liability to issue advocacy. As a reminder, the first line was actual progress, which could man-ifest in policy or behavioral changes or in awareness-raising.

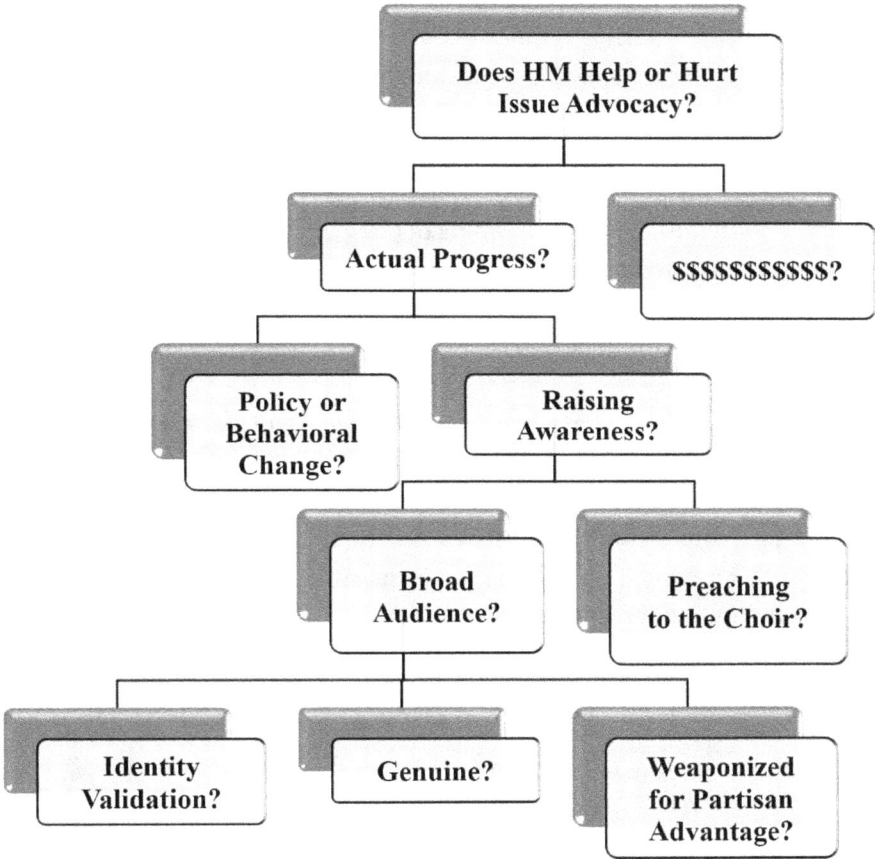

Figure 5.2: HM and Issue Advocacy Efficacy

Money

The second line is analogous to trying on the shoes of officers and board members of commercial media outlets. Not-for-profits have boards too. Agendas for every board meeting include discussing organizational finances.

How does HM with ideologically segregated audiences financially affect issue advocacy? The second line of inquiry is money. Actual progress and money are the two lines.

The answer to both lines of inquiry is: It depends on the issue, people, and organizations involved. Not all issues and organizations appear regularly on POEP. I can think of several reasons for this. Some organizations and issue advocates may take their nonpartisan status to heart and aren't comfortable being used as weapons in partisan warfare. POEP shows may have learned which issue advocates are more willing to play partisan politics and therefore are more likely to invite them.

Actual Progress versus Money

Let's examine the financial advantages for issue advocates appearing regularly on POEP. Before doing that, I need to highlight a relevant distinction between actual progress and fundraising. Actual progress in democracy may require convincing a majority of the electorate. With actual progress, the "too clever by half" phenomenon or negative feedback loop is in play. As a media outlet becomes more partisan and oriented toward advocacy, overall credibility to broader audiences for presenting objective information diminishes. Blatant partisan advocacy hamstrings the outlet's ability to reach a democratic majority.

This isn't a problem for fundraising. It's an advantage. With fundraising or marketing, a large part of the battle is identifying target audiences. You don't want to waste time with people who aren't going to contribute. You want to find supporters and make your pitch. Segregation solves a marketing dilemma. The target audience is everyone watching.

Segregation of HM audiences can be understood as target audience identification for fundraising. Regular POEP appearances for certain issue advocates is good business. The issue ideologues watch. Some may think, "I'd like to support that group."

Once again, with hyperpartisanship, "dysfunction" is contextual. Financial incentives for its perpetuation abound.

Lateral Expansion and Adaptation

The creep of hyperpartisanship across the landscape feels inevitable. I'm tempted to say media is the vanguard of lateral expansion but given our discussion of the chicken and the egg and the dynamics of feedback loops, I'm reticent. Concepts of visibility and vanguard are easily muddled. In battle, officers have been known to remove distinguishing regalia to avoid being targeted.

Given our evolutionary framework, the notion of vanguard seems incongruous. The first seed a flower disperses may fall on pavement, whereas the last seed may find rich soil. Segregation along ideological lines coupled with limitless political spending provides a fertile environment for partisanship. In such an ecosystem, hyperpartisan behavior is adaptive. Visibility, on the other hand, isn't necessarily malignant or benign, but it *is* an environmental factor.

Another way of understanding visibility is by considering media a tool. It can be a tool for good. Raising awareness about the struggles of marginalized communities during the last half-century has been positive, especially if you broaden the concept of media beyond news to include Hollywood and TV drama. Dramatically humanizing the traditionally disenfranchised genuinely raises consciousness across broad audiences.

However, a hammer is not limited to driving nails. Alleging influence for positive change while claiming to be a mere reflection of negative phenomena is childishly self-deceptive, spineless, or deliberately deceitful. Only the goofiest of media partisans could endorse that analysis. It defies reason. Visibility is an environmental factor. Visibility matters, always.

Increased partisan content in media is obvious to anyone above a certain age. I outlined this expansion while introducing changing environmental factors relevant to evolving hyperpartisanship. To ready our examination of lateral expansion, I briefly reiterate.

There used to be a handful of television stations, and all were free. The entire TV audience divided among as few as three channels. Competition between a handful of channels precluded programming narrowly tailored for partisans of any ilk.

Programming expanded to hundreds of channels, and extra channels required monthly fees to cable or satellite providers. Fees along with media conglomerates owning dozens of channels made expansion profitable. The audience divided among hundreds of channels instead of a handful.

As alternatives increase, fragmentation increases. Providing narrowly tailored content becomes economically feasible with increased fragmentation. As narrowly tailored content becomes possible, political content narrowly tailored for partisan or ideologically segregated audiences becomes economically feasible.

A Few Channels → Hundreds of Channels → Fragmentation of Viewing Audiences for Non-Political Programming → Partisan or Ideological Segregation of Political Programming.

None of this seems unusual. You could say partisan or ideological segregation for political analysis in an environment including hundreds of channels was inevitable. Twenty-four seven POEP is no stranger than 24/7 cooking, sports, or retro TV. If that's what you're into, that's what you're into.

But that's not what this section is concerned with. It's about the next step–lateral expansion. Why is partisan content infiltrating programming that was traditionally either apolitical or marginally political and nonpartisan, and what's the impact of such infiltration?

The process is plain. Just combine natural selection with commercial media. Evolution uses trial and error. Try something. If it works, it sticks. "Works" means enough people tune in for commercial viability.

But why are people tuning in, and why do they persist? I was one of those people, and the short answer is *tribalism*. Before I expound through unflattering self-examination, I need to mitigate an apparent contradiction.

Isn't the success of traditionally apolitical programming infused with partisan content evidence that audiences changed, and partisan programming simply reflects that change? It's one thing to cast about fancy feedback-loop theories for news. People watch news, at least in theory, to stay informed. News disproportionately informing on stories emphasizing partisan division or advantage affects audiences' perceptions. Through proportionality alone, it's easy to recognize POEP doesn't simply reflect. It also affects.

POEP attracts a specific set—partisan political junkies. I was one of them. I was a heavy user.

But we're trying to understand lateral expansion. Late shows, comedy/variety programming, awards shows, even TV dramas and sitcoms incorporate partisan and ideological content. I initially considered lateral expansion as partisan and ideological content infiltrating non-POEP shows. Lateral expansion can also be considered different varieties of POEP. POEP can take the form of news shows, late-night variety shows, talk shows, movies, sports talk, sitcoms, TV dramas, or awards shows. POEP is mutating into different strains. POEP is multiplying. Everything is becoming POEP.

But audiences for these shows are too broad, aren't they? There aren't that many political junkies out there. Do political junkies multiply with POEP? Are there different strains? This seems to substantiate reflection theorists. Partisan programming in all its guises is growing. That can't happen unless audiences are changing. That can't happen unless audiences, i.e., the public, are becoming more partisan.

The Enigma of Change

Consider the concept of change in general and difficulties showing causality, especially from the perspective of a participant or one impacted by change, which we all are. It's like trying to capture a landscape in watercolor during a rollercoaster ride.

This is a suitable time to fulfill my promise of unflattering introspection. I used to be into late-night variety and comedy shows that mercilessly ridicule the other team with aggressive humor. I was addicted to POEP and a variety of its mutations.

I confessed my desire for affirmation, but it goes deeper. I used to run with a politically active crowd. I did government relations in Albany, N.Y., and Washington, D.C., for a not-for-profit. It was my job and the job of my colleagues to pay attention to what was happening on the political landscape.

I got a kick out of partisan humor. But it was more than just a kick. I was bonding with my colleagues—with my tribe. We watched the same stuff. We repeated some of the funnier jokes to each other. It reminds me of memorizing *Monty Python* sketches to enact with my friends during high school. Only I wasn't in high school anymore.

Ego-boosting is also implicated. Partisan humor is painted with a veneer of erudition. I get the jokes because I'm well-informed. Look how politically sophisticated I am.

But my job was to be well-informed. Audiences I'm referring to are significantly broader. Not everyone tuning in to POEP or its mutations have political jobs.

When I left the not-for-profit, I became less interested in politics. My sabbatical lasted several years. During the Obama candidacy and administration, I gradually allowed myself to be reinfected. My infection peaked during the Trump administration.

As I began drafting this book in earnest while grappling with my POEP addiction, I became less enamored. At first, I watched incessantly. I told myself it was research. But as I wrote and watched and analyzed and wrote, I lost my appetite. My analysis of the subject matter, which required a fair amount of self-analysis concerning HM, precipitated change. I no longer viewed my obsession with POEP as evidence of political sophistication. I understood it as addiction, and I was beginning to kick the habit. I was evolving. Isn't that wonderful?

But it was more than that. In truth, I was identifying less with the humor. I felt more like I was taking the brunt. It's all passing me by. I'm getting old. I'm becoming an old man. I'm becoming a target. I'm being made fun of.

What's all this change then? Am I just getting old? The world is continuously changing and always too fast for the aged. Hyperpartisanship is just the latest in an extensive line of elders' observations.

But what is maturity for, if not perspective? Changes have occurred that can't be written off as shadows beneath gathering cobwebs of an aged mind. Private political spending has increased to industrial proportions. The number of TV channels has exploded. The internet and social media have come to be. Audiences have fragmented. But is audience fragmentation evidence that audiences changed, and if they have, what does this have to do with hyperpartisanship?

Initially, I take the position audiences have not fundamentally changed. Thus far, I've said that audience segregation according to political affiliation contributes to hyperpartisanship, and media is more than mere reflection. Segregated media influences society toward hyperpartisanship. Maybe that's true in a much gentler way than I've implied. I'm going to tie this idea to the concept of visibility, which I left hanging.

Perhaps audiences, i.e., the public, were always just as partisan or ideo-logically segregated as now, at least in their minds, and if not their conscious minds, within their souls. In evolutionary terms, seeds of hyperpartisanship eternally present within humanity await favorable environmental conditions. Media explosion into hundreds of TV channels plus internet and social media transform the ecosystem to allow our hyperpartisan natures to germinate and bloom. It's wonderful when you think about it. Better TV and social media freed us from repressing our true hyperpartisan selves. Yay!

Of course there are more sides to this story. Most people believe we should work toward a fairer and more civil society, and most Americans believe that requires some form and level of democracy. But functional democracy de-mands collaboration awkwardly juxtaposed against the freedom of ideological diversity and segregation.

Also, and this idea is explored in subsequent chapters, organizing forces funnel the myriad of newly unrepressed and diverse ideological souls into an essentially binary, i.e., polarizing paradigm. In other words, the ideological freedom and diversity provided by new media is illusory.

Just to recap, we're examining media influence or visibility and the concept of change as it pertains to the relationship between changing media, segre-gated audiences, and hyperpartisanship. What has changed, and how does it relate to hyperpartisanship?

Partisan Content and Identity

In addition to increased political spending and partisan media segregation, one more element of change must be introduced before we complete our anal-ysis. It concerns the relationship between partisan affiliation and self-identity. Regardless of whether Americans are more or less divided according to party or ideology, they are more likely to self-identify that way.

The portion of identity people attribute to political or ideological affilia-tion has increased. Or at least we think that way, or at least we talk that way. When asked about our values, partisan or ideological affiliation creeps into our answers more than it did forty years ago.[25]

25 Pew, "Values Surveys."

Through identity, political disagreement becomes existential. Linking identity to partisan affiliation transmutes political disagreement into personal attack. This has at least two effects.

First, compromise becomes less palatable. In a hyperpartisan atmosphere, compromise translates to selling out one's identity. Second, it's a boon to PI. The product being pushed, partisanship, is usurping consumer identity. That's a marketing coup.

Visibility and Identity

Distribution of partisan content throughout the media landscape facilitates a deeper identification with partisanship. Everyone's doing it. Belittling fellow Americans who think differently than we do with aggressive humor is fine. All the hip cats on TV do it. They may be bona fide celebrities in fields other than politics, but when they appear on POEP, they are their political affiliations. They are their ideologies.

This is powerful from an indoctrination perspective, especially with POEP mutations. Observing blatant partisan advocacy from PPs within the context of political news-programming is mundane. Watching beloved celebrities engage in ideological proselytizing as part of a variety or comedy show is considerably more powerful. It does a better job of normalizing hyperpartisanship. Regardless of your lot in life, partisanship is quite fashionable.

I don't mean indoctrination into specific ideology, but into the concept of profound identification with partisan affiliation. Media explosion sets up safe spaces for intense partisan identification. Increased media choice effectively segregates audiences according to partisan affiliation, while galvanizing personal identity along partisan or ideological lines.

Die-hard partisans probably think, "Good. My personal politics and ideology becoming more visible throughout the media landscape means my team is winning!"

First off, if you believe you're winning, making fun of the other team is poor sportsmanship. It's a character flaw.

Second, you're not winning. You're *too clever by half*. From the perspective of progress, hyperpartisan segregation has resulted in policy stagnation. Progress in a democracy requires compromise. In a hyperpartisan environment, compromise is regarded as an existential threat to personal identity. Your clever jokes drive segregation. Segregation inhibits constructive communication. Democracy is awkward even *with* constructive communication. Without it, you get dysfunctional hyperpartisanship, keeping in mind "dysfunction" is a matter of perspective.

In other words, there *are* winners. The entertainment subsector expands laterally to occupy more niches as revenue for the campaign subsector rises. From the perspective of those profiting from presenting partisan content, the system functions magnificently. Watching programs featuring your politics in a creative and seemingly irrefutable manner may persuade you to believe you're making progress, but you're not. You're watching TV targeting your demographic. You're a ratings data point.

Conclusions

Free press is not the enemy of the people. But where is the free press?

Sometimes I speculate about journalism in academia. I imagine a journalism professor saying, "Let facts dictate story. However, you may be more successful in today's environment if you impose a partisan narrative." You probably wouldn't hear that, but those inclined to view or frame the world according to partisan viewpoints may be preferentially selected for, naturally.

What principles of journalism are divined from consuming POEP? How would those principles align with those prescribed in a journalism curriculum?

Claiming media presentations merely reflect audience desires or societal values doesn't pass the straight-face test. The relationship between content and constituents is complex and dynamic. Hyperpartisanship factors into the dynamic as both input and output. It's both ingredient and product. It results from processes it helps shape. As content, it reflects and penetrates, and its penetrations modify sources of reflection.

Free press is critical to functional and sustainable democracy. Could it be so as mere reflection? The public experiences free press. Along with inherited biology, experience shapes us.

A commercial press, as well as one dependent upon donations, is not free from revenue considerations. Therefore, revenue considerations affect content.

Partisan content effectively generates revenue in a media environment segregated according to partisan affiliation or ideology. The public policy discussion is framed, at least in part, in consideration of ratings generated from partisan content. Public policy discussion in America is a ratings-driven discussion colored by partisan advocacy conducted under the banner of journalism.

The economic viability of partisan programming allows lateral expansion of PI's entertainment subsector. Partisan content infiltrating traditionally apolitical or nonpartisan formats increases partisanship's visibility.

Visibility matters. We identify with what we see. Partisan content infiltrating more of the landscape magnifies its impact on our individual and cultural identities.

Remedy?

The First Amendment doesn't permit legal remedy, nor should it. The absolute necessity of a press free to publish without government infringement carries vagaries of human personality. Legislating away frailties such as vanity and greed without defiling the virtue of candor is impossible.

The remaining potential remedies are media and audience self-regulation. In an environment where audiences segregate according to partisanship, media self-regulation transmutes into tribalism. Partisan media outlets are regiments in tribal warfare. The ruse of accountability provides partisan content. It's another way of playing to partisan audiences. "Our journalism is superior to theirs." That's not self-regulation.

Self-regulation can work, but it depends in part on the profession being regulated and for what it's being regulated. Because its commercial success is independent of its reliability for honesty or accuracy, POEP self-regulation for the qualities of honesty or accuracy rings hollow.

I don't see much evidence society values honesty. It's given lip service. But what does it mean to value something? Time spent watching TV, exploring the internet, or reading are definitive valuation criteria. In the context of commercial media, value means ratings, clicks, or subscriptions.

People enjoy a good story, especially if they can imagine it's their story or if they can easily identify with one of the main characters. We could conceive of some nongovernmental independent nonpartisan regulatory entity funded through contributions from media corporations. The entity, with input from journalists and academics, could develop a code of professional responsibility for journalism. The entity could rate "news outlets" and individual "journalists" by their adherence to the code and widely publish results.

The independent entity could sanction bad actors for cherry-picking facts, presenting stories driven by narrative instead of fact, skewing presentations to support narrative, disproportionately reporting stories supporting narrative, presenting opinions as fact, framing stories to emphasize narrative, manipulating human psychology to market narrative, and so on. Sanctions could take the form of public shaming for less egregious offenses or actual fines for making shit up. Failure to comply could mean losing accreditation from the nongovernmental professional entity.

So what? You don't need any stinking accreditation. You just need to tell a good story—one your constituency prefers.

Responsibility, the Apparent Contradiction Revisited, and Choice Dynamics

Are you capable of humility? Here, I explore the relationship between responsibility and humility.

In commercial settings within free societies, the choice of consumption rests with the consumer. The consumer chooses. We choose. You choose. You are the subject of that sentence. We are the subject of this media chapter. You are the subject of this book. It's about us.

The contradiction appears implicated. The media really is mere reflection. Media reflect consumer choice.

Why do we choose, and what are the impacts of our choices on ourselves? We compartmentalize. Compartmentalization can facilitate getting by but can interfere with understanding. Analyzing the foundations of our choices may disturb our enjoyment. Awareness of the impact of those choices can be stifling. Sitting next to someone in a theater who insists on sharing insight as the movie unfolds is a drag. It ruins the experience.

I want to ruin the POEP experience. I want to ruin POEP for everyone. But I can only do it with your help. Your assistance comes in the form of humility. I'm begging for humility.

We know, on an intellectual level, advertising works. We know it statistically. But that's a far cry from admitting we are data points contributing to those statistics—that it works on us. We like to think we only buy what's needed. Advertising works on the weak-minded. I'm not a victim of repetition. I don't succumb to peer pressure. Celebrity endorsement is vacuous. Nostalgia is Pollyannaish. I'm immune to storytelling. I know for damn sure these *are* the droids I'm looking for. Jedi mind tricks don't work on me.

A free society implies consumer choice, but choice can be manipulated. The first step in destroying POEP is admitting we're susceptible to manipulation. *I* am capable of being manipulated. Please summon the humility necessary to take this first step.

The second step also requires humility. It's an admission of vulnerability. In the abstract, the concept isn't too difficult. To a certain extent, we are the choices we make. This one may be easier for older folks. Looking back, we appreciate how choices we've made fashioned our identity. We're defined by opportunities we've taken advantage of as well as ones we've let slip away.

Let's apply that theory of identity construction to media consumption. It's easy to perceive, or at least acknowledge, how twenty years in a specific vocation or relationship has influenced our character. But are we capable of acknowledging that our media choices infiltrate our identities? Consumer regulation of media requires such an acknowledgement.

Who we are is a product of both nature and nurture. The relationship is dynamic. Our nature guides our choice of experience, which contours our inheritance. Experience modifies our brains.

Sometimes personal evolution is palpable. We come upon something we enjoy, and we know it's good for us. It resonates. Something wonderful within us awakens to the experience. We let it nurture us. On the other hand, sometimes we experience something and say to ourselves, "that's not for me."

Usually, it's not so obvious, especially concerning media and virtual reality. Compartmentalization and the way we categorize experience are implicated.

We distinguish active participation from watching or reading. There's a difference between climbing Everest and watching a documentary about mountaineers ascending its summit. We tend to categorize the first as experience and the second as watching the experience of others.

But watching does not rule out active participation or experience. Sure, it's possible to sit in front of the TV and completely space out. Whether or not programming successfully infiltrates on some unconscious level is not presently germane. But if you're paying attention, your brain actively takes part. You're experiencing the program. You're having an experience.

Experience nurtures character. *Every time we make a media choice, we're making a decision affecting our character and identity.* Consumer regulation of media flows effortlessly from that acknowledgement. What do I wish to nurture within myself? Do I want to stoke negative emotions toward those I perceive as political opponents, or would I like to exercise my empathy muscles? Do I want to feed adversarial perceptions by emphasizing differences or challenge my prejudices by seeking common ground? Do I want to coddle myself with identity validation, or would I like to evolve?

Substantial impediments to acknowledging the gravity of media choices exist. Our egos obstruct our efforts in at least two ways. First, we don't like to concede vulnerability. It's like admitting we're manipulated by advertising. It may work statistically, but not on me. I'm too solid to be tricked like that.

The second involves tension between identity validation and personal evolution. There's a part of us, the ego, which likes to think we don't need to evolve. That's why identity validation is such a powerful ratings tool. You're perfect just the way you are. You don't need to change one iota. Those others are the problem. They're the ones needing change.

Identity validation is ego intoxication. Pushing it is like pushing smack. Kicking it is like kicking smack. The first step is admitting its impact. But admitting an addiction to righteousness affirmation and acknowledging that addiction interferes with personal evolution is admitting you need to evolve—that you're not perfect—which requires humility.

Our talent for compartmentalization also hinders our recognition of the role media choices play in our personal evolution in at least two ways. First, we tend to categorize media as entertainment. We're just relaxing. Because we're in entertainment or relaxation mode, we're immune to experience. If your brain engages in the activity, you're experiencing the activity, and that experience affects you.

Second, the way we distinguish mind from body or mental from physical is flawed and frustrates personal evolution. Around the holidays each year, many of us look in the mirror and decide on a plan of action for our bodies. This past New Year, I gave up soda, desserts, and between-meal snacks. I'm eating less junk food.

Identity validation is junk food for the brain. It's worse. It's brain junk. It's crack. How about quitting brain junk for the New Year? Let's resolve to consciously acknowledge that every single time we engage media, we make a mind-nurturing decision.

There's no magic mirror that so plainly reveals the figure of our minds as common sense. Either your mind is in perfect shape or not. Which is more likely? Does your current understanding of the universe conform with your understanding as a fifteen-year-old? Was the evolution of your teenage mind the product of righteousness affirmation, or was it through challenge, mistake, experimentation, and hardship? Can you pinpoint the moment in your life when evolution of your mind consummated? Are you a Buddha?

Enter humility and responsibility. Having humility to acknowledge your mind can still evolve and to appreciate that media driven by identity validation retards evolution provides a foundation for audience regulation of media. You regulate media by evolving yourself. Media regulation is a secondary outcome of personal regulation. Media regulation is an ancillary benefit of a personal ambition to grow. Personal growth benefits from humility—acknowledging you can improve and are vulnerable to experience. The result is more responsible stewardship of society. It's up to us. It's up to you. Turn off POEP. Wreck their ratings, but not out of vindictiveness. Do it for yourself.

Remedy Redux

Media: Consistently present facts that contradict your narrative.

Consumer: Don't consume narrative-based content that omits contrary facts or content whose primary purpose is to emphasize differences between groups of people.

Generations

Perhaps it's simply a matter of adaptation. Maybe we haven't fully adapted to the new paradigm. But how could we? Media is evolving explosively. Its cosmos is a hot plasma coalescing into unfamiliar forms. The advancing universe outpaces wisdom. Obsolescence continuously looms on an ephemeral horizon. Relevant experience sets with each day's sun.

Maybe it must run its course. Like children with a new toy, we've gone overboard. But we need to try it out, don't we? Let's take it for a spin. Responsibility and moderation are for later, after we break some stuff. Surfing for moderation on the internet is like ordering cornflakes at a four-star restaurant. It's like driving a Ferrari around a parking lot. The internet is extreme, dude!

What about kids? Maybe birth into a world of evolving media technologies confers immunity. I have my doubts. We were all exposed to television commercials before we could speak, yet we remain susceptible. Contagions elegantly evolve to exploit vulnerabilities. Commercial algorithms adapt faster than we do.

Future generations will develop within ecosystems fully integrated with extreme partisan content. Consumerism mingled with evolving media technologies can indoctrinate the public into hyperpartisanship as easily as any fashion obsession. I doubt that immunity can be conferred through unconscious exposure. Only through awareness and deliberate effort can we develop resistance to sophisticated manipulation.

Surrendering to psychological predispositions without inspection is lazy. Inspecting a compulsion makes it less compelling or reduces its malignancy. We must become conscious of the role our psychological predispositions play in our choices. Algorithms that map our preferences and offer, with an unconscious click, titillating versions of the desires found at the extremities of our awareness challenge aspirations to consciousness.

The bottom line is: We're customers. Consider it a business transaction, but the merchandise is not accurate information. The product provided is that which will induce us into becoming sustaining customers. That's the product—that which brings us back.

What brings you back? When you read a newspaper, do you jump to opinion pages? Why? POEP displays opinion on the front page, page two, and throughout. I was in denial of the allure of righteousness affirmation. In the instant I became aware of its effect, its hold on me dissolved.

We're all just trying to make our way in the world. That includes media correspondents, publishers, producers, owners, etc. The way media makes its way in the world isn't necessarily helpful to society because media's bottom line doesn't require it. Identity-validating content provides a solid foundation for tribalism as well as being fundamental to partisan segregation. Partisan segregation undermines the communication necessary for functional democracy.

It's perfectly natural to prefer stories validating your identity. But don't mistake righteousness-affirming narrative for journalism.

— 6 —

Playing with Extremism

The tree of liberty must be refreshed from time to time with
the blood of patriots and tyrants. It is its natural manure.
—Thomas Jefferson

Hyperpartisanship couples with extremism. Their mutual purpose is survival. Segregation insinuates itself into the ménage. Extremism, hyperpartisanship, and segregation conspire in lucrative procreation.

Relationship between Extremism and Hyperpartisanship

Extremism lends reason to hyperpartisanship by rendering compromise repugnant. Questing for common ground becomes ludicrous.

Hyperpartisanship, which subsumes segregation, provides an environment amenable to proliferating extremism. Free from the mitigating effects of contrary opinion, ideological segregation nurtures the extreme.

As partisans coalesce at the extremes, ideological distance between political parties increases. Greater ideological distancing translates into clear-cut product differentiation, helping PI's campaign subsector.

Characterizing opposition as extreme is a traditional partisan tactic. In addition to clear-cut product differentiation, extremism makes working with the other side seem impossible. If working with the other party is impossible, the only path to progress is partisan victory. From an electoral perspective, actual or perceived extremism is of great utility.

Extremism also works for the entertainment subsector. On the internet, algorithms ascertain human preference for extreme content to profitably gratify users. On TV, partisan clowns make great sport of opposition extremism. Segregated partisan audiences are untroubled by their laughter or finger-wagging. Extremism frees judgmentalism from conscious inhibition.

The discussion until now isn't meant to intimate that PI deliberately instigates extremism. But PI is at least an ancillary beneficiary. Extremism, along with partisanship, is financially incentivized.

Extremism as Compensation

People employ compensation mechanisms to offset or mask inadequacies. It has been postulated that men carrying big guns are compensating for a specific deficiency. That's how I perceive extremism. The pertinent inadequacy is a general feeling of impotence, and engaging in extremism is an attempt to compensate for it.

I'm reminded of the type of unconscious bragging we used to undertake as children concerning sports or rock 'n' roll fandom. Endless discussions around who knew the most about a team or a band. Tireless boasting about who watched the most games or attended the most concerts. We made our cases for being the most extreme fan. As children, we were mostly unconscious of our motivations for engaging in the mindless competition.

Unfortunately, as an adult environmental professional, I engaged in analogous gamesmanship. Who is the greater environmentalist? Who is the better progressive? Who is the truer conservative? Who is the real American? An extreme line of reasoning leads inexorably to conclude that whoever's proposals are the most extreme wins. "Ten-percent reductions over twenty years? And you call yourself an environmentalist? I want twenty-percent reductions." "Oh yeah? I want fifty-percent reductions over ten years. I win. Look at me. I'm the best." Really? You sound like a child in the school yard bragging of your fandom.

Extremism Systematics

I divide extremism into two general categories: *substantive* and *procedural*.

Substantive

Substantive extremism is further divided into three categories: facially extreme, extreme by quantity, and extreme by time frame.

Facially extreme means substantive policy that's obviously extreme or extreme on its face, such as banning people who practice a certain religion from entering the country, or defunding police.

Extreme by quantity means reasonable substantive policy changes that become unreasonable by amount or quantity, like asking for 100-percent reduction in greenhouse gas emissions.

Extreme by time frame means reasonable substantive policy that becomes unreasonable through speed of implementation, like asking for reasonable reductions in greenhouse gas emissions by Friday.

Procedural

Procedural extremism implicates manner or process of advocacy rather than policy substance. Using violence or destruction is procedural extremism. Terrorism is an extreme form of procedural extremism.

Conspiracy Theory

I considered including this subsection in Chapter 22, which deals with religion and hyperpartisanship. Engrossing oneself in pursuit of something located between insubstantial and nonexistent requires at least a modicum of faith. However, one could similarly describe the pursuit of theoretical physics, so we need to mind our judgmentalism. Along those lines, this subsection is not about schizophrenia or any psychological impairment causing hallucination without psychedelics. Conspiracy is engaged in too broadly to be explained away exclusively by severe mental illness. At least I hope that's the case.

Consider conspiracy as extreme political narrative. It's not substantive extremism. It's not asking for too much along an unrealistic timetable.

It seems procedural, but not like throwing Molotov cocktails. It's more like a hunger strike, like the Mahatma. It's a *reality* strike!

However, Gandhi consciously undertook hunger strikes for specific reasons, such as protesting religious intolerance and British colonial rule. Whether or not reality-strikers are consciously aware of the political underpinnings of their protest is a question for professional psychologists. Nonetheless, reality-strikers' political message, if there is one, is clear. They'd rather chase unicorns than take part in a system that marginalizes them.

Also, conspiracy-theorizing gains a foothold in ideologically segregated media as a partisan tactic. It's simple. When you lose, or better yet, when you perceive the likelihood of losing, engage in conspiracy-theorizing.

To better understand the dynamic, please resist harshly judging PPs promoting conspiracy. Whether or not agents of conspiracy are true believers is only marginally relevant to our analytical framework. If a profitable niche is found, it will be inhabited.

Conspiracy in this context is better understood as a manifestation of partisan media with segregated audiences. If viability required appealing to integrated audiences, partisan conspiracy wouldn't fly. Partisan media segregation permits normalizing partisan conspiracy-theorizing. More generally, fragmentation opens the door for the fringe to enter the mainstream.

Extremism Efficacy

This discussion is analogous to our examination of the "Effect of HM on Issue Advocacy" in the preceding chapter, depicted graphically in figure 5.2. Figuring out efficacy requires contextualization that considers objective. For example, if the purpose of the 9/11 attacks was to promote Islam as a religion of peace, it failed. On the other hand, if the intent was to escalate a cycle of violence, the attacks succeeded.

With hyperpartisanship, analyzing impacts of the different forms of extremism separately makes sense. I begin with the substantive variety.

Substantive Extremism

Substantive extremism works best as partisan electoral strategy. Introduce legislation or propose policy extreme enough to prevent opposition support. Then argue the only way to progress is voting the other team out.

However, substantively extreme proposals prevent majority support from either team. But with partisanship, discretion is the better part of honesty. Loose lips sink ships. Disclosing information means betraying party, unless you're forced into a primary and your zealot opponent brandishes purity.

Substantive extremism aligns with partisan purification. "If my primary opponent were a real Democrat, she would support an eighty-eight-percent reduction in greenhouse gas emissions within ten years." Now it's OK for the moderate to spill the beans and point out the unrealistic nature of the proposal. The zealot's response will imply her opponent sounds more like a Republican than a Democrat. "Stop using Republican talking points."

Partisan purification is a movement from center to extreme. HM abets using substantively extreme proposals to divide and purify. When partisan identification and ideological faith trump a pragmatic desire for compromise, unrealistic proposals gain theatrical traction.

Targeted fundraising also benefits from substantive extremism. Whether well-heeled targets are naïve enough to believe substantively extreme proposals have a realistic chance or they're politically sophisticated enough to recognize partisan scheming doesn't matter. Money is fungible.

In sum, the utility of substantive extremism is to advance partisan electoral strategy, partisan purification, and targeted fundraising. What about procedural extremism?

Procedural Extremism and HM

Procedural extremism is mostly about grabbing attention and only works with media complicity. That's not a problem because procedural extremism provides outstanding visuals. The possibility the media could turn up its nose at rioting, conflagration, eye-popping vandalism, or recorded violence isn't worth considering. That's OK because we're not interested in prohibiting the media from documenting reality. The issue is contextualization of procedural extremism by HM outlets with ideologically segregated constituencies.

If I were prone to engaging in procedural extremism, I might object to my initial characterization of the activity as attention grabbing. No, it's for raising awareness. It focuses attention on injustice, successfully. Every media outlet in the entire country is playing the clips. They're not just playing the clips. They're playing the clips in the context of the injustice my procedural extremism was designed to accentuate. Procedural extremism works!

Once again, I reference the earlier discussion concerning "Effect of HM on Issue Advocacy" in the preceding chapter, depicted graphically in figure 5.2. No doubt procedural extremism focuses attention on the extreme acts as well as their alleged rationalizations. But what is the impact of that attention parsed through HM?

I've observed a disturbing trend in media that implicates and transcends both procedural extremism and media. It's as fundamental to the presented subject matter as the Constitution is fundamental to our country's laws. To answer the question about the impact of attention on extreme acts, I embark on a (hopefully brief and instructive) constitutional excursion.

The First Amendment begins:

"Congress shall make no law respecting an establishment of religion . . ."

The "Establishment Clause" focuses our consideration. Congress can't pass laws directly or indirectly establishing a religion of state or favoring one religion over another. As a legal matter, the Bill of Rights is concerned with government action and doesn't prevent private actors such as the media from playing favorites.

However, the Constitution reflects, and to a certain extent guides, societal norms. Disparaging or favoring one religion over another by private actors breaches those norms. I'm aware that strict adherence to the code isn't universal. Infringement is occasionally direct, but more often in the form of tropes and dog whistles.

There are no such proscriptions or unwritten rules for partisan causes or ideology. I'm not suggesting amending the Constitution or that society through media shouldn't have robust or even discourteous discourse around ideology. But when it comes to procedural extremism, we should take care. We should be mindful of Establishment Clause principles concerning violence and destruction.

The disturbing trend is for "free press" to treat procedural extremism according to its substantive mission. In other words, HM treats destructive acts differently depending on their underlying rationale and who committed them. If procedural extremism constitutes speech, ideologically segregated media spit on content neutrality.

It's not necessarily overt. I haven't heard anyone in mainstream media state, "because I approve of their cause, destroying property is OK," although I've heard guests on certain POEP shows come close.

It's more subtle and effective. It's accomplished through the concept of understanding. It's a seductive appeal to our understanding, and the appeal is to ideologically segregated and sympathetic audiences.

Use of the word "understandable" can be tricky and manipulative. Understandable does not mean "excusable" or "desirable." Let me use a striking example to illustrate my point. That a victim of child abuse might grow up to be an abuser is understandable, but not excusable. We cannot excuse abuse from one who has been abused. We must prosecute.

But combining "understandable" with sympathetic vocal intonations and facial expressions appears to excuse extremism. By focusing on underlying rationale to sympathetically segregated audiences, destruction begins to sound like legitimate activism. And look, we're all talking about the issue, so it must have worked. Extremism works!

Extremism "Works" to Establish Hyperpartisanship

It works to establish partisan affinity and the ideological underpinnings of media outlets. It establishes double standards. It erodes the credibility of "free press." It establishes that the press is not free from factionalism.

It does not broaden support for causes. It does the exact opposite. Procedural extremism broadens opposition. It broadens support for the opposition, i.e., *too clever by half.*

I cannot help but contemplate the efficacy of the civil rights movement under Martin Luther King, Jr. The establishment labeled him an extremist. Eventually he embraced the epithet for tactical reasons, but the procedural activism of his movement was not extreme. They did not engage in procedural extremism. They engaged in peaceful protest, civil disobedience, and intelligent discourse.

Horrific extremism greeted those civil forms of advocacy. By this time almost every American has seen footage of police force response to the courageous civility of the activists. Police often reacted with violent extremism, including beating peaceful protesters with batons and flattening them with high-pressure jets from fire hoses. Police dogs brutalized activists with the encouragement of their helmeted handlers.

The excessive force used by police was ineffective in gaining support for their cause. Their unreasonable tactics were unpopular. The violent extremism of the police was effective in garnering sympathy for that which they opposed. It was both immoral and stupid.

Procedural extremism resulting from either religious or ideological fundamentalism should be condemned universally, regardless of the religion or ideology of culprits or perceived righteousness of the cause. To tacitly coddle or explicitly condemn perpetrators to complement media narratives or audience preferences is tantamount to religious or ideological establishment.

It's not trivial or academic. It sends the message that engaging in violent or destructive acts is OK if you believe in the cause, in other words, as long as your faith is righteous. This sentiment undermines rule of law and begins a slippery slope toward theocracy or its ideological equivalent, which are both totalitarian. It undermines a fundamental tenet of civilization. Allowing religious or ideological faith to establish justification for criminality is antithetical to democracy.

Even in our current hyperpartisan environment, this should be common ground. This should be neutral territory. This should be a demilitarized zone between warring media factions.

Regardless of media outlet and regardless of stated cause or political or ideological motivation, the reaction to violent or destructive acts in the name of social protest must be consistent. If you can't do that, you're not a journalist. You're doing ideological activism under the banner of journalism. In other words, you're a fraud.

Revolution

Revolution is the most extreme form of substantive extremism. Overthrowing government or the existing order is facially extreme and requires procedural extremism. Overthrowing government is by force, not with letter-writing campaigns. Using force, i.e., killing, to take over is the most extreme form of procedural extremism. Revolution combines substantive and procedural extremism in an extreme way.

Sometimes "revolution" means radical or fundamental change, like getting rid of capitalism in favor of socialism. Replacing free markets with government takeover of the economy won't be carried out through civil forms of activism.

Overthrowing government by force requires military or substantial paramilitary. Let's assume for argument's sake the second type of revolution, radical or fundamental change, can be carried out without overthrowing the government. Well, if you're not overthrowing, then you're working within the existing constitutional framework.

Let's say the existing constitutional framework is the problem, and you want to scrap the current version and rewrite considerable portions. You have two choices. You can overthrow the government by force, or you can work within the current framework to rewrite the Constitution.

Article V provides two methodologies for amending the Constitution. Either two-thirds of both Houses of Congress can propose an amendment, or two-thirds of state legislatures can apply for an amendment. Then the amendment requires ratification by three-fourths of the states, either by state legislatures or state conventions. Three-fourths is a supermajority.

Even if radical or fundamental change could be carried out without amending the Constitution, such as by just passing laws, legislatures aren't going to make radical change without overwhelming popular support.

So how does procedural extremism fit this dynamic? Generally, deteriorating conditions enhance opportunities for radical change. Popular support for revolution is hard to come by if the majority is doing fine. System functionality and institutional reliability are also relevant. If the system functions for a majority or a majority perceive the system to be functioning, the case for radical transformation is problematic. If faith in institutions is high, revolution is unlikely.

If revolution is your game, you prefer deteriorating conditions or perception thereof, dysfunctional systems or perception thereof, and untrustworthy institutions or perception thereof. In this context, procedural extremism makes sense. While procedural extremism doesn't effectively gain sympathy for a particular issue or cause, it's destabilizing. Images of destructive and violent rioting create the perception of dysfunctional systems and failing institutions.

Procedural extremism may not advance the issue or cause for which extreme acts were allegedly committed, but it strengthens the rationale for radical transformation. Revolutionary ambition subordinates issues and causes.

Revolutionaries would argue that radical transformation is the only way to make progress on their issue(s). Notice parallels in arguments made by revolutionaries and PPs. PPs assert that making progress requires voting out the other team. For PPs, lack of progress serves partisan electoral strategy. For revolutionaries, lack of progress provides justification for procedural extremism in pursuit of radical transformation. Both revolutionaries and PPs collect issues the way a necklace-maker collects pretty little seashells.

Problems with Progress

This is why progress is problematic for both revolutionaries and PPs. Progress disarms revolutionaries. Progress achieved through established frameworks undermines arguments for radical transformation. Even the perception of progress sabotages revolution. Revolutionaries, and to a certain extent PPs, engage in an extreme form of propaganda to combat the perception of progress. Statements like, "no real progress has been made" or "things are worse than they have ever been" exemplify revolutionary or PP propaganda and are a form of procedural extremism in service of radical transformation or electoral hyperpartisanship.

Another positive feedback loop lurks in the midst. Perceptions of deteriorating conditions, dysfunctional systems, and untrustworthy institutions bolster justification for extremism. Engaging in procedural extremism heightens perceptions of deteriorating conditions, dysfunctional systems, and untrustworthy institutions.

Relationship between Decentralized Movements, Extremism, and Hyperpartisanship

I've disparaged HM. I've also asserted issues or causes can be subordinated to partisan electoral desires as well as revolutionary ambition. Being fair, sorting complex relationships between issue advocacy and either partisan politics or radical aspiration and effectively communicating those relationships to the public can be exasperating even for talented nonpartisan journalists. That's because the relationships are complex and a bit tricky. In addition, activist communications can be inconsistent, and figuring out whether inconsistencies are strategic or due to different activists arriving at the table with different understandings and motivations is challenging. I'll use a couple of examples to illustrate the muddle, or perhaps delineate parameters of confusion. Or at least impart the flavor of befuddlement.

Occupy Wall Street

To make a not-so-long story shorter, in the early part of the twenty-first century, banks issued mortgages to borrowers with poor credit ratings. These "subprime mortgages" were bundled and sold as subprime-mortgage-backed securities. As borrowers defaulted on loans, the value of the securities tanked, resulting in a cascading devaluation of investment portfolios that caused the Great Recession, which began at the tail end of the George W. Bush presidency to be inherited by President Obama. Welcome to the White House.

Over Labor Day weekend, 2011, I launched a blog. Within weeks, Occupy Wall Street (OWS) began. I went to Zuccotti Park in lower Manhattan to interview Occupiers for my blog. This was my first and only foray into journalism.

I was going to simply convey what I found, but once again, recalling the episode precipitated introspection. Even before OWS, I was convinced our financial regulatory framework was flawed because "Wall Street" had disproportionate influence over our political processes because they could afford to, and our political spending laws were obliging.

In other words, I arrived at Zuccotti Park with a predetermined narrative. Here I spent an entire chapter criticizing media for engaging in narrative-driven tribalism, yet my only foray into journalism involved looking for stories I already wrote. I guess it's human nature. We should be aware of that nature while consuming media content. Inspecting a compulsion makes it less compelling or at least mitigates damage.

As I approached the park, I slowed my pace to appreciate the cacophony. Occupiers packed the park and surrounding sidewalks, and the overflow spilled into streets. Groups of people shouting and drumming were magnets for the cameras of media outlets as well as for my unconscious attention.

Figure 6.1: Guy Fawkes Mask

I made a deliberate effort to see past noise. I saw groups of young people in ordinary garb sitting and chatting. Ordinary except for the ubiquitous Guy Fawkes masks worn by members of "Anonymous." I learned the protests were "organized" by two groups: Anonymous, which was described to me as a group of activist computer hackers, and Adbusters, which was described as an anti-consumerism socialist group from Canada. At the same time, some Occupiers insisted OWS was an organic uprising focused on wealth and income inequality, as embodied by the slogan, "we are the 99 percent." Examination of top-down centralized control versus organic and democratic decentralization associated with OWS is fascinating and holds some relevance but will not be spotlighted here.

I must admit that sitting among masked individuals who conducted cyber-attacks on powerful institutions was a bit unnerving. But with the heat of the day and duration of the event, the masks transformed from facial coverings to hand props as anonymity yielded to comfort. I spoke with the young humans, some of whom were masked and some held masks, but most were maskless and unaffiliated with any political organization predating OWS.

Toward the beginning of OWS, there was much talk of the movement culminating with "one demand." I knew what that demand would be if I had anything to say about it. My discussions with Occupiers were framed by pre-conception and influenced by predisposition.

I never spoke with an Occupier who thought financial institutions *didn't* have disproportionate influence over political processes. Many thought that curbing that influence should be the focus. While talking with some like-minded Occupiers, I learned of amending the Constitution to solve the problem.

During the next decade, that idea evolved into Chapter 17. The Occupier pitched an amendment that would end corporate personhood. I chewed on that for several years. I've concluded that eliminating corporate personhood is both substantively extreme and too broad. I argue for a narrowly tailored amendment.

At that time, I thought of industrial political spending in terms of fairness rather than partisan division. I've come to appreciate them as two sides of the same coin. (More on that later.) Here, I explore the rationale for, and impact of, "decentralized" movements having extreme or revolutionary facets and their relation to hyperpartisanship.

Unanimity on how Wall Street dropping bundles of cash in D.C. corrupted political processes to an extent that mocked equal representation coincided with much broader concerns for many Occupiers. For them, the entire system was corrupt. An economy based on consumption was not sustainable. Disproportionate influence was merely a symptom. Capitalism was the problem.

In America, getting rid of capitalism can be fairly characterized as substantively extreme. While the dispositions of Occupiers were diverse, the diversity included would-be revolutionaries. For some, disproportionate influence and wealth inequality represented issues to be addressed head-on. For others, they were useful devices for effecting radical transformation. In other words, the financial collapse and Great Recession represented opportunities for those seeking some form of revolution.

Some OWS-sponsored direct actions evinced revolutionary intent. The Obama Administration, in accord with the consensus of mainstream economists, concluded economic stimulus was the proper remedy for recession. But OWS shut down West Coast seaports. Closing seaports shuts down a part of the economy. It's the opposite of stimulus. Shutting down ports depresses the economy. It sabotages economic recovery. It prolongs recession. It's throwing gasoline on the fire.

Toward the end of 2021, I spoke with a former Occupier I met through my yoga practice. I told him of the book I was working on, and we agreed that political parties adversely influence our politics. But we didn't agree on everything.

OWS came up, and he told me he had recently attended a ten-year anniversary meeting. I made my argument about how shutting seaports was not helpful in fixing the American recession. He responded flat-out that "we" weren't trying to "fix America"; "we" were trying to overthrow the system. I understand he wasn't speaking for everyone involved, but based on my conversations with Occupiers, he was speaking for a significant portion.

Back in 2011, I was caught up in the notion of "one demand." Speaking with Occupiers, I learned of a discussion hosted on an OWS website. I joined threads and posted comments focused on the disproportionate influence of Wall Street, corporations, and the well-heeled. I was motivated by my desire to influence the "one demand" and to call attention to my newly minted blog, which featured more extensive OWS coverage.

Although some online participants agreed with me, the discussion lacked focus. Anti-capitalist revolutionaries, 9/11 conspiracy theorists, antiwar activists, environmentalists of all types, rants against the one percent, and a whole lot of antisemitism derailed productive discourse. It didn't take long to realize consensus on "one demand" wouldn't arise from such a forum.

Some of us, in addition to advocating for a reasonable "one demand," carried on a meta-discussion around the online discussion. Whenever promising and reasonable threads evolved, trolls blew them up. It was frustrating. Some theorized the trolls were CIA operatives deliberately undermining productive dialogue. My take: In addition to trolls trolling for trolling's sake, genuine antisemites, conspiracy theorists, and radical extremists used the forum.

I also think the agenda for some trolls was to derail the movement because they were opposed to it. Whether or not these trolls worked for government or Wall Street is impossible to say. But given the nature of phenomena like OWS in the context of an ideologically segregated society goaded by revenue-driven media, you could argue that trolling by government agents is superfluous.

The scene at the park wasn't much different from online, although I don't remember running into blatant antisemitism during my face-to-face encounters. Internet anonymity frees closeted repulsiveness.

Everyone else sported their colors. Media presence was irresistible to those incapable of generating press. It was a publicity bonanza for marginalized advocates. How segregated media and OWS responded to the multiplicity of activism is most relevant.

Portions of the media concentrated on the disparity of wealth and the disproportionate influence wealth could purchase in our political system. Other portions fixated on the desire of anti-capitalists to overthrow the system. Inertia of familiar dialectics, i.e., lazy thinking, entices us to conclude that the truth inhabits space between the two portrayals, but that is false.

The truth is OWS included protesters who wanted to work within the system to address issues illuminated by the Great Recession, as well as those with radical intent who wished to burn the whole thing down. Truth does not lie between the two; it includes both. I know this because I spoke directly with Occupiers. If I had relied on media, I would have concluded either one part of the media was lying, or truth was somewhere in between. But in reality, all portions of media reported part of the truth.

All media fragments reporting part of the truth is the everyday manner in which partisan segregation corrupts free press and undermines democracy. It also confounds our ability to appreciate intricacies of decentralized movements such as OWS. I think advocates operating under the banner of journalism worry that intricacy might deflate purpose. But the best journalists appreciate the opportunities for contextualization that intricacy provides.

However, I must concede some common ground was found. The overwhelming majority of media outlets, regardless of partisan affiliation, tended to point their cameras at the noisiest and most visually provocative protesters. People sitting around attempting informed discourse can't compete with shouting, marching, dancing, or drumming.

What interests me most is the way Occupiers themselves dealt with the multiplicity of activism. Reckless trading of flimsy securities by financial professionals on Wall Street caused financial collapse, which brought global attention to wealth inequality and a system that bends to wealth in mockery of representative democracy. Yet gatherings, both in person and online, included people dissatisfied or outraged about anything and everything.

You could argue disproportionate influence on our political process by corporations and wealthy individuals is fundamental to all dissatisfactions, and more fundamental than the myriad of actual dissatisfactions, because you can't successfully address dissatisfactions through a system corrupted by disproportionality. In other words, disproportionate influence is more fundamental and urgent than global warming, health care, clean water, education, sustainability, poverty, wealth inequality, crime, clean air, gun violence, healthy food, etc.

But that's not the argument Occupiers made. No organized effort to focus the outrage and dissatisfaction on a single issue or "one demand" manifested. Instead, the movement collected the outraged and dissatisfied and focused their outrage and dissatisfaction on direct actions such as closing ports, marching on Wall Street, and taking over public spaces.

Whether the form of the movement resulted from organic evolution, design, or some combination thereof is hard to say. For argument's sake, let's assume the answer is design, and let's try to discern intelligence behind the design. I'll provide a brief midstream summary and focus my examination on a single question.

A specific triggering event, the Great Recession, with specific causes and theoretically specific solutions, inspired a movement initially suggesting it would produce a specific demand, but instead amassed the generally dissatisfied who were outraged about a multiplicity of problems and focused that outrage and dissatisfaction on provocative direct actions instead of specific policy initiatives. The question is:

Why Would a Movement Born of Specificity Refuse to Promote Specific Policy Recommendations?

My initial inclination is to imagine myself among Occupiers and assume an appropriate spirit of camaraderie and simply conclude that promoting a specific policy recommendation would alienate a significant portion of my siblings in the cause whose cause was not exactly the same as mine, but that's OK because we're all in this together, sort of.

Even without adopting the perspective of dispassionate examiner, the rationale unravels.

It's as if building a broad coalition supersedes tangible results.[26]

---

26 For a connection to this concept see Chapter 21, section, "Unaffiliated Origins Story," subsection, "Affiliation Options."

That can't be right. We must be missing something. Let's reexamine our premises in the context of the question we wish to answer. Why would a movement born of specificity refuse to promote specific policy recommendations?

Because the premise that the "movement was born of specificity" is false. The movement was not born of specificity. Remember that although OWS espoused "decentralization" and "direct democracy," groups with broader agendas than curbing the disproportionate influence of the wealthy instigated the movement. Centralized organizers were international and primarily concerned with the effects of capitalism and unbridled consumerism. To them, the Great Recession was symptomatic of a flawed system that should be overthrown. Rather than being born of specificity, the movement visibly manifested in a specific manner, OWS, following a specific event, the Great Recession, but the movement is broader and predates both OWS and the Great Recession.

When the cause is as monumental as getting rid of capitalism, focusing the outrage of broad coalitions of the dissatisfied on direct actions to disrupt or depress the economy and destabilize the social order, rather than focusing on specific policy recommendations, makes sense.

First, making specific policy recommendations tacitly acknowledges the current system can effectively address issues. That's a no-no for those seeking radical transformation. You could lose membership in the hipster revolution club for implying real problems can be solved by working within existing frameworks.

Second, conditions need to get far worse for revolution to be possible. Sensible policy carries the hazard of improving conditions, thereby deferring prospects of revolution. For revolutionaries, enacting sensible policy within existing frameworks is just kicking the can down the road.

Crowds thinned as weather turned cold and police cracked down. Central organizers represented a larger percentage of hangers-on. I finally spoke with a couple of representatives from Adbusters. One was a young woman from Canada who I would guess was in her early twenties. The other was a slightly older man, perhaps in his late twenties.

I pressed about the "one demand." The young woman deemed an economy based on consumption unsustainable. As someone who studied environmental science and whose gateway into political awareness was environmental activism, I couldn't argue. But considering context, I didn't think she was on point. We went back and forth a few times. As I recall the conversation, I appreciate that within the framework she used to make sense of the world, nothing was more essential than our economic system. That was her focus, and I have no doubt that fundamentally changing our economic system was the primary focus of many Occupiers.

The young man displayed media savvy and political tact. His resolution for "one demand" was pragmatically conciliatory with an aftertaste of democracy. He said we should each work "on our own piece of the puzzle." It was a neat answer. I knew my piece. But upon reflection, I wish I had asked what the completed puzzle was supposed to look like. He probably would have replied with something appeasing like, "that's up to all of us." But if that's true, I don't see capitalism disappearing any time soon. It's going to have to get much worse for that to happen.

My OWS Takeaways

We're not blank slates. Concepts derived from experience form the framework through which we experience. Past experience embeds preconception into our future experience. Narrative predisposition is human nature. Journalists are human. We perceive and convey perception via preconception. Adult responsibility includes awareness that predisposition colors the content we consume as well as provide.

- The utility of internet forums open to the public without qualification is either entertainment or tactical opposition. Using such forums to advance policy is demoralizing. If I opposed a movement, I would encourage the best and brightest of that movement to focus their energies on participating in such open online forums. The spectacle of wildly popular movements coupled with anonymity is irresistible to trolls regardless of agenda. The sites suck life out of the genuine and well-meaning.
- Movements attracting media attention attract those who seek media attention.
- I suspect movements that resist concrete recommendations. I suspect the issue for which the movement allegedly evolved is pretense for an

insidious agenda.

- Movements focused on specific policy initiatives capitulate to the system. Movements focusing outrage on extreme actions are for overthrowing the system.
- Movements espousing decentralization while employing centralized control or organization are inherently deceitful.
- With partisan media segregation, incorporating movements that inherently transcend partisan affiliation, and require such transcendence to succeed, into partisan programming and partisan warfare neutralizes those movements. Partisan incorporation neutralizes revolution.
- Motivations for using precipitating events that raise legitimate societal concerns as rationale for executing procedural extremism, i.e., throwing gasoline on the fire or engaging in destructive acts, include the following:

  1. You're a troll and you get a kick out of blowing stuff up;
  2. You're an opposition insurgent trying to discredit the movement;
  3. You have no genuine desire to work within the system to make progress on the immediate issue. Instead, the immediate issue or triggering event serves as a stepping stone for overthrowing the system; or
  4. You genuinely believe engaging in extremism will aid efforts to make progress within the current system.

- Partisan filtration by media corrupts awareness-raising. As stated, OWS inspired my interest in a constitutional amendment proscribing corporate political spending and permitting Congress to fairly limit political spending by individuals. But I didn't get that from media. Inspiration came directly from Occupiers.

The media skewed coverage either toward radical extremism or toward reasonable responsiveness to economic and political injustice. Skewed analysis jettisons relevant content. OWS offered an opportunity to explore complexities within our society, such as movements espousing decentralization. Using a partisan lens to explore those complexities is like using a hand-held magnifying glass for particle physics. The partisan lens is best used for studying the hand that holds it.

Black Lives Matter

Unlike OWS, where I traveled to the encampment to interview Occupiers, my knowledge and understanding of BLM comes from media, mostly TV viewing and internet research. Despite differences in how I experienced each movement, parallels are worth noting. While examining resemblances, hold onto the notion of decentralization, which is the thematic key to understanding connections and enigmas within each movement, as well as their tie-ins to hyperpartisanship.

Media characterizations of BLM are partisan. Outlets describe the movement's purpose as either an effort to redress documented racial bias in our society, especially with respect to policing, or as an effort to overthrow the system by Marxist revolutionaries. Depending on the media outlet, BLM employs methodologies that are "mostly peaceful" or "destructive rioting."

A logical pathway toward resolving contradictions might be to ignore media characterizations and attend to what BLM activists have to say. However, because of decentralization, messages from movement members are inconsistent and at times contradictory. Decentralization doesn't resolve contradiction; it enables it.

Contradiction can be evidence of misunderstanding, i.e., flawed construction of the framework used to analyze the phenomenon. If not misconstruction, the question becomes: Are contradictions deliberate or simply an effect of diversity? I'm going to argue for misconstruction, but before doing so, I'll establish apparent contradictions.

While unequal treatment of Africans and African Americans including enslavement, murder, torture, rape, and Jim Crow is centuries in the making, the current movement expressed by BLM is born of specifics indicating that although equal treatment under the law has been ratified in the Constitution and formalized in statute through civil rights legislation, actual treatment, as evidenced by statistics and video, remains disparate. The criminal justice system, beginning with police encounters, treats African Americans, especially Black men, more harshly than the rest of society.

Excessive force by police causing death, and the blasé treatment of offending officers by the same criminal justice system to which offending officers belong, are of particular concern. There's little dispute over the existence of the problem. Only a small percentage of people who saw the recording of officer Derek Chauvin kneeling on George Floyd's neck concluded it was an accidental death resulting from good policing.[27]

However, like OWS, BLM is all over the place, or at least bifurcated, as to specific policy recommendations. Some associated with or publicly supportive of BLM advocate policy change. Others seem more interested in keeping public attention focused on the problem through protest and are a bit standoffish about committing to specific policies.

Exploring policy recommendations, the potential and realized impacts of those policies, BLM commentary on those policies, and relevant media coverage will help illustrate the complexities of decentralization and provide a suitable analytical framework by zeroing in on the misconstruction.

Campaign Zero[28] concentrates on police violence and proposes ten specific policy solutions. I reduce my advocacy to "one demand" by highlighting two recommendations. My "one demand" is effectively prosecuting police who commit crimes. Two specific recommendations are independent prosecution and filming police, including universal body cams.

In addition to providing evidence for prosecution, filming police helps build and broaden the movement. Here, I distinguish filming police from protests including destructive acts.

BLM peaked in popular support shortly after the recording of officer Derek Chauvin killing George Floyd by kneeling on his neck was made public. Protests erupted throughout the nation. Such widespread protest evinces popular support. But protests didn't cause popular support. The recording did that.

The movement's popularity waned as media documented destructive acts associated with protests. No doubt antagonistic HM outlets disproportionately focused on anarchy. But "mostly peaceful" is also a characterization bolstering a specific narrative. The reality is protests included peaceful demonstrators *and* rioters.

---

27 Jordan Williams, "Poll: Number who think George Floyd's death was murder down more than 20 percent," *The Hill*, March 5, 2021, https://thehill.com/blogs/blog-briefing-room/news/541788-percentage-that-thinks-george-floyd-death-was-murder-down-more/.

28 About," Campaign Zero, accessed Oct. 4, 2023, https://campaignzero.org/about/what-we-do/.

The assortment of responses by BLM supporters in the media to occasional rioting and property destruction associated with protests confounds fundamental characterization. One narrative attributes aggressive behavior solely to counter-protesters or police. A similar narrative suggests that, by definition, those engaging in violence or destruction are criminals, not protesters.

However, some BLM activists embrace a "diversity of tactics," which includes nonviolence but permits disruptive use of force.[29] Some BLM advocates in the media suggest that given police murdering unarmed Black men, some property destruction is understandable and not outrageously disproportionate.

So which narrative represents BLM? Because of decentralization, the answer is: all of the above. In decentralized movements, protesters devoted to peaceful methods march side-by-side with those believing more aggressive tactics are necessary and appropriate.

Attempting to Appreciate a Decentralized Movement under a Single Narrative Is Nonsensical

The "defund the police" tempest illustrates the futility of media's convoluted efforts to impose unity of meaning and purpose on a decentralized movement. For starters, actually defunding police is at the extreme end of substantive extremism. Taken literally, defunding police means getting rid of police departments.

Characterizing such a proposal as a specific policy recommendation is disingenuous. Eliminating publicly funded policing is revolutionary. It's a radical transformation of our system.

Permanently ending public funding for police departments through democratic processes is highly unlikely because it's unpopular. Using the system to radically transform the system to get rid of police is fanciful.

The injection of an unpopular idea into a movement swelling with approval and attention while flirting with mainstream acceptance in the wake of the

29 "Black Lives Matter," Wikipedia, accessed Oct. 5, 2023, https://en.wikipedia.org/wiki/Black_Lives_Matter; "Diversity of tactics," Wikipedia, accessed Oct. 5, 2023, https://en.wikipedia.org/wiki/Diversity_of_tactics.

documented murder of George Floyd by police caused the heads of media partisans to spin like pinwheels in a hurricane. The contortions necessary to rationalize the notion were spectacular: "They don't literally mean defund police. They mean repurpose or reform. They mean funneling some police funding toward programs better suited to handle some of the things police are currently forced to deal with, such as domestic disputes or people with mental illnesses. Armed police don't need to perform routine traffic stops," and so on. Yet occasionally, someone associated with decentralized BLM will insist they really do mean defunding police. In truth, the decentralized movement contains factions advocating for police reform as well as abolitionists. But rather than exploring the nature of and reasoning behind decentralization, HM simply presents the movement according to narrative.

Symbiosis between Decentralized Movements and HM

Which story do you prefer? If you prefer the story that BLM stands for rational response to documented injustice, characterize protests as "mostly peaceful" and interpret "defund the police" to mean sensible reform. If you prefer the story that BLM fronts for Marxist revolutionaries wishing to overthrow the system, focus on destructive episodes within protests and interpret "defund the police" to mean abolishing our current policing system. Decentralized movements provide an assortment of particulars supporting multiple and conflicting narratives. Media fragments report fragments of available particulars according to narrative preference.

The relationship between decentralized movements and HM is deeper than symbiosis. It's familial. They're akin. Media and audience segregation according to ideological narrative is a form of decentralization.

When there were only a few networks and no internet, news was, in a sense, centralized. While opinions varied, there was general agreement about factual occurrences. Media watchdogs and activists lamented the conformity of a centralized corporate media oligarchy.

Hundreds of channels and tens of millions of internet sites later, those lamentations have been transposed. More immediate apprehensions displace old concerns, which remain unaddressed. Decentralized media is profitable appeasement. It's a corporate con. It's three-card monte. Keep your eye on the conformity. It's deeper now than ever.

Stories likely to be covered conform to a single type—stories that can be leveraged for partisan advantage or that facilitate ideological differentiation. Pressure to conform to tribal doctrine has never been stronger. As the opportunity to locate your opinions in a decentralized media increase, the incentive to collaborate decreases.

As for media, decentralization is targeted marketing. Decentralized movements are a buffet. Select according to taste. Which story do you prefer?

Decentralized Movements Incorporate and Utilize Ideas and Factions That Appear to Be at Odds

Therein lies frustration and perhaps misconstruction. To be clear, abolishing police is at odds with reforming policing. They're not the same. No amount of spin or punditry can reconcile the discord. Different factions within BLM advocate for irreconcilable goals.

Different factions advocating for irreconcilable goals is a foreseeable consequence of decentralization, inevitable in fact. I think advocating for irreconcilable goals reduces the likelihood of achieving any.

The opposing argument is that police reform appears reasonable alongside abolition, and therefore factions calling for abolition make reform more likely. Reformers appear to stand on sensible middle ground between status quo and radical transformation. I think it unlikely that dynamic is operating for a couple of reasons.

First, I doubt abolitionists voluntarily take part in a relationship subordinating their status. More importantly, advocating for abolition does not build support for reform. It allows BLM opposition to characterize the movement as extreme while cultivating mistrust within the targeted community. Why should police believe the goal is reasonable reform? Because BLM is decentralized, who's to say the real agenda isn't abolition? How can we expect rank and file police officers to be fluent in the nuances of decentralization, when society at large, and especially the media attempt to synthesize decentralized movements into a single narrative?

We're predisposed to using centralized frameworks to understand our universe. Rather than conceding inevitable dissonance associated with decentralization, we insist on imposing unity. It must be one or the other. It can't be both reform and abolition. That doesn't make sense.

We also focus on the bigger threat. From a threat perspective, abolition is the one to guard against. Threat of abolition builds resistance and causes opposition to dig in. The extremism of abolition intensifies opposition and clears compromise from the table while reducing mainstream support.

This can be frustrating for those seeking to work within the system to achieve reasonable reform. It also helps explain the contortionism of partisan spinmeisters in addition to narrowing in on the fundamental misconstruction.

Imagine yourself a civil rights activist seeking progressive reform within the system. You want improvement. Since the system requires democratically elected legislators to change policy, you assume a premise:

> The greater the public support, the more likely democratically elected legislators are willing to make progressive change.

You believe you're part of a movement that understands this premise. But factions of your movement propose radically unpopular ideas. Other factions undertake destructive forms of activism, eroding popular support. These factions appear to undermine your efforts. Why would people within your movement deliberately undermine the movement?

Your first response is: the people who seem to be working against you aren't part of your movement. You are correct! But they're not counter-protesters either. They are BLM.

Decentralization

A decentralized movement is not *a* movement. It is *movements*. A decentralized movement is a collection of movements. Appreciating a collection of movements under a single narrative is nonsense.

We fixate on the singularity of names—BLM or OWS. It's tempting to say that although proposed solutions vary, a cohesive rationale exists. But even that is false. Participants in decentralized movements come to the table for various reasons. The variety of recommendations reflects the variety of ways participants see the problem.

Not everyone is working on the same problem. Some wish to fix specific problems within the system. Some perceive the system itself as the problem. Some viewed the 2008 financial collapse as evidence Wall Street was improperly regulated. Others viewed it as an inevitable consequence of capitalism and an opportunity to promote a socialist agenda. Some within BLM have responded to specific injustices with specific recommendations, such as independent prosecution of police officers accused of committing crimes. Others view injustices as an inevitable consequence of an inherently racist system that requires radical transformation including abolishing publicly funded policing.

Although I've said that appreciating a decentralized movement or collection of movements under a single narrative is nonsensical, singular takeaways are worth articulating. To put it another way, the concept of a decentralized movement or the concept of a collection of movements is singular. Cohesive understanding of decentralization that avoids misconstruction is possible:

- Decentralization helps partisan-driven media narratives. Decentralized movements encompass disparate particulars supporting disparate partisan narratives. Each media fragment reporting selective particulars fortifies partisan segregation and impairs collective understanding.
- Participants in decentralized movements perceive problems differently, and so envision different solutions. Solutions originating from different factions within the movement can be irreconcilable. Therefore, a decentralized movement is better understood as a collection of movements.
- Decentralization spotlights tensions between those wishing to work within the system to make progress and those who want to change the whole system. This is the crux! Refusing to explore the effects decentralization has on the relationship between reasonable reform and radical transformation is media failure. Simply latching on to specific particulars supporting preferred narratives is bankrupt journalism. It's not journalism at all. It's tribalism. It's hyperpartisanship.
- Decentralized movements are more adept at focusing the outrage of the dissatisfied on attention-grabbing direct actions or protests than on specific policy recommendations.
- Voluminous coverage of problems and protests coupled with minimal exploration of specific policy solutions—in part because "the movement"

cannot reach consensus on specific policy recommendations—undermines faith in the system and sows the seeds of radical transformation.

- As participation in direct actions or protests increases, media attention, at least in the short run, also increases.
- Media is better suited to illustrating problems and documenting discontent than to aiding progress. Problems and protests provide eye-catching media content, in contrast with discussing potential solutions. Problems such as police murdering unarmed Black men by kneeling on their necks, and protests organized around that problem, can be recorded and conveyed directly to the public in a compelling manner. Problems and protests are action blockbusters. Discussing solutions is all dialogue and no action.
- As the number of factions within any movement increases, likelihood of policy agreement decreases.
- As the number of causes associated with the movement increases, likelihood of agreement on reasonable reform decreases and likelihood of demanding radical transformation increases.
- Decentralization mocks accountability because segregated and sympathetic media outlets can always find factions who can honestly say, "that wasn't us."
- Extremist factions in a movement together with those seeking reasonable reform within the existing system could either improve or undermine the chances of reasonable reform. If extremism can be leveraged as a bargaining position, then chances could be improved because reforming the system emerges as reasonable compromise between extremism and status quo. However, because the public isn't versed in decentralization nuances, there's a danger the entire movement acquires a taint of extremism, thereby reducing popular support and undermining progress within democratic processes. Procedural extremism, e.g., property destruction, raises visibility. Whether or not visibility associated with procedural extremism facilitates reasonable reform within the existing system is open to debate.
- In a segregated media environment, the presence of reforming factions in a movement including extremists mainstreams extremism. This is especially true if reforming factions within the movement and in the media are reticent to criticize extreme acts or proposals or to simply name them for what they are: *extreme*. This reticence is understand-

able. People seeking reasonable reform understand the value of coalition-building. People seeking reasonable reform understand coalitions contain elements across a broad spectrum. People seeking reasonable reform tend to be reasonable people who don't want to throw hand grenades, real or metaphorical, that sabotage coalitions.

- Extremists, on the other hand, recognize popular movements as opportunities to insinuate themselves into the mainstream, and some people seeking reasonable reform are quite calculating. After all, extremists excel at attracting attention. Perhaps the old adage, "there's no such thing as bad publicity" attributed to circus huckster P.T. Barnum has merit. Perhaps the relationship between reformers and extremists is mutualistic. Perhaps.
- It's easier to organize a disparate collection of disaffected people to protest than to find policy consensus among a disparate collection of disaffected people.
- The broader the movement, the less specific policy recommendations make sense.

Whether decentralized movements evolve organically or result from intelligent design is beyond the scope of this analysis. Either way, decentralization seems better suited to protest than reform.

We Need to Change the Whole System

Sometimes you hear someone declaring that with great commitment—commitment that is, to the declaration. I think nearly 100 percent of the time, the sentiment is either meaningless or at best figurative. I also think most of the time the person making the declaration is oblivious to its futility.

It sounds good though. It's chest-beating. When someone on TV passionately proclaims, "we need to change the whole system," I imagine audience members thinking, "wow, he sounds serious," or "wow, she sounds like she's dedicated to progress."

The dedication, however, is to a provocative but hollow sentiment. It makes for entertaining content. It may get you airtime. But if you say it and genuinely believe it, you're either extraordinarily vain or blessed with exceptional unconsciousness.

However, for the sake of analysis, let's take it at face value. The pronounce-ment has three operative words: "change," whole," and "system." Here, the focus is "system." What constitutes "the system?"

At a minimum, the system consists of the legal framework, i.e., the U.S. Constitution, all federal law, all state constitutions, all state law including state statutes and state common law, and all local law.

But the legal framework is only part of the system. Our economic structure and cultural aspects such as organized religion, charitable organizations, and foundations are parts of our system.

Some elements of our system span multiple categories. For instance, fast food or convenience is part of our economic system as well as our culture. Some people think fast food is a bad idea. Getting rid of all fast food would sub-stantially change our system. Yet fast food is a small part of the whole system.

Some parts can be changed without legislation. For instance, if a large enough portion of our society simply stopped eating fast food, the fast-food industry would cease to exist.

But regulating Wall Street or substantially changing policing requires legis-lation. Legislation requires majority support in the legislature, which requires a certain amount of popular support, depending on the magnitude of change.

Modest change, like tougher oversight of the financial industry or more effectively regulating risky securities such as subprime-mortgage-backed securities, requires popular support. But radical change like converting our economic system to pure socialism would require the kind of overwhelming support that's hard to find in a diverse, multicultural, free, and democratic society.

Moderate change, like diverting a part of the police budget to government agencies better suited to deal with the community problems police currently face, requires popular support. Radical change, like abolishing publicly fund-ed policing, requires overwhelming support.

Even converting our economic system to pure socialism or abolishing publicly funded policing doesn't change the *whole* system. They qualify as changing subsystems of the system. While many who blurt, "we need to change the whole system," have no idea what they're saying, some might mean changing subsystems of the system. Alternatively, some may actually believe amending our entire legal framework and converting our economic system, in addition to changing our culture, is the way to go.

Whether the goal is changing subsystems or the whole damn thing, you run up against the how. Without rehashing the process for amending the Constitution, working within the system to change entire subsystems requires supermajorities difficult or impossible to find in a diverse, free, and democratic society.

Radical Change versus Democracy

Fascinating dynamics exist between substantive extremism, or the desire for radical transformation, and democracy. Compromise is a fundamental instrumentality of democracy. But compromise is anathema to radical transformation. There's no compromise in converting our entire economic system to socialism. We're already living the compromise. We have a mixture of free markets and publicly funded programs such as public education.

Extremists denigrate compromise. Extremists spit upon modest progress. Extremists reject the instrumentalities and outcomes of democracy, and for good reason. Democracy and its institutions are roadblocks to changing the *whole* system.

The system of democracy prevents changing the entire system. Changing the whole system by working within the system of democracy is impossible. Elevating the impossibility of changing the entire system over the possibility of modest progress through compromise is another way of perceiving extremism.

This analysis helps to clarify a fundamental tenet of extremism:

The institutions of democracy are inconvenient to radical transformation.

January Sixth: *Viva la Revolución vía Corrupción*

Perhaps no American in history has more profoundly understood the frustrating nature of democratic institutions to those seeking radical transformation than our forty-fifth president, Donald J. Trump. You might say, "we've never seen anything like it." No one has. Totally.

Trump's ultimate solution to maintaining presidential power in contravention of the Constitution doesn't require the popular support needed to amend the Constitution nor the destructive power of the U.S. military or armed militia. I'm not saying he didn't explore using military force, but on this occasion, the U.S. military functioned as an institution of democracy. What a drag.

His use of militia was provocative and mortally dangerous, but he didn't have the numbers to actually overthrow the government. The extremism of January sixth eroded support within his party, family, friends, and allies, and cemented to him the caption of "danger to our democracy" at least for the rest of his administration for some, and beyond for others. In other words, January-sixth extremism undermined his legitimacy and wrecked his legacy without advancing his ambition.

But the story doesn't end there. President Trump enlightened us to the fragility of our democracy. He revealed a feasible pathway to authoritarianism through corruption.

As a former New York real estate developer, he is uniquely qualified. He brought those talents to bear to achieve his ambition. I've come to think of him as a corruption savant.

Being fair, not all his efforts were radical exercises in corruption. He initially worked within the legal framework. He used courts to challenge election results in closely contested states. But arguments crafted to incite mobs are ill-suited to courtrooms, bank robbers lose patience waiting for the next available teller, and democratic institutions don't condone authoritarian revolution.

He then embarked upon a series of ploys more befitting a crooked mogul. He pressured state Republican officials, including governors and secretaries of state, to decertify election results. He conspired to have Republican state legislators appoint Trump electors in states Biden won. He rolled out an aggressive misinformation campaign including allegations of hacked voting machines, rigged elections, and widespread voter fraud. He pressured the Justice Department in a failed attempt to get it to declare it was investigating fraud to lend legitimacy to his misinformation campaign. He pressured Vice President Pence to use the formality of the Electoral College roll call to reject votes for Biden. He conspired to use military force to seize voting machines and ballots to prove fraud and force a "do-over."[30] Finally, he riled a mob that

----

30 Helderman, Rosalind S., "All the ways Trump tried to overturn the election— and how it could happen again." *The Washington Post*, Feb. 9, 2022. https://www. washingtonpost.com/politics/interactive/2022/election-overturn-plans/.

included armed militia prepared to overthrow the government.

The institutions of democracy held because key individuals, including Georgia Secretary of State Brad Raffensperger, refused to capitulate to Trump's radical ambition. But Trump exposed a pathway to radical transformation requiring neither majority endorsement nor armed insurrection.

Corruption can be used as procedural extremism to achieve substantive extremism. It may be as simple as installing a few officials willing to ignore popular election results in key positions in battleground states to create the appearance of electoral dispute to throw the decision to the House of Representatives to decide the presidency along partisan lines. Trump pursued this strategy by endorsing election deniers for governors and secretaries of state in battleground states to prepare for another run. Using corruption to change a substantial portion of the system is plausible.

Let's take a moment to touch home base. We're examining corruption as a species of procedural extremism used to carry out the extreme result of circumventing constitutional elections. Extremism is relevant as it pertains to hyperpartisanship. Extremism enables hyperpartisanship by making compromise less likely and relegating common ground to fantasy. Because corruption links to extremism and extremism to hyperpartisanship, corruption is worth a brief exploration.

Interestingly, corruption connects to partisanship without the intermediary link of extremism. Corruption and partisanship share at least two causal factors. The first is obvious, and we'll dispose of it briefly. Both corruption and partisanship are financially incentivized. We've extensively discussed financial incentivization of partisanship through product differentiation in PI's campaign subsector and through presenting partisan content by the entertainment subsector. In addition, everyone is familiar with the concept of bribing public officials. Corruption and partisanship are money.

Segregation, Corruption, and Political Machinery

The second causal factor of segregation merits more time. We've established that partisan segregation facilitates hyperpartisanship. It also enables political corruption.

A political machine is "a party organization, headed by a single boss or small autocratic group, [which] commands enough votes to maintain political and administrative control of a city, county, or state."[31] While segregation is not explicit in this definition, it's implied. Commanding enough votes to keep control requires a fair amount of partisan segregation. If the city, county, or state are politically integrated, in other words, if the split between Democrats and Republicans is anywhere close to 50/50, political machinery is improbable.

Political machinery, which requires significant partisan segregation, invites various forms of corruption, undermining functionality and faith in the system. Patronage rewards those who deliver votes with advantageous jobs. But the skill set and ambition needed to deliver votes may not be a good fit for the patronage job. Sitting in an office collecting a good paycheck without necessary qualifications or even the desire to perform isn't in the people's best interests. Machine control of elected and appointed offices invites kickback schemes. Machines accept "donations" from businesses in return for zoning concessions or highly profitable public-works contracts. Political machines have been known to accept bribes from criminal organizations in exchange for legal protection.[32]

Corruption through political machinery transcends partisan affiliation. Both Democratic and Republican machines have corrupted political systems. The longer a single party controls an administrative division, whether Democratic or Republican, the greater the likelihood of corruption. The ability of the minority party to hold the majority party accountable diminishes as the magnitude of the majority increases and as the time the machine maintains control lengthens.

Regardless of the ideological underpinnings of radical ambition, our best defense against extremism, including the extremism of radical corruption, is maintaining the integrity of democratic institutions. Democratic institutions are more likely to maintain integrity if they're integrated and balanced with respect to partisan affiliation.

~~~~~~~~~~~~~~

31 "political machine," Britannica, accessed August 11, 2022, https://www.britannica.com/topic/political-machine.

32 Britannica, "political machine."

Neither Dysfunctional Hyperpartisanship nor Disunion Requires
Egregious Corruption

Corruption's connections to hyperpartisanship through extremism in the
previous subsections are somewhat tenuous. I admit them as content in part
to make this next point, which I expound upon in the following sections.
Corruption facilitating both hyperpartisanship and extremism is mundane,
yet more profound and pervasive than fraud or bribery.

It's not against the law to fund partisanship or extremism. It can be argued
that corruption is absent. Is the assignment of extremism-justifying righteousness to our causes intellectual corruption, or basic psychology allowing
us to act on our impulses? Human psychology cannot be legislated away. But
surrendering to inclinations without inspection is lazy and enables extremism.
Inspecting compulsions renders them less compelling.

Extremism Is Glamorous

Extremism commands a closeted allure. I confess to experiencing its seduction. Its heat melts restraint. Its purpose taunts moderation. To do something
spectacularly extreme to advance the righteous cause is heroic—the stuff of
dreams.

Charisma and moderation combine awkwardly if at all. You don't pitch a
movie about a moderate to a studio in need of a blockbuster. The middle way
isn't sexy. It's boring. *Ce n'est pas chic.* Extreme circumstances call for extreme
measures. That's the philosophy of heroes. That's what sells tickets.

We identify with the hero, and the hero does whatever it takes . . . in pursuit
of the righteous cause. The cause *must* be righteous. That's the key.

Once we're convinced of the righteousness of the cause, we're free to do
whatever it takes. The end justifies the means. In other words, righteousness
can be liberating.

But how are we convinced of the righteousness of our cause, and who
does the convincing? As far as who, we must convince ourselves. True, the
eccentricities, charm, and intelligence of the charismatic may seduce us. Yes,
charismatics are intelligent. Charisma is a form of intelligence. The charismatic is psychologically adept. But if we're to commit to extremism, we must allow

ourselves to be convinced of our righteousness. We must be self-righteous.

The psychological underpinnings of the sanctimonious, along with complexities associated with appraising their deeds, merits volumes. I limit this treatment to a few paragraphs providing a bare-bones framework for analysis.

The internal struggle takes many forms. To act or do nothing is a familiar expression. To be certain or tentative of one's righteousness is presently more relevant but less well-known. What internal factors influence the appointment of righteousness?

Both a desire and fear of freedom vie within us. The desire to act freely, to do whatever it takes, abets the appointment of righteousness to our causes. Fear constrains such appointment. In other words, an allure as well as apprehension of extremism exist independently of the righteousness of any cause. Allure or apprehension may affect our psychology to convince us as to the morality of our undertakings. Allure of extremism tilts internal decision-making toward a finding of righteousness in our cause. Fear sows doubt.

Many spellbound by extremism are closeted. They disguise their obsession to the outside world and to themselves with a cloak of righteousness. Rather than admitting that their compulsion for extremism drives them to righteous classification, they proclaim that the righteousness of their cause demands extremism. Extreme circumstances call for extreme measures. Heroic. Stuff of legends.

Sanctimony rationalizes extremism. Awareness of the psychological underpinnings of our rationalizations comes with maturity. Consciousness through examining our motives is part of growing up.

Get 'Em While They're Young

Predatory grooming is not exclusive to pedophilia. Radicalization adheres to a recipe that similarly works best with pliable ingredients.

Identity in Flux

Desire for new experience can be exploited. Human development includes experimentation: Try it out. You might like it. The relationship between experience and identity is dynamic. A well-timed introduction to extremism may blend seamlessly into self-discovery.

The Excesses of Youth

If a little is good, a lot must be better. Youthful physiology permits excess. Some die, true, but those who survive come away with the lesson that they can survive excess. X-games are extreme. Extreme sports were not invented for the aged.

Perceiving the extreme as virtuous is fashionably youthful. Nonviolent resistance is so twentieth century. Civil disobedience is old-fashioned. MLK and Gandhi are passé. Smash some windows dude!

Youthful Ambition

Ambition can be tricky. We just examined the allure of extremism independent of the righteousness of the cause. Ambition is similar. Popular philosophy rationalizes unqualified ambition: It doesn't matter what you do as long as you do it well. Ambition, like the allure of extremism, can assign righteousness to our causes. You want to make a difference, don't you? You want to make a name for yourself, don't you? We need people willing to take action. Are you one of those people? Are you willing to do what's necessary?

Here, I take a brief excursion to distinguish "old" from "previous generations." Blaming older generations for a plurality of the world's ills is stylish. I accept the premise for argument's sake as well as the insidious tautology. Since everything happening flows from prior conditions according to nature's laws, it must be that the present results from the previous. In other words, crediting older generations for a plurality of the world's blessings is equally insightful.

But all previous generations were, at some point, young and ambitious. Accepting the premise, what percentage of the world's ills caused by previous generations were born of youthful ambition? The rhetorical question is meant to inspire reflection.

Now, I distinguish "idealistic" from "concerned about the consequences of our actions."

Confession: When I was younger, I was more idealistic and less concerned about the consequences of my actions and more likely to have stars in my eyes. Idealism and ambition combine to assign righteousness to our causes, condoning extremism.

Certainty

A certain anxiety associated with uncertainty is also a youthful quality. Parents comfort children with assurances concerning matters they can't be certain of. That's hard to shake. It's as if we're conditioned to feel a moral obligation to be certain.

But like ambition's and extremism's allure, the need to be certain can be tricky. If we really want to do something, we can con ourselves into certainty.

Genuine feelings of certainty can be misleading. All humans have experienced genuine feelings of certainty, only to learn they were wrong. Certainty is like an emotion. Feeling certain doesn't guarantee a certain outcome.

As a teenager, I was certain about many things, and when I wasn't, I spoke as if I was. Within weeks I would be equally certain about things directly contradictory to the things I was previously certain about and spoke with equal conviction while asserting contradictions. Realizing that life demands action without certainty is part of growing up. Many of us develop a healthy skepticism surrounding the concept of certainty. That's healthy skepticism, which is another way of saying healthy uncertainty. Uncertainty is healthy. It's natural. It's harmonious with life.

Unfortunately, our politics glisten with a veneer of certainty. The media is complicit. The people just want to be assured—like children—by fairytales of certainty.

The political discussion treats the electorate like children. The meaning of "certainty" transmutes to "strength" while "uncertainty" translates to "weakness." The reality of uncertainty yields to the propaganda of certainty. The perception of strength defeats honesty.

This is a danger of allowing PPs to conduct public discussion. An honest discussion admits uncertainty, but political ideologues manage discussion with religious certainty.

On the other hand, certain acts beseech certainty. I'm almost certain that the 9/11 hijackers were certain of their righteousness. In other words, moral certainty expedites extremism and healthy uncertainty restrains it.

If you feel compelled by circumstances beyond your control to front an avatar of certainty, be uncertain inside and you've inoculated yourself against extremism. When circumstances change, get out. On the other hand, if you publicly front an avatar of certainty to manipulate circumstances to your advantage, shame on you. You're part of the problem. Lastly, if certainty about your righteousness is eternally genuine, you're psychologically impaired. If you're a child, growing up should dissolve the impairment. If you're an adult, get help.

Peer Pressure Facilitated by Segregation

In addition to pliability, excess, ambition, and certainty, susceptibility to peer pressure, especially in segregated environments, enhances the appeal of targeting the immature. When I reflect upon some of the stuff I did as an adolescent to impress my peers as to the level of reckless behavior I was willing to undertake, the words "humiliating," "shameful," and "embarrassing" come to mind. I refuse to share details at this time. (They're details only shared under the influence of impressive amounts of alcohol, and I've quit drinking.) But under the influence and in the mindset of the reckless adolescent, stories are told with pride.

Segregation can turn peer pressure to the purposes of management. Consider military prep schools or private religious institutions. Think of work retreats organized under the pretense of collegiality but used to reinforce hierarchy and managerial canon.

It's one thing to pull that crap with adults whose fully formed identities provide buffering against indoctrination, but instituting ideological segregation for children or adolescents is perverse. Subjecting developing individuals to narrow experience sequestered from healthy antithetical experiences retards the evolution of a balanced and complex identity.

The extremist guru isolates his flock from moderating influences. Integration provides a vigorous environment, promoting evolution and protecting against extremism.

Physics of Extremism

Imagine two forms. The first has the bulk of its mass located near its center like the object in figure 6.2. The structure appears stable because the preponderance of its substance sits near its center of gravity.

Figure 6.2: Structure of Stability

The second has the bulk of its mass at the extremes, like the object in figure 6.3. This structure appears unstable because most of its material is far removed from its center of gravity. It looks like it could easily topple. The unstable structure also appears prone to teetering in perpetual oscillation between the two extremes.

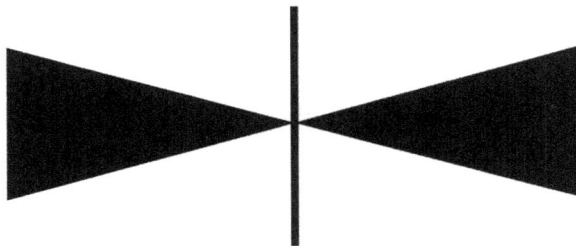

Figure 6.3: Structure of Instability Prone to Oscillation

So, a structure or system locating its majority at the extremes has two qualities—instability and a tendency to oscillate. Topple a system or object by pushing as much to the extremes as possible and begin to rock back and forth. Leading the majority toward the extremes makes perfect sense if your goal is overthrowing the system. Revolutionaries benefit from instability.

Perks associated with oscillation implicate more traditional calculus. As the system leans far to one side, the other side can manipulate fear to profitable advantage. Oscillation from one extreme to the other is rejuvenating from a fundraising perspective. PI's campaign subsector benefits from oscillation.

The entertainment subsector also benefits. Oscillation provides excellent content. It's scary and exciting. A stable system never straying too far from its center of gravity is ho-hum. Oscillating instability delivers. It makes for good POEP.

In a system financially incentivizing oscillation, the extreme left helps maintain the extreme right and vice versa. Movement toward extremities exacerbates oscillations. Only in the center can a movement amass sufficient gravity to stabilize the system and defuse extremism. The threat to the extreme left is not the extreme right, and the threat to the extreme right is not the extreme left. The threat to both extremes comes from the center.

The Internet Effect and Extremism

The internet is an excellent tool for redistribution toward the extremes. The internet learns our desires and predicts, through algorithms, the most gratifying content. Statistically, humanity has shown an appetite for the extreme. Because our eyes are in the front of our head, we tend to move in the direction we're looking. Capturing our gaze is the first step in determining our direction.

The internet is a private affair. It's also an exploratory vehicle. Is it reasonable to assume we're going to use a private exploratory vehicle to seek what is available at the library?

I'm certain some of you temper private searches with moral, ethical, or exploratory discipline, which is to say either you behave privately as if you're being watched or you're exceptionally boring. A valid response to that insulting analysis is you've reached a level of maturity beyond the prurience of adolescence. Bravo to you. I've made clear the relationship between extremism and immaturity. I fear technology races far ahead of the pace at which society matures.

The internet is an expanding universe. Our human predispositions coupled with algorithms written to maximize traffic and trade by predicting and inciting desire lead us inexorably to the outer reaches of the expanse. The force of the internet is away from center. The population relocates to the extremes as the center hollows out. Common ground is becoming a commodity without value.

Will the force of expansion rip us apart or will we pull back toward the center? If we're to assemble in the commons once again, it won't be via the internet. Virtual reality lacks the necessary gravity.

Conclusions

Happy for us that when we find our constitutions defective and insufficient to secure the happiness of our people, we can assemble with all the coolness of philosophers and set it to rights, while every other nation on earth must have recourse to arms to amend or to restore their constitutions.
—THOMAS JEFFERSON

For governing a country well
there is nothing better than moderation.
—LAO-TZU, *Tao Te Ching*

Extremism supports and helps sustain hyperpartisan systems. The further both sides move from center, the more difficult it is to compromise, and the more absurd seems common ground. If you're just left of center, and you perceive the right to be dominated by extremism, then lefty extremism seems a more palatable alternative, and vice versa. In other words, if you're a lefty extremist, righty extremism helps the cause. The more extreme both sides become, the less likely is functional accord.

In a tribal environment, but where democratic institutions still hold, even barely, partisan electoral politics incorporates extremism, blunting its ability to trigger radical transformation or advance specific policy. The potential energy of extremism dissipates in partisan warfare as potential supermajorities acquiesce to the institutionalized polarity of party allegiance.

PI's campaign subsector uses fear of opposition extremism to motivate and mobilize the partisan electorate. Extremism provides compelling content for the entertainment subsector's segregated audiences.

Partisan extremism sustains partisan extremism. Far-right and far-left extremism maintain and justify one another. They accommodate each other. Developing a more robust center disturbs that comity by reducing oscillation thereby reducing extremism's profitability.

Irrespective of the ideological underpinnings of radical ambition, our best defense against extremism is maintaining the integrity of democratic institutions. That includes a free press calling balls and strikes according to the strike zone as opposed to partisan narrative or tribal nepotism.

Figure 6.4 encapsulates relevant features of extremism:

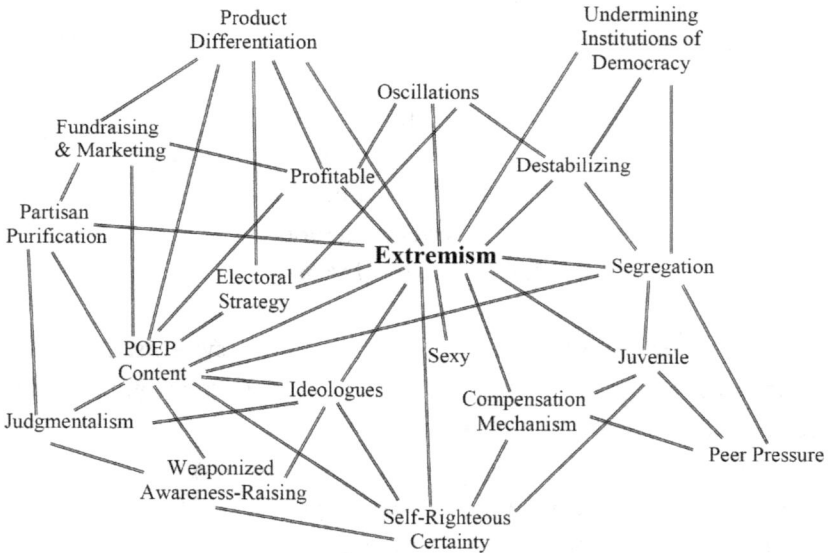

Figure 6.4: Extremism Sub-web of Hyperpartisanship Web

Now its antithesis: The Web of Moderation!

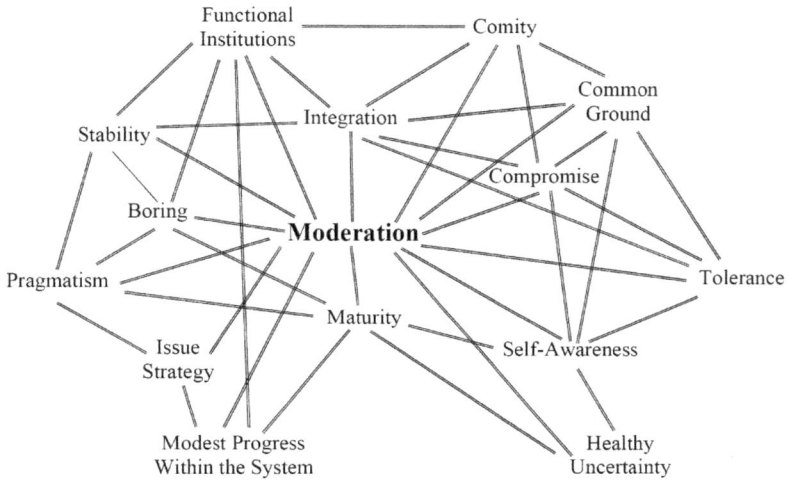

Figure 6.5: Web of Moderation

7

Echo Chamber Effect

E cho chambers (ECs) are environments "in which participants encounter beliefs that amplify or reinforce their preexisting beliefs by communication and repetition inside a closed system and insulated from rebuttal."[33] ECs are generally discussed in the context of partisanship.

ECs implicate partisanship. However, focusing on the addictive lure of ECs rather than their partisan implications has greater utility.

In addition, while our definition leaves the door open for real-world ECs, I focus on virtual expressions, which are more fecund and poignant. Reverberations of one's opinions saturate ECs, and access tends to be through media, especially via flat screens. We seem predisposed to ponder echo effect, but the virtual setting may be more relevant.

Red Herring

The idea that we must make pilgrimages to foreign ECs to expose poor souls within those dark spaces to contrary opinion in hope of propagating enlightenment like some Johnny Appleseed casting pearls of wisdom is delusional hubris, off the mark, and self-defeating.

We need to get out of ECs for our own sake. Consuming our own opinions fattens our egos while starving our wit. The gluttony is addictive, and we should treat it as addiction. Managing ECs as a partisan problem feeds the

---

33 "Echo chamber (media)," Wikipedia, accessed Oct. 16, 2023, https://en.wikipedia. org/wiki/Echo_chamber_(media).

beast. It's a psychological problem with partisan implications.

Jonesin' for Validation

The psychology of insecurity is a reservoir of profitability from which the advertising industry has wet its beak for decades. Celebrity endorsement, skin care, makeup, fashion, health, automobiles, you name it—you yearn to be better than you are, and if you buy our product, you will be.

Partisan marketers dip into its reservoir as well. However, instead of pushing products guaranteed to make you better, they hawk validation. "Independent analysts" provide unconditional righteousness affirmation while panels of "experts" confirm your opinions.

The Matrix Conundrum

ECs exploit contrary opinion. The first version of the Matrix was too perfect. It lacked credibility. It was easily distinguishable from real life. People woke up.

By deliberately introducing imperfections into the imagined lives, the system functioned at a higher level. People were more effectively conditioned to think their fantasy existence was real. The machine exercised superior control by programming a little, but not too much, strife into the illusion.

So it is with contrary opinion within ECs. A little, but not too much, makes it more compelling. Divergence is ephemeral, and deep down, everyone knows it. At some level, even if it's unconscious, everyone is in on the game. Deviants are either outnumbered, outmatched, or out-programmed. The majority corpus relentlessly whittles away antagonistic validity until it dissolves into the ether. Time and resources belong to the house, and in the long run, the house always wins.

Red Herring Redux

This is why descending upon foreign ECs to bestow enlightenment is misguided, unless *you* are the house, the house employs you, or you profit from appearing. If you're a player, by all means, feed the beast. For PPs, both problem and solution are partisan. Don't dwell on audience insecurities. For profit's sake, steer clear of self-examination. Do you want people changing the channel?

No, if you're a pro, the path is well-defined. Suggest your audience is faultless. The problem is with those other ECs. We just need to expose the people trapped in those other ECs to our truth. That's how we save them. That's how we save society. Be brave. Speak out. In the end, our superior worldview will win out—if we could just reach them, if we could just rescue them from malevolent ECs.

People with differing ideologies should routinely converse. We should work to normalize such a thing. But ECs aren't the proper venue. If the house is rigging the game, don't play.

The Camouflaged Mirror

In reality, mirrors manifest plainly. They stick out. They interrupt panorama with reflection. Our image and backdrop replace the foreground. Unless we're shaving, or spying, we gaze momentarily and move on.

Not so in the virtual world. Within ECs, our opinions reverberate and reflect. But neither our visual nor auditory cortex processes the data as echo or reflection. A part of our brain concludes: "It's not us," though in a sense, it is.

The design is unapparent. Consequences are insidious and implicate the relationship between insecurity and affirmation.

We start by perusing accessible media. Deliberately seeking like-mindedness isn't necessary. A conscious search for validation is unlikely and not needed. We chase some form of satisfaction.

Satisfaction is felt through diverse antecedents. Amusement, information, cooking, escape, artistic or athletic expression, etc. may trigger the desired feeling. ECs exploit escape and affirmation to seduce their prey.

Escape and affirmation form a potent yet bewildering mixture. Like oil and water, they resist combination. But by the enchantment of the camouflaged mirror, they transmute into an addictive and noxious potion.

We seek either to escape disagreeable realities or to escape ourselves. Consciously discerning the difference may be difficult. Am I trying to escape the reality that I'm continuously forced to deal with difficult people or escape the fact I do not play well with others? Either way, enter the camouflaged mirror.

Using a mirror to escape oneself sounds like nonsense. But parts of our brains do not recognize the mirror as such. Our visual or auditory cortex, depending on the medium, concludes it's not us. We're not perceiving ourselves.

Within ECs, we're not mindful of smart algorithms or seductive advertising delivering our attendance. We just know it feels right. Affirmation caresses our spirit. Like overindulgent parents, unconditional reinforcement spoils objective self-evaluation. Who needs it? Not us. Not me. Those other people who don't think like me need to take a good look in the mirror.

But you *are* looking into a mirror: a funhouse mirror disguised as the consensus of the brilliant and insightful. The illusion that the euphoria of affirmation was not self-induced and the deception that the desire of our unregulated ego wasn't in play helps make escape of oneself into a mirror possible. Escaping ourselves or our lot in life while bathing in affirmation is dangerously addictive.

Professional Counterargument

Assembling like-minded individuals provides an organizing foundation. Successful advocacy requires such congregations. True, but deflecting. I'm sure some owners, hosts, and participants are organizing and conducting advocacy, but let's not forget the house rakes in a profit and pays its employees, and many participants are paid professionals.

Some of the audience or participants may use ECs for organizing or advocacy. Some may be gathering information for their efforts. Some may tell themselves they're practicing citizenship. But most of the habituated simply provide the basis for advertising revenue. Like a pyramid scheme, a small percentage at the top profit, and everyone else is just a supporting brick—a ratings data point or subscriber.

Red Herring III

Visiting foreign ECs to spread the word enables addiction by providing rationalization. Look at me. I went on a mission. Now it's OK for me to slip back into my warm bath of validation. PI thanks you for your unpaid service. How does it feel to be a pawn?

You can't beat a gambling addiction by stepping onto the floor of a new casino. The house still wins, and you still lose. Stop being a brick in someone else's pyramid scheme. Be more than a ratings data point for a well-heeled industry's advertising revenue. Don't be duped by the camouflage—rip your gaze from the mirror.

ECs, Hyperpartisanship, and Extremism

EC ecosystems are soft. The selective pressures induce adaptation to pre-conceived notions, i.e., no adaptation required. The like-minded coddle feeble thoughts. In a petri dish pushing an addictive medium inside a laboratory with optimal temperature and humidity, hopes and desires of the disaffected transmute into mirages of valid argument. Ideas that wouldn't survive the scrutiny of more rigorous environments evolve and perpetuate. Radical concepts germinate and fester. The progeny of the fanatic's untethered manipulations can range from harmlessly disconnected to abomination. Hyperpartisanship and extremism flourish in ideologically congenial ecosystems.

However, some effects are more subtle yet have broader consequences. Within ECs, humility is a vestigial affectation. It's superfluous. It's neither exercised nor instilled.

The real world relentlessly engenders humility. We wait in lines, we settle, we enthusiastically volunteer wrong answers, we clumsily engage people we're attracted to, we fail … in so many ways. But as a result, *we evolve*. We learn to take care. We learn to be mindful of others. We learn our intelligence and even our memories are flawed. We're not perfect. We make mistakes. Sometimes we're flat-out wrong.

Humility Is the Soul of Civility

Therefore, ECs corrode civil discourse. If civil discourse could be measured quantitatively, I would predict the following relationships:

As the time an individual spends within ECs increases, his or her desire and ability to conduct civil discourse decreases, and as the time humanity spends within ECs increases, the desire and ability of humanity to conduct civil discourse decreases.

Evolutionary Impacts

Virtual-world algorithms guide us to environments suiting our nature. Virtual reality adapts to us. It's engineered to keep us in our comfort zones. The internet is *Westworld* continuously evolving to better understand and catalogue human predilections while we stagnate in the comfort of our predictable patterns. No need to stretch. No need to grow.

Stagnation and self-destruction incubate, threatening viability of individual and species. The narcotic of escape through self-induced, unconditional affirmation can immobilize. Potential withers in stillbirth. Mesmerized by the camouflaged mirror, with our eyes wide open, we contentedly slumber.

Or the disaffected zealously embark upon destructive irrationality, convinced of their righteousness by sympathetic reverberations of depravity or psychosis, resulting in impairment, death, or confinement. Regardless, addiction curtails promise and opportunity. Our extinction appears plausible.

ECs Redefined in Terms of Effect

ECs are media constructs designed to ensnare the public, preying on and profiting from insecurity by providing escape through the narcotic of self-induced affirmation. Sequestration from reality through intoxication by self-induced affirmation may reduce civility, cause radicalization, extremism, stagnation, or some combination thereof depending on the personality or character of the ensnared.

Isolation Chambers

At last, you've found a place where everyone thinks like you. It's not the real world, of course, but you know what I mean. Everything is grand, until one day the discussion broadens. You're no longer in perfect harmony with the consensus. The dialogue troubles you.

But not only you. Others perceive deviation. Suspicion develops. One of the disgruntled endorses an alternative site, a place of greater purity, of loftier distinction.

Secession ensues, and the process regenerates. ECs propagate to become better targeted. The more specifically tailored ECs become, the more the market fragments. Finally, boutiques cater to single individuals. The isolation chamber comes to be.

The financial viability of isolation chambers is problematic and impossible with respect to TV or radio. A channel or station broadcasting to an audience of one goes out of business. But through clever programming, the internet is potentially lucrative.

Imagine a super-intelligent bot able to communicate like humans without making innumerable uncalculated errors. However, occasional mistakes without discernable pattern are desirable.

It must have profound facility to divine the user. Like a courtesan maestro, it communicates whispers of affirmation through a multitude of conjured personalities. Each fictitious participant, unique in style, massages distinct facets of the user's complexion.

But let's not forget *The Matrix*. Remember the psychology of habituation. Rewarding every interaction with affirmation dilutes compulsion and diminishes efficacy. The bot must deduce optimal frequencies of dissonance, which vary by user. Occasionally, the bot, through one of its avatars, must invoke dissension. Then the user, with help from bot-avatar allies, can conquer the deviant. How delightfully satisfying! How euphorically affirming!

The economics work because the same program can be used endlessly. Imagine a single site hosting ten million individuals, each in his own isolation chamber. What a wonderful world!

I lack programming skill and possibly the moral turpitude to pull it off. AI makes it possible.

Final Thoughts

As stated in the introduction, this book was conceived in part through self-examination. I've known addiction. I recognize its tug. Treating ECs exclusively as partisan artifices or virtual incubators of radicalization will fail—the way the "war on drugs" fails.

Addressing phenomena harboring addictive qualities requires dealing with both supply and demand. Public policy seems better suited to dealing with supply. Let's go after drug dealers. Let's outlaw online gambling. Let's do a better job of regulating the internet.

Let's acquire perspective. Politically, confronting supply is a no-brainer. Consumers outnumber suppliers by a wide margin. Think votes. I'm not suggesting prosecuting users. I'm thinking more along the lines of vaccination—metaphorically—don't panic.

Addiction transcends vice. Advertisers and marketers, etc. understand categorically. Phenomena perpetuated through addiction exploit traditional economic systems involving consumers and suppliers. Regulating suppliers makes political sense, but it leaves consumers vulnerable to the next debilitating, habit-forming trend.

As a society, we need to do a better job of understanding the fundamentals and triggers of addiction to boost our immunity. It requires developing awareness of potential sources of addiction and recognizing its onset symptoms to consciously deploy protective psychology. That's a lot of hassle for a convenience-based society. That's why we should integrate addiction-resistance training into educational curricula. Manipulating dependence to market self-destruction and disunion should be harder.

But most media discussions of ECs are conducted and moderated by PPs. Political marketers incorporate the subject matter into partisan warfare. HM examines ECs principally because they provide a refuge for the enemy to multiply and radicalize. The enemy's extremism provides justification for extreme counterpoint, reinforcing and escalating a cycle of partisanship that profits PPs.

The wrong people are conducting the discussion.

8

Red/Blue Cognitive Impairment

If in the 1960s we had applied physics that placed Earth at the universe's center, space exploration would have been grounded. Shedding archaic physics theories allowed us to walk on the moon. Analytical frameworks evolve.

They also depend on subject matter. For example, to figure out the kinetic energy of a baseball hit for a home run, one multiplies its mass times the square of its velocity and divides by two: $KE = (1/2) \, mv^2$. However, articulating an exciting home-run call requires rules of grammar instead of Newtonian physics.

Applying incongruous analytics impairs problem-solving, and problem-solving capacity is an element of intelligence. To be blunt, trying to solve a physics problem using grammatical rules is stupid. Consequently, clinging too assiduously to a single analytical framework or refusing to apply alternative analyses retards our intellectual potential. Different problems require different analytical frameworks. Diverse sets of problems require diverse analyses.

Viewing life through red/blue glasses diminishes fitness by blunting one's ability to glean relevant information from experience. Some readers may wonder: Is he on Team Red or Team Blue? Do his ideas help blues or reds? If you are nodding yes in your head, or for that matter nodding your head yes, you may have a touch of RBCI, applying an inappropriate analytical framework that prevents you from getting maximum value. Reading this book while wondering if its ideas help the red or blue team is like pouring water onto a lidded jar. Don't waste your time. Get yourself a rah-rah red book or a rah-rah blue book.

Wedding oneself to a single paradigm impairs cognition. Red/blue is simply a subcategory of binary paradigms that hook us all. Binary thinking is constantly reinforced in game shows, sports talk, political talk, drama, etc. It's simple. It's a toss-up. It's one or the other.

Framing discussions from the outset for issues like the economy, crime, or education in terms of Republican and Democrat skews the analysis to lose or ignore potentially valuable content. Foundational discussions about issues relevant to the functioning of society should ignore partisan politics and be conducted the way we would discuss engineering a bridge. What's the best way to get the job done?

Election day imposes choice, and typically that choice is binary. But between now and then, framing every issue as Democrats versus Republicans confounds problem-solving. It's as if we're shooting ourselves in the foot for entertaining TV. One of the most nauseatingly overused phrases is: "Think outside the box." The binary paradigm is the box. It's a prison. Abandoning binary thinking opens the box. Free yourself. Crush the box. Take the lid off the jar.

Our society has fallen in love with, and is wedding itself to, the red/blue analytical framework (RBAF). This is especially true for POEP. In the chapter on media, I discussed the incentivization of partisan analytical frameworks without referencing RBCI or RBAF. As partisan affiliation becomes more significant to personal identity, validating programming becomes more compelling.

Stories pitting red against blue are effective at validating identity via partisan affiliation. This is achieved either by cherry-picking naturally partisan stories or by imposing partisan analytical frameworks on stories that would benefit from alternative analyses.

Trump

> When the Master governs, the people are hardly aware that he exists.
> —Lao-tzu, *Tao Te Ching*

Framing every story in partisan terms jettisons relevant content. Paradigm subordinates content. This is backwards. Content should determine analytical framework.

Using pejorative classifications and excessively relying on the word "simple" when ascribing adjectives to former President Trump's motivations and actions is tempting. But if we're being honest, accurately placing him in context of the present subject matter involves complexities.

First, I agree he is "a symptom, not the cause" of what's dividing our country, as former President Obama stated.[34] I presented data earlier showing the evolutionary explosion of partisanship predates the Trump administration. But as a symptom, he presents grossly. Trump is the most noticeably polarizing public figure I've witnessed.

Our evolving hyperpartisan ecology created conditions permitting the election of Donald J. Trump as POTUS. As president and former president, he is an instrumental factor in the hyperpartisanship web rippling through the evolution of society. Feedback loops perpetuate dispassionately.

Obsession with his influence on our republic also perpetuates and ripples. Here, I discuss how media's partisan obsession degrades news content and undermines constructive discourse.

Saudi journalist Jamal Khashoggi was murdered by Saudi nationals at the behest of Saudi leadership in the Saudi embassy in Türkiye. Instead of vigorously condemning the Saudis, Trump called attention to American jobs associated with outstanding weapons contracts with Saudi Arabia, implying a severe denouncement might put those contracts at risk. Trump's rationale for his tepid condemnation spotlighted our brokered relationship with Saudi Arabia.

The primary framework for debate as presented by Trump himself was whether a proper reprimand was worth potentially losing the jobs and money America was to garner from weapons contracts. Unfortunately, the media accepted this paradigm, with the anti-Trump team arguing our nation's principles demanded a firm rebuke, potentially accompanied by sanctions, whereas Team Trump argued that thousands of American jobs were worth more than a single journalist who wasn't even an American citizen.

Team Blue's position suggests previous presidents would've done the noble thing and condemned the Saudis with suitable righteous indignation. They're half right. Condemnation would have been broadcast, but there would have been nothing noble in it. Political expedience demands rebuke. But our expedient relationship with Saudi Arabia would have continued unabated. Flaunted

---

34 President Barack Obama, "Full speech: Obama brands trump as 'symptom not the cause of division,'" Sept. 7, 2018, https://www.nbcnews.com/video/full-speech-obama-brands-trump-as-symptom-not-the-cause-of-division-1315294787749?v=railb&.

rebukes help obscure our dependent relationship. Public displays of revulsion distract us from and ease our unsavory relationship with Saudi Arabia.

Trump's framework was surprisingly honest. How rare for an American president to acknowledge the seamy nature of our Saudi relationship. Even after 9/11, when eleven of fourteen hijackers were identified as Saudi, our national leaders made sure to focus our attention on Osama bin Laden, in Afghanistan, and eventually on Iraq. The Saudi discussion never happened. Trump presented us with an opportunity to have that discussion. Although the discussion paradigm presented by Trump and adopted by the media raised a principal issue, it was fatally flawed.

Arming Saudi Arabia isn't about jobs. It's about protecting our Middle East interests. We prop up Saudi Arabia, warts and all, because of Iran and oil. Saudi Arabia's record of human rights abuses is longstanding, deep-rooted, and well-documented.

The issue isn't whether Trump, or any president for that matter, should condemn or reprimand Saudi Arabia. The issues are: What sustains our un-savory relationship with Saudi Arabia? Should we end that relationship, and if so, how, or how can we make that relationship less unsavory?

Let's deal with the latter first. Our relationship with Saudi Arabia becomes less unsavory if they end government-sponsored human rights abuses and institute democracy. Whether or not the U.S. can play a productive role, per-haps as part of a coalition of democratic nations, in helping another nation peacefully transition from abusive authoritarianism to democracy is open to debate. We haven't had much success in that regard, but that doesn't mean we should give up. One thing is for sure. Media PPs aren't going to help get us there. I guess it's possible that public condemnation coupled with behind-the-scenes relationship maintenance is part of the strategy, but I have my doubts.

Can we end the relationship, and if so, how? At least two pretexts abet the relationship. First, Saudi Arabia is our regional geopolitical ally, at least in part, because they oppose Iran, our regional geopolitical enemy. The enemy of our enemy is our friend. This begs the question: Does aligning with Saudi Arabia truly help neutralize Iran? In other words, does aligning with Saudi Arabia serve U.S. geopolitical interests? I don't know the answer, but it's worth asking and discussing publicly.

If aligning with Saudi Arabia serves U.S. geopolitical interests, the question becomes, how can geopolitics change so we don't need Saudi Arabia as a regional ally? This is an extremely complex question whose answer seems to involve changing our relationship with Iran. I suppose it's possible, but highly unlikely, at least in the short term.

Let's say geopolitics can change so there's no benefit to having Saudi Arabia as our ally. In a world connected through economy, ecology, and geopolitics, do we want to discard allies inconvenient to our democratic sensibilities?

Second, oil dependency incessantly lubricates our relationship with Saudi Arabia. The inflationary period following COVID saw gasoline prices top five dollars a gallon, precipitating a visit by Trump's successor, President Biden, to Saudi Arabia. We're addicted to oil. The global economy is an oil economy, and our unsavory relationship with Saudi Arabia continues unabated regardless of any administration's partisan affiliation.

The complexities surrounding Middle East geopolitics and oil addiction merit substantive analysis and discussion. Rather than publicly rebuking Saudis, President Trump clumsily spotlighted the expedient nature of our Saudi relationship with his offhand remarks on American jobs. This was an opportunity to engage in an adult conversation about the nature of that relationship.

Instead, the media reduced the episode to whether or not President Trump should condemn Saudis, and if so, how strongly. It's elementary school, current-events discussion framing. "Well class, should the president have condemned Saudi Arabia? What do you think? Yes, or no? Oh, I see Jesse has raised his hand. Tell us what you think Jesse."

"I think he should have."

"Why Jesse?"

"Because what they did was bad."

"Excellent!"

I would describe our relationship with Saudi Arabia as follows: Saudi Arabia is a Middle East ally regardless of human rights or democracy concerns, but we'd rather they didn't publicly murder journalists and stuff like that because it puts us in an awkward position. However, if we're put in such a position, some of us may feel compelled toward public condemnation. But don't worry Saudi government, the condemnation mainly provides content for partisan media. Just ignore it so our relationship may continue unabated. Also, when media frame the issue with partisan simplicity, some of the awkwardness is alleviated because the critical examination that should be directed toward the relationship between our countries is diverted to America's internal partisan circus.

Media imposing a less-than-optimal analytical framework wastes substantive content. RBAF isn't always best. Common sense dictates it can't be. The media's dogged insistence on it erodes substance from public discussion, thereby undermining democracy while institutionalizing polarity.

Rationale for Media's Dogged Insistence on Imposing Less-Than-Optimal RBAF

Identity Validation

As partisan affiliation becomes a more conspicuous part of identity, content affirming the righteousness of the audience's partisanship becomes more desirable. Partisan analytical frameworks facilitate validating segregated audiences' partisan affiliations.

RBAF Reduces Chances of Wandering into the Hazardous Territory of Audience Self-Examination

Boiling our seamy relationship with Saudi Arabia down to elementary school issue-framing perfectly illustrates this phenomenon. Audiences, i.e., the American people, benefit from our Saudi relationship. The relationship increases access to inexpensive oil and provides national security benefits. High gasoline prices at the pump can lose and have lost elections.

Our relationship with Saudi Arabia persists despite human rights abuses and murdered journalists because of *us*, not Donald Trump. Our Saudi relationship, like hyperpartisanship, predates the Trump presidency and will persist long after. Biden's visit with Crown Prince Mohammed bin Salman proved that.

The manner in which the media dealt with Trump's response to Jamal Khashoggi's murder pinpoints something essential about Trump, media, and self-examination. If Donald Trump is in the picture, self-examination becomes nearly impossible. It reminds me of the restaurant scene in the movie *Scarface*, where an intoxicated Tony Montana, a Miami gangster played by

Al Pacino, fights with his girlfriend, played by Michelle Pfeiffer.[35] After she storms out, Tony notices restaurant patrons staring, and says:

> What are you lookin' at . . . You need people like me. You need people like me so you can point your fucking fingers and say, 'that's the bad guy.' So what that make you? Good? You're not good. You just know how to hide and lie. Me, I don't have that problem. Me, I always tell the truth, even when I lie. So say good-night to the bad guy. C'mon. The last time you gonna see a bad guy like this again, let me tell you. C'mon. Make way for the bad guy here. There's a bad guy comin' through. Better get out his way!

You might argue that with Trump, he always lies even when he tells the truth. But you get the idea. Trump is the gift that keeps on giving for HM.

The psychology of introspection is inapposite to hyperpartisanship. Self-examination provides a pathway toward assuming responsibility. Hyperpartisanship requires blaming others. Trump is a magnet for finger-pointing. He interferes with, or depending on perspective, alleviates, inclinations toward introspection. For hyperpartisanship, this is Trump's most relevant quality.

He fits HM perfectly. It doesn't matter which side you're on. If Trump is in the picture, there's nary a chance of constituent introspection. "I don't want to think about it" enables dysfunctional hyperpartisanship. If you don't want to contemplate your complicity, Trump's your guy. I hope it's the last time we're gonna see a partisanship guy like this again, let me tell you. "I'm winning," Trump replies. Self-examination is a loser.

RBAF Matches PP Expertise

In addition to validating partisan identity while reducing the peril of audience self-evaluation, there's a more mundane, yet equally relevant, rationale for the media to consistently rely on RBAF. It's what they know how to do. The expertise of POEP hosts, analysts, and guests is divining and arguing for partisan advantage. That's what they're good at.

---

35 *Scarface*, directed by Brian De Palma (Universal Pictures, 1983), 2:50:00.

The same pool of hosts and analysts examine every story. If the same people analyze everything, and those same people excel in partisan analysis, chances that any given story is conveyed via RBAF are high. They're just staying in their lane. And why wouldn't they? They're getting paid. Sponsors are happy. Networks make money. If it ain't broke, don't fix it.

So what if media occasionally fails to glean maximum value from stories due to applying less than ideal analytical frameworks? The media business model doesn't require optimal analysis. The bottom line of the business ledger doesn't include an entry for substance or insight.

Notice the feedback loop. As media professionals develop expertise in partisan analysis, their incentive to cover stories suitable for partisan advantage increases. As incentive to cover stories suitable for partisan advantage increases, incentive to staff media with experts in partisan analysis increases, and so on. Stories that divide along partisan lines or can be used to gain partisan advantage or highlight partisan differences are in partisan analysts' wheelhouse.

Content is more compelling if coverage is in the wheelhouse of central characters—hosts, analysts, and guests. If occasionally you're forced to cover stories that would fare better under different analytical frameworks, oh well. What are you going to do, get rid of central characters? I don't think so. Beloved central characters are going to have to do the best or only thing they can: impose RBAF regardless of optimality.

RBAF Is Entertaining

It transforms political discussion into competitive sport. We love it. The psychology and business model underwriting partisanship are deep-rooted and wide-ranging.

Effects of the Media's Dogged Insistence on Imposing RBAF Regardless of Optimality

RBAF Is Polarizing

The choices are diametrically opposed. That's what polar means. Either you think President Trump should've condemned the Saudis or you don't.

Adopting polarizing frameworks necessitates confrontation. Confrontation makes for good POEP, but that's not necessarily what society needs. Even if the adult conversation I suggested doesn't solve our unsavory relationship with Saudi Arabia, it's uniting. Regardless of partisan affiliation, we all share a country that benefits geopolitically from our Saudi relationship. If you don't think that's true, that's the discussion we should have. Regardless of ideology we share an economy underwritten by oil. If you don't like it, that's the discussion we should have.

Sharing a country benefiting geopolitically and economically from our Saudi relationship means we're all in the same boat. None of us can claim moral high ground. That's a poisonous notion from a PP perspective. It undermines the game by interfering with righteousness affirmation. That could be extremely disturbing to audiences segregated according to partisan affiliation. Nobody tunes in to POEP to find they're no better than anyone else. Adopting nonpolarizing analytical frameworks undermines product differentiation and threatens PI profitability.

RBAF Is Profiling

Employing RBAF from the outset skews decision-making toward less-than-optimal results. RBAF severely constrains the universe of outcomes. Either Team Red or Team Blue wins, or nothing happens. The dynamic makes it more likely policy will be decided according to partisan muscle rather than optimization. If a single party controls both houses of Congress along with the White House, then policy results are according to partisan ideology rather than pragmatism.

In other words, RBAF prejudices the process, which is symptomatic of profiling. All we see from the outset is red or blue. That level of reductionism is hurtful.

Media don't have to play along, but by and large they do. We've discussed how media benefits. RBAF polarizes the investigation, suiting it to partisan validation while reducing the peril of audience introspection.

But it does something more—something that gets us back to the media being more than a mere reflection of society.

RBAF Is an Insidious Form of Conditioning

HM conditions audiences to perceive society, all its issues, and all its people as red or blue. We're developing an implicit bias for RBAF. Everyone's doing it. We're all red/blue profiling. It's both cause and effect of PI lateral expansion. RBCI resulting from ubiquitous use of RBAF is one reason lateral expansion is debilitating.

Reiteration is powerful, but the issue is more than just repetition. There's a qualitative aspect as well. It's prime time. Prime-time partisan demagogues have achieved bona fide celebrity status, and bona fide celebrities see partisan demagoguery as a pathway to social status transcending entertainment celebrity.

RBAF seems clever. People we tend to idolize, i.e., people who appear on TV, use RBAF. They sound informed. You, too, can sound smart if you analyze everything in red/blue terms.

Maybe it is clever. Clever like a one-trick pony. But it's not smart. Smart distinguishes situations where partisan analysis makes sense from situations where it doesn't. Applying incongruous analytics impairs problem-solving, and problem-solving is an element of intelligence. Using grammar to solve physics problems is stupid.

COVID Illustrates RBAF/RBCI

We used partisan analysis to solve a pandemic. Results were less than optimal. Decisions on whether to congregate, wear masks, open schools, open small businesses, and get vaccinated correlated with partisan affiliation as much as with medicine.

HM is responsible for part of the problem. COVID bulletins differed according to the partisan inclinations of outlets. But it went deeper than that. Some medical professionals seemed infected with at least a mild case of RBCI.

Medicine is grounded in science, and opinions among medical professionals vary and evolve. Even consensus opinions on the efficacy and appropriateness of specific treatments and prophylactics change with time as the latest information becomes available. This is understandable.

Therapeutic philosophy also varies. Some medical professionals emphasize preventative care including diet and exercise, while others focus on treatment. But opinions on both diet and treatment have changed with time.

Some medical professionals have raised alarms over the ubiquity of highly resistant strains of bacteria resulting from the overuse of antibiotics in food production and blasé prescription practices. Even before COVID, opinions among medical professionals about routine vaccination diverged.

Throw profit motive into the mix. Drug companies profit from selling drugs. Duh. Doctors who receive incentives from drug companies are more likely to prescribe brand-name medications.[36] An undergraduate friend of mine, while in medical school in the 1980s, told me a pharmaceutical company was offering frequent flier miles to doctors prescribing its drugs. Acknowledging that profit motive impacts medicine is reasonable. When considering treatment, adult responsibility demands appreciating profit motives within the medical profession.

When a pandemic bursts on the scene, uncertainty is certain. That understanding will evolve is certain. That recommendations will change is also a certainty. Diagnostics will improve. Treatments will be refined. But profit motive is eternal. The reliability of the profit motive transcends the medical profession, extending to media outlets that provide platforms for medical professionals to address the public.

Most conscious adults understand these dynamics. Medical professionals speaking to the public should understand that audiences understand. But let's put aside the galling practice of medical professionals patronizing laypeople.[37] This is about hyperpartisanship and RBAF's debilitating impacts.

---

36 Colleen Carey, Ethan M.J. Lieber, & Sarah Miller, *Drug Firms' Payments and Physicians' Prescribing Behavior in Medicare Part D*, National Bureau of Economic Research, accessed Aug. 17, 2024, https://www.nber.org/system/files/working_papers/w26751/w26751.pdf.

37 For those particularly annoyed by medical professional patronizing, I highly recommend the "Me Doctor" sketch by Monty Python's Flying Circus. Rylxyc, "Monty Python—Me Doctor," YouTube, accessed Aug. 12, 2023, https://www.youtube.com/watch?v=BQSbKBTuQBc&ab_channel=rylxyc.

RBAF Injects an Element of Intractability That's Especially Harmful in Situations Demanding Fluidity

People don't like admitting they were wrong. Medical professionals, media personalities, and public officials occasionally get it wrong. That's understandable. But by imposing RBAF, situational understanding meant to be temporary takes on the gravity of a partisan platform.

While changing partisan platforms is possible, the time frame for doing so doesn't suit pandemics. Partisan positions develop from snapshots in time of phenomena that are best understood through movement and change. Information meant to grow, demographic analysis meant to be refined, diagnostics that must develop, treatment that must be improved, understanding that will evolve, and recommendations that will change should not become rigid for partisan advantage.

Partisan positioning undermines efficient response in at least two ways. First, politicians, media personalities, public officials, and yes, even medical professionals, build strongholds around positions they've staked out. Staking out positions for phenomena such as evolving pandemics makes no sense.

Second, as understanding evolves, early public statements look uninformed. This must be. Early statements are relatively uninformed in pandemics because early on less information is available. Statements based on less information are less informed than statements based on more information. PPs utilize early statements to discredit the other side, thereby retarding evolution of understanding and response.

Potentially productive discussions deteriorate by perpetually relitigating early and necessarily less-informed statements rather than concentrating on what's current and relevant. Throw a finger-pointing magnet, i.e., Trump, into the mix, and discussions go off the rails. The number-one priority for the anti-Trump team is opposing anything coming from his mouth. Team Trump makes opposing the opposition its number-one priority. That's no way to deal with a pandemic. Imposing a partisan framework sabotages competency.

Proving RBCI

My hypothesis as a non-medical professional is that at this time in America, RBAF is applied too often, resulting in cognitive impairment at both the individual and societal level. I can't prove it, and I'm not sure it's provable, but it's worth looking into. If I were a well-heeled foundation, I would make grant money available for research in this area.

Proving societal impairment, or dysfunction if you like, might prove diffi-cult because of confounding factors. For example, with COVID, our response was less than optimal because of RBAF. On the other hand, pharmaceutical companies produced vaccines in record time. Technological advances in med-icine confound efforts to measure the negative impacts of RBAF in pandemics.

Individual impairment is easier to prove. Imagine an experiment involving 100 individuals. Divide them randomly into two groups of fifty. Each group would be asked to solve a series of problems and answer a series of questions on a wide variety of subjects, similar to aptitude tests such as the SATs. Prior to testing, researchers would provide the control group with a substantial series of warm-up questions similar in scope to actual test questions.

In contrast, warm-up questions for the experimental group would focus on partisan politics. I'm willing to bet all your money the control group would outperform the experimental group to a statistically valid extent.

Conclusion

The partisan mindset is communicable. Our vulnerability to habituation and our infatuation with fashion make us susceptible. Partisanship is trendy. It's also easy. It's like learning a single chess opening. You can get by in most cir-cles with a single chess opening. But a single opening, like a single analytical framework, preordains mediocrity. It's lazy.

There's something suspicious about RBAF. It's in the "too good to be true" category. If you apply an analytical framework invariably leading you to con-clude fault lies exclusively with a group you don't belong to, that's too good to be true. It sounds more like self-pleasuring than objective analysis. If, on the other hand, your analytical framework occasionally forces upon you an undesirable self-examination and realization of complicity, that's evidence you're on the right track.

RBAF is both cause and symptom of dysfunctional hyperpartisanship. Kicking such a habit is demanding work. It begins in the mind with genuine desire to beat it. But it's featured in prime time. It must not be that bad. I can get over with a single stylish paradigm, and I can feel righteous about it. Conscientious self-evaluation is a drag. Who needs it? Let's watch some POEP.

9

Political Parties

The essence of political parties is difficult to fathom through definition or structure. According to the encyclopedia, a political party is "a group of persons organized to acquire and exercise political power."[38] But what type of organization and how does it function?

According to ThoughtCo, "Political parties are neither corporations nor political action committees, nor super PACs. Nor are they nonprofit groups or charitable organizations. In fact, political parties occupy *a vague space* in the U.S.—as semi-public organizations that have private interests (getting their candidate elected to office) but play important public roles. Those roles include running primaries in which voters nominate candidates for local, state, and federal offices, and also hosting elected party members at presidential nominating conventions every four years"[39] (emphasis added). Now we know what type of organizations political parties are not.

I like the "vague space" concept from ThoughtCo. I think that's right. It's interesting that entities with ubiquitous influence over politics function within a "vague space." But here, we're mostly interested in the effect of political parties, especially concerning hyperpartisanship. Our exploration of effect begins with abstract graphic analysis.

Imagine the circle in figure 9.1 to be a single policy issue circumscribing

---

38 Maurice Duverger, "Political Party," Britannica, accessed June 14, 2023, https://www.britannica.com/topic/political-party.

39 Tom Murse, "How Political Parties Work in the United States: The Functions and Responsibilities of the Republicans and Democrats," ThoughtCo., July 3, 2019, https://www.thoughtco.com/political-party-definition-4285031.

the universe of positions on that issue. Symbols within the circle represent six people with nuanced positions.

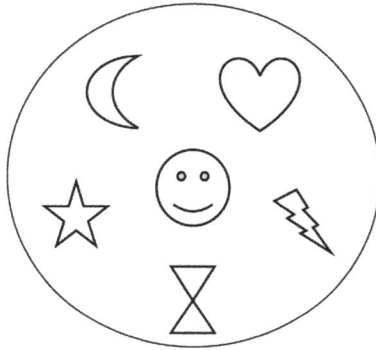

Figure 9.1: Individuals with Nuanced Positions

Now imagine a bill introduced in Congress on the issue. The bill doesn't accurately reflect any of the nuanced positions represented in the figure but has elements of all six. The six must vote yea or nay on the bill.

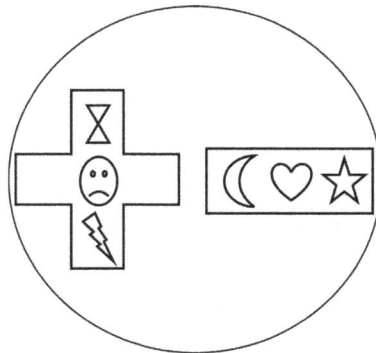

Figure 9.2: Polarizing Configuration

The three within the plus sign in figure 9.2 voted for the bill, and the three within the minus sign voted against. Notice how organizing within the binary construct of yea or nay necessarily polarizes the configuration. People divide into two sides.

By spending some more time with the simple diagram, we can discern the consequences of organizing within a binary construct beyond the polarizing effect. All six individuals moved off their nuanced positions to fit themselves into the new framework. Individuals changed. They changed their positions. They made a choice, and to a certain extent, we are the choices we make.

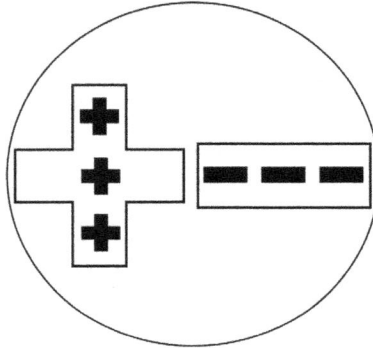

Figure 9.3: Hyperpolarization

So, this piece of legislation created by humans affects humans, but not solely through policy implementation. The bill itself, before passage, is an environmental factor influencing the behavior and nature of people. The construct we shape, shapes us. It's hyperpolarizing. Because stipulated configurations obligated the six to conform, each sacrificed individuality.

But human beings are complex and resilient. Modifying one's position on a single issue isn't a big deal. Besides, in America, representatives vote on bills. The rest of us vote in elections. We don't have to modify or even take positions on legislation. We only need to take positions on candidates, and we only have to take those positions once every two, four, or six years depending on the elected office.

Let's expand our single-issue analysis to examine political parties.

Parties and Platforms

Political parties take positions on dozens of issues in fashioning a platform. To begin, notice the word "issues" is plural, "platform" and "party" are singular. Keep that in the back of your mind.

The likelihood of complete and natural agreement wanes as the number of topics or issues increases. This makes intuitive sense. But let's briefly examine "natural" in this context.

We begin life with different biological brains. From birth, the organ of thought is uniquely our own. Then, information accrued through experience uploads. Our experiences continuously change our biological brains, affecting the way we experience and upload future experience. The relationship between our brains and experience is dynamic. Our experiences affect our brains, and our affected brains affect our experience of reality.

Our thought organs as well as our experiential uploads are unique. We grow up in different homes with different families emphasizing different values. We have different friends with different personalities. We play different games and sing different songs. We go to different schools, have different teachers, and read different books. Even identical twins who grow up in the same household do not experience life identically. One goes first.

Different brains plus different experiences means different thought patterns. It means we aren't going to agree on everything. That's OK if we can agree on some things some of the time. There may be some things we can all agree on. For instance, if:

$1 + 0 = 1$; and

$1 + 1 = 2$; and

$1 + 1 + 1 = 3$; then

$2 + 1 = 3$.

I hope so. I hope we can all agree on at least that. But for most things, even if we limit the universe to two people, there will be some agreement and some disagreement. That's the *natural* condition. If we increase the number of people in the universe, likelihood of universal agreement on even a single issue decreases.

Based on the discussion thus far, we can plainly state two rules:

1. As the number of issues increases, likelihood of agreement on *all* issues decreases; and
2. As the number of people increases, likelihood of universal agreement on any single issue decreases.

We can state a third rule based on our abstract graphic analysis:

3. As the number of possible nuanced positions on a single issue increases, likelihood of universal agreement on that issue decreases.

There's another rule which should be self-explanatory:

4. The more issues, the greater the likelihood a person will be interested in at least one of the issues.

Political parties include tens of millions of people concerned with dozens of issues with handfuls of nuanced positions on each issue. How do parties finagle functional accord under such conditions? Parties have three operational elements—people, issues, and positions. We'll dispose of the first element at once. The more people, the better. It's a no-brainer. It's a premise. The question for political parties becomes: How can issues and positions be manipulated to maximize membership and member participation, including voting and financial contribution? For ease of analysis, we'll assume maximizing membership is compatible with fundraising objectives.

Now let's apply our rules. Our premise, "the more people the better," diminishes the importance of rule two: more people supersede universal agreement. So, we're talking about rules one, three, and four. It appears rule four supports the premise. The more issues, the more people will be interested.

However, at least two factors restrain rule four. The first is rule one. More issues mean more people, but more issues reduce likelihood of agreement. The second is emphasis. Not all issues carry the same weight with the electorate. At some point, increasing the number of issues becomes unwieldy distraction.

The concept of platform ameliorates discord between rules one and four. Platform is a singular entity encompassing a multitude of issues. But how could that possibly work? It works because few of us concern ourselves with party platform details.

Amorphous discussions conducted by segregated media manage our limited insight, blunting nuance. My impression is there are only two positions on every issue and at most two relevant bills. Either there is only one bill, which one party supports and the other opposes, or there are two bills representing the positions of the two parties. If multiple bills with nuanced positions exist, public discussion as framed by media keeps it secret.

In the absence of detail, the conglomerate must suffice. Without specifics, we're left to generalize. Without inspection, we surrender to packaging. So, we submit to the binary construct of party affiliation.

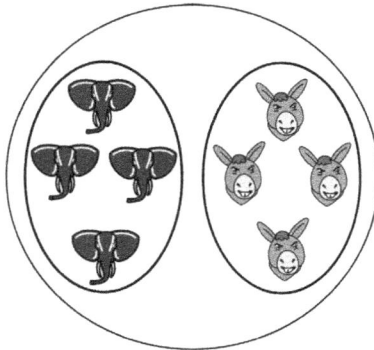

Figure 9.4: Partisan Conformity

But it doesn't end there. Though for some of us, it does. Some of us couldn't give a hoot what our party's platform is. There may be one or a few issues we concern ourselves with, and one party seems a little more in tune with our positions on those few issues, but we couldn't care less what our party's position is on other issues. Some of us wish to vote in primaries, and some states require party affiliation to do so, but that's as far as it goes.

Some of us are secure in our identities independent of political ideology or party affiliation, but that bucks the trend. Ideology and party affiliation are gaining prominence as characteristics for self-identification.

Rule: As importance of party affiliation for an individual increases for self-identification or self-worth, the sway a party wields over that individual increases.

The more vulnerable one is to tribal bullying and the more partisan tribes infiltrate one's identity, the more likely one is to conform to the construct. You may be a star-shaped peg, but available holes are shaped R or D. Think COVID: for many, partisan affiliation determined vaccine status.[40]

Psychological Effect on the Electorate

What are the impacts of personality contortion? How does it feel to conform to ideals of an ill-defined and little understood entity existing within a vague space? As your party pulls further away from the other party, are you pulled with it? Do you go along for the ride? As extreme elements of both parties become more powerful, do you stand and cheer, or does it make you a little nervous? Are you comfortable with hatred, or does it upset your stomach? When you find yourself squeezed into a position not of your making, do you blame yourself, or does resentment kindle? How do you handle resentment? Do you identify its source? Are you more likely to blame your own tribe for coercion or condemn the other?

Relationship between Political Parties and PI

This one isn't easy. Examining this part of the web is a bit like looking at a kaleidoscope of discordant devotions. To avoid vertigo, we must ration our examination into digestible portions while maintaining our purpose of realizing hyperpartisan effect within the complexities of the relationships.

First and foremost, political parties are not a part of the PI. It's counterintuitive because "party" and "partisan" share the same root. The concept of party is embedded within partisan and vice versa. But PI is a private sector,

40 William A. Galston, "For COVID-19 vaccinations, party affiliation matters more than race and ethnicity," BROOKINGS, Oct. 1, 2021, https://www.brookings.edu/articles/for-covid-19-vaccinations-party-affiliation-matters-more-than-race-and-ethnicity/.

for-profit business complex, while political parties occupy a "vague space" between private and public sectors. Maybe the best way to understand political parties is as a conduit between those sectors. I bet you can guess what flows through the conduit.

Money forms the filaments connecting nodes in this part of the web. But the relationship isn't binary. It entangles fundraising entities such as PACs and super PACs, donors both large and small, and political candidates. PI's campaign subsector is featured here. As a reminder, the campaign subsector largely comprises political consultants who expertly spend political contributions.

The players:

1. Political parties
2. Other fundraising entities
3. PI campaign subsector
4. Politicians
5. Large donors
6. Small donors

Campaign spending can easily ditch us in the weeds. Due to the murkiness of both the framework and enforcement of campaign finance laws, the wisdom of "follow the money" is like directions for navigating a blind alley. Concerning political parties, the concept of coordination is somewhat relevant. Coordination among fundraising entities, political parties, and politicians is legally restrained, but nobody can claim with a straight face that coordination is absent. Political parties have a say in spending the money.

The relevance of coordination is de minimis for our analysis; I mention it only to facilitate picturing the process.

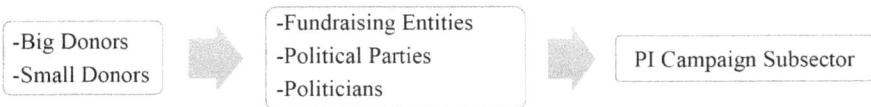

| -Big Donors -Small Donors | ⇒ | -Fundraising Entities -Political Parties -Politicians | ⇒ | PI Campaign Subsector |

Figure 9.5: The Process

Big donors are corporations, unions, and well-heeled individuals. Small donors are individuals either not so well-heeled or cheap. Donors contribute to any or all entities in the center frame. Political parties and fundraising entities influence to which campaigns money flows. PI consultants hired by campaigns expertly spend on TV advertising, social media, phone banks, door-to-door canvassing, direct mailing, etc.

Regardless of outreach medium, the message is the same. Our guy is different and better than the other guy. It's product differentiation. It's highlighting differences. It's emphasizing the gulf between sides. It's advertising discord. It's normalizing polarity. It's making the case for a type of segregation. The other side is crazy, stupid, extreme, or evil.

Donors' Intent Is Irrelevant

Whether paying for future access or motivated by ideology or circumstance, money channels to PI for product differentiation. Even moderates supporting compromise and pursuing common ground finance polarization by donating. An exception might be donating directly to a campaign where the candidate genuinely runs on moderation and civility.

With respect to parties and fundraising entities, some involved endorse hyperpartisan behavior, and some stand opposed. Either way, money flows to campaigns, where it flows to PI and is spent on product differentiation. Money spent by fundraising entities subsidizes polarity.

So, what's the relationship between political parties and PI? It's not exactly employment. Politicians' campaigns employ PI. Political parties collect, distribute, and influence money distribution to campaigns. Political parties are a conduit between donors and campaigns, but campaigns deal directly with PI. It's like political parties are mommy and daddy and campaigns are the children. No matter how money is distributed, it's all going to the candy store.

Money Is Its Own Reward

Occasionally, media experts proclaim outspending opponents doesn't guarantee victory. Hillary Clinton, for example, outspent Donald Trump in 2016, yet lost the election by a wide margin. This suggests that concerning elections, money is overrated. This is a red herring distracting us from scrutinizing actual motivations, true value, and the ultimate effect of money on politics.

More money is better than less money. This is true for every participant, regardless of election outcome. More money is better than less money for a donor wishing to buy access. More money is better than less money for a politician. More money doesn't guarantee victory, but it doesn't hurt. More money means better consultants, more media buys, more robust grassroots outreach, etc. It means the politician goes to war with a larger, better trained, and better funded army. A bigger war chest is better than a smaller war chest.

More money is better than less money for political parties and other fundraising entities. It means more power and influence. Billions of dollars flow through these entities from donors to political campaigns. Authority to influence distribution of such treasure is regal.

More money is better than less money for PI, duh. The campaign subsector is a for-profit business complex receiving and spending political contributions. More revenue increases the intensity and ubiquity of partisan product differentiation.

Each participant is incentivized to maximize money irrespective of election outcomes. The intricacies of cash flow merit inspection from a democracy perspective. But we know, without looking further, it all ends up with PI. PI grows with revenue. As PI grows, so does distribution of its product. As political spending grows, the volume of partisanship distributed by PI increases.

A New Definition

Now let's combine our abstract graphic analysis with our examination of the financial relationship between parties and PI to define the effect of political parties on society.

Political parties are conduits for cash flow between the private sector and political campaigns. They institutionalize polarity and diminish individuality by restricting ideological freedom and diversity for the financial benefit of PI.

Polarity Is Different from Organic Disagreement

Before moving on, let's hammer home why political parties *must* be polarizing. Without parties, millions of people have nuanced positions on dozens of issues. Every single person agrees with other people on some things, and every single person disagrees with others about other things. Progress within a free and democratic society requires robust public discussion premised on a natural distribution of ideas and opinions.

This does not describe polarity. The natural distribution of ideas and opinions isn't binary. Polarity is binary—polar opposites: north and south, plus and minus, D and R.

Political parties are organizational structures designed to function in opposition to one another.

Rule: Funneling the universe of ideas, opinions, and people into two opposing constructs that exert conforming pressures—"stop using Republican talking points"—intended to minimize intraparty diversity of thought and expression, while maximizing interparty differentiation, generates and entrenches polarity.

Political parties deeply embed polarization within our society through institutional structuring.

Recommendations

I would like to get rid of political parties. Third parties or more parties won't solve the problem. The power dynamic eventually transforms added parties into subsidiaries of the two dominant parties, leaving the binary construct functionally intact. The polarizing effect persists undiminished. This is especially true since alternative parties trend toward the extremes pulling further from the center, further from where common ground can be found.

However, government action prohibiting political parties would contravene the First Amendment's assembly clause. We're stuck with the constructs, but we can diminish them. We can reduce their power and influence without government action because they persist through our patronage.

Defund and Unaffiliate

Political parties subsist on money and membership. Stop writing checks to parties and PACs. If there's a particular candidate or politician you believe in, then by all means donate to that candidate. But stop transferring your hard-earned money into "vague spaces." Money within vague spaces is the lifeblood of opaque power–distribution, financially incentivizing partisanship and lending institutional structure to polarity.

Resource management is also a factor. Why fund dysfunction? It's not working. Partisanship and legislative dysfunction increase with political spending. Unless you're a big donor paying for access, there's no return on your investment. You're throwing money away. Worse, you're funding the growing rift within society. Spend locally on programs you're familiar with, or better still, that you're involved with. Stop underwriting expansion of vague spaces.

I don't wish to discourage participation in politics. I am, however, discouraging participation in institutionalized polarity. Political parties structure polarity through our membership, and PI finances polarity through our donations.

One Final Thought on the Relationship between Political Parties and PI

While parties funnel money to PI, the relationship is at times incongruous. For example, consider the effect of large candidate fields during presidential primaries. Financially, it's a no-brainer both for political parties and PI.

Large fields clearly benefit PI's campaign subsector. Each candidate hires her own consultants and conducts his own fundraising. As the number of candidates within a party increases, the slices of pie may get thinner, but the pie gets larger. PI revenue increases.

Multi-branding works financially for political parties, too. Potential voters are more likely to identify with at least one candidate in a large field, precipitating more donations.

A large field not only works financially for parties and PI's campaign subsector, but it also works for the entertainment subsector. Intraparty squabbling makes for great TV because squabbling of any kind makes for great TV. From a financial perspective, conflict works.

However, with respect to election results, the effect of large fields isn't clear. A large field may have candidates attracting electorate members who normally keep politics at arm's length. Like finicky shoppers enticed by exclusive boutiques, fussy voters are duped into taking a peek. They may invest some time or reach into their wallets during the primary, only to eventually recognize the item they admired was for display only. The carny trick may bring people into the tent for primaries, but the long-term effect may be disillusionment or resentment.

Intraparty wrangling can debilitate a candidate's chances in general elections. Candidates with legitimate chances in the general may feel pressure to adopt fanciful positions during primaries to compete with seductively extreme elements within their party. Securing raucous applause from partisan audiences during a primary is electoral fool's gold. Large primary fields provide greater opportunity for the opposition to mine those fanciful nuggets for weaponization during the general election.

Smaller primary fields bring fewer people and less money into the tent. But smaller fields are less likely to cultivate disillusionment or resentment. Debates will be less likely to wander onto the pages of children's fairytales. The opposition will have less material to exploit during the general election.

In conclusion, the financial interests of political parties and the financial interests of PI's entertainment and campaign subsectors are simpatico. However, the electoral interests of parties can be at cross purposes with the financial interests of both PI and parties.

More money is better than less money. However, certain approaches to securing more money, for example large primary fields, may clash with electoral ambitions.

10

Definitions, Formulas, and Relationships

Definitions

Partisanship

Prejudicial allegiance or opposition to a political party, faction, group, tribe, person, ideology, or cause.

Hyperpartisanship

There's no consensus definition for "hyperpartisanship," however, prevailing definitions tend to focus on combative division or the inability of parties to compromise or find common ground. Those definitions are concerned more with systemic dysfunctional results rather than rationale or incentive. I propose the following:

> Prejudicial allegiance or opposition to a political party, faction, group, tribe, person, ideology, or cause *to an extent that substantially alters or determines the opinions, beliefs, ideals, principles, behavior, or personality of those so aligned.*

In other words, as a consequence of joining a group, following a person, or obsessing on an ideology, the individual conforms to that with which he aligns. This is not unusual. People want to fit in. But details matter, as does degree. Factors including identity, group size, and group administration can transform a rather benign desire to conform into a perversion of democracy. We've touched on identity, and we'll spend more time with it here. We'll examine group size and administration in Chapter 21. But just so we're clear, making vaccination decisions according to partisan affiliation is perverse.

We can analyze *hyperpartisanship* as a relationship of dynamic equilibrium. In figure 10.1, the left side of the equation contains the individual partisan, and the right side has the group or individual to which the individual aligns.

Individual Partisan ⬅➡ Partisan Entity

Figure 10.1: Dynamic Relationship between Individual and Partisan Entity

The arrows represent the relative influence individuals have on the group compared with the influence the group has on the individual. In 10.1, comparative influences are relatively equal.

Individual Partisan ➡⬅ Partisan Entity

Figure 10.2: Dynamic Relationship Favoring Individual

In figure 10.2, individuals influence the group to a greater degree. This is the desirable relationship for political parties: the party reflects the interests of its members.

Conversely, figure 10.3 represents hyperpartisanship. The group exerts disproportionate influence on the individual, elevating the partisan entity to preeminence.

Individual Partisan ⬅➡ Partisan Entity

Figure 10.3: Dynamic Relationship Favoring Partisan Entity

Notice we can treat the ailment by working with either or both sides of the equation. Treating the left-hand side means making individuals less susceptible or more resistant to group manipulation. Treating the right-hand side means reducing the power and authority of political parties. I believe in a comprehensive approach, as is reflected in my recommendations throughout this book.

"Dysfunctional" Hyperpartisanship

Promotion of or opposition to the particular interests of a political party, faction, group, tribe, person, ideology, or cause to an extent that communication or cooperation with those not similarly aligned is unworkable—except in crises, where, nonetheless, collaboration may be impaired to an extent that undermines crisis management.

First, we're keeping in mind throughout that "dysfunctional" is contextual. While legislative progress stalls, faith in democratic institutions deteriorates, and civility fades, PI functions like a Swiss watch. PI's campaign subsector revenue has never been higher. The entertainment subsector continues to expand and profit by delivering content that either provides partisan advantage or is polarized along partisan or ideological lines. In other words, the industry moderating public discussion on hyperpartisanship profits within the hyperpartisan environment.

Second, most of the PI-facilitated discussions surrounding "dysfunctional hyperpartisanship" tend to focus on dysfunctional results. We need to spend more time examining underlying causes and how specific components of society nurture and connect to it. Presently, factionalism and tribalism supersede patriotism.

I resist the temptation to assert patriotism is passé. If we were to ask people who put their group before country why they do, we'd get two types of answers. The first is along the lines of: "I care more about my particular group than my country." I like that answer because it's honest.

But there's a big problem with that answer for electoral politics. You can't win elections with the slogan, "my group is more important than my country," at least not yet. That tells me the spirit of patriotism breathes within a majority of the electorate.

The second type of answer is along the lines of: "What my group wants is better for the country than what the other group wants. So, my personal membership in this group, my advocacy on behalf of this group, and my unwillingness to compromise or work with the other group is patriotic. My refusal to recognize any legitimacy to the aspirations of the other side is a manifestation of my patriotism."

Within any group exists a range of naiveté and cynicism. Some within a particular group may believe intransigence and incivility are righteous and patriotic. Others view any group as an opportunity to coalesce power to their advantage. Some are straightforward and unapologetic about ranking group above country: Is it so terrible to put family, friends, and loved ones before country? Can't the same logic apply to any group you closely identify with?

The key phrase in the last sentence is "closely identify with." What are the mechanisms and psychological underpinnings of close identification or identity? What is the balance of power between individual and group?

I'll use a contract-law analogy for brief analysis. There's an implicit contract, in a nonlegal sense, between group and individual. In consideration for enlarging group size and influence, membership should benefit the individual.

It doesn't have to be tangible such as helpful policy or power. It could simply be a place to belong. There's nothing wrong with that, unless . . .

Unconscionability can negate a contract. Did the group mislead the individual? Was there duress? Was bargaining power between group and individual severely out of balance?

Of course, there's no real contract between political parties occupying "a vague space" and their members. Next, I was going to say, "we expect to be misled by political parties to their advantage." Then I thought, "maybe we don't."

Some of us expect to be misled by political parties because of experience. Here's where identity and unequal bargaining power, product differentiation, and "Get 'em while they're young" all come into play.

Formulas and Relationships

> As a person derives an increasing share of individual identity from a group, psychological pressure to conform to group identity increases.

Notice how marketing and/or recruitment incentivize group identity. Fusing individual identity with a product is a marketing coup. It's the holy grail of partisan marketing.

At a fundraiser in September of 2016, presidential candidate Hillary Clinton said, ". . . you could put half of Trump's supporters into what I call the basket of deplorables."[41] The warmth of the audience's response to the implicit compliment was exposed in laughter tickled from self-satisfied grins that couldn't be contained. The message was clear if not stated explicitly. You're better than them. Simply by virtue of your presence in this room, you're not deplorable. By virtue of your support for me, you're better than they are. The holy grail! Self-righteous identity validation through membership alone.

A critical factor referenced throughout this book was working seamlessly during the fundraiser. The audience was segregated according to partisan affiliation. The audience consisted of Hillary Democrats. This brings us to our next formula.

> The probability a person will derive an increasing share of individual identity from a group increases with segregation.

A primary concern with ECs and POEP is identity impact. To counteract conforming inertia requires an opposing force. Without diversity of identity or contrary opinion, group absorption is more likely.

Briefly review our hyperpartisanship definition in light of the two formulas. Prejudicial allegiance to a group to an extent that substantially alters or determines opinions, beliefs, ideals, principles, behavior, or personality of

---

41 The laughter I refer to in the following sentence can be heard on the video included at this link. Katie Reilly, "Read Hillary Clinton's 'Basket of Deplorables' Remarks About Donald Trump Supporters," *TIME*, September 10, 2016, https://time.com/4486502/hillary-clinton-basket-of-deplorables-transcript/.

the partisan requires profound identification with that group by the partisan. Segregation facilitates identification. Therefore:

> As segregation according to partisan affiliation or political ideology within society increases, probability of "dysfunctional" hyperpartisanship also increases.

Now let's bring money into the equation and derive some formulas using the hyperpartisanship definition and identity formulas from this chapter combined with earlier PI discussions.

- As PI's entertainment subsector expands, partisan identification strengthens;
- As revenue for the campaign subsector increases through increased political spending, spending on differentiating candidates, politicians, and ideology of the parties increases; and
- As the wealth of partisan entities like political parties or PACs increases, their influence over individual identity within partisan groups strengthens.

Now we have the core of the hyperpartisanship web:

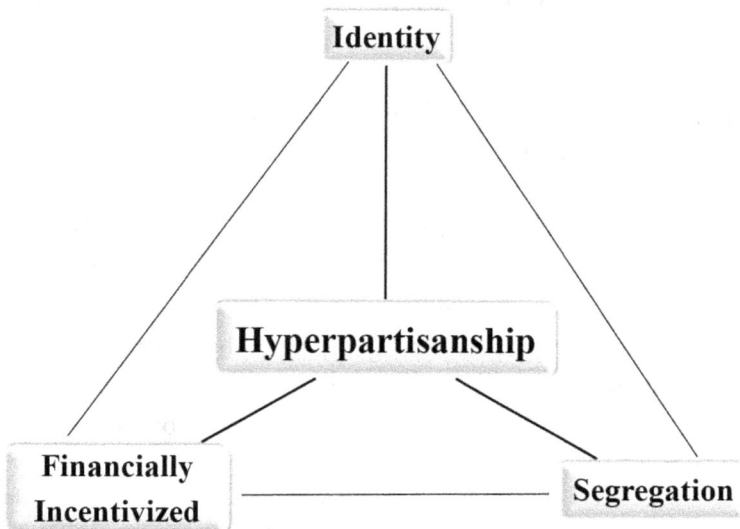

Figure 10.4: Hyperpartisanship Web Core

Before leaving this chapter, let's top it off with a few more formulas derived from earlier discussions.

You could make an argument for including extremism in the core. I have it one level removed, but it's close. In any case, it's worth stating:

Extremism increases with partisan or ideological segregation.

In addition to making intuitive sense based on EC effect, Fair Vote found, as was noted in the introduction, competitive or integrated voting districts were more likely to elect moderates, and non-competitive or segregated districts were more likely to elect representatives toward the extremes of their respective parties.

As extremism increases, so does partisanship intensity.

I consider this a tautology worth stating. I might present evidence by saying Fair Vote found moderates more likely to vote across party lines, and more extreme representatives from both parties less likely to do so. But more moderate implies greater willingness to cross party lines.

Finally, I would like to present one more relationship implicating money and segregation, especially through media and the internet.

Fortifying the independent viability of ideological or partisan fragments within society obscures the urgency of interdependence and strengthens division.

A financial investment in a particular fragment is an investment in division. Building a network of like-minded people on the internet undermines cooperation across divides. Building a network of like-minded people builds an army preparing for war, not compromise. Spending money on product differentiation builds walls. Sanctimonious validation of partisan identity repudiates alternatives. Buttressing individual fragments by monopolizing righteousness makes it harder to sew fragments together.

11

Presidential Campaign Programming: Primaries and Debates

> . . . it is a custom
> More honour'd in the breach than the observance.
> —WILLIAM SHAKESPEARE, *Hamlet*

Subject matter for presidential primaries as determined by questions posed by debate moderators reflects television priorities rather than presidential priorities and exacerbates partisanship. I base my argument on my reading of the Constitution, my extensive observations of presidential campaigns, and most importantly, wide-ranging ruminations.

Primary Focus

The principal powers and responsibilities of POTUS include:

1. Administering the executive branch of government, which includes executing laws, implementing executive programs, and commanding the military;
2. conducting foreign policy, which includes the power to make treaties;
3. making appointments; and
4. signing bills Congress has passed into law.

The first two duties partially subsume the appointment power, because POTUS appoints domestic officers as well as ambassadors, public ministers, and consuls. POTUS also appoints SCOTUS justices and federal judges. This category figures prominently in selecting presidential candidates, in addition to implicating partisanship. However, appointment of justices occupies a suitable share of TV programming and won't be examined further in this section. Instead, I discuss the other three categories in order of significance.

Administering the Executive Branch of Government Is by Far the Most Important Presidential Job, Deserving a Plurality If Not a Majority of Allotted Debate Time

According to President Biden's budget for fiscal year 2024, the U.S. is expected to spend nearly seven trillion dollars.[42] That money comes from me and you. It's our money. In my humble opinion, the most important presidential responsibility is to make sure our money is spent properly, as Congress intended.

This philosophy is expressed best by phrases such as "put your money where your mouth is" or "money talks, bullshit walks." I want our money spent wisely, and I want to know which candidates propose to ensure it is. How do candidates plan to make sure every federal program is efficiently implemented without theft or fraud? How will candidates identify obsolete programs?

According to the Associated Press, "fraudsters potentially stole more than $280 billion in COVID-19 relief funding [and] another $123 billion was wasted or misspent."[43] Roughly ten percent of the $4.2 trillion in relief the government disbursed thus far was stolen or wasted. The continuing investigation is expected to reveal even greater malfeasance and/or incompetence.

---

42 Office of Management and Budget, *Budget of the U.S. Government Fiscal Year 2024*, https://www.govinfo.gov/content/pkg/BUDGET-2024-BUD/pdf/BUDGET-2024-BUD.pdf.

43 Richard Lardner, Jennifer McDermott, and Aaron Kessler, "The Great Grift: How billions in COVID-19 relief aid was stolen or wasted," AP, June 12, 2023, https://apnews.com/article/pandemic-fraud-waste-billions-small-business-labor-fb1d9a9eb24857efbe4611344311ae78.

Was that a one-off? Do you believe fraud and waste is particular to COVID? Think ecology. Our ecosystem includes seven trillion per year in government sustenance. Expecting scavengers or grifters to ignore such bounty is unreasonable. As more nourishment flows through a leaky pipeline, available niches for fraudsters increase.

But new programs are like shiny new presents. Finding fraud is like dad fixed up your old bike, put a ribbon on it and said, "happy birthday."

I like and support renovation projects. But shiny new toys are better for ratings, especially if you're trying to attract shiny new viewers.

Look me straight in the face, metaphorically, and tell me you're just assuming existing programs all run properly. Government workers are, by and large, honest and dedicated. But they're human, right? And they're not all civil servants. Some are political appointees. An annual budget of seven trillion dollars presents considerable opportunity. Debates should reflect that reality.

Before getting excited about new laws like children anticipating the contents of beautifully wrapped presents, scrutinize existing laws and programs. The priorities of every president should be to make sure government programs run in the best interests of the U.S. and its citizens, and existing laws are enforced as Congress intended. I want presidential debates to reflect those priorities. But that would fall short of compelling television.

I put foreign policy second, but you could make a good case that conducting foreign policy is the president's most important job. Many Americans rank national security as the government's highest priority. I would point out successful national security combines sensible foreign policy with efficient administration of executive programs, both foreign and domestic.

Signing bills passed by Congress into law is dead last among presidential priorities as far as I'm concerned. It's interesting that this presidential power isn't in article II, which is the constitutional section describing the presidency. Instead, it's in article I, section 7, which describes the legislative powers of Congress.

Presidential debates spend too much time discussing stuff that will never make it to the president's desk. That may be poor time management with respect to learning about presidential candidates, but it's great TV and contributes to hyperpartisanship.

Big Is Better than Small and New Is Better than Old

The Constitution limits the president with respect to changing policy, especially domestic policy. POTUS may have some leeway in how programs are implemented or by what means laws are enforced if the authorizing legislation passed by Congress permits it, but great, sweeping changes require congressional action—as the Framers intended. Giving that much power to a single person is autocracy. We have a president, not a king.

What a quandary for media. Not really. The choice is easy. Producing a presidential primary miniseries requires blockbuster content. If you focus on material exclusive to the presidency, you have a flop. If you're shooting a blockbuster, you're gonna need Congress. Start theme music and roll opening credits.

Blockbuster issues include immigration, health care reform, gun control, climate change, criminal justice reform, income inequality, minimum wage, voting rights, reforming the tax code, education reform, controlled substance reform, judicial reform, military reform, funding priorities for national security, subsidies, and more. Substantial progress on these blockbusters requires congressional action.

If I were running for president, my response to questions from debate moderators concerning any policy changes requiring congressional action would be the same: "I will sign any bill crossing my desk into law, on any issue, so long as the legislation, in my opinion, improves the current situation—no matter how small the improvement." I would vote for a candidate with the chutzpah to offer such a response stipulating the absence of outrageous disqualifications.

Conflict and Control

Focusing on issues that require congressional action in presidential debates benefits media by escalating partisanship. Conflict is money from a programming perspective. Folding Congress into presidential debates enhances conflict opportunities for media during the campaign miniseries and beyond.

By reviewing the grand policy issues listed above, you can see the real action is in Congress. It's ground zero for partisan conflict. But from a TV programming perspective, Congress is unwieldy. The overwhelming majority of its 535 members are unfamiliar. They're extras. Blockbusters need stars. Putting it all on POTUS is neater.

The President Is Leader, or De Facto Leader, of His Party

How many times has the American public heard that one from media? How many times have we swallowed that little gem without inspection? It's precisely such traditions that we've taken for granted for so long that they've insinuated themselves into our political DNA, despite being extraneous to the Constitution, that we must reevaluate. The ones self-servingly pushed by partisan media are especially ripe for reexamination.

Media states it as truth, a premise for all that ensues. They've been doing it for so long, it may pass their lips without awareness of implications, without the faintest notion that its status as premise is not only undeserved but malignant. On the other hand, some may know exactly what they're doing. Regardless of motivation, our interest is the suitability of the concept, its impact, and its merit as premise.

The president's job is party leader. Parties are at war. Therefore, POTUS is commander-in-chief of partisan warfare. By stating as premise that the president is the leader or de facto leader of his party, the media assigns POTUS an extra-constitutional duty.

Not only is this duty extraneous to the Constitution, but it also impedes POTUS from faithfully or efficiently executing the office and contributes to hyperpartisanship. It's a conflict of interest. Leading a political party conflicts with leading a nation. Assuming the mantle of supreme party leader conflicts with faithfully executing the office of the presidency.

Presidents are expected to discharge conflicts before assuming office. But the media and PPs consistently heap this conflict upon the presidency. Through this assigned duty, the media expands its influence on the presidential narrative and institutionalizes partisan conflict. The unexamined premise is a boon to media, for which partisan conflict is content, but it undermines our republic by assigning an extra-constitutional burden on POTUS that conflicts with his actual and substantial constitutional duties.

Before I get deeper into my argument, I provide a neutral rationale for heaping everything on the president during the campaign miniseries. It would be unfair of me not to. Analyzing evolutionary factors perpetuating hyperpartisanship should be without bias.

Every four years, the presidential primary miniseries presents an opportunity for parties to articulate platforms to a captive national audience—a lollapalooza for partisan marketers. 'Tis the season of abundance. It's harvest time, and the most profitable produce can't be found in the presidential aisle. Effective management of the executive branch is a dud. Efficient administration of executive programs is a clunker. Successful enforcement of existing laws? Don't waste my time. We need to excite the base!

Forget POTUS. This has nothing to do with the president. This is about money, and the real moneymakers are blockbusters requiring congressional action. Big, new, bold, systemic, revolutionary, woo-hoo! Now we're talking. Who cares if most of it doesn't have a chance in hell of making it to the president's desk? Better still if there is no chance. No chance means disagreement. Why in hell waste partisan lollapalooza on stuff parties agree on? It's harvest time. "Stop using Republican talking points!"

Let's not forget marketing principles. Focusing on areas of disagreement— stuff that won't make it to the president's desk—is product differentiation. We need a clear choice. Why do we need a clear choice? So during the general election, PPs can say, "the choice is clear." PPs want clear choices. I, on the other hand, want choices to be less clear. We'll get to that.

There are at least two reasons why media accedes to partisan lollapalooza for their presidential primary miniseries. We've discussed the first: media likes blockbusters as much as professional fundraisers do. Better ratings for the networks staging the miniseries means greater product visibility for professional fundraisers. The business interests of the entertainment and campaign subsectors are simpatico.

Flip the Script

The second reason extends beyond the election. The election miniseries, which includes both primary and general elections, is contrived prologue. Media uses the miniseries to impose a self-serving framework to cover and judge the future president, thereby extorting a certain amount of control.

The policy debate is most visible during the presidential election season. It's like the playoffs. Casual fans watch. But casual fans as well as a significant proportion of diehards aren't concerning themselves with constitutionally appropriate division of responsibility among branches of government. Whatever moderators and media pundits focus on must be essential to the presidency. After all, they're the experts.

We've seen the trailer. The specific plot is immaterial. Whether the hero fails or succeeds is irrelevant, as long as it's a blockbuster.

Conflict is essential to blockbusters, and making the presidency about Congress ensures perpetual conflict in a variety of attractive styles. There's your red/blue conflict within the House. There's your red/blue conflict within the Senate. There's red/blue conflict between House and Senate. There's red/blue conflict between Congress and POTUS. There's intra-blue and intra-red conflict between moderates and zealots within both House and Senate. There's intra-blue and intra-red conflict between moderates or zealots in the legislature and POTUS. And no matter the substance of conflict, it can all be presented as part and parcel of the presidency. The election miniseries groomed us for it.

So, during the presidential primary miniseries, the focus is on issues only Congress can address. Then, after the inauguration, the focus is on what POTUS is doing about those issues. There's too much attention on congressional issues during presidential campaigns, and for actual governing, there's too much attention on the president. I would flip the script. During presidential campaigns, I would focus on issues exclusive to the executive branch. But between elections, I would pay more attention to Congress. I guess that's why I'm not in the TV business.

But being fair, isn't the president's job to lead Congress? Isn't congressional failure to put a bill on the president's desk a presidential failure when all is said and done? When Congress fails to make progress on a blockbuster issue, isn't that a failure of presidential leadership?

Lincoln and LBJ

This is one of my favorites: "The president should lead the Congress." Let's throw out the Constitution for the sake of argument. Forget about separation of powers and different branches of government and all that guff. The fact that Congress has its own leaders is irrelevant. After all, Lincoln and LBJ led Congress, didn't they?

It depends on your definition of "lead." They moved Congress on issues to which it was initially disinclined. Lincoln got the 13th Amendment prohibiting slavery and LBJ got civil rights legislation. These are two of the most profound advancements in American history. You might say they were exceptional.

But can't we learn from the exceptional? If we could learn from the exceptional, we could consistently make progress. How did Lincoln and LBJ move Congress?

They got dirty! They grimed their way to success. They laid down with the other side and made deals. They compromised. They strategically misled. There was nothing pure about those cats. They'd sell out their parties in a heartbeat to get what they wanted. They rolled around in river muck with adversaries to make progress.

To tell the truth, it is swampy—in a good way. Swamps, or as environmentalists like me refer to them, wetlands, are some of the most biologically productive ecosystems on Earth. They teem with life. Life proliferates in the dinge. Impurities are referred to as nutrients. Impurity nourishes ecosystems. Cross-pollination is inescapable. Birds do it. Bees do it. Political hybrids do it.

Except the swamp has been drained—not of the obscene amounts of money incentivizing polarization—but of complex ecology or impurity supporting higher-functioning life. Rich river muck baked and cracked. Partisan zealots have trampled the earth into hardpan. Fecundity has surrendered to sterility. No mixing. Keep to your own. "Stop using Republican talking points."

Sterility designated as virtue is dysfunction. Neither Lincoln nor LBJ would have a chance today.

We Need to Excite the Base

"She wants to turn out the base." "We need to motivate the base." "He's playing to the base." We hear such phrases incessantly during harvest time. But what is the base, and why does it need to be excited, turned out, motivated, or played to?

The base is the portion of the electorate consistently voting for one party. They're loyal to one party. Intuitively, I supposed the base is likely to vote in every election, contribute financially to their respective parties, volunteer for campaigns, and tune in to partisan media. But apparently, loyalty does not necessarily imply participation, contribution, or involvement, otherwise exciting or turning out the base would be superfluous. Part of the base, though loyal to one party, only occasionally votes, contributes, or participates at a higher level.

Part of the electorate votes occasionally. But not all occasional voters are loyal to one party. Some occasional voters swing from one party to the other depending on candidates. But not all swing voters are occasional. Some swing voters take part in every election.

The final category, which necessarily wanes as Election Day approaches and more votes are cast, is undecideds. Media professionals tend to speak of this last group with a fair amount of scorn, as if any attention directed their way is undeserved. Maybe they're right. For our purposes, the swing category includes undecideds. Undecideds cannot be a part of the base by definition because the base is loyal to one party, unless undecided means undecided about whether to vote, in which case undecided means occasional.

So, the categories of voters include:

1. The regular base;
2. The occasional base;
3. The regular swing; and
4. The occasional swing.

Now, let's talk election strategy, keeping in mind our opening remarks on exciting the base. We can ignore category one for voter turnout. They vote in every election, and they always vote your way. From a resource management standpoint, I wouldn't concern myself with category four either. They don't always vote, and if they do, they might not vote your way.

Let's focus on categories two and three. If you can turn out category two, they will always vote your way, and if you can convince category three, they will always vote. The question is whether turning out the base is congruous with convincing swing voters.

Not everyone in the base is the same, and not all swing voters are the same. Part of the base is near the political center, and part inhabits extremities. It's tempting to place all swing voters in the center. However, in 2016, a significant number of Bernie supporters swung to Trump after Hillary received the Democratic nomination. That seems like an outlier. In any case, we've narrowed our voter turnout targets to the following categories:

1. Occasional base moderates;
2. Occasional base extremes;
3. Regular swing moderates; and
4. Regular swing extremes.

Identifying messages appealing to all these categories is challenging. But what if we broaden our decision-making paradigm to include other factors, such as money and participation, instead of focusing exclusively on turnout? What does "excite the base" mean when you bring money into the equation? Do you really think it has anything to do with turning out or convincing moderates?

Imagine harvest contributions coming with little sticky notes. Which of the following are the sticky notes more likely to say?

a) Please exercise moderation; make a genuine effort to find common ground; and compromise with members of the opposing party whenever possible; or
b) Hold your ground; Stand firm; Don't give in; Go big or go home.

Exciting the base has nothing to do with moderation. It means concentrating on those big, transformative issues requiring congressional action and unlikely to reach the president's desk—blockbusters. That's where the money is. People may vote for moderation, but nobody pays for it. Moderation is a loser for fundraising and ratings. Once again, the business interests of PI's entertainment and campaign subsectors are simpatico.

What does it mean that blockbusters won't make it to the president's desk? It means we need to win Congress, too! It's not about picking the best person to sit in the Oval Office. It's partisan lollapalooza. Presidential primary and general election miniseries are staging grounds for partisan warfare. Focusing on blockbusters where differences between parties are greatest, i.e., on issues least likely to make it to the president's desk, is partisan electoral strategy. PP's goals are to accomplish product differentiation while maximizing ratings and revenue. The business interests of entertainment and campaign subsectors are simpatico. Providing a forum focused exclusively on presidential responsibilities to enhance the odds of picking the best president isn't legitimate PI business.

Primary Alternative

The nominating process for president should be an open tournament without party-run primaries. I'll discuss the advantages after stating proposed rules.

1. Each state would host a website that only registered voters in that state can access. Each registered voter in a state could nominate up to six candidates for president. Each state would set their own nominating threshold for ballot access for the tournament. For example, New York currently requires 45,000 signatures on a petition for independent or unaffiliated candidates to gain ballot access. Under my proposal, the top six on the ballot-access website, along with any candidate meeting the minimum threshold, would be eligible to take part in the first round of the tournament. Party nomination would not guarantee ballot access;
2. Candidates meeting constitutional eligibility requirements for president would register their intentions to run by February fifteenth of a presidential election year;
3. Round 1: On the first Saturday of April of a presidential election year, an election would be held in all the states, and all qualified candidates for president would be on ballots regardless of party affiliation, including candidates not affiliated with any party. All registered voters, regardless of party affiliation, including registered voters not affiliated with any party, would be eligible to vote for up to three candidates without ranking. The top six candidates according to the popular vote qualify for the next round;
4. Round 2: On the first Saturday of September after Labor Day, an election

would be held in all the states, and the six qualifying candidates who want to be president would be on all ballots. All registered voters would be eligible to vote for up to two candidates without ranking. The top two candidates according to a popular vote who desire to be president qualify to be on the ballot for Election Day; and

5. Finals: On Election Day, the two remaining candidates who want to be president shall be on the ballot. Early/mail-in voting for president may begin after the results of round 2 have been determined. The winner would be decided according to the Constitution; and

6. Any candidate may campaign at any time, and debates may be held at any time.

The Open Tournament Nurtures Democracy and Reduces Partisanship

It Diminishes Party Control of Political Processes

Parties govern primaries, which turns the process for deciding the presidential ballot into partisan lollapalooza. Eliminating party control reduces opportunities for using the system for partisan advantage.

The Open Style Tournament Reduces Partisan Fragmentation of Society

All candidates being on stage throughout, regardless of party affiliation, produces a more integrated process. Viewing audiences will be less segregated according to party or ideology, enhancing political experiential commonality and diminishing EC effect. All who watch debates will see the same debates. Political water-cooler moments will be more inclusive.

The Open Tournament Delegitimizes Political Extremism

The primary system generates a destructive dance normalizing extremism and fortifying partisanship. Primaries incentivize appealing to the more extreme elements of both parties. But during the general election, candidates tend to moderate positions and distance themselves from extremism.

Both media and the electorate have come to expect and accept this recurrence. Considering this phenomenon from the perspective of partisan voters, especially the ones inclined toward, or vulnerable to, extremism, provides insight: We spent the whole primary focused on terribly exciting partisan blockbuster proposals only to be forced to the center for the general. Why? Because of the other side. Because of them. Our extremism is righteous. After all, we just watched the primary miniseries orchestrated by mainstream media focus on extreme proposals from our side. That means they're legit. If barely our side of center is good, extreme our side is better. Who could argue with that?

With a tournament open to all candidates and voters regardless of party affiliation, extremism is less likely to gain a mainstream foothold. Candidates can't afford to play to party extremes because of the risk of alienating a majority of the electorate. This has the added benefit of undermining partisan fundraising, further reducing party influence over the electoral process. Even media run the risk of appearing detached or incoherent if questions skew toward extremes in front of integrated audiences viewing an inclusive candidate array.

Tournament Style Is More Egalitarian and Reduces Systemic Partisanship

Many states, including my home state of New York, exclude unaffiliated registered voters from primaries. Voters must register as either Republican or Democrat to vote in primaries. The system forces voters to make a polarizing choice in order to take part in a significant part of the electoral process. The primary scheme institutionalizes partisanship and reduces voter participation. Where are the voting rights advocates on primary exclusion? It appears they're putting partisanship before country.

The Tournament Devalues Ideological Differences and Elevates Competence and Character as Determinative Voting Criteria

Without partisan segregation of primaries, candidates will have to aim closer to center to maximize appeal. In other words, from an ideological perspective, products will be less differentiated and choices less clear.

Extreme ideological product differentiation distracts us from examining qualities more relevant to governing. It's like meeting two people of the same gender and ethnicity who are dressed the same, compared with meeting two people whose genders and ethnicities diverge and whose fashions clash. With one set, differences are so dazzling, distinguishing the two requires no effort. But with the other set, we must look deeper to perceive distinction.

Extreme Ideological Product Differentiation Promotes Laziness, Increasing the Likelihood of the Electorate Neglecting Competence and Character

Looking deeper requires effort. When choices aren't clear, we must engage at a higher level to decide. Engaging the electorate at a higher level benefits democracy. Perceiving competence and character becomes more likely by piercing the ideological veil through deeper engagement.

Focusing on ideology allows other qualities to slip our notice. Character flaws plainly manifesting in a president chosen on the basis of ideological kinship shouldn't be surprising. Expecting a contest decided by ideology to produce competence is naïve. Exclusionary preoccupation with ideology is voter negligence, and the open tournament will reduce the likelihood of ideological fixation, while wasting less time on candidates who are unable to transcend ideology.

Closing Thoughts and Reality Check: Defund and Unaffiliate

The open tournament could produce the same finalists. That's OK because it provides a less fragmenting electoral process. The open style undermines party control. The process is more inclusive because it's integrated. The tournament reduces extremism because candidates must consider the entire electorate from the get-go. Character and competence are elevated as determinative criteria, while ideological differences are devalued. In its entirety, the open tournament is more democratic and less partisan.

However, and unfortunately, political parties—which the Constitution doesn't mention—have a death grip on our political processes. Because an open tournament would improve democracy and reduce partisanship, it would diminish parties. Parties won't diminish themselves. Unless such an idea gains the type of popular support capable of impacting elections, it's unlikely to materialize. Defund and unaffiliate.

—12—

Politicians

You can only understand people if you feel them in yourself.
—JOHN STEINBECK

Peace cannot be kept by force; it can only be achieved by understanding.
—ALBERT EINSTEIN

Learning to stand in somebody else's shoes, to see through their eyes,
that's how peace begins. And it's up to you to make that happen.
Empathy is a quality of character that can change the world.
—BARACK OBAMA

Understanding abets efficacy, and understanding
without empathy is pretense.
Manufacturing empathy for sympathetic characters is as challenging
as eating your favorite flavor of ice cream, but a lot less useful.
—THE AUTHOR

Synthesizing the preceding epigraphs suggests empathy is fundamental to both peace and efficacy. Empathy also restrains partisanship. But first, let's challenge ourselves to understand politicians. Let us be genuine in our application of empathy.

The Critical Distinction

While an undergraduate, one of my friends told me he knew he wanted to be a doctor in seventh grade. He went to college, took the MCATs, graduated college, attended and graduated medical school, completed his internship, and became a doctor.

On the other hand, the would-be politician can attend all the finest schools, graduate top of the class, build a captivating résumé, perform requisite volunteer work, and diligently pay proper dues within the political framework only to get crushed in an election. Lose several elections and it's bye-bye dreams and aspirations. "So what," you say. Few of us get to realize our dreams. That's life. Suck it up. OK, but fairness requires recognizing the distinction. And by the by, where's your empathy?

If the Only Requirement to Attaining and Keeping Your Job Is Winning Elections, Your Job Is Winning Elections

Take a moment. Take it in. This is the crux. It's an examination for your class in empathetic understanding. Many will instinctively reject the notion outright. Many will label the concept a cynical heresy to democracy. I understand. I really do. There was a time I would've been with you.

But remember, empathy is fundamental to efficacy. This isn't cynicism. This isn't about rationalizing cutthroat behavior. I'm not excusing corruption. I'm counseling understanding as a precursor to peace, efficacy, and partisan restraint.

Imagine you have a job paying $174,000.00 a year.[44] The job is warehouse manager. Managing day-to-day operations, including personnel management, describes your duties. However, to keep your job, all you must do is win an annual election. The electorate is not limited to warehouse employees or clients. It's a statewide election. What would you do? How would you spend your time?

---

44 The salary for rank-and-file members of Congress in 2023.

Doing the Job to the Best of Your Abilities Maximizes Chances of Winning Elections

Hah. Do you even know who your representatives are, let alone how they're doing? Let's pretend for argument's sake you know the names of all your representatives on the local, state, and federal level. How do you know what kind of job they're doing? Let's review some common ways you might learn of representatives' job performances.

They Tell You

Yes, they do. They mail or email to inform you about what they're working on and how hard they're working for you. They regularly put out press releases to inform you through the media of the job they're doing. If you believe those self-serving communications are objective assessments, you shouldn't be left alone, be allowed to answer the door or phone, have a social media account, or respond to emails without review by a loved one.

Voting Records

Thousands of bills are introduced into Congress each year. Nobody reads them all. Congressional members are most familiar with bills they've introduced or personally worked on. Representatives must also familiarize themselves with party talking points for bills that precipitate media frenzy. But all members vote along party lines for most bills. Does that inform in a substantive way about job performance or character?

The Free Press Comes to the Rescue

Theoretically, this is the correct answer. However, as discussed, although the press is free to chat about anything, media isn't free from tribalism, partisanship, ratings, revenue considerations, etc.

Relying on media to inform about your representatives' job performances is flawed in two ways that implicate partisanship. First, there's a tendency to offer greater coverage to PWs. The modest centrist unwilling to lambaste colleagues across the aisle is either ignored or cornered by partisan media in such a way that their refusal to deride opposition party members looks weak.

The media's inclination to favor more combative representatives shouldn't surprise. Every industry supports helpful politicians. The oil industry backs representatives good for oil. The television industry prefers politicians good for TV. Dynamic personalities seeking confrontation and fomenting outrage pull ratings. Humble moderates seeking compromise . . . not so much.

The media rewards PWs for hostility with airtime. The media encourages conflict. War rates. Media PPs refer to partisan attacks as "calling out" the opposition. "We need to call them out." HM can't get enough of "calling out."

As a result, constituents get the idea that the job of elected officials is conducting partisan warfare. Zeal for partisan advantage supersedes legislating. HM preferentially cover and portray most favorably those most willing to rip members of the other party.

The second way relying on media to evaluate job performance is flawed concerns EC effect or tribal media as discussed. Portraits of representatives' performances and characters on competing media outlets can be facially contradictory.

What about your media outlets? Do they affirm your predispositions? Do representatives from your district appear regularly in outlets you patronize? If they're covered, what's the context? Did they screw up? Are they on the attack? Are they recommending compromise with the opposition? Are they seeking common ground? Are they more interested in legislating or partisan warfare?

Fly on the Wall

What if you could be a fly on the wall of your legislator's office? You could see whom she's meeting with. You would be privy to meeting subject matter. You could hear her discuss meetings with her staff, and by those discussions you could tell which meetings were of greatest importance. You could see her, or her chief of staff, allocate work assignments. You could deduce the genuine priorities of her office by its allocation of staff time and resources. But you can't see any of that, because you're not a fly on the wall. You're outside.

Let's bring the press back in and pretend they're free from partisanship or petty concerns about ratings or revenue. Imagine free press as the paragon of journalism. The fanciful archetype has contacts within your representatives' offices. They can get the real inside dope—maybe, sometimes.

What's the makeup of the contact providing inside dope? Is he loyal to his boss? Does he want to keep his job? If the answer to either of those questions is yes, then he'll deal inside dope selectively. He'll want to keep his boss in office. You won't get an objective overall appraisal of your representative's job performance that way.

What about a disgruntled contact? Chances are he will also deal inside dope selectively. He'll supply the media with hand grenades. You won't get an objective overall appraisal of your representative's job performance that way either.

What if the contact is neutral and detached, like an android who can perform its assigned duties all day and after work relay comprehensive objective information to the press in a manner that, when viewed in its totality, will provide an accurate depiction of the representative's job performance? OK, let's imagine that. Even an exemplary member of the quintessential free press must edit the android for public presentation.

The free press isn't a fly on the wall. But that's all right. We know what your representatives do. They work on keeping their jobs, just like you would. And if the only requirement to keeping your job is winning the next election, your job is winning the next election—empathy.

Framers' Intent

> Power attracts the corruptible. Suspect any who seek it.
> —FRANK HERBERT, *Chapterhouse: Dune*

The Framers' genius was insight into human nature. They understood flesh and blood representatives would come with facilities and foibles and, to varying degrees, be susceptible to the corrupting influence of power. Constitutional checks and balances concede human nature.

The Framers didn't expect representatives to be perfect, or even good. They constructed a constitution assuming human imperfection and dispersing power. Our representatives aren't supposed to be better than us. They *are* us—empathy.

However, they are supposed to be accountable . . . to us. The only concrete means of accountability residing exclusively with the people is the vote exercised in free and fair elections. Like it or not, that's what we have.

They Should Do What We Want

There's nothing in the Constitution requiring elected officials to do what we want, or to even listen to us. Our government is a democratic republic, or representative democracy. We elect representatives, and they govern. We don't vote on the thousands of bills introduced each year; they do.

I'm not suggesting disengagement except on Election Day. We're working toward greater efficacy through empathy, with an eye toward systemic sources of partisanship. While voting is the people's only rightful power over our representatives, we should absolutely engage between elections. We should send emails, make phone calls, write letters, use the press, and peacefully demonstrate, but not because representatives should do what we want or because they should listen to us.

Malignant Red Herring

An unscrupulous pundit might infer, I think, that our representatives should not do what we want or listen to us. This is false. I'm advising an alternative paradigm to enhance citizenship efficacy and reduce partisanship.

Whether our representatives should or should not listen to us isn't relevant to our form of government. It's a red herring. It's a television talking point deterring us from taking responsibility and practicing citizenship. It breeds disaffection and apathy by setting us up to fail. Failure generates blame and blame targets others.

Let's revisit the premise that most elected representatives wish to keep their jobs and act accordingly—empathy. The job of the citizen activist is to convince representatives that complying with the activist's proposal will enhance reelection odds and/or opposition will impair those odds. At a minimum, advocates must be able to ameliorate any concerns representatives might have concerning potential negative impacts.

For arguments' sake, let's say the representative's job is to do what's best, or at least good, for his or her district, state, or country. Then the job of citizen activists is to convince the representative that compliance will be good for the district, state, or country. However, what's good for the country, etc., is a matter of opinion, and in a democratic republic or representative democracy, representatives' opinions determine policy.

If a Majority of Constituents Feels a Certain Way, Representatives Must Go Along

This is blatantly false on many levels. First, as stated, the Constitution doesn't require representatives to comply with constituents' desires. More importantly, not all issues grab the same attention or hold sway with voters.

Hypothetical

Polling shows 100 percent of voters in a hypothetical district think the U.S. should do more to reduce the global problem of childhood slavery, and 60 percent believe the U.S. should do more to develop alternative sources of energy. In the same district, 48 percent of voters think government should spend more on pre-K education, and 52 percent believe government should maintain or reduce current spending levels.

The representative of that district opposed greater participation by the U.S. in reducing childhood slavery, opposed spending more on renewable energy, and voted for legislation to increase spending on pre-K education, yet was re-elected by a 60-percent majority. Post-election polling suggested his position on abortion was decisive, even though no abortion bills were pending in the legislature.

Consider an activist in the district working on renewable energy. Lamenting her team's loss is understandable. Then what? One way to go is to indulge in a tantrum disguised as undertaking public accountability. It involves finger-pointing, name-calling, and blaming others.

Another approach is self-evaluation. Not the type concluding the activist's team made no mistakes and was righteous to the core, or the kind concluding her team's only failure was to underestimate the other team's wickedness and public ignorance. Not the sort that views the letdown as anything but a transitory obstacle laid in the path to test and instruct.

An honest and productive self-evaluation might ask: Did we understand that although renewable energy is popular, voters did not consider it important enough to decide an election? Did we do enough to convince voters? Did we do enough to convince constituents to contact their representative about renewable energy? Did we do enough to convince the representative his support would increase his popularity? In other words, what did we neglect, and what can we do better?

Which approach do you think PI favors—the approach examining our shortcomings or the one accusing the other side?

What about the representative? He did his job. He kept his job. He's doing his job.

What about a constituent who supports renewable energy and was aware of her representative's opposition, but is not an activist? She must have voted against him, right? Maybe, maybe not. Was she aware of his positions on other issues? Is renewable energy the most important issue in her life? Maybe she figured the best thing to do is just vote her party.

Big Picture and Easy Mark

Consider a constituent who isn't aware of specific policy initiatives involving his representative or specific proposals at issue in the election. He may be vaguely aware of his representative's name. For whom will he vote?

He has no idea what his representative does, but he knows Congress is doing a lousy job. He knows the country is heading in the wrong direction, and he knows whose fault that is.

It doesn't matter who's in power. If the other team is in power, they're pulling in the wrong direction. If his team is in power, the other team is obstructing. The choice is clear. He'll vote his party.

In the absence of detail, the conglomerate must suffice. Without specifics, we're left to generalize. Without inspection, we surrender to packaging. So, we submit to the binary construct of party affiliation.

The moderate's drab apparel challenges perception. PW is packaged conspicuously, and easy marks crave distraction.

Due Diligence

Remember the fly on the wall? We must practice citizenship without its intimate perspective. Action without perfect knowledge describes human experience. However, responsibility demands due diligence. The substance of a citizen's due diligence is acquiring relevant knowledge.

But what knowledge is relevant? I'll assume since you've gotten this far in a book titled *Subordinating American Democracy*, your relevant knowledge exceeds party membership. Otherwise, party membership is on the ballot. Simply show up on Election Day and vote your party. Boom. Done. Next.

Anecdotal tangent: Remember times when you had to move your apartment and couldn't afford to pay professionals. Whom did you go to for help? Did you cross-examine candidates about their political affiliations? I used people I could count on to show up and pitch in. In other words, it was more about character than partisan affiliation or ideology.

I learned the same lesson as a construction laborer. While perched on a roof's edge or clinging to a building's side, there was no space or justification for contemplating the political ideologies of my colleagues, whose vigilance I depended on for my safety.

They Should Be Better

With a government of, by, and for the people, the only way our representatives get better is if we get better.

They Should Be Better than Us

They are us.

Character and Ideology

> Hence it comes that faith alone makes righteous and fulfills the law.
> —MARTIN LUTHER, *Commentary on Romans*

I understand character and ideology to be independent. Both corruption and virtue transcend partisan affiliation. These traits are human. History confirms this. In addition, I've known people across the political and ideological spectrum. There are some whose company honors me and some I wouldn't answer the door for. Party affiliation isn't relevant to that distinction.

With respect to my vote, I now seek knowledge on character. I say "now" deliberately. This marks change. I could gild the lily and claim personal growth or evolution. Perhaps, but I prefer the neutral version. I've changed.

I want to linger a moment on the concept of change before diving into the subject matter. We seek change in many ways. We must. Hyperpartisanship impairs society and undermines democracy. I seek to change that.

Partisans pursue a different sort of change. Winning hearts and minds or defeating or vanquishing opponents is change. Even those frightened by rapid transformation desire a type of change—to decrease the rate of change.

Sometimes we're confronted by philosophies designed to smother prospects of change. "People don't change." "The more things change, the more they remain the same."

My realization of change specific to the present subject matter was spontaneous. Most of us don't walk around noting data points indicative of personal change. But as I began this section, introspection intervened. I've changed. Change is possible.

In the past, ideology determined my vote. It's tempting to plead that fathoming character through the gauze of media hype is impracticable—that when all is said and done, all that tangibly remains is a candidate's stated positions on issues, suggesting ideology. Maybe, but in truth, ideological purists mesmerized me. No longer.

Let's revisit the concept of empathy intermingled with marketing, character, ideology, and the power of identity validation. Professionals know voters consider character relevant, at least to a certain degree. But elements of character create quandaries for candidates and marketers. Two that come to mind are honesty and humility. We'll use the first as example, but nearly the same line of reasoning could be used for either.

Character demands sometimes telling people things they don't want to hear. But winning elections requires appealing to electorate desires. Industry professionals don't call it: "telling voters what they want to hear, even if what they want to hear is unworkable." They use phrases like "tapping into" or "having the pulse" or "connecting."

Yes, character can be quite vexing. But, with respect to political candidates in an increasingly segregated society, there is an elegant marketing solution:

Character = Party Affiliation or Ideology

If party affiliation determines character, the pathway to superior character becomes a whole lot easier. Just check the correct box on the voter registration.

By virtue of partisan affiliation, you're a fundamentally better person— the holy grail of partisan marketing. This goes way beyond exclusive or unqualified product adoption. The product integrates itself into consumers' biology. It becomes a human organ. I'm a better person because I have the correct faith. Registration or membership justifies the righteousness of my identity.

What an easy mark you've become. Partisan evangelists sing ideological hymns, and the artificial organ placed by partisan marketers within your body begins to resonate. Hallelujah. I am good. My candidate is good because of our shared faith. And when I vote for my candidate who believes what I believe, I will have done good. I am good because of who I vote for and for what I believe. These things make me good and confirm my goodness. And those people who don't vote the way I do or believe what I believe, well, if I'm good, then ...

Forget quality control. Ideological proclamation subsumes both character and competence. Winnowing out the unqualified or corrupt takes a back seat to extinguishing heretics.

Is it possible to divine character through media presentation? Maybe you can get a glimpse—but you must want to. Your desire to perceive character at the expense of ideology must be genuine. Adopt the aspect of an interrogating detective. Sure, what they say counts for something, but not everything, not by a long shot. Which candidates simply tell you what you want to hear? Which promote lack of humility as virtue? Am I allowing aesthetics to supersede substance? Who risks ideological heresy by telling it like it is?

Make the Picture Small

I suggested falling in love with the concept that elected officials being obligated to do what we want or listen to us contributes to partisanship through blame, deters us from taking responsibility, and sets us up to fail. There is a pathway that helps us avoid those pitfalls while simultaneously providing insight into the character of elected officials and our democratic process.

Practice Citizenship

In case you missed it, the emphasis is on "practice." We need to take it down a notch. We just need to practice. There's no failure in practice other than failing to do so. We can't sub out our practice by writing checks to professionals. We just need to practice.

What does practice mean? It means different things to different people. I liken it to working out. The danger is overreach. Imposing a workout routine on yourself that's too demanding becomes unsustainable. Instead of looking forward to it, you fashion excuses. You feel like a failure. You look for gimmicks and use your credit card. But that doesn't work either. Fashion more excuses. Not enough time. Why not enough time? Others. Resentment. Blame.

We must practice citizenship. Start small, start local, and do it yourself—a stop sign, a speed zone, a dog-waste problem, etc. It doesn't matter, because the goal is practice. You can't fail. Maybe you get what you ask for and maybe you don't. Either way, you did your practice. You worked out. You learned something—about process, about an elected official or her staff, or about yourself. You practiced.

This isn't an advocacy 101 book, but a brief discussion may promote visualization. Begin with a phone call. Where do you start? It doesn't matter. An administrative action not requiring a new law involves the executive branch. That means mayor, county executive, governor, or president, or their departments, such as sanitation, public works, police, etc.

If a new law is needed, you're dealing with the legislative branch: town council, county legislature, state assembly, state senate, U.S. Senate, or U.S. House of Representatives. Whatever level you're dealing with, start with your district.

Don't Worry about Making Mistakes

You're just practicing. Begin with guessing whom to call. Call them. Say something like: "I'm calling about such and such and want to know if you're the right person to speak with, or should I speak with someone else, and who might that be?" Write down the name of the person you're speaking with. Having pen and paper is part of your practice.

Can you find the right person, office, or department for your particular concern? Think of it like a game. Finding the right place is a tremendous accomplishment.

You've found the right place or person. You might be able to get it done over the phone, or you could ask for a meeting. Why meet? Does it enhance chances of succeeding? It depends upon what you mean by success. You're just practicing, and learning is one reason to practice. Getting a meeting is a higher level of practice because of enhanced learning opportunities.

There's an academic and psychological component to preparation. The academic element calls for a cogent argument. Put it to paper on letterhead, including contact information. Psychologically, you're not getting ready for a fight. You're preparing for the next level of practice. Your professor assigned some field work instead of boring classroom stuff. How exciting!

Take it all in. The office, manner of the receptionist, just take it in, like a child. Be receptive without reaching, like reading a good book. Let it take you.

After introductions, state your case. Be brief. This is who I am. This is what I want, and this is why I want it. This is why it will help my community. Note their response. It may be a prompt for further information. Give it to them or tell them you will get it for them. Get the business cards of people you're meeting with.

Chances are the representative or staff will not immediately accede to your request or proposal. If they do, thank them, and ask about timeline and if there's anything you can do to help. But if they don't, that's OK because of your psychological preparation. You're practicing. Ask them what next steps are. Let them know if you don't hear from them in a couple of weeks, you'll reach out to them. Be polite. Be civil. Be professional.

Don't Explode

Don't lecture on your democracy perspective. Don't suggest that if they don't comply, they're corrupt. Don't hurl insults like, "all you care about is getting reelected." Those tactics will cement your status as persona non grata. More effective means of turning up the heat exist. The foundation of any escalation should be understanding, and understanding without empathy is pretense.

Watching PPs on TV gives the impression that having a tantrum every time you don't get what you want is appropriate. Civility is for suckers. That makes for good TV. But I guarantee when meeting with representatives in private, the demeanor of those same TV heroes is respectful.

After meeting is note-taking time. It has a twofold purpose. First, you want to make sure you document next steps, including your understanding of time-lines, as well as correct contact information. The second purpose is broader. For a brief period, you were almost like a fly on the wall. I say almost because flies go unnoticed. In other words, meetings may have an element of production akin to campaigning. That's OK. It's the best you can do at this point.

Create a meeting narrative. Weave feelings into narrative. What did you feel before stepping into the office? How did you feel after being greeted by the receptionist while waiting for the meeting? Did your feelings change during the meeting? What prompted that change? How did you feel after the meeting?

Describe physical elements of the office and the seating arrangement for the meeting. These trivialities may spark insightful revelations, the way scents trigger memory.

Convey the meeting's substance. Don't separate elements. Merge substance, physical description, and feeling into a cohesive narrative. What did you learn? Keep in mind that office and staff reflect the boss. Were you treated respectfully? Were you patronized? Were you given the runaround? Did they make you feel like you should give up? Did they cast blame elsewhere? Did you gain any insight into character and process that transcends party affiliation? I hope so.

Conclusion

If more of us practiced citizenship with an emphasis on the practice itself, supported by empathetic understanding, rather than being frustrated by make-believe expectations and subbing out work to professionals who are paid to operate within a partisanship-incentivizing framework, then our democracy would function at a higher level, and our society would be less factious. Start small, start local, and do it yourself.

Farewell to Moderates:
A Partisan Allegory

Once upon a time in days of yore, there were moderates. Moderates took reasonable positions between the extremists. They introduced proposals advocating modest advances, thereby garnering support from both sides and causing occasional aisle-crossings that resulted in intermittent bipartisan support for modest progress. In other words, they were terrifying troublemakers.

Their unfortunate proposals were honestly characterized as implementing modest improvements in the issue at hand. But moderates themselves would have to admit their puny proposals couldn't dispose of the issue entirely and for all eternity, as extremists claimed their proposals would. Even more frustrating, extremists had a difficult time making the case that moderates' proposals were not only not as ambitious as extremists' proposals, but essentially made things worse. Part of the problem was these independent entities, admittedly caught between a rock and a hard place, or honesty and ambition. The independent entities were required, in order to maintain appearance of independence, to provide independent analyses, which invariably substantiated moderates' claims of actual, albeit modest, improvement.

So, Money stepped in. And partisans wanted Money to step in, because they were beneficiaries of Money, and because every partisan knows proposals worth money are proposals the other side cannot accept. But independent entities also wanted money. Money was in a quandary. But this is the business of Money. To Money, quandaries are opportunities. Opportunities to use money to consolidate power define the rationale of Money.

Money looked back in time for remedy, before they crossed the sea, to the time of kings, when they were kings, when wars and alliances were forged by blood and through blood. So, Money resolved to arrange, with their money, through their money, and by their money for independent entities to be mated to partisans.

And partisans mated the independent entities. And the mating was as consensual as a bordello assignation with a conscripted harlot. Consequently, although independent entities were still legally nonpartisan, they became functionally conjoined with partisans. Then Money, using its money, decreed that henceforth:

All issue of the mating shall be partisan.

Through fecundity, their issue was begotten and proliferated.

Furthermore, Money decreed:

All issues advocated for shall serve partisan interests, which are primarily the acquisition of power by and for partisans, and interests of partisans shall be supreme, and issues not serving partisan interests, be those interests electoral or financial, shall not be issues of interest henceforth. Henceforth, issue advocacy shall be partisan advocacy.

Thus, Money rebuked moderates. Scant praise for their modest proposals dwindled like the meager flame of a dying candle until snuffed. Soon their modest proposals were being compared with what could be instead of what is. And things can always be imagined to be better. Their modest proposals had no chance against the fantastical imagination of extremists. And just like that, there was no longer any place or reason for moderates. Money canceled them.

And Money was well pleased. Money, seeing its purpose fulfilled—consolidation of power—beamed at its wisdom. Content with the solution, Money opened the floodgates, and flowed to partisans. But as more and more money flooded the system, less and less happened, because that is the nature of partisanship. Too clever by half. So in the end, Money mated itself, as it always has, in the end. And PPs beamed at their providence.

—14—

The Eternal Game

The answer to all your questions is money.
—Tony Kornheiser, *ESPN*, quoting former
NBC executive Don Ohlmeyer

As a kid, I was a huge sports fan, especially football. My father, who grew up in western Pennsylvania, taught me how to fire out of a three-point stance as soon as I could walk. Sports, especially playing sports with my friends, was my joy. It was my Saturday afternoons. It was my free time. Dreams of making spectacular plays alongside my heroes transitioned my consciousness to slumber every night.

I can still recall being young enough to imagine playing professional sports for real. But as I grew up in the late '60s and early '70s, my country's understanding of professional sports was growing up as well.

At first, the sentiment spat forth as if an evangelical preacher were cleansing his palate of a satanic heresy. "They're treating it like a *business*." As a child, I knew better. It's not supposed to be like that. It's supposed to be fun! They're supposed to play for fun. Trading my favorite players all over for more money was ruining it. They were ruining the game.

At that time, I didn't know the game for what it was. Many of us didn't. Not just children; plenty of adults didn't get it. Over time, that's changed. Now most adults understand sports is a business. But understanding something is a business isn't the same as understanding the business.

Game on the Field versus Game at Large

The relationship between the game on the field and game at large is the crux of our inquiry.

Thesis

I'll state the conclusion up front and work back.

It's not that the game at large can be played without some version of the game on the field. But the way the game on the field is played isn't determined by the game on the field. It's played according to the game at large.

The Sports Industry, i.e., Game at Large

The sports business is a human system evolving to increase revenue. That's just another way of saying, "the answer to all your questions is money." But let's stick with the evolutionary framework for now.

Revenue increases by enlarging existing revenue streams, developing new ones, or some combination of the two. Revenue streams for the sports industry include ticket sales, concessions including food, beverages, and souvenirs, off-venue souvenirs, commercial broadcasting of games, streaming games (Amazon, etc.), sports betting, including fantasy leagues, and sports talk/journalism. Some revenue streams were present from the outset. Others, like fantasy leagues, are new. All continue to grow with the industry.

I want to focus on one stream to transition back to hyperpartisanship. Can you guess which? I want to spend a little time with sports talk/journalism.

Sports talk/journalism is part of the industry. It's not separate. Sports talk/journalism depends on the game on the field. The more people pay attention to the game on the field, the better for sports talk/journalism. The more people pay attention to sports talk/journalism, the more they're invested in the game. The relationship between games on the field and sports talk/journalism is mutualistic, and they're both part of the game at large. In other words, "the answer to all your questions is money" is not a sentiment exclusively belonging to sports commentators for describing the motivations and machinations of owners, players, and executives. It applies to journalism as well.

Holding the Industry Accountable versus Taking Care of the Game

In truth, the relationship involves complexities, but ultimately, "the answer to all your questions is money." Initially, I was going to assert that "caretaker" best describes sports media, as opposed to "watchdog" whose primary responsibility is holding the industry accountable. Instead, I'm going to argue that by adopting an amenable perspective, taking care of the game holds the industry accountable, up to a point. I begin with some premises.

1. The goal is maximizing sports industry revenue without killing the game on the field;
2. Professionals take care of the profession to which they belong;
3. Maintaining integrity, or the appearance of integrity, is good business; and
4. Members of the sports industry, including sports journalists, depend on the game on the field for their livelihood.

My argument involves contextualizing "accountability" and implicates the concept of incorporation. In the abstract, we imagine accountability implies separation. But often, targets of accountability include its agents or enforcers. Before leaping to conclude "conflict of interest," review the premises. An arm of the sports industry, sports media, holds the sports industry, to which it belongs, accountable only to an extent that protects revenue generation for the industry.

Three issues I use to illustrate my point are sexual assault and domestic violence by players and traumatic brain injury. I'll distinguish the first two from the third.

Sexual assault and domestic violence aren't exclusive to the late twentieth or early twenty-first centuries. But open discussion by sports media on those issues is relatively new. It's possible sports reporters intimately covering athletes in the late nineteenth and early twentieth centuries were unaware of criminally abusive behavior. I think it more likely there was occasional awareness followed by looking the other way and cover-ups.

The motives for cover-ups transcend the game and implicate broader concerns like rights and opportunities for women. Now sports journalism includes women. Women change the equation for the calculation of what is off-limits, in a good way.

Technology is relevant. Cell phone cameras are ubiquitous, and anyone can post footage.

But something else has changed. We now know that sexual assault and domestic violence by players, in addition to talking about it, doesn't hurt the game one iota. In fact, talking about sexual assault and domestic violence by players has become part of the game at large.

Sexual assaults and domestic violence by players provide sports talk content. You can't talk about it all day long. But with 24/7 sports talk on TV, radio, podcasts etc., ten- or fifteen-minute segments on the latest incidents of sexual assault or domestic violence are fine. It's similar to the self-righteous identity-affirmation effect associated with POEP. Discussing sexual assaults and domestic violence by players provides opportunities for shows' panelists and audiences to scrutinize and judge others. It's solid programming.

Discussions may deal with whether the team or league issued appropriate fines or sanctions. Was a ten-game suspension enough? What about criminal or civil liability? Notice, there are no right or wrong answers, just discussion opportunities, i.e., content.

Sexual assault and domestic violence transcend sports. Incidents of sexual assault and domestic violence by players provide opportunities to talk about broader societal issues. At least the sports industry is talking about it—right? Look at us. We're not brushing it under the carpet. We're raising awareness on real problems in our society—right? Maybe.

Let me be clear about a couple of things. Sexual assaults and domestic violence by players are not good for the game, good for society, or good in any way. I don't even think talking about sexual assaults and domestic violence by players is good for the game. What I've said and what I'm contending is that talking about sexual assaults and domestic violence by players is part of the game. The eternal game—the game including sports media—*incorporates,* through discussion, sexual assaults and domestic violence by players.

Incorporation Neutralizes Potential Threats

To use a deliberately offensive metaphor, the media turns lemons into lemonade. This may be the most adaptive feature of media in a free society driven, in part, by market principles. The media identifies malignancies within society, gives them a uniform and says, "suit up, you're in." Let's make a movie. This could be a docuseries. You get the point. The entertainment industry, which includes sports and sports talk, turns potential negatives into profitable programming.

On the other hand, remedy demands conversation. Society progresses by discussing issues, and media helps. Whether or not discussing sexual assaults and domestic violence by players as part of sports talk reduces sexual assault and domestic violence is open to debate.

But this isn't a morality play. It's not about right and wrong. It's about under-standing—empathetic understanding. We're trying to understand the game, from the perspective of the eternal game, as a stepping stone to understanding hyperpartisanship in a different game.

The eternal game incorporates sexual assaults and domestic violence by players through sports talk. Whether or not such discussions lead to remedy isn't relevant to the game. The game doesn't care. However, such discussions allow participants and audience members to feel as if they're part of a process that could lead to remedy. That's good for the game!

Traumatic Brain Injury Resists Incorporation

The takeaway from the movie, *Concussion*,[45] was that "it is the repeated, mi-nor head trauma that occurs regularly in football that appears to lead to CTE, as opposed to the more violent hits that lead to concussions."[46] "Repeated minor head trauma" is worth reiterating. Key words are *repeated* and *minor*.

The response by professional and college football has been to concentrate on "the more violent hits that lead to concussions" rather than "the repeated, minor head trauma that occurs regularly." Focusing attention on "spectacu-lar" and "occasional" as opposed to "repeated" and "minor" is good business.

Sports talk/journalism is on board. During a game, when a particularly

---

45 *Concussion*, directed by Peter Landesman (Sony Pictures Entertainment, 2015).

46 Ashley Welch, "The real doctors behind 'Concussion' movie speak out," CBS NEWS, Dec. 24, 2015, https://www.cbsnews.com/news/concussion-movie-doctors-speak-out-nfl-cte/.

violent hit occurs, announcers bring in the rules expert to discuss legality and consequences. Was it targeting? Should the recipient go into "concussion protocol?" No one on the broadcast says, "you know, that may have been a spectacularly violent hit, but it's actually the repeated minor head trauma that occurs on *every single play* that is believed by medical experts to cause Chronic Traumatic Encephalopathy (CTE)."

During 24/7 sports talk, game highlights include spectacularly violent hits. Discussions focus on whether a flag was appropriate, etc. No one says, "you know, that may have been a spectacularly violent hit, but it's actually the repeated minor head trauma that occurs on every single play that, according to medical experts, causes CTE."

It's the fundamental conflict discussed in Chapter 5. Singularly spectacular, violent hits occurring throughout the season don't threaten the game. They can be managed with rule changes and vindicating sports talk. But repeated minor head trauma occurring on every single play resists incorporation.

Dr. Omalu, portrayed by Will Smith in the movie, argues that "children should not be allowed to play football until the age of 18."[47] The notion that little children, on every single play, are subjected to minor head trauma, the effect of which accumulates and accumulates until . . . *That* notion threatens the game.

If sports talk/journalism weren't part of the game, journalists and commentators would consistently point out that focusing on concussion-causing violent hits is misdirection. It's a trick play. But they're fundamentally conflicted. They don't want to kill the game that lines their pockets. The way in which the game on the field is played isn't determined by the game on the field. It's played according to the game at large—the eternal game. Or if you prefer, "the answer to all your questions is money."

Hyperpartisanship

During my lifetime, I've seen the American public transition from resistance to the notion that sports is a business to mainstream acceptance. Politics is a different story. Before widespread acceptance of sports as a business, I re-

47 Welch, "Concussion."

member adults expressing mistrust of politicians. Acquiescence to big money buying politicians predates widespread acceptance of sports as a business, as well as our current affair with hyperpartisanship.[48]

We acquire relevant perspective by itemizing the purchase of a politician by a special interest as a single play in the game. We've previously described this play from a different standpoint. Purchasing a politician by a big donor is political spending. The special interest donates to a politician's campaign, political party, or alternative fundraising entity such as a PAC, in return for access or policy. But instead of focusing on politicians' ethics or what big donors receive in quid pro quo, we followed the money. The special interest's donation went to a fundraising entity or politician to end up with PI's campaign subsector to be spent on product differentiation.

Recall this graphic:

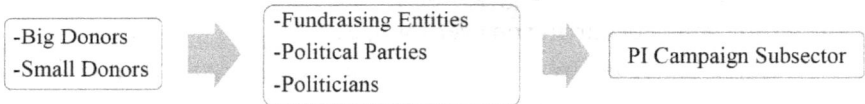

| -Big Donors
-Small Donors | ➡ | -Fundraising Entities
-Political Parties
-Politicians | ➡ | PI Campaign Subsector |

Figure 14.1: The Process Revisited

So rather than obsessing on beneficiaries of a singular and spectacularly corrupt play, we examine the impacts of running that same play over and over, whether or not it leads to quid-pro-quo corruption of politicians. Incessantly running that play incentivizes polarization and is incentivized beyond the specific benefits accrued to special interests.

It may be tacky, but I'm going to explicitly clarify the sports game metaphor. With respect to hyperpartisanship, the game on the field is the legislative or policymaking process. It's what's happening in Congress. Congress is the playing field.

PI manages the game at large or eternal game. Both subsectors take part.

---

48 See *Mr. Smith Goes to Washington*, directed by Frank Capra (Columbia Pictures, 1939).

Central Thesis

Policymaking processes run according to PI. Congress operates according to PI, at least sometimes.

We must parse "dysfunction." Regardless of how "dysfunctional" our policymaking is, PI revenue continues to increase. The game is growing. From the eternal game's perspective, there's no dysfunction.

How can we allow this game to devastate policymaking? The industry profiting from devastation manages both the devastation and public discussion of the devastation—the fundamental conflict.

Let me restate the thesis. PI's desires determine our policymaking process. Let's moderate. At least occasionally, PI determines policymaking.

Focusing on Quid-Pro-Quo Corruptions Is Psychologically Incentivized, but Distracts Us from Understanding the Game

This goes way beyond corruption of politicians via financial contributions, which most voters understand. Understanding quid-pro-quo corruption is psychologically palatable. It's something we can compartmentalize.

It's more difficult to separate ourselves from the eternal game. We like to watch. We're fans. We like to blame the other team—not just the other team's players, the other team's fans as well. In other words, we take part. We can't separate ourselves from the game as easily as we can separate ourselves from the singularity of a corrupt politician.

This brings us closer to the sports metaphor contextualizing sexual assault, domestic violence, and CTE. The sexual predator is like the corrupt politician. He's not us. We can deal with that by outlawing that single play. But being fans of a sport which, on every play, features repeated minor head trauma that causes permanent and debilitating brain injury, well, I'd rather not think about that.

Regardless of donor or recipient intent, every single donation ends up with PI's campaign subsector to be spent on product differentiation, i.e., the other side is crazy, evil, or stupid. Insulating oneself either morally, psychologically, or intellectually from quid-pro-quo corruption does not shield against polarization. Even if we could eliminate quid-pro-quo corruption from politics, every donation would still subsidize polarity. It happens on every play.

My thesis is not an endorsement. I provide perspective in aspiration of greater understanding.

Mitch McConnell

> The single most important thing we want to achieve is
> for President Obama to be a one-term president.
> —U.S. Senator Mitch McConnell (R-KY), 2010

The statement of gamesmanship is plain. It couldn't be clearer. McConnell's view is that the field of play, i.e., Congress, should be used first and foremost to defeat the Democrat in the White House. Passing legislation to help Americans or make America stronger is not Congress's purpose. The way the game on the field is played isn't determined by the game on the field. It's according to the game at large. It's according to the eternal game.

PPs argue the only way to help Americans or make America stronger is to vote out the opposition. This is another way of saying the representative's job is to use the office to gain partisan advantage for the next election. So, from day one, immediately after taking office, the representative's primary purpose, in addition to getting reelected, is to use that office to gain seats for his party for the next election.

Working with the other party to pass legislation to help Americans or make America stronger undercuts the primary purpose. The eternal game supersedes the game on the field. Partisan electoral interests supersede legislative progress.

Consider functionality. Legislative progress is functional. Congress consistently passing legislation beneficial to our country evinces that the game on the field is functioning. But consistently passing legislation that helps America requires more than occasional bipartisanship.

It means the two sides are working together. From the perspective of the eternal game, this is dysfunctional. PI profits from hyperpartisanship, not bipartisanship. Working with the opposition undermines product differentiation. Blaming the other side is more difficult when you pass laws with them. Passing laws with the other side means agreeing with them. That's partisan heresy.

Legislative functionality is PI dysfunctionality. There's more money in opposition than collaboration, and "the answer to all your questions is money."

Impeachment

This concerns the first impeachment of President Trump, for trying in 2019 to use congressionally approved military aid to Ukraine to extort advantage over his political opponent, Joe Biden, in the upcoming election. It was abuse of power, and I supported impeachment. But the game is in the details.

The game on the field is impeachment. According to article I, section 2, clause 5 of the Constitution, the "House of Representatives . . . shall have the sole power of impeachment." Representatives were doing their job according to the Constitution. They were playing the game on the field the way it was meant to be played. They were playing the game on the field according to the game on the field . . . up to a point.

Witnesses with Firsthand Knowledge

House committees interviewed witnesses, most of whom did not have first-hand knowledge of Trump's dealings with Ukrainian President Zelenskyy over congressionally approved military aid. Some potential witnesses who were higher up in the White House food chain, and therefore more likely to have firsthand knowledge, refused to testify except if subpoenaed or under court orders.[49]

One potential witness was former national security adviser John Bolton.[50] According to a former adviser to POTUS on Russian affairs, Fiona Hill, who did testify, Bolton referred to the administration's dealings with Ukraine on this matter as a "drug deal."[51] Bolton was either fired or resigned on September 10, 2019, which was during the relevant time when Trump was withholding military aid. Bolton was the type of top administration official who would

~~~~~~~~~~~~~~~~

49 Jonathan Turley, "How the House lost the witness battle along with impeachment," *The Hill*, Feb. 1, 2020, https://thehill.com/opinion/judiciary/481015-how-the-house-lost-the-witness-battle-along-with-impeachment/.

50 Turley, "Impeachment."

51 "Impeachment inquiry against Donald Trump," Wikipedia, https://en.wikipedia.org/wiki/Impeachment_inquiry
_against_Donald_Trump.

have been able to describe the smell from the smoking gun.

Two other key administration officials who refused to appear were acting White House Chief of Staff Mick Mulvaney and Energy Secretary Rick Perry. Witnesses who did testify "implicated Mulvaney in seeking a quid-pro-quo arrangement with Ukraine, testifying that Mulvaney appeared to have approved a White House meeting between Trump and Zelenskyy, on the condition that Ukraine's government investigate Biden."[52] Perry was allegedly involved in unofficial back-channel communications with Ukrainian officials to push for investigations into the Bidens.[53] In other words, Mulvaney and Perry may have been holding the smoking gun.

Yet Democratic House leadership chose not to use the courts to compel Bolton, Mulvaney, or Perry to testify. How strange. After all, nothing short of our democratic republic was at stake. The idea that a president, to gain electoral advantage, could use congressionally approved aid to solicit foreign interference in our elections is offensive to American democracy and a perversion of U.S. sovereignty.

This is the purpose of separation of powers. It's what the Framers had in mind: coequal branches of government. It's why we don't have a king with limitless power. It's why POTUS is accountable to Congress through impeachment.

Merry Christmas Deadline

Congressional oversight of the executive branch is fundamental to constitutional democracy. That's why Democratic House leadership decided to wrap things up by Christmas, 2019. *What?* Compelling testimony from key White House officials with firsthand knowledge of presidential abuses could have taken several months. It would have violated the sacred "Merry Christmas Deadline" (MCD).

The justification for MCD revolved around the notion of protecting the

---

52 Nick Robins-Early, "These Key Witnesses Won't Appear At The Impeachment Hearings," HUFFPOST, Nov. 19, 2019, https://www.huffpost.com/entry/impeachment-hearings-bolton-mulvaney-trump_n_5dd4691be4b0fc53f20a529b.

53 Robins-Early, "Key Witnesses."

integrity of the 2020 elections. House leadership was allegedly alarmed about "crime in progress," so there was "no time to delay a submission [of articles of impeachment] to the Senate."[54] This was utter bullshit.

But to say their bullshit made no sense is different from saying their actions made no sense. First, here's why their bullshit made no sense. Everyone on Earth with media access, including the media, knew the Senate wasn't going to convict. Trying POTUS without testimony from top administration officials with firsthand knowledge, such as Bolton, Mulvaney, and Perry, made the Republican-led Senate's job of refusing to convict that much easier. MCD did nothing to protect the integrity of the 2020 presidential election or prevent "crime in progress." All it did was provide Trump with an opportunity to declare his innocence.

Let's imagine the House had taken time to compel testimony from key administration officials by using the courts. I'm not going to pretend such testimony would've altered the probability of conviction. If God came down from heaven or through coalesced omnipresence physically manifested before Congress to accuse Trump of abuse of power, the Republican-controlled Senate would have proclaimed it was actually Satan in disguise and refused conviction. Conviction in the Senate was never on the table, and all the players knew it.

So why impeach at all? I began this section stating Trump clearly abused his power and should have been impeached. The House was correct to impeach, regardless of Senate outcome. It wasn't about preventing "crime in progress." That was partisan rhetoric enabling MCD.

The integrity of our republic was at stake. Using congressionally approved foreign aid to extort foreign interference in our elections perverts the American system of government. The House was correct to hold impeachment hearings to lay bare that abuse and perversion for all to see. The House was doing its job as described in the Constitution. It was upholding its responsibility as a coequal branch of government. It played the game correctly . . . until it didn't.

Playing the game correctly, laying bare the abuse and perverse machinations of the Trump administration, performing according to the Constitution, according to the game on the field, would have required the House, with all the power the Constitution provides, including using courts, to zealously

---

54 Turley, "Impeachment."

pursue testimony by key administration officials with firsthand knowledge of Trump's actions.

Time Frame Is the Key

An honest pursuit of this nature determines its own time frame. Imposing MCD pulled back the curtain. Partisan media tried to close it up, but we got a peek. Let's open it back up. Let's examine the time frame to better understand the game.

Some professional analysts proclaimed MCD made no sense, or it was a tactical mistake. I disagree with that sentiment with every fiber of my being. The idea that the House, under the leadership of Speaker Nancy Pelosi (D-CA), would impose a nonsensical deadline just doesn't make sense. It's absurd. The rationale of a "crime in progress" or of protecting the integrity of the 2020 election doesn't make sense. The rationale was bullshit, but that's different than saying the timeline didn't make sense. It was no mistake.

The essence of this section involves making sense of the timeline. Let's analyze the timeline from the perspective of Trump's reelection chances. In other words, was the timeline a Democratic partisan electoral strategy for defeating Trump? That may be part of it, but that analysis is incomplete.

The Senate acquitted Trump in February of 2020, allowing Trump to proclaim his innocence prior to Election Day 2020. The two other choices would have been to compel testimony from Bolton, Mulvaney, and Perry, and postpone Senate acquittal to either before or after Election Day.

You could make arguments, which can neither be proved nor disproved, that all three time frames would have either helped or hurt Democrats' chances of unseating Trump. Let's explore the pros and cons of all three options to make sense of MCD to better understand the game.

Option 1

Imposing MCD, thereby completing impeachment proceedings in the House without the testimony by key administration officials with firsthand knowledge of the alleged scheme to trade congressionally approved foreign aid for personal political advantage, leading to Senate acquittal in February 2020.

This option actually happened. The disadvantage is that the official impeachment record lacks testimony from key administration officials. This isn't trivial. It allowed Republican PPs to claim the whole thing was based on hearsay. Future historians will look back to find a giant hole in the record. They might wonder why the House didn't bother compelling testimony from administration officials with firsthand knowledge. They might think it doesn't make any sense or it was a mistake. But we in the present know better.

There are at least two pros to option 1. First, it maximized the length of time between Senate acquittal and Election Day. Everyone not domiciled in a vacuum conceded the inevitability of acquittal. Acquittal in February gave Democrats nine months to take the sting out of it. Democrats, in conjunction with sympathetic media, used those nine months to focus on their election narrative, which included their conclusions about Trump's alleged scheme, absent testimony from key officials.

Second, it cleared the table of impeachment business so House members could focus on reelection campaigns. House leaders, including the Speaker, hold positions with the consent of the majority caucus. My guess is the majority of the Democratic caucus was all well and good with MCD.

I said there were at least two pros, but let's bring another character in our drama to center stage. Consider MCD from PI's perspective. The entertainment subsector had a presidential primary miniseries to produce, and the Iowa Caucuses were to be held on February 3, 2020. I mean, impeachment hearings were interesting and all, but did we really need more of the same? Initially audiences loved it, but it was beginning to feel like reruns. Democrats had twenty-seven candidates for president. OMG! And they were so diverse and interesting or crazy. The media, by and large, was OK with MCD.

For PI's campaign subsector, it was harvest time. Yeehaw! Billions upon billions flowing through power-brokering fundraising entities for advertising to remind Americans how different and crazy the other side is. The campaign subsector could have made prolonged hearings work for them, but it was risky. Not everyone was writing checks based on impeachment. Impeachment is unidimensional. Professional competence requires fundraising diversification. SCOTUS nominations, immigration, crime, the economy, etc. are tried and true moneymakers. Exclusive obsession with impeachment is bad business.

While we can't say for certain what prompted MCD, terminating impeachment proceedings without testimony from key officials, we've identified beneficiaries.

Congressional representatives had campaigns to run, and prolonged impeachment proceedings would've interfered with those efforts. In other words, if the only legal requirement for keeping your job is winning the next election, your job is winning the next election. The game on the field—legislative branch holding executive branch accountable as the Framers intended—was played according to the game at large. Reelection efforts, fundraising concerns, and ratings considerations superseded impeachment diligence.

Option 2

The second option is fully embracing constitutional responsibility as a co-equal branch of government by pursuing impeachment with all the diligence and rigor a constitutional crisis demands by using courts to compel testimony from key administration officials with firsthand knowledge of the alleged scheme, leading to inevitable Senate acquittal closer to, but still prior to, Election Day.

This time frame allows the House to develop a more complete record of the Trump administration's abuse of power and perversion of our republic, including testimony from key administration officials with firsthand knowledge. It's not exclusively about Trump. Conspiratorial schemes require coconspirators. Details of coconspirator complicity are essential to the historical record.

Why let coconspirators off the hook? Forcing acting White House Chief of Staff Mick Mulvaney and Energy Secretary Rick Perry to testify under penalty of perjury would have, in and of itself, been a triumph of democracy.

The counter argument was: Even if top administration officials had testified, the Senate would've acquitted anyway, so it was time to move on. If that's the argument, why impeach in the first place? Everyone above ground knew acquittal wasn't in the cards. Republicans argued from the get-go that impeachment had nothing to do with protecting the republic or election integrity. They alleged it was a Democrat electoral strategy. MCD lent credence to that accusation.

Some analysts have argued testimony from key administration officials with firsthand knowledge would have increased conviction chances in the Senate. I don't believe it. But it would have undermined the Republican talking point that impeachment was based on hearsay.

It also would've penalized coconspirators, which could have had positive reverberations into our future. If you conspire in a corrupt scheme, you're gonna pay. "Don't do the crime if you can't do the time." Instead, the takeaway is: If you're going to aid a powerful figure in corruption, the higher up the food chain and closer you are to the corruption, the more likely you'll get away with it. That's just great.

Option 2 has drawbacks. The first is the proximity of Trump's declaration of innocence to Election Day. Imagine an October surprise of Senate acquittal. "I'm innocent. See, it was all a witch hunt, just like I said. They can't stand to see me win. But I am winning, and I'm innocent, and I'm going to win. It was just a witch hunt, like I said." This time frame would've been more difficult for lefty PPs to manage. Getting acquittal over with in February reduced the magnitude of its effect on the November election.

The other drawbacks concern competing priorities during campaign season. Impeachment occupies congressional time and resources, as well as significant media attention, including live programming. MCD allowed incumbents to focus on their jobs of getting reelected. Impeachment proceedings interfere with campaigning and fundraising activities. Also, impeachment may have been a liability in closely contested swing districts. MCD allowed representatives in those districts to focus on more promising issues.

From a media perspective, impeachment was fall 2019 programming. Spring 2020 programming was to feature the presidential primary miniseries, starring twenty-seven diverse and sometimes wacky candidates. MCD cleared the schedule for spring programming.

Whether it's winning elections, fundraising, or ratings, the law of diminishing returns is relevant. Impeachment's impact curve was on the wane. At some point, even if sources get closer to POTUS, it begins to sound like "same old, same old." Unlike a jury sequestered for the duration, the public can change the channel.

In addition, as Election Day approaches, focusing congressional resources on impeachment begins to look more like an election strategy. It begins to look, dare I say, like a witch hunt. There's a lot to be said for MCD.

Option 3

Option 3 is to fully embrace constitutional responsibility as a coequal branch of government by pursuing impeachment with all the diligence and rigor a constitutional crisis demands by using courts to compel testimony from key administration officials with firsthand knowledge of the alleged scheme, leading to inevitable Senate acquittal sometime *after* Election Day.

Here, the time frame may appear helpful to Democratic electoral strategy by denying Trump the opportunity to declare his innocence before Election Day. But Team Trump could have easily argued that Democrats delayed sending articles to the Senate because they knew the Senate would acquit. "They know I'm innocent. It's just a witch hunt."

This could've been a valid argument. If Democrats could contrive MCD, they could just as easily contrive a post-Election Day deadline. Otherwise, the same pros and cons discussed under option 2 are valid. Prolonged impeachment devours valuable campaigning, fundraising, and programming time as impact wanes. The public jury wanders from the box.

Diligence and Conviction

House leadership understood and will always understand the politics from the get-go. Impeachment by the House doesn't require the likelihood of Senate conviction. Impeachment knowing the Senate will inevitably acquit is valid because it lays bare corruption of office and abuse of power for all to see, including future generations, as well as holding coconspirators accountable.

However, whether deciding to impeach is based on the probability of Senate conviction or to lay bare and create a public record of abuses and corruption, once that decision is made, *go for it*. Commit to playing the game according to the duties and responsibilities of a coequal branch of government. Follow evidence all the way to the top. Secure testimony from everyone involved in the corruption, as was done for the Nixon impeachment. If you're not committed to compelling testimony from those closest to the president, don't bother to impeach. The diligence necessary to complete the job determines the time frame. Play the game on the field the way it was meant to be played, according to constitutional responsibility, according to the game on the field.

Unfortunately, evidence suggests the game on the field, the game in Congress, is played according to the eternal game. Eternal game priorities subordinate congressional duty. Electoral politics, campaigning, fundraising, and ratings superseded impeachment integrity.

"Dysfunction"

Let's go back to sports for a second. Major League Baseball implemented substantial rule changes in 2023. To quicken the pace, pitchers and batters were placed on a clock. A thirty-second limit between batters and a fifteen-second limit between pitches reduced breaks in the action. In addition, limits on defensive shifts increased the probability that batted balls would fall for hits. Finally, larger bases increased safety and led to more stolen bases. How exciting!

Whether or not rule changes improve the game on the field is a topic for sports talk and is largely irrelevant except as sports talk. Whether or not rule changes enhance revenue is the essential issue. Some diehard fans who have yet to come to grips with "the answer to all your questions is money" may wish to argue that improving the game on the field enhances revenue. In other words, the better the game on the field functions, the better for the eternal game.

But how the game on the field functions is a matter of opinion. Did the three-point shot improve basketball by putting a premium on the outside shot, or ruin it by transforming the game into one in which the ball endlessly moves around the perimeter? It doesn't matter! Ticket sales trump aesthetics. Ratings are undeniable. Receipts from concessions can be counted. Gambling proceeds are fact. Revenue is measured with certainty. How the eternal game functions, which is calculated precisely through accounting and without opinion, determines the game on the field.

There's much lamentation and gnashing of teeth in contemplation of government dysfunction. Government isn't effective. It's not working for the people. It isn't even working for the country, which is truly strange. There's something wrong with the game.

Some people put part of the blame on hyperpartisanship like it's a fly in the ointment. As if we could only grasp it's in our best interests to work together. You know—no red states or blue states just the United States.

But hyperpartisanship is not a fly in the ointment. It's a key component of a powerful industry. I don't approve of the fact that society takes a back seat to PI. I don't endorse pursuing campaign revenue and TV ratings over functional accord. However, I kind of admire an industry capable of destroying society. I choose "admire" because it relates to empathy.

Most concerning themselves with hyperpartisanship tend to focus on the dysfunctional effects it wreaks upon society. That's not helpful. Examining functionality leads to greater understanding.

To use a brutal analogy, consider how historians tell the tale of Nazi Germany. The Holocaust is only part of the story. How Nazis came to power and how they functioned is more instructive. To prevent something similar from happening again, dissecting functionality is at least as useful as spotlighting atrocity. I counsel understanding hyperpartisanship as an essential component of a highly functioning system to identify its remedy.

Policy Issues

According to quantum theory, simultaneously knowing both location and momentum of subatomic particles such as electrons is impossible. It's also said quantum matter exists as both particle and wave.[55] It's similar with policy issues.

Issues have two natures or functions. Before exploring that duality, let's make sure we're on the same page as to what exactly "issues" are. Listing some issues will prove more useful than a definition. Let's take another look at what I referred to as "blockbuster" issues. Examples include immigration, health care reform, gun control, climate change, criminal justice reform, income inequality, minimum wage, voting rights, reforming the tax code, education reform, controlled substance reform, judicial reform, military reform, funding priorities for national security, subsidies, etc.

Issues requiring congressional action involve substantive policy that engages the electorate. Policy issues bring people to the table. Desire for progress on

---

55 John D. Norton, "The Quantum Theory of Waves and Particles," Department of History and Philosophy of Science, University of Pittsburgh, Feb. 6, 2022, https://sites. pitt.edu/~jdnorton/teaching/HPS_0410/chapters/quantum_theory_waves/index.html.

issues generates activism and interest in government. People vote according to candidates' positions on issues.

Issues also include government procedures, such as whether to impeach. They also implicate other branches of government, such as SCOTUS on abortion rights, or the executive branch on foreign policy matters such as whether a treaty is in our best interests. However, our discussion mainly concerns congressional dysfunction, and we'll keep congressional blockbusters in mind while dissecting the game.

Dual Nature of Issues

Like quantum matter, issues have both a particular and wave or energy nature. Issues exist as either particles or energy waves. Perhaps they can exist as both simultaneously, but as energy waves, their particular nature is compromised.

Their particular nature is how most of us know them. An issue's particular nature is plain. It exists for itself. The particular function is to advance itself, i.e., to make progress on the issue.

As a wave, the issue doesn't exist for itself. Its energy is used for other purposes. As waves, issues advance partisan interests, either by generating revenue or differentiating products. As waves, issues serve the eternal game.

The theory of simultaneous existence asserts that issues can be used to energize partisan interests without losing particular integrity. I am dubious. Campaigning along the lines of: "The only way to make progress on this issue is to vote out the other side," or "if you care about this issue, you should donate your time or money to our party," undermines an issue's particular integrity and reduces likelihood of advancement through bipartisan collaboration.

PPs have no problem with this. With the repetitive force of a jackhammer, PPs promote the message that bipartisan cooperation on your issue(s) is impossible. Voting out the other side is the only hope for progress on issues you care about.

While knowing an issue's prospects with certainty is impossible, indicators providing insight into their nature and function exist. For instance, are key players genuinely willing to compromise, or is compromise off the table? If compromise is off the table, the issue's particular integrity has fully transformed into energizing partisanship.

How effectively can an issue "energize the base?" If an issue proves exceptional for energizing the base, then for a partisan electoral strategy, progress through compromise is self-defeating. It's wasting the energy of a blockbuster. It's throwing away pocket aces before the flop. Progress through compromise undermines partisan rhetoric and strategy.

Wedge Issues

Definitions for "wedge issues" vary, but I'll provide one to kick off the discussion. A wedge issue is "a sharply divisive political issue, especially one that is raised by a candidate or party in hopes of attracting or disaffecting a portion of an opponent's customary supporters."[56]

This is an example of how relying exclusively on labels interferes with understanding. Notice in the definition that wedge issues are raised "in hopes of attracting or disaffecting a portion of an opponent's customary supporters." In other words, the wedge issue manifests as energy and its particular function disappears. The particular purpose of the issue, to advance itself, takes a back seat to partisan electoral advantage.

This reminds me of our CTE discussion in football. Using the term "wedge issue" without contextualization helps normalize a phenomenon benefiting PI at the expense of legislating. Imagine every time media uses "wedge issue," it's accompanied by: "when we say, 'wedge,' what we mean is the issue is being used purely for partisan advantage, as opposed to making any actual progress on the issue itself." I wonder how constituents would feel about their issues being used as wedges if the implications were fully explained each time the term was uttered. Its casual use dulls us to its insidious implications.

The Dual Nature of Issues Is Asymmetrical

Transforming issues from particle to energy is easier than from energy to particle. I propose the following rule:

---

56 "wedge issue," The American Heritage dictionary of the English Language, https://www.ahdictionary.com/word/search.html?q=wedge+issue.

The longer and more completely an issue serves primarily as a wedge or as part of a partisan electoral scheme or as a fundraising vehicle for political parties, the more difficult is its transformation back to an issue whose primary purpose is to advance itself through the legislature via compromise and bipartisanship.

In other words, spending too much time as a wave energizing partisanship defiles the issue's particular nature, leaving it broken. Can the particular nature of an issue revive? Is redemption possible? Of course! But the more time spent under a corrupting influence, the deeper its spell.

Here's a second rule that follows:

As the percentage of issues used primarily to advance partisan interests increases, legislative functionality decreases, and PI functionality increases.

Restatement of that second rule:

As the percentage of issues used primarily to advance partisan interests increases, the more the game on the field suffers in favor of the eternal game.

One final restatement:

As the ratio of issues manifesting as energy to issues manifesting as particles increases, PI profitability increases.

PP rapture occurs when every issue serves primarily to advance partisan interests. More and more issues are serving as vehicles for partisan advantage rather than existing for their own advancement. We're approaching PP paradise.

The question is whether PPs and partisan entities such as political parties exist to advance issues, or whether issues exist to advance partisan interests. Are political parties subordinate to issues, or are issues subordinate to parties?

Hyperpartisanship Enables Issue Subordination

We have defined hyperpartisanship as prejudicial allegiance or opposition to a political party, faction, group, tribe, person, ideology, or cause to an extent that substantially alters or determines the opinions, beliefs, ideals, principles, behavior, or personality of those so aligned.

If an individual aligns with a partisan entity to an extent that entangles their identities, then issue subordination to the partisan entity appears equivalent to issue subordination to the aligned individual. To be clear, issues *should* serve individuals. People support or advocate for issues because they believe issue progress will help them or their society.

But that's different from saying issues should serve partisan entities. Ideally, political parties should serve individuals by making progress on their issues. But the entanglement of personal and group identity muddies analysis.

A hyperpartisan environment enables issue subordination to a partisan entity because the individual identifies with the entity to an extent that the individual cannot distinguish between that which serves the entity and that which serves the individual. They become one and the same. Therefore, as hyperpartisanship increases, as the identities of more individuals become entangled with partisan entities, the more issues will exist primarily to advance partisan interests. As hyperpartisanship increases, the more difficult it will be for any issue to exist with the primary purpose of advancing itself through legislatures via compromise and bipartisanship. Hyperpartisanship enables issue subordination.

Extremism Is Good for the Game

Not the game on the field, of course, but for the eternal game. Extremism sabotages legislating by making compromise more difficult and reducing common ground to quaint fancy. But it's titillating.

Extremism provides undeniably compelling content for PI's entertainment subsector. Procedural extremism, like rioting mobs, provides marvelous images for visual media. Substantive extremism of far-out or insane ideas perfectly fits POEP shows that use identity validation to seduce audiences. Moderation, on the other hand, is boring. It's a loser. It would be canceled weeks into its first season.

The campaign subsector also profits from extremism. Fear sells, and extremism is scary. If you don't want those scary people on the other side running our country, you should write us a check. Extremism is good for business.

Extreme Oscillations Are Good for the Game at Large

In general, violent oscillations destabilize systems. Imagine a giant wrecking ball hanging from a thick chain in the middle of Washington, D.C., equidistant from the White House, Capitol, SCOTUS, and all ancillary office buildings. It swings back and forth, rotating ever so slightly, to carve out 360 degrees of destruction. But devastation is limited to the elevation of the hanging wrecking ball. The point from which the chain hangs remains unscathed and unmoved by havoc below.

So it is with the game on the field and the eternal game. Oscillations from one extreme to the other that sabotage legislating, undermine continuity of federal programs, interfere with enforcement of federal law, injure morale of federal employees, and gradually erode faith in, and functionality of, our institutions, occur at an altitude that cannot destabilize the eternal game. The pendulum dangles from a thread firmly grasped between the thumb and forefinger of PI, which looms far above the game on the field. The back-and-forth motion barely distorts the shadow of the looming colossus, to its contented delight.

Small Steps Are Less Likely to Precipitate Overcorrection

Moderate progress in any direction dampens the oscillating effect. However, moderating the amplitude of oscillations to achieve functional equilibrium below disturbs the dominant system. Moderation can lead to fundraising complacency. The pendulum must swing as far right as possible to loosen purse strings on the left, and far left to motivate the right. Oscillation maximizes PI revenue, while undercutting government functionality.

The Overuse of Executive Orders Amplifies Oscillation

An executive order "is a directive from the President that has much of the same power as a federal law."[57] Every president has used executive orders, although the Constitution does not explicitly mention them. But constitutionality is only tangentially relevant. Executive orders with authorizing congressional legislation supporting them are not at issue.

On the other hand, presidents frustrated by congressional stagnation, dysfunction, partisan gamesmanship, or intransigence substituting executive orders for legislation catalyzes a feedback loop of oscillation subordinating societal health to hyperpartisanship.

The politics are a no-brainer. POTUS has constituencies wanting action on their issues. The opposition party in Congress demurs. POTUS signs an executive order and receives praise: "At least he did something."

But absent congressional authority, executive orders are ephemeral, symbolic gestures to appease partisan constituencies. Either courts will find they violate separation of powers because they are obvious end-runs around the legislature, or the next president of the opposing party will sign countermanding executive orders. Executive orders epitomize partisan overreach.

Coupling a symbolic-gesture-obsessed entertainment culture with legislative dysfunction perpetuates an escalating cycle of executive orders followed by revocation. Conversely, legislation passed by Congress through deliberation and compromise and signed into law is more likely to withstand court challenges and cannot be canceled via subsequent executive action, and therefore endures. Congressional functionality dampens oscillation.

Over-Reliance on Courts Has a Similar Effect

Getting *our* judges in place through partisan victory supersedes legislating. Consider the psychology of two branches of government. In the legislature, adults get together to talk, argue, deliberate, and compromise to advance

---

57 "Executive Orders 101: What are they and how do Presidents use them?" National Constitution Center, Jan. 23, 2017, https://constitutioncenter.org/blog/executive-orders-101-what-are-they-and-how-do-presidents-use-them.

national interests. Legislating is collaborative. Not so with the judiciary. We use courts when collaboration fails. Legislatures require working relationships. Judiciary is for divorce.

But there's no partisan divorce in a constitutional republic. We're stuck with each other for the duration.

PI Is Not Partisan

PI markets partisanship. Some or most individuals and entities within PI are partisan, but the industry itself isn't. It's not the Partisan Industry. It's the *Partisanship* Industry. From the financial perspective of PI, who wins or is winning the war is irrelevant. PI's business model requires conflict. It's like a weapons manufacturer arming both sides. Escalating conflict grows the industry.

Marketing Partisanship Is Exploiting Segregation and Maximizing Oscillation

The rotating pendulum plays no favorites with compass points. North, South, East, and West matter not. They're relevant as positions on the perimeter of a circle separated by the amplitude of a swinging pendulum. The further apart, the greater the diameter of the circle through which the pendulum swings, maximizing its potential for energizing revenue generation.

Dominant or Governing System

This gets us back to the central thesis. Our public processes run according to PI profit motives.

Functionality reveals hierarchy. If system A functions at the expense of system B, system A is the dominant system. System A controls the dynamics between systems. System A governs.

PI profitability increases at the expense of functional policymaking. PI governs. Our political processes accord with PI priorities. The eternal game dictates the game on the field.

Perhaps you wish to argue PI profitability and political dysfunction are coincidental. That seems unlikely because of interdependent components and processes.

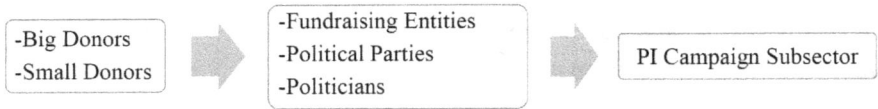

| -Big Donors / -Small Donors | ⇒ | -Fundraising Entities / -Political Parties / -Politicians | ⇒ | PI Campaign Subsector |

Figure 14.2: The Process Reprised

Which way does money flow and what's it used for? Divisive politics, i.e., product differentiation, enhances PI profitability while undermining government functionality. PI governs.

Hyperpartisanship undermines government functionality while enhancing PI functionality. Entanglement of personal identity with partisan affiliation facilitates media segregation through the enchantment of identity validation. Segregated hyperpartisan environments, free from the mitigating effects of contrary opinion, incubate extremism. Hyperpartisanship enables issue subordination.

Positive feedback loops work to the advantage of the dominant system. For example, as segregation increases, the financial incentive to provide partisan content grows. As more and more fragmented partisan content is provided, more and more people migrate toward a fragment, and so on. In addition, hyperpartisanship causes legislative dysfunction, which leads to public finger-pointing, which escalates partisanship, which causes greater legislative dysfunction, and so on.

Hyperpartisanship functions for the dominant system. This explains its persistence and expansion. Interference with the profitability of a dominant system would've led to diminishment or extinction. Appreciating hyperpartisanship as an essential part of a highly functioning and governing system, instead of as a factor in a subordinate system's dysfunction, is illuminating and useful.

Ancillary Beneficiaries of "Dysfunctional" Hyperpartisanship

This will always remain one of the best jokes of democracy, that it
gave its deadly enemies the means by which it was destroyed.
—JOSEPH GOEBBELS

By definition, the primary beneficiary is PI, but others profit. Before identifying "ancillary" beneficiaries, let's distinguish potential processes by
which benefits accrue, or rather the specific nature of hyperpartisanship that
provides benefits.

One way to benefit from hyperpartisanship is riding PI coattails. In other
words, allow hyperpartisanship to work for you, similarly to the way it works
for the highly functioning and governing system. Use entanglement of individual and group identity to sell products. Find ways to profit from identity
validation similar to POEP. We could file this under PI lateral expansion.

The other way to benefit is to take advantage of societal dysfunction arising
in part from hyperpartisanship. In other words, use it to divide and conquer.

Hyperpartisanship can support marketing strategies or be exploited for
dysfunction.

Enemies Foreign

How easy we've made it. Providing our enemies with means to destroy us.
We've published the roadmap for infiltration. X marks the spot.

Hyperpartisanship is key, and the internet, of course. It doesn't take much.

We're already organizing into a circular firing squad. Just a little push from the outside.

Just a little more extreme, on both sides. Work both sides. Aggravate wounds. Pick at scabs. Focus on the most divisive issues. Provoke. Who benefits from civil war or talk of civil war? Do we? Do you?

Hamstring the functionality of our institutions. Undermine faith in our institutions—government, media, elections. Our elections! Plant seeds on the internet and watch them grow. Help them fly.

Violence! Violence and destruction. Destruction is good. Incivility is good. What good is civility? What can you hope to achieve through civility? Civility is passé. Civility has gotten you nothing.

Compromise? What a joke. Civility and compromise are for old-timers confined to wheelchairs in nursing homes. Youth know better. Radicalize the young. Time for action. The time for talk is over. Sick of civility. Sick of compromise. Let's smash some windows. Let's break some glass.

Like a twisted crack of thunder, deliberate laughter from the Nazi Propaganda Minister reverberates through time.

Enemies Domestic

Those who wish to tear us down from within in pursuit of noble revolution fueled by either unconscious self-righteousness or lust for power, benefit, like our foreign enemies, from hyperpartisan dysfunction. Every time the current system works, or solves a problem through bipartisanship and compromise, arguments for radical change diminish. In other words, revolutionary ambition incentivizes dysfunction.

As discussed in Chapter 6, institutions of democracy supported by majority rule block radical change. Even after January 6, 2021, institutional failure to the extent of permitting revolution may be difficult for most Americans to envision. But electoral fundraising benefits from movement by both sides toward the extremes.

Irresponsible Resource Management Creates Ancillary Casualties along with Beneficiaries

More private sector capital diverted toward organizations or causes peddling radical change means less money for organizations or causes working through the system to achieve gradual progress. Note the embedded positive feedback loop. As more resources are dedicated to radical change, opportunities for modest progress within the system diminish, and as opportunities for modest progress diminish, arguments for radical change gain traction, and so on.

Resource management isn't trivial. As discussed, changing the whole system within a democratic republic requiring approval of three-fourths of the states for a single constitutional amendment isn't realistic. Functioning democratic institutions supported by majority rule resist revolutionary change. Therefore, achieve revolutionary change by subverting institutions of democracy. Therefore, sending donations to organizations or causes peddling radical change or revolution is sending donations either to organizations peddling nonsense—the concept that revolution can be achieved by working within the system—or to organizations legitimately working to undermine our democratic institutions. Our money can be better spent.

So, while actual revolution may be presently impossible, fundraising or campaigning for revolution or providing radical content to garner ratings, clicks, and subscriptions is happening. The revolution may not be televised, but revolutionary content is compelling. It's good business.

PI Neutralizes Revolution through Incorporation

Nonviolent revolution requires majorities unachievable along partisan lines. Incorporating radical change and revolutionary intent is solid business. PI incorporates radical dissent into partisan war through ideological segregation. Even the most revolutionary PPs are thus relegated to revenue generators for the machine. PI's business model and the intent of actual revolutionaries are at cross-purposes.

Entrenched Power and Non-PI Corporate America

How can entrenched power along with those seeking radical transformation benefit from the same phenomenon? In short, "the answer to all your questions is money." Before fleshing that out, I'd like to take a moment to marvel at corporations. Corporations can take advantage of both the dysfunctional and functional aspects of hyperpartisanship. Yay, corporations!

Maintain Status Quo via Legislative Dysfunction

Entrenched power wishes to maintain status quo, i.e., hold on to its power. Passing laws is change. Change threatens status quo. I'm not talking about the type of laws or policies that are solicited benevolences in recompense for financial contribution. Those quid pro quos deepen entrenchment. I mean regulations, such as those designed to curb toxic pollution, that benefit society, but may have at least temporary negative impacts on the bottom lines of certain corporations.

Here, corporations benefit from the negative impacts of hyperpartisanship on legislative processes. Threats of new regulation diminish as hyperpartisanship increases. If the two sides are unwilling to get together and compromise, nothing happens. Bravo entrenched power!

Identity Function

Corporations also market to identity similarly to POEP.[58] Understanding the partisan or ideological demographics of the market may permit positive hyperpartisan strategies. This is the product your side buys. This is the service everyone in your group uses.

However, it's not a no-brainer. Michael Jordan once said, "Republicans

---

58 Jason Brooks, "Identity Politics: A Lesson for Brands," LRW Resources, April 10, 2017, https://lrwonline.com/perspective/identity-politics-lesson-brands/; and Transformation Marketing Admin, Politics, "Ideology and Identity in Marketing," Transformation Marketing, Jan 25, 2016, https://www.transformationmarketing.com/politics-ideology-and-identity-in-marketing/.

buy sneakers, too."[59] The point is spot-on. Appealing to demographics with specific partisan affiliation or ideological inclinations may alienate portions of the potential market.

On the other hand, if the market is already segregated, like POEP audiences, marketing according to partisan identity may strengthen connections between your brand and your market slice. Corporate branding according to partisan affiliation strengthens hyperpartisanship by integrating political divisions into traditionally nonpartisan components of our culture—lateral expansion.

So entrenched power and non-PI corporations can benefit from legislative dysfunction while piggybacking on the private sector profitability of identity validation endlessly and successfully promoted by PI. Well done!

Entrenched Power versus Radicals and Revolutionaries

Now let's get back to the apparent contradiction of how those seeking radical transformation and entrenched power can both simultaneously benefit from the same phenomenon. Actual revolution ravages entrenched power. If you don't believe me, ask Marie Antoinette.

But we're not quite there yet, are we? Extremism is chic, no doubt. You'll get no argument from me. Exclaiming "we need to change the whole system," will garner approving applause with coordinated head-nodding from the most fashionable of check-writing audiences.

Radical content is fresh. Whether one is hunting clicks, ratings, readers, listeners, or subscriptions, fanatical quarries are best lured with fresh bait.

But while revolutionary dialogue is a viable fundraising tactic and makes for profitable media content, we're not there yet for actual revolution. Perhaps January 6, 2021, is the closest we've come. Perhaps it's the closest we'll ever come, perhaps.

It's a fine line though. Rioting and property destruction aren't good for business . . . other than media business. But as long as it happens infrequently,

---

59 Tim Bontemps, "Michael Jordan stands firm on 'Republicans buy sneakers, too' quote, says it was made in jest," ESPN, May 4, 2020, https://www.espn.com/nba/story/_/id/29130478/michael-jordan-stands-firm-republicans-buy-sneakers-too-quote-says-was-made-jest.

it's not so bad. Here and there, now and then, we can deal with that. What are the hazards of conciliation compared with the probability of revolution? Not conciliation to right or left, but to functionality. Functionality carries the hazard of legislative compromise, which means progress, which means change, and change threatens entrenched power. Functionality also undermines the rationale for radical change.

Revolution still seems a long way off, though. All that radical nonsense on the internet is just, well, nonsense.

Warning Signs

On August 1, 2023, Fitch downgraded the U.S. government's top credit rating from AAA to AA+. According to a statement by the ratings agency, "there has been a steady deterioration in standards of governance over the last 20 years [and] repeated political standoffs and last-minute resolutions over the debt limit have eroded confidence in fiscal management."[60] This echoes Standard and Poor's rationale for its 2011 downgrade citing "political polarization and insufficient steps to right the nation's fiscal outlook." In other words, ratings agencies downgrade America for congressional dysfunction.

Corporate America needs America. Parameters of that dependency concern short-term profitability versus longevity. There's a short-term profitability bias. It makes sense. Demands of shareholders, plus taking America for granted for so long, equals short-term profitability bias. Can we still take it for granted? Can American corporations afford to take the longevity of America for granted?

Maybe it doesn't matter to them. I'm not talking about patriotism, not that. We're not that naïve. I mean corporate self-interest. American longevity benefits American corporations. Maybe it's time to step up.

By stepping up, I don't mean taking partisan positions. There's plenty of that already. We need to reduce PI lateral expansion.

---

60 Davide Barbuscia, "Fitch cuts US credit rating to AA+; Treasury calls it 'arbitrary'," *Reuters*, Aug. 2, 2023, https://www.reuters.com/markets/us/fitch-cuts-us-governments-aaa-credit-rating-by-one-notch-2023-08-01/.

Paying for Bipartisan Influence Bankrolls Partisan Warfare

Giving money to both sides doesn't work either. I mean, it works for the short-term profitability of corporations by either preventing inconvenient regulation or securing amenable policy. But all that money ends up with PI to be spent on advertising incessantly advising us as to how crazy and evil the other side is. Financing polarity through political spending destabilizes society and threatens American longevity.

The reason I'm appealing to non-PI corporate America is because it has power—more power than PI. However, there are at least two catches. First, PI controls public discussion. Second, as just discussed, corporate America profits from legislative dysfunction, at least in the short term.

Framing this analysis is the concept that the United States is a nation of laws. The issue for non-PI corporate America I'm desperately trying to get at is:

> Does corporate America believe the longevity of America "as a nation of laws" is in the best interests of corporate America?

I suspect a lack of consensus on that one. Non-PI corporate America is not monolithic.

There are undoubtedly masters of our universe who imagine corporatocracy as a better way to go. In a sense, I've argued we're already there. PI subordination of legislative processes describes a type of corporatocracy. But things can always get worse.

Corporations benefit from our laws. I don't mean laws they've paid good money for. I mean more fundamental laws providing our civilization's framework—laws permitting the beehive of civilized economic productivity such as roads, national security, contracts, currency, and police. So, corporations benefit from both our union and the phenomenon of hyperpartisanship threatening that union.

The Fine Line

What endures in the aftermath of revolution? Uncertainty. Are profits guaranteed, or will the new government take over your economic sector? Will people still have enough resources to make your business profitable? It seems a little risky, doesn't it?

Undermining faith in elections is dicey. Profiting from disunion is a dangerous game. There comes a point where returns diminish. Beyond that, economic wasteland.

Your infernal game is played at the expense of the game on the field, the game we love. Your neglect leaves us to speculate. Why is our nation of laws failing?

Because we are Americans, we identify who profits from polarization. We follow the money. While a large chunk of corporate America benefits to a certain extent from government dysfunction, PI directly profits. Is it worth it? What is the calculus, non-PI corporate America?

There comes a point where no one believes the game on the field anymore. It begins to look like professional wrestling. It begins to look like scripted drama rather than honest competition. If it's not real—if our representatives aren't playing according to the Constitution—if, instead, PI revenue concerns dictate their play, then why not revolution?

Your infernal game depends on public buy-in. The game on the field matters. It must appear real. It doesn't necessarily have to *be* real, but it at least needs to appear real. Corporate masters of the universe should know this. We're moving across the fine line. Can't you see that? What I'm trying to say is: *Help us non-PI corporate America, you may be our only hope.*

—16—

Reflections

> It may be that we are puppets—puppets controlled by the strings of society. But at least we are puppets with perception, with awareness. And perhaps our awareness is the first step to our liberation.
> —STANLEY MILGRAM, 1974

I've been living in a dream. Many of us have. The dream arises from a psyche steeped in the mythos of American exceptionalism. The notion has morphed from an idea into a sense of permanence. America is eternal.

But the universe disdains creeds of intransience. We are mortal and our systems provisional. The pandemic and January sixth were like memoranda from the cosmos: *Nothing is forever.*

Hyperpartisanship Hastens Our Evanescence

Within a civilized and cohesive society, optimal response to crises entails coming together. But teaming up to fight a common enemy is apparently reserved for invading forces. The cocktail of disease and discord failed to reveal our best.

In a hyperpartisan environment, crises exacerbate polarization. Instead of coming together, we doubled down on division. Instead of circling the wagons and gathering in the center, we circled the firing squad and fled the center. We stoked instability and exposed our transience.

Who benefits from crisis and instability? I'll give you a hint. It involves a clicker. Watching TV during the pandemic was a curriculum in polarity. Upon reflection, the main takeaway based on POEP was how incredibly different red states are from blue states. That was the emphasis. Differences were a point of emphasis.

It wasn't simply that HM emphasized our differences the way a scientist might emphasize differences between two insect species. Differences were emphasized tactically for partisan advantage. PPs used pandemic response as evidence of tribal superiority. The crisis was weaponized for partisan utility. The red/blue holy war incorporated the pandemic. PI engaged in crisis profiteering. Solving the pandemic took a back seat to partisanship. PI subordinated crisis management.

Let's revisit our definition of "dysfunctional" hyperpartisanship:

Promotion of the particular interests of a political party, faction, group, tribe, person, ideology, or cause to an extent that communication or cooperation with those not similarly aligned is unworkable except in crises, where, nonetheless, collaboration may be impaired to an extent that undermines crisis management.

Clearly, hyperpartisanship impaired pandemic management. But the impact was not unidirectional. The relationship between crisis management and hyperpartisanship is dynamic. The pandemic didn't cause hyperpartisanship, but pandemic management affected the hyperpartisan environment.

We're more fully integrated with hyperpartisanship. Its essence has infected us more profoundly. It's part of our biology, like COVID antibodies. We developed a greater resistance to recognizing our commonalities. Our herd immunity is to compromise. We're fully vaccinated against common ground.

The perception *was* America shined in crises. Now . . . not so much. Evidence of our transience builds. Doubts about the eternal nature of our exceptionalism creep in as hyperpartisanship strengthens.

That which damages our ability to deal with crises is strengthening. Amazing! A particular segment of society profits from our failure, and we respond by watching it unfold on national cable news, which contributes to our decline. We are ratings data points for the industry profiting from our disunion.

Evolution

Either we must evolve, or our systems and institutions must evolve, or both. Great care is needed in this regard. The danger is incorporation. I fear partisanship is so financially incentivized or adaptive in the current environment that any evolution or change will result in even greater partisanship. PI will simply incorporate evolutionary efforts into partisan warfare.

Its adaptive nature is our focus. We marvel at its functionality. The organism is highly successful. It didn't simply appear. But blooming so magnificently, it threatens to overtake our ecosystem like a voracious weed without natural constraints. Where did it come from, and why is it suddenly blooming out of control?

It comes from within us, and it blooms because the ecosystem changed to allow it.

We Must Evolve

How does it come from within us, and how can individuals evolve to curtail its devastation? Our predilections for understanding differences as threats and our yearning for the safety of resemblance evolved within tribal units. I'm not suggesting we can biologically evolve beyond our contemporary natures any time soon.

However, surrendering to psychological predispositions that evolved during our tribal existences without inspection is lazy and confounds awareness. Examining compulsions makes them less compelling. The evolution I speak of for democracy's fundamental unit doesn't require altering our genetic code. Instead, we must cultivate a consciousness that engenders functional democracy.

Cultivating consciousness is a practice. In Chapter 12, I hailed *practicing* citizenship. Emphasizing practice reduces chances of failing. As long as you practice, you succeed.

Unless you live in a monastery, and possibly even there, you can't practice consciousness all day. It's tiring. Most of us are out of shape. We can get into shape. But how?

Let's practice when we're engaged by media in political analysis. There's no danger of offending through a screen or being rude to print. Let's make productive use of these commodities.

Introspection starts at the most basic level. Why are we engaged? Are we being seduced? Maybe we tell ourselves we're keeping informed. But is that what it feels like? Does it feel like reading a science text? Do authors of science texts ensnare you in "us versus them" narratives?

What is the utility of "us versus them" frameworks? Longtime POEP viewers take the structure for granted. I know I did. I accepted it without inspection. What's the big deal? It's us versus them. That's the way it is.

But there's purpose and value beyond simply conveying information. There's a little bit of diddling going on. We've discussed the seductive power and purpose of righteousness affirmation. Are you really tuning in for news?

"I don't want to think about it. I don't care why I like something." These refrains bring joy to PPs. The choruses nurture a mindset blockading awareness. Surrendering to primitive psychology without inspection is lazy and undermines consciousness evolution.

"I don't need to change or evolve!" Does you not changing at all make sense to you? Is that your experience? Have you lived your whole life that way? Do you remember the moment your evolution concluded? What is the anniversary of your perfection?

"It's other people who need to change!" So it *is* you. You're the one. You're the center. The universe revolves around you. Astrophysicists got it all wrong. *You* are the constant. Everything must conform to you. If you believe that, you're either a spoiled child or in serious need of therapy.

My purpose is not insult. I'm pessimistic about institutions like media evolving beyond a business model that successfully exploits primitive psychology. On the other hand, our own evolution is beyond their control. It begins with genuine desire.

Our Systems and Institutions Must Evolve

Institutions evolve partisan natures because entities competent in partisanship are better adapted for securing resources in a hyperpartisan ecosystem. Partisanship is selected for, while both bipartisanship and nonpartisanship are selected against. In the current environment, partisanship is adaptive.

Here again, assessing functionality promotes understanding. Appreciating that the evolution of institutions or individuals toward increased partisanship is adaptive is the functional paradigm.

Alternatively, the phenomenon may be understood as corruption. All people as well as all peopled institutions are susceptible in varying degrees to corrupting influences of power.

Notice that whether we interpret evolution of democratic institutions toward greater partisanship as adaptive or corrupt, the analysis doesn't change. In other words, "the answer to all your questions is money." Institutions either adapt by evolving partisan natures to secure more money, or institutions are corrupted by profit motive. Either way, within our ecosystem, resources are more easily secured by entities skilled in partisanship.

We must modify the environment to disincentivize partisanship.

Defund PI

To disincentivize partisanship, reduce resources permitting it to thrive. Stop underwriting PI.

As to the entertainment subsector, i.e., POEP and its mutations, it's up to consumers. As discussed in Chapter 5, the First Amendment proscribes government action compelling responsible journalism.

Impacts of partisan news and entertainment aren't trivial. Remember the feedback loop. Media doesn't simply reflect society. It affects it as well. It's part of the environment determining our complexion. Cut that loop.

Remedy POEP's effect by refusing to consume polarizing content. Awareness that POEP exploits tribal psychology curbs our appetite for it.

Consumer activism divests the campaign subsector as well. Cease and desist all political spending. Contributions to PACs, political parties, and individual politicians end up with PI, to be spent informing the public how crazy, evil, and extreme the other side is. Defund and unaffiliate.

However, as to the campaign subsector, consumer responsibility is not the only option.

Constitutional Amendments

JOINT RESOLUTION

Proposing an amendment to the Constitution of the United States to prohibit corporations, organizations, and associations from political spending, and to permit Congress or any state to reasonably limit political spending by candidates or their supporters, and to require reasonable documentation of such spending.

WHEREAS discord is more marketable than harmony.

WHEREAS extremism is more marketable than moderation.

WHEREAS campaign contributions ultimately end up with the partisanship industry's campaign subsector to be spent advising Americans how different, crazy, evil, or extreme the other side is.

WHEREAS political parties institutionalize polarity through a society-wide template.

WHEREAS reducing funding to partisan combatants is de-escalating.

WHEREAS reducing funding to partisan combatants reduces the financial incentive to subordinate issues of public interest to partisan electoral concerns.

WHEREAS allowing partisan associations to aggregate immense wealth to influence elections strengthens hyperpartisanship by bankrolling associations' authority over individual identity.

WHEREAS too much money is in the pot to rely on voluntary civility or reason.

WHEREAS corporations are legal persons *not* subsumed in the preamble's "We the people of the United States."

WHEREAS "in a functioning democracy the public must have faith that its representatives owe their positions to the people, not to the corporations with the deepest pockets."[61]

WHEREAS corporations and entrenched power benefit in the short term from legislative dysfunction and cannot be relied upon to voluntarily forgo quantifiable short-term profitability for intangibles such as the longevity of America.

WHEREAS the principle and spirit of "one person, one vote" should not be circumvented, defiled, or mocked through financial fiat.

WHEREAS equal treatment under the law is mocked when well-heeled individuals or associations disproportionately secure favorable lawmaking through campaign contributions.

WHEREAS the principle of equal opportunity, which includes equal access to political processes, is mocked when well-heeled individuals or associations disproportionately secure access and favorable lawmaking through campaign contributions.

WHEREAS the corrupting consequences of independent expenditures by corporations and unions for electioneering communications[62] are well documented.[63]

WHEREAS valuable societal resources are diverted to finance our disunion.

WHEREAS America's enemies, both foreign and domestic, benefit from our disunion through the financial incentivization of partisanship.

WHEREAS self-government within the structure of a democratic republic as outlined in the Constitution requires functioning institutions, and financially incentivized partisanship undermines institutional functionality.

---

61 *Citizens United v. Federal Election Commission*, 558 U.S. 310, 446 (2010), available at https://tile.loc.gov/storage-services/service/ll/usrep/usrep558/usrep558310/usrep558310.pdf.

62 "An electioneering communication is any broadcast, cable or satellite communication that refers to a clearly identified federal candidate, is publicly distributed within 30 days of a primary or 60 days of a general election and is targeted to the relevant electorate." "Making Electioneering Communications," Federal Election Commission, accessed Oct. 31, 2022, https://www.fec.gov/help-candidates-and-committees/other-filers/making-electioneering-communications/.

63 *Citizens United*, 558 U.S. at 448.

WHEREAS partisanship has been financially incentivized to the extent that partisan advantage subordinates government functionality.

WHEREAS America's ability to make progress or manage crises has been compromised by the financial incentivization of partisanship.

WHEREAS the Congress serves as the primary battleground for partisan warfare, rather than as an institution of deliberation and compromise for the betterment of America and the benefit of Americans.

WHEREAS through financial incentivization of partisanship America is transforming from the paradigm of functional democracy to the exemplar of dysfunction.

WHEREAS in order to preserve electoral integrity and de-escalate partisanship: Now, therefore, be it

Resolved by the Senate and House of Representatives of the United States of America in Congress assembled (two-thirds of each House concurring therein), that the following article is proposed as an amendment to the Constitution of the United States, which shall be valid to all intents and purposes as part of the Constitution when ratified by the legislatures of three-fourths of the several States:

"Article —

"_SECTION 1.

Rights of corporations, organizations, and associations shall be maintained, except the right to contribute money to candidates for public office either directly or through intermediary persons or entities such as political parties or political action committees, or to finance express advocacy for candidates or electioneering communications, is hereby extinguished and reserved exclusively for natural persons.

"_SECTION 2.

Neither the First Amendment nor any other provision of this Constitution shall be construed to prohibit the Congress or any state from imposing reasonable limits on the amount of money candidates for public office, or their supporters, may spend in election campaigns.[64]

"_SECTION 3.

All such spending henceforth shall be reasonably documented.

"_SECTION 4.

The Congress shall have power to enforce this article by appropriate legislation.

Mock Congressional Record

Congressional Representative from Right Field (CRF): "I conspicuously object to section one because it unfairly handicaps American corporations."

Congressional Representative from Left Field (CLF): "Of course you do."

CRF: "Do I detect sarcasm from my esteemed colleague?"

Congressional Representative from Center Field (CCF): "OK, let's cut the crap and get on with it. How does section one 'handicap' American corporations?"

Corporations, Organizations, and Associations

CRF: "Corporations are the backbone of American ingenuity and economic productivity. We should provide them with every right to weigh in on policies affecting their productivity and innovative capacity. Through innovation, America has distinguished itself as the greatest of all nations."

CCF: "I agree innovation or evolution is essential. However, I respectfully disagree with your interpretation of section one. The amendment doesn't preclude corporations from speaking publicly on issues of concern, or lobbying or meeting with representatives or public officials to provide insight about existing or proposed policy. The amendment prohibits bolstering such insight with cash."

CRF: "I don't know what any of this has to do with evolution."

CLF: "Can I say something? Corporations aren't people. This amendment

---

64 Erin Fuchs, "6 Constitutional Amendments That Could Dramatically Improve America," *Business Insider*, Jun. 27, 2014, https://www.businessinsider.com/john-paul-stevens-six-amendments-2014-6. Section 2 is taken almost verbatim from an amendment proposed by retired SCOTUS Justice, John Paul Stevens.

should abolish corporate personhood!"[65]

CCF: "As persons, corporations have rights to own property, make contracts and use courts to sue or defend against suit. Removing those rights would extinguish corporations altogether."

CLF: "Well, couldn't we eliminate corporate personhood and enumerate specific rights of corporations?"

CCF: "Section one has the desired effect without the rigmarole. Besides, the purpose of this amendment is to improve electoral integrity and reduce financially incentivized partisanship by reducing money available for divisive campaigning. It's not an anti-corporation amendment. Don't allow the kitchen sink to be the enemy of the narrowly tailored."

CRF: "I don't care for any of it. Corporations consist of people. Corporations are simply associations of people guaranteed First Amendment protections, including the right to donate to campaigns."

CCF: "I agree corporations are associations of people, and every one of those people, including every shareholder, every board member, every officer, and every employee shall maintain their right as natural persons to contribute to candidates for public office."

CLF: "Hold on a second. Aren't unions associations of people?"

CCF: "Yes, and all union members shall maintain their right as individuals to contribute to candidates for public office. Either contributing money to candidates for public office is a right exclusive to individuals, or it extends to associations of individuals. We shouldn't impose double standards for partisan advantage."

CLF: "What about political parties?"

CCF: "All political party members shall maintain their right as individuals to contribute to candidates for public office."

CRF: "Why would anyone contribute to a political party if it can't fund campaigns for public office?"

CCF: "Is my esteemed colleague from right field suggesting that funneling money to candidates is the primary purpose of political parties? It's an

---

65 For a synopsis of corporate personhood as well as corporations as associations, see Adam Winkler, *Corporate Personhood and Constitutional Rights for Corporations*, 54 New England Law Review 23 (2019)."

excellent question deserving serious contemplation by all involved, including every citizen."

CLF: "We're getting a bit off track, I think …"

CCF: Interrupting. "I respectfully disagree. The role of political parties in distributing campaign funds gets to the very heart …"

CLF: Interrupting. "OK, OK, respectfully, I'm changing the subject. Instead of amending the Constitution, why don't we get the Supreme Court to overturn *Citizens United*?"

Citizens United

CCF: "Your use of 'get' is revealing. My esteemed colleague from left field knows that as a coequal branch of government, Congress cannot 'get' the Supreme Court to overturn cases.

"Before exploring my fascination with your use of 'get,' if *Citizens United* made one thing clear, it's that the Constitution must be amended to distinguish the ability of associations to affect political and electoral processes through financial contribution from that of natural persons.

"Even before *Citizens United*, corporations and unions could form PACs for express advocacy or electioneering communications. Voluminous independent expenditures, regardless of whether they come from general treasury funds or PACs, threaten electoral integrity and financially incentivize partisanship."

CRF: "You're trying to end free speech for corporations. This is outrageous!"

CCF: "No. Speaking on issues of public or corporate interest is easily distinguishable from financing political campaigns. Speech intended to promote or prevent election of specific candidates should be reserved for voters."

CLF: "That's why we need to overturn *Citizens United*."

CCF: "Pursuing overturning *Citizens United* subordinates relevant issues to partisan electoral concerns."

CLF: "How so?"

CCF: "The argument goes: The current makeup of the Supreme Court won't allow for overturning *Citizens United*. The only way to overturn *Citizens United* is by changing the Supreme Court's membership. The only way to change Supreme Court membership is by electing presidents who will nominate justices likely to overturn *Citizens United*. However, even if court membership changed to the extent you wish, there's no guarantee a relevant case will be heard."

CRF: *Unconstrained guffawing.* "I wonder what is less likely, passing this amendment or the Supreme Court hearing a relevant case?"

CCF: "Your sarcastic ruminations aren't amusing."

CRF: "There's no accounting for taste."

CCF: "The point is, the legal framework for political spending shouldn't depend on the Supreme Court's partisan complexion. The way we can do something is by amending the Constitution."

CRF: "So how do you see this all playing out? Who's going to run my re-election ads and where will the money come from?"

CCF: "Only you will be able to run ads and the money for those ads must come from individual contributors."

CRF: "What the #!*##!*..? Are you **!##ing kidding me? Why?"

CCF: "The benefits to public discourse are plain. The most hatefully divisive ads funded through independent expenditures accompanied by disclaimers will be eliminated. Candidates can only remain above the fray by campaigning civilly. A campaign going negative or getting dirty will be attributed directly to the candidate. You won't be able to subcontract out filth. The need for disclaimers will be obviated."

CRF: "How will people know whom to vote for? Those ads allow citizens to make informed voting decisions."

CCF: "I think it's my turn to laugh. But all kidding aside, my esteemed colleague from right field is correct to assume that TV ads leading up to Election Day will be reduced, elevating the relative importance of televised debates and interviews. That should make it more difficult for candidates to unfairly smear opponents with misleading rhetoric, for two reasons.

"First, as discussed, portrayals of opponents' character or positions on issues will be coming directly from the candidate, instead of from sketchy third-party ads. I say, 'sketchy' because, although the ads clearly benefit a particular candidate, disclaimers provide plausible deniability for nastier content.

"Second, political TV ads are ephemeral ECs. They impart biased ideas and opinions without contrast. Both debates and interviews provide opportunities for contrary opinion and follow-up questions, thereby improving chances candidates will be fairly presented to the electorate."

CLF: "You say third-party ads will no longer be funded through independent expenditures. But my reading of the amendment is that neither corporations nor other associations can pay for express advocacy or electioneering communications. Couldn't an individual so-called 'natural person' pay for a TV ad for a candidate for public office?

Reasonable

CCF: "That's where section two comes in, giving us and states the right to place 'reasonable limits on the amount of money candidates or their supporters may spend in election campaigns.' While I concede the amendment theoretically permits such an independent expenditure from an individual, reasonable spending limits should make such a venture impracticable. A 'natural person' might be able to finance a print ad in a newspaper or on the internet or a pamphlet for distribution, but producing a TV ad and paying for airtime by a single well-heeled individual is unlikely."

CRF: "What exactly is your idea of reasonable?"

CCF: "I will answer. But before I do, let me point out it's not my idea of reasonable that's relevant. It's for Congress on the federal level and state legislatures to figure out. In making that determination, consider the amendment's purposes, which are to preserve electoral integrity and de-escalate partisanship.

"As to electoral integrity, it's about fairness and the appearance of fairness. The public must have faith that its representatives owe their positions to the electorate, not to the individuals or associations with the deepest pockets. I think limiting contributions from an individual to a particular candidate to something like $1,000 is fair. Also, we should limit the total amount an individual can contribute to all candidates on the federal level to something like $15,000. States can enact similarly reasonable limits."

CRF: "We clearly have different ideas about 'reasonable.' You're trying to destroy an entire industry along with the exceptionally charming American tradition of the two-party system."

CCF: "As I said, Congress and the states will decide what's fair. Besides, the relative value of money changes. I have faith in my esteemed colleagues, both now and in the future, to determine what's fair."

CRF: "I can't tell whether you're trying to make me laugh or run to the toilet. What about reasonably documenting all contributions? If somebody gives me five bucks, do I have to write it down?"

CCF: "Once again, that's for Congress and states to determine. I think candidates should have to report total amounts raised, plus document individual contributions above a certain amount."

CRF: "OK, OK, I get it. I want to move on to something else. I'm not sure I buy your whole premise that campaign contributions finance polarization. You can't prove any of that."

Financially Incentivized Disunion

CCF: "I submitted several hundred pages of supporting documents to this committee on that issue."

CRF: "You mean that manifesto titled *Subordinating American Democracy* or some such nonsense?"

CCF: "Maybe."

CRF: "Ha. Yes, some of us regrettably took time to familiarize ourselves with your opus. By my calculations, you owe me a week of my life. I wonder what my esteemed colleague from left field thinks."

CLF: "No comment."

CRF: "I don't know what your problem is with campaign financing. It's sound American business. It creates jobs. The more spent on campaigns, the more injected as stimulus into the economy. We're not forcing people to make campaign contributions. It's voluntary. It's a manifestation of American freedom. It creates jobs, stimulates the economy, educates voters on candidates, and it's all voluntary. It's a win, win, win, win situation."

CCF: "We can distinguish, without hypocrisy, various conduits to profit and approaches to economic stimulus. On the other hand, money fungibility produces origin-obscuring intermingling that can appear to render manner irrelevant. Nonetheless, as a representative of the people, I am loath to endorse fear and sponsor gang violence to bolster gun manufacturer profitability. I would veto a war whose singular purpose is augmenting military-industrial complex revenue. Similarly, I oppose our disunion to stimulate the economy and create jobs.

"I'm not suggesting potential donors tie their purse strings. However, I believe their money would be better spent patronizing local businesses or funding charities working within their communities. Writing checks to political parties or PACs transfers resources from local economies to finance a cold civil war that is maiming society. It's our job to identify and support policies disincentivizing our demise.

"Opposing the other side shouldn't be so damn profitable."

CRF: "Well I believe I shouldn't shoot myself in the foot. This amendment will reduce my war chest while resulting in a policy windfall for my esteemed colleague from left field."

CCF: "I don't believe it. I know that's the rhetoric, but simply reducing private money in politics won't result in partisan or ideological policy imbalance. People who claim that either don't understand our country or are deliberately spouting rhetoric for partisan advantage.

"The benefits for America won't accrue disproportionately to extreme factions of either party. If there is a windfall, it will be for moderation as well as . . ."

CLF: Interrupting. "Excuse me. I would like a brief sidebar with my esteemed colleague from center field."

Sidebar

CLF: "What do you think you're doing? How am I supposed to get my party to support the means to its own bankruptcy without unequivocal policy victory?"

CCF: "I don't want your party to support this amendment."

CLF: "*What*? Why?"

CCF: "Because support from your party will result in opposition from the other party. Proposing a constitutional amendment requires two-thirds of both houses of Congress. Ratification requires three-fourths of the states. There's not enough registration within a single party to amend the Constitution along partisan lines.

CLF: "If support from either party will kill the amendment, how could it possibly pass?"

CCF: "Individual representatives from both parties must support the amendment. Generating that amount of support means convincing an overwhelming majority of Americans that it's important enough to decide their individual votes. Amending the Constitution needs to rise to the level of an election issue throughout the country."

CLF: "But if my party controlled two-thirds of Congress and three-fourths of the states, we could pass it."

CCF: "Let's pretend for a second your party . . . how did you put it . . . was willing 'to support the means to its own bankruptcy' for good of country. I don't believe it for a second. But for argument's sake, let's pretend it's true.

"Here's a cautionary note for true believers out there. A Democratic representative from West Virginia or Louisiana or Montana is, first and foremost, a representative from West Virginia, Louisiana, or Montana. Putting a 'D' in front of the name doesn't change that. You yourself know this because you remember when your party controlled the White House and both houses of Congress, and you couldn't get votes for comprehensive climate-change legislation or a public option in the Affordable Care Act (ACA)."

CLF: "Then there's no hope."

CCF: "The hope is that a majority of Americans recognizes partisan warfare is at the expense of a majority of Americans. Passing this amendment won't be a victory for left *or* right. Those who profit from partisanship will suffer defeat. The rest of us win.

"Framing the debate as right versus left incorporates issues of electoral integrity and de-escalation of partisan warfare into the partisan war. Red versus blue subordinates issues to a partisan electoral strategy, and these fundamental issues cannot be solved through partisan victory. The math doesn't work.

"It's not red versus blue or right versus left. It's those who profit off partisanship versus the rest of us. In that configuration, we have the numbers. When the people organize themselves accordingly, the math works."

CLF: "Good luck with that."

CCF: "Look on the bright side. Your party can still raise private money on the issue of getting private money out of politics."

CLF: "F*** you!"

Sidebar Ends

CRF: "Did you two work it out?"

CLF: "Not quite. I have one more question for my esteemed colleague from center field. If we could get this passed, are you certain it will work?"

CRF: "Good question. Here's another. Can you guarantee no negative consequences?"

Certainty, Guarantees, Implications, and Consequences

CCF: "As a politician, I'm not supposed to respond this way, but the answer to both your questions is unequivocally, 'no.'"

CLF: "So you expect support from two-thirds of Congress and three-fourths of states, even though you're not certain it will work, and you can't guarantee there won't be negative consequences?"

CCF: "I have no such expectations. But I know something of certainty and guarantees and consequences or implications. We must stop pretending."

CLF: "Stop pretending what?"

CCF: "That we're certain of all implications of our actions and can guarantee desired outcomes."

CRF: "Do you want the people to lose faith in our capacity to govern?"

CCF: "Many already have, and the pretense of certainty contributes to the erosion of that faith."

CLF: "Explain."

CCF: "Certainty is soothing. Desire for certainty is desire to be soothed. When parents wish to soothe their children, they adopt an air of certainty for situations for which they couldn't possibly be certain.

"A political philosophy never explicitly articulated is that the electorate should be treated like children—that the electorate wishes to be soothed with fables of certainty. So, we place a premium on a knack for appearing certain, which is plainly an expression of deceit."

CLF: "What's your point?"

CCF: "Knowing all implications or consequences of any proposed policy is impossible. We never know."

CRF: "And you think telling the American people that is a good idea?"

CCF: "Most adults know this."

CLF: "Then why does certainty triumph over uncertainty in electoral politics?"

CCF: "Because people compartmentalize. We relegate adult cognizance that certainty is a con to our unconscious, especially if we feel less qualified on a subject like politics than the speaker who speaks with an air of certainty. But at some level, the electorate understands they're being conned.

"In addition, the unwitting mark can claim exemption from liability. Some self-deception is psychologically incentivized. This dynamic is inapposite to democracy where representatives allegedly derive their power from the people.

"We must encourage the electorate to grow up for at least two reasons. First, it would render con artists hawking certainty impotent. Second, it would be more difficult for voters to exempt themselves from liability. The electorate is ultimately responsible, and responsibility demands taking an adult view of certainty and guarantees. Only children should be vulnerable to fables of certainty and guarantees of intended consequences.

"Amending the Constitution, or simply passing a law, is change. Change carries anticipation of uncertain outcomes. We must act without perfect knowledge of consequences."

CLF: "So 'in order to form a more perfect union,' we must make imperfect policy changes based on imperfect knowledge of consequences. I'm not sure that makes sense."

To Form a More Perfect Union

CCF: "It makes perfect sense as long as you understand 'more perfect' means 'less than perfect.'"

CRF: "I can't wait to hear this one."

CCF: "The phrase, 'more perfect,' cannot tolerate a plain reading and must be interpreted.

"First, it cannot mean perfect. That would render 'more' as a modifier superfluous and the Framers weren't prone to superfluity."

CRF: "I wish I could say the same for my esteemed colleague."

CCF: "Second, 'more perfect' cannot mean 'more than perfect' or 'better than perfect' because there's no such thing. Perfect cannot be improved. It doesn't need to be 'more perfect.'

"Since 'more perfect' means neither 'perfect' nor 'more than perfect,' we are left with one possibility. It means closer to perfect than we are now, but not quite perfect, i.e., 'less than perfect.'

CLF: "Scalia would be proud."

CRF: "Ha. Perfect."

CCF: "This isn't trivial. There's a relationship between unrealistic expectations of voters and hyperpartisanship. Setting unrealistic goals divides us into factions. Maintaining status quo, going back to a previous time, and achieving perfection are all childishly unrealistic.

"It's not government's job to construct a perfect society. Government inevitably not working perfectly for any group or individual sets the stage for blame and partisan scheming. Democracy needs adults. We must move forward with the goal of improvement."

CRF: "In other words, we shouldn't let the perfect be the enemy of the good."

CCF: "That adage holds a false premise. For society, perfect doesn't exist. To use a concrete example, because of entropy, infrastructure perpetually degrades. Things wear out. Conditions continuously change.

"The goal isn't perfection. It's improvement. We must relentlessly work to improve society. A constantly improving society can never be perfect. Quest for perfection impedes efforts to become more perfect."

CRF: "So my esteemed colleague asks us to introduce and ratify a less-than-perfect amendment without certainty of consequences or guarantees of efficacy."

CCF: "Well put. Let the experiment continue."

The American Experiment and Evolution

CLF: "What's that supposed to mean?"

CCF: "With all my heart and as a patriot, I believe the American Experiment should continue. Acting without perfect knowledge, without certainty of consequences, without guarantees of efficacy is experimentation. We must experiment to evolve and avert stagnation and decay.

"We should ratify every policy in the spirit of experimentation and let the people in on it. Treat them like adults. Policy conceived as experimental facilitates course correction. Institutional and programmatic inertia will be slower to develop if the legal authority for programs is understood to be experimental. It's more difficult for a boondoggle to find enduring refuge in an experiment.

"The recipe for policy should be:

1. Experiment;
2. Monitor the experiment; and
3. Make appropriate adjustments."

CLF: "That sounds risky."

CCF: "A system that eliminates risk impairs evolution. Nothing in the Constitution even hints that policymakers should legislate a risk-free system. Fair doesn't mean risk-free.

"The Framers understood the necessity of acting without perfect knowledge. The Constitution admits a deficiency in clairvoyance. That admission provides logic for amending the tentative. Stipulation to modify the provisional is prophetic. The tentative achieves duration through modification.

"The alternative path is a dead end. A concerted effort to avoid mistakes at all costs formulates extinction. Evolution is by trial and error. The system must run through permutations to identify potential. Problem-solving necessitates mistake-making. We must evolve. We must experiment.

"My colleagues who have graduated to tying their shoes and matriculated to responsible leadership understand this perfectly well. The specter of uncertainty is conjured with deliberate cynicism to frighten the child psyche. Even the consequences of designating a park cannot be fully understood, because time can tarnish the most hallowed of names. The burden of certainty terminates the American Experiment."

So ends the mock Congressional Record.

Electoral College and Gerrymandering

Amending the Constitution to abolish the Electoral College or to stop gerrymandering would also reduce partisanship. A popular vote would make the red-state/blue-state dynamic extraneous to presidential elections. The entire electorate would decide outcomes. Under the current system, that privilege is exclusive to voters in swing states. There would be no swing states, or, if you like, every state would be a swing state. Candidates would be ill-advised to appeal to extremes of their respective parties for fear of alienating independents, moderates, swing voters, and undecideds.

Gerrymandering effectively institutes an Electoral College dynamic for legislative districts. Drawing districts that segregate and concentrate voters according to partisan affiliation means legislative candidates can afford to ignore large portions of the electorate and simply conform their dispositions to partisan talking points. Ending gerrymandering would mean more districts where the partisan breakdown approaches fifty-fifty. Again, this would result in more campaigning toward the center rather than the extremes.

Notice how all three amendments target PI's campaign subsector, albeit in different ways. Ending gerrymandering and abolishing the Electoral College shifts campaign messaging from extremes toward the center by restructuring the electorate in a more inclusive way. This makes product differentiation more challenging for campaign professionals.

Functionally organizing the electorate according to partisan affiliation, either through gerrymandering or red-state/blue-state, allows campaign professionals to easily differentiate candidates according to partisan talking points. Product differentiation is easier the further apart candidates are on issues.

But shaping voting districts so candidates must compete for the center impairs cookie-cutter product differentiation. As partisan affiliation becomes less important, character specific to individual candidates rises in prominence. Generalizing or packaging according to the partisan conglomerate begins to look lazy and feel tone-deaf. Simply entering the voting booth with the intention of submitting to the binary construct of party affiliation is insufficient.

Campaign finance reform, on the other hand, reduces revenue to PI's campaign subsector and political parties. It's a capacity-reduction strategy. The quantity of advertising reminding us how different, crazy, and extreme the other side is will be greatly reduced. Abolishing the Electoral College and ending gerrymandering incentivizes aiming closer to center, while campaign finance reform turns down the volume on divisiveness.

I chose to highlight campaign finance reform because as an American who has lived in America his whole life, I can't help but "follow the money." Persistence of phenomena in this country implies profitability. "The answer to all your questions is money."

Reality Check and Conclusions

In addition to targeting PI's campaign subsector, all three amendments instigate moderation. The reputation of such proposals is that implementation favors the left. That reputation is overblown. While the suggested amendments could facilitate modest progress on issues like renewable energy, health care, or immigration reform, ratification would reduce substantive extremism from both sides. Proposals like "Medicare-for-All" or "Green New Deal" would remain disconnected from political reality.

Speaking of political reality, the likelihood of two-thirds of Congress and three-fourths of states supporting any amendment in this hyperpartisan environment is fanciful. If I had a not-for-profit exclusively dedicated to making these amendments election issues and the not-for-profit had an annual operating budget of 100 million dollars, I could imagine generating the type of support necessary within two to five decades. I probably won't live that long.

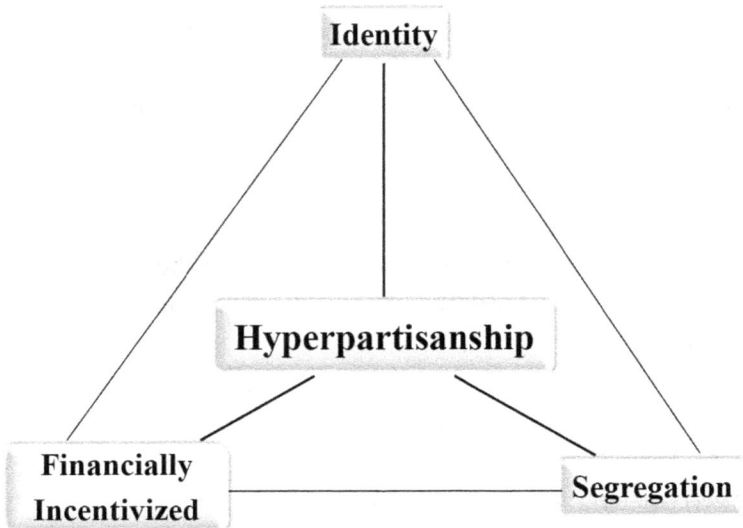

Figure 17.1: Hyperpartisanship Web Core Reprise

Before sliding further down what feels like an inevitable slope of pessimism, let's revisit our hyperpartisanship web core. While I indicated that the proposed amendments target PI's campaign subsector and financial incentivization, they also affect segregation and identity. Abolishing the Electoral College and stopping gerrymandering is integrating. The same could be said for transforming the primary system, as discussed in Chapter 11. Segregation according to ideology or partisan affiliation facilitates hyperpartisan identification.

However, as to the entertainment subsector, i.e., POEP, whether the suggested amendments would moderate content is unclear. Could functionally integrating the electorate by going to a popular vote for presidential elections and eliminating gerrymandering nurture a broader desegregating movement, dissolving ECs? Could disincentivizing partisanship by defunding political parties and the campaign subsector translate to programming not dominated by partisan narrative? Maybe, but I'm dubious.

The lure of POEP isn't information. Identity validation underwrites the business model. We're back to evolving the fundamental units of democracy. Can enough individuals free themselves from their addiction to affirming their own righteousness to disrupt the cycle of partisan hostility in an environment dominated by media that markets validation?

Approaching that question requires us to recognize we're not just confronting industrial or institutional financial incentivization. The dilemma incriminates human psychology and culture.

Part II: Psychology and Culture

Our behavior affects our environment. We are environmental factors within our environment. Likewise, our environment influences our behavior. Our nature, developed through evolution within environments carrying selective factors, drives our actions. Our actions modify the landscape, and so on—the feedback loop.

While Part I underscored institutional financial incentives, Part II emphasizes relationships between human predispositions, our culture, and hyperpartisanship. I say "emphasize" because many elements to be explored in greater detail have been insinuated, and ensuing explorations will implicate components previously examined. All relevant factors naturally operate and intermingle concurrently. This is the nature of evolution and the web.

18

Emphasizing Differences

*Surrendering to psychological predispositions evolved during our
primordial existences without inspection is lazy and sabotages democracy.*
—The Author

Perceiving and emphasizing differences isn't just marketing. It's a survival
strategy. It's adaptive. It's engrained.

It makes sense. Treating something suddenly manifesting in your environment as a threat until proven otherwise is prudent. Different = potential
threat. Focusing on differences enhances survivability.

Although hyperpartisanship mostly involves the senses of seeing and hearing, the olfactory suitably illuminates. Smell is judiciously ephemeral. Our
sensitivity to persistent odors fades, until we can't detect by smell something
that was pungent moments before. But introduce a new odor, and it bursts
on stage to steal the spotlight like a self-absorbed ham.

The construct embraces adaptive logic. Identified as non-threatening, the
persistent odor isn't relevant to survival. Obsessing on the persistent odor
could prove fatal. The fresh scent of the stalking predator might be missed
or undervalued. We're programmed to notice and fixate on differences, and
we're wired to presume those differences to be threatening.

Nature and Nurture

Our totality stems from biological inheritance and experience. Our experiences include diet, education, interactions with others, vocation, stress,

exercise, catastrophe, culture, etc. We inherit a body, which includes a brain, and our experiences upload to the template biology provides.

> Different biological inheritance + different experiences → different person with different physicality, thought patterns, inclinations, ideas, aspirations, and opinions

Since no two people have the exact same experiences, we can each be unique.

But on the genetic level, we're almost identical. The Human Genome Project tells us all humans share 99.9 percent of the genome.[66] On the genetic level we are 99.9 percent the same. A single troop of chimpanzees has greater genetic variability than the entire human race. Approximately 70,000 years ago "the world-wide population of human beings skidded so sharply we were down to roughly a thousand reproductive adults,"[67] which explains our genetic uniformity. Humans retain so little genetic variability that the Adam and Eve myth is almost plausible. Yet we emphasize our differences.

Expressions of this propensity are not etched in stone. Intolerance or antipathy for differences are destructive manifestations, which can result in bigotry or an inability to endure those with different opinions. On the other hand, the obsession can appear affectionate. Some people make careers out of studying our differences because they find differences fascinating. But why? Whether obsessing on differences results in bigotry or an academic career, the underlying propensity is the same.

Different = Potential Threat

Why obsess on differences? As to human motivations, the answer is often fear. People who are different can frighten us. We may perceive people who think

---

66 "Part 2: Revolution in the Treatment of Disease." *The Gene: An Intimate History.* Ken Burns. PBS, April 14, 2020.

67 Robert Krulwich, "How Human Beings Almost Vanished From Earth In 70,000 B.C.," NPR, October 22, 2012, How Human Beings Almost Vanished From Earth In 70,000 B.C. : Krulwich Wonders... : NPR.

differently as threatening. Some people shut down and close their minds, others hate, and others conduct research. Still others exploit programmed human predispositions to drive people apart, market differences, and profit handsomely.

Genetic Programming Is Not Immutable

The totality of our being derives from biological inheritance and our experiences. We can learn. Yes, we are programmed to learn. But learning can eclipse programming. People jump out of airplanes, voluntarily! Overcoming programmed fear is possible.

Hyperpartisan culture exploits programmed fear. A culture of judgment and condemnation opens chasms of distrust, constricting pathways to understanding. Our innate response to judgment and condemnation is to point the finger right back with equal or greater judgment and condemnation, deepening chasms. But surrendering to psychological predispositions without inspection is lazy and undermines civilization.

PI, the industry with a substantial role in framing political discourse, nurtures this culture. PI profits from the cycle of escalation. Can we learn to create a different culture? I hope so. I disdain the culture of escalating partisanship for profit. I advocate for widespread disdain of this hyperpartisan culture as a step toward evolving functional democracy-consciousness.

19

Understanding Differences

H uman beings can understand one another.

In the context of hyperpartisanship and group identity, the apparently innocuous preceding sentence may be the most controversial idea in this entire book. Before analyzing, let's review the hyperpartisanship web core.

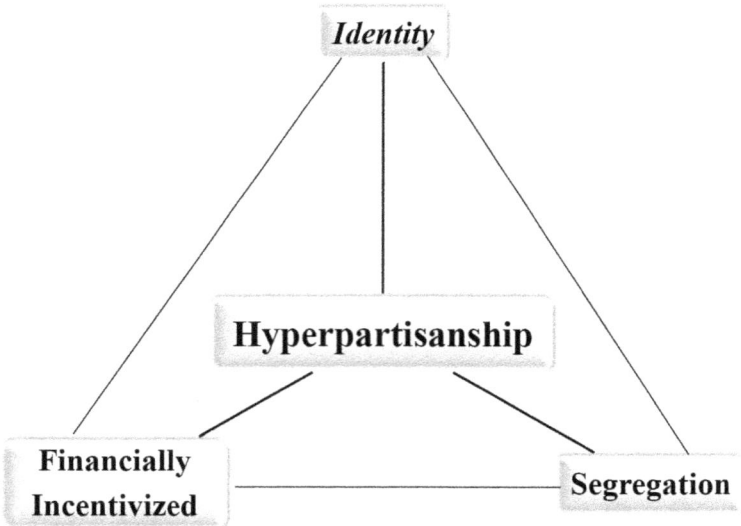

Figure 19.1: Hyperpartisanship Web Core Redux

Here, and in much of the remaining material, I focus on identity as it relates to hyperpartisanship. However, identity implicates segregation, and we'll also keep in mind that manipulating human psychology concerning identity is proven marketing strategy, i.e., it's financially incentivized. All relevant factors naturally operate and interact concurrently.

Identity and Understanding

The philosophy that only members of a group defined by race, gender, sexual orientation, culture, or ethnicity can understand other group members, and someone external to a group so defined couldn't possibly understand people within the group, is regressive, antithetical to democracy, and bolsters hyperpartisanship.

I preface my argument with four premises:

1. Biological inheritance exists on a continuum;
2. Human experience exists on a continuum;
3. The capacity for understanding is determined in part by biological inheritance and in part by experience, and the variance of that capacity exists on a continuum; and
4. "Understand" and "experience" are two different words with two different meanings.

Now let's revisit the introductory proposition: "Human beings can understand one another." The premises temper and provide context, but I stand by the concept.

Within the fourth premise is the rub. Can we understand people whose experience of life is different from our own? Are different life experiences an insurmountable barrier to understanding? Can we understand someone who has experienced life differently than we have? I think so, and the contrary position doesn't make sense either pragmatically or logically.

"You couldn't possibly understand me" undermines efforts to broaden progressive coalitions. As a former grassroots organizer, my success depended on my ability to make issues for which I was seeking support understandable. Approaching the public with a message intimating I wanted their support without their understanding would have severely reduced my efficacy.

Consider Empathy

The following definitions are functionally equivalent, but use different words, raising underlying concepts helpful to our analysis. Empathy is:

> the action of understanding, being aware of, being sensitive to, and vicariously experiencing the feelings, thoughts, and experience of another of either the past or present without having the feelings, thoughts, and experience fully communicated in an objectively explicit manner.[68]

Alternatively, empathy is "the ability to emotionally understand what other people feel, see things from their point of view, and imagine yourself in their place. Essentially, it is putting yourself in someone else's position and feeling what they are feeling."[69]

Both definitions begin with understanding. The first includes "experience," and the second uses "imagine." A synthesis of the definitions implies we can use our imagination to understand another's feelings about an experience without sharing the precise experience ourselves. "Understand" and "experience" are two different words with two different meanings.

There are differences in degree and kind. Experience provides deeper understanding. Do you understand yourself better than I do? I would hope so.

But if we can only be understood by those who have shared our exact experiences or experienced life precisely as we have, then we've rendered "empathy" meaningless, and it should be scrubbed from all human dictionaries because it inconveniences certain ideologies.

Art and Imagination

If "you couldn't possibly imagine what it's like to be me," I wonder if art is meant to be communicative. What's the point of a documentary about an-

---

68 "Empathy," Merriam-Webster, accessed November 15, 2022, https://www.merriam-webster.com/dictionary/empathy.

69 Kendra Cherry, "What is Empathy?" Verywell Mind, updated Feb. 22, 2023, https://www.verywellmind.com/what-is-empathy-2795562.

other culture if we couldn't possibly understand what it's like to be a member of that culture? Why write about members of historically disenfranchised groups who, through extraordinary effort, overcome institutional prejudice? What's the purpose of crafting a tale of warring factions whose humanity transcends their differences? Is it not implicit within such efforts that human beings are capable of understanding, at least at some fundamental level, that which they have not specifically experienced?

Through imagination, we connect to what appears distinct. Imagination allows us to penetrate what seems impervious. We imagine what is beyond our senses. Before enjoying your favorite piece of music, it was imagined. Before genes were discovered, a biological mechanism for inheritance was imagined. Before Einstein's theories were published and accepted, the hypothesized relationships between gravity and space-time were imagined. Are you more difficult to fathom than General Relativity?

We disparage imagination at our peril. Disparagement can curtail or closet the expression or practice of human talent. "You couldn't possibly imagine..."

Empathy Is Adaptive

There is a dark side to human imagination as well. Our imagination appears indiscriminately efficacious as applied to problems. We excel at creating them. Weapons of mass destruction and ingenuity applied to subjugation color our appreciation for human imagination.

We are both predators and prey. Our ability to empathize with both aids our survival. Empathizing with prey makes us more efficient hunters, and empathizing with predators makes us harder to trap. It is precisely this that instills in me the confidence to assert we can understand one another.

Explaining, Understanding, and Being Understood

A few paragraphs ago, I posed the rhetorical question: "Are you more difficult to fathom than General Relativity?" Taking it literally, you could answer: "Yes. I believe I'm more difficult to understand than Einstein's Theory of General Relativity." Then what's the point of explaining yourself? That question is not rhetorical.

Both desire to explain and desire to understand are easily distinguishable from desire to be understood. Within established hierarchies, explaining and understanding occupy dominant stations. The professor explains to the student because the professor possesses superior understanding of the subject matter. The entomologist understands the moth beneath the glass; the moth is understood by the scientist.

Most of us would rather be scientist than moth. Permitting oneself to be understood is scary. It feels threatening and makes us vulnerable. In the psychological context of threat and vulnerability, the phrase, "you couldn't possibly understand me," could be understood as, "I don't want you to understand me or even be able to understand me. I understand you. You can't understand me—and don't you forget it!"

Understanding the act of explaining oneself is complex. Let's assume for argument's sake we're capable of understanding ourselves. Complexities associated with explaining oneself absent self-knowledge is beyond the scope of this discussion.

In explaining oneself, we occupy both the dominant station as explainer and the subordinate station as one being understood. We are simultaneously scientist and butterfly if the point of explaining oneself is to be understood. But, if we can only be understood by those within our group, those who have experienced life as we have, what's the point of explaining our experience of life to those outside our group?

It only makes sense if the purpose of explaining is something other than being understood. For example, explaining oneself can be an opportunity to put your best foot forward—like a sales pitch. Someone applying for a job or campaigning for office might relish the opportunity to "explain" himself.

On the other hand, some people can't help themselves. They love explaining anything, including themselves. Not necessarily to be understood, but because during any explanation of anything, they get to hold the mike. Explaining puts them at center stage.

Another reason to explain oneself, other than for being understood, links to hyperpartisanship. Explanation can be weaponized. It's an opportunity for proselytizing. The subtext of such explanation is: "If you don't belong to my group, you are ignorant and incapable of understanding or imagining what it's like to be a member of my group." The tenor of explanation is lecture, but not the sort given by a professor to a class. Rather, the type eliciting the response, "don't lecture me." The explanation is combative. It's for combat rather than understanding.

Hyperpartisanship

The philosophy that only members of a group defined by race, gender, sexual orientation, ethnicity, or culture can understand other group members, and someone external to a group so defined couldn't possibly understand people within the group is regressive, antithetical to democracy, and reinforces hyperpartisanship.

The philosophy is segregating, and segregation is regressive. Understanding constructs bridges between tribes. Constructive understanding derives its efficacy from empathy, or a genuine desire to understand, as well as unreserved acquiescence to being understood. The sentiments "you can't understand me," or "you couldn't possibly imagine what it's like to be me," are walls.

Notice the feedback loop. Barriers to understanding segregate, and segregation creates barriers to understanding. Communication between segregated populations becomes more challenging as the depth and duration of segregation increases. As communication degenerates, understanding becomes more difficult. As barriers to understanding grow, segregation becomes more entrenched, and so on.

The zealous pursuit of common ground, in addition to an authentic disposition toward compromise, is essential to functional democracy. Where is the common ground between groups whose differences erect insurmountable barriers to understanding? How do you compromise with the incomprehensible?

Segregation, disdain for common ground, and contempt for compromise all support hyperpartisanship. In addition, the philosophy of group identity to an extent that understanding between groups disappears discharges civic responsibility. If understanding between members of groups with different experiences is impossible, why try?

You Couldn't Possibly Understand What It's Like to Be Me, but You Should Try Anyway

No offense, but while I live and breathe in a free and democratic society, I'm going to focus my time and energy in what I believe to be the realm of the possible. Thanks for the suggestion, though, and have a nice day.

—20—

Dealing with Differences

Democracy isn't instinctual. It's a grind.
—THE AUTHOR

There are three basic approaches for dealing with differences between groups and/or individuals. Differences can be moderated, dealt with as they are, or some combination thereof. I support the combination featuring an overwhelmingly disproportionate emphasis on dealing with our differences as they are, while applying an extremely light touch with respect to moderation.

Moderating Differences

Moderating differences means reducing our differences. It means becoming more similar to one another, especially with respect to our understanding of society. What is the purpose of society? What are optimal relationships between individuals, groups, cultures, private enterprises, the government, and society?

Let me state from the outset that one of my core principles is: Long-term survival of our species depends on diversity. Furthermore, of all diversities, diversity of thought is most essential. We *must* think differently from one another if we're to survive. Different thinking solves different problems. The mind solving space travel reasons distinctly from the mind shaping song. Each of us has vision interposed with blind spots. Different perspectives increase vision and reduce blind spots of the collective, as long as we listen to one another.

On the other hand, differences predominating without a collective understanding of their value undermines democratic societies, which in turn threatens long-term survival of our species. Maybe different times call for different measures. Maybe this time calls for moderating differences. Maybe not. I approach the subject with great trepidation.

As noted, we're a combination of our biological inheritance and experiences. If there's work to be done, it's through experience. I'm opposed to moderating human differences through biology, both for moral reasons and because it's a bad idea, which is to say it won't solve our problems or facilitate our long-term survival. However, I go through the exercise to illustrate.

Moderating Differences through Biology

Contemplating inherited differences in the context of hyperpartisanship without considering "race" is difficult. It has been asserted, and I have at times acceded to the assertion, that so long as racial differences are perceived, racism will persist. Therefore, racism can only be solved through biological integration. Only when every child on the planet is at least biracial can we make a dent in racism. Racial purity facilitates racism. Moderating racial differences through integration impedes racism—perhaps.

I have no problem with racial integration. People should get with whomever they wish. But before we consider racial integration as a strategy for moderating biological differences, we should take a gander at the science.

"Race" Is Not Genetic

"Social scientists have long understood race to be a social category invented to justify slavery and evolutionary biologists know the socially constructed racial categories do not align with our biological understanding of genetic variation."[70] As part of the Human Genome Project, scientists found "humans are 99.9 percent identical at the DNA level;" "there's no genetic basis

---

70 Theresa M Duello, Shawna Rivedal, Colton Wickland and Annika Weller, "Race and genetics versus 'race' in genetics: A systematic review of the use of African ancestry in genetic studies," *Evolution, Medicine, & Public Health* 9, no. 1, (2021), https://academic. oup.com/emph/article/9/1/232/6299389#eoab018-BOX1.

for race;" and there's "more genetic variation within a race than between them."[71] Furthermore, human genetic variation exists on a continuum, and "genetic isolation, sharp boundaries and distinct evolutionary lineages of 'races' do not exist." Finally, "there is no genetic basis for 'self-identification.' One may "self-identify one's cultural, religious and sexual identity, but not one's DNA."[72]

Furthermore, skin color, which is a primary trait of focus for racial discrimination, will continue to vary regardless of integration. Scientific evidence suggests skin tone significantly varied hundreds of thousands of years before humans migrated from Africa.[73] Even if all humans undertook a strategy whereby they chose mates in an effort to moderate differences in skin tone, the nature of biological inheritance would foil the effort. The human race will persist with a continuum of skin tone variability.

Some people concern themselves with genetic legacy, racial purity, and racial dilution. Those apprehensions are unfounded. A child receives half its chromosomes from each parent regardless of "race." Each parent contributes equally to the genetic makeup of the child. It's fifty-fifty regardless of "race." A parent's genetic legacy will survive within the child regardless of the "race" of the other parent. A white parent's genetic legacy will persist within the child to the same extent whether the other parent is white or black. A black parent's lineage will persist within the child to the same extent whether the other parent is black or white.

If you have a child, your child will be genetically half you regardless of the "race" of your partner. Your genes will survive throughout human existence to the same extent regardless of the "race" of your partner. As long as your children survive to have children and their children survive to have children and so on, your genetic legacy will persist regardless of the "race" of your partner or the "race" of your children's partners or the "race" of your grandchildren's partners and so on.

---

71 Duello, "Race & genetics."

72 Duello, "Race & genetics."

73 Colin Barras, "Gene study shows human skin tone has varied for 900,000 years," *New Scientist*, Oct. 12, 2017, https://www.newscientist.com/article/2150253-gene-study-shows-human-skin-tone-has-varied-for-900000-years/.

Racial purity and racial dilution are red herrings because "race" is not genetic. Genetic legacy of any individual is unaffected by "race" of partners. Pursuing racial integration and diversity from a genetic perspective makes no sense because there is as much genetic diversity within a "race" as there is across "races" and because "race" is not genetic. Pursuing racial purity, integration, or diversity from a genetic perspective is pointless.

Nevertheless, in a historically and contemporaneously racist society that obsesses on race and emphasizes racial differences, pursuing diversity and integration from a social perspective has merit. If the identity groups to which we belong constrain our capacity for understanding, then a more integrated society will function better.

In other words, although there is no genetic basis for "race," racism is alive and well because race endures as a social concept. Imposing arbitrary demarcation is human nature. Continuums defy consumption. Partitioning rainbows is irresistible. But surrendering to psychological predispositions without inspection is lazy and undermines comprehension.

It's Curious That Science Undermining Racial Constructs Is Not Regularly Publicized

I only remember hearing it twice, in two separate PBS documentaries. The first time, I thought, "what a tremendous strike against racism." Yet compared with the deluge of coverage implicating racism, science on "race" is barely whispered. It's as though relevant science is being suppressed.

Why is the most profound scientific discovery concerning the hottest of all hot-button issues broadcast with such diffidence? I can think of several possibilities. First, it's easy to understand why victims of racism would not want to hear that suddenly race doesn't exist. It's too convenient. Victimization based on an unsound construct is, nonetheless, victimization.

Second, if personal identity intimately and inexorably links to race, reticence to deem the construct as human fabrication is understandable. Science undermining racial constructs seems like an assault on personal identity.

Next, identity is not exclusive to natural persons. Race bequeaths institutional and organizational inertia. Government programs run in consideration of race. Federal agencies funding research "require scientists to report the race and ethnicity of their study populations."[74] Not-for-profits fundraise off the concept of race. Race-based content in media guarantees audiences. Race is money.

Maintaining the racial construct is financially incentivized. Economics of division discussed throughout this book apply to race. Racial segregation supports partisan and ideological segregation and vice versa. Thriving hyperpartisanship depends on divisions based on group identity. The science of "race" undermines the profitability of division. For PPs, the utility of science is political expedience. If scientific reality provides partisan advantage, then "we should listen to the science." On the other hand, if scientific reality interferes with partisan advantage, then not so much.

The issue is whether publicizing the science of "race" to a greater extent will lead to greater progress on the issue of race in our society. The fear is that if we allow scientific understanding to predominate, we might not devote proper resources to combating racism.

I think the fact that race is not genetic is a weapon in the arsenal against racism, and that fact should be more broadly publicized. However, the truth that racism and race as a social construct persist should be equally publicized. I give the human race credit for being able to simultaneously grasp all three concepts. I would teach all three concepts in schools. I would hope within a few decades, every human is aware race is purely a social construct.

Moderating Differences through Experience

Before beginning this section, I reemphasize the importance of thought diversity to human survival, and that moderating differences might be at the expense of problem-solving at the societal level. However, at this time in America, one could argue that our inability to deal with our differences weakens society, and that we could function better by moderating differences to some extent. If that's true, our best chance is through shared experiences.

While I support voluntary biological integration, I oppose in the strongest way possible government enforcement to that end. On the other hand,

---

74 Duello, "Race & genetics."

I don't oppose either government or private actions that enrich experiential commonality.

I also wish to point out that while I chose to focus on race in the previous section, experiential integration applies to partisan affiliation, political ideology, and anything else factionalizing society, including, but not limited to, race.

Enriching commonality of experience involves the experience and the individuals experiencing. I discuss each.

Human Experience Is Represented on Continuums

Choosing a suitable framework for analysis is arbitrary, but we must choose or submit to the infinite, for which we lack time. I pick the concept of "extreme." One end of the continuum includes extreme activities such as skydiving, surfing giant waves, climbing Everest, or going to war. The other end comprises activities such as walking on the beach, watching the sunset, or listening to music.

The less extreme activities are more inclusive. Almost anyone can participate in at least one of them. On the other hand, more extreme activities are less inclusive, but more impactful. Interactions are more substantial. More extreme experiences have greater integrating potential. And it's not just experiencing the activity, but preparation as well. More extreme experiences require planning and practice. They're more like collaborative projects.

The sweet spot for moderating differences through commonality of experience lies somewhere between.

Individuals Are Also Represented on Continuums

For individuals, I choose "age." We know what that continuum looks like. Working too near the margins of either end is a poor investment, but for different reasons. Without further elaboration, young adults or mid- to late teens through early to mid-twenties seem like optimal target populations: old enough to contribute to meaningful projects and young enough to realize societal dividends.

Greater incentivization for programs like AmeriCorps is a good investment. Providing free college tuition or trade apprenticeships for national service makes sense for several reasons. First, implementing programs improves the quality of American lives. Second, it enhances access to practical educational opportunities. Third, it provides commonality of quality experiences, breaching partisan factions. It's experientially integrating, and it makes America stronger.

Moderating Differences and Group Identification

The hyperpartisanship web core traps this central thesis. Our hyperpartisanship definition suggests it, and it deserves more than a subsection within a chapter. I raise it to touch home base, as a reminder of material previously covered, and to frame what is foreshadowed.

Temper group identification either by disempowering the group or by empowering individuals. Defunding parties disincentivizes partisan grouping and can be understood as an effort to moderate differences by discouraging group identification. Defunding a group reduces its power and undermines its lure and sway. Empower individuals through self-awareness and awareness of group dynamics, which will be explored more thoroughly in subsequent chapters.

But within the preceding discussion, I introduced a logical inconsistency. Did you catch it? If moderating differences means reducing our differences, or becoming more like one another, discouraging group identification seems to be at cross-purposes.

Our definition of hyperpartisanship implies groups have conforming impacts on their members. Through group identification, members adopt similar points of view. Differences within a group are moderated through conforming pressures associated with group dynamics.

Nonetheless, I continue to assert that discouraging group identification moderates our differences. But it's not moderation in quantity. It's moderation of intensity and effect.

Without identity groups, the U.S. has 350 million categories—one for each person. Organizing into twenty distinct groups reduces the number of categories. In a sense, we've moderated the quantity of our differences. Twenty is less than 350 million.

But each of the twenty categories is more potent than a single individual.

By reducing the number of categories or organizing according to identity, we empower our differences. Group identity intensifies our differences.

Dealing with Our Differences

While experiential integration might have some moderating effect on our differences, the real work is in learning to deal with each other, especially those outside our groups. Without relitigating hypothetical concepts surrounding understanding those whose experience of life is different than our own, as a pragmatic matter, we must achieve a functional understanding of one another. Functional democracy requires a pragmatic understanding of our citizen colleagues.

We achieve pragmatic understanding by looking at society as a whole in concert with individual motivation. At the societal level, the team of misfits is a useful metaphor. We've all seen movies where the team of misfits wins the day because each misfit brings some unique quality to the ultimately collaborative effort.

Human diversity, especially thought diversity, is essential to human survival. But we are wired to perceive differences as potentially threatening, and threats provoke fight or flight. Our instinctual reaction to contrary opinion is anger or disengagement.

Imagine yourself confronted with contrary opinion. Before responding, think to yourself, "one of my societal teammates has a different opinion than me. My society is strengthened through such diversity. I'm lucky to be on a team where each member brings unique perspective, even if I strongly disagree with that perspective in the moment." Then respond. Feel free to disagree with your teammate. Is anger or the desire to disengage still present?[75]

At the risk of sinking into pure sap, unifying fundamentals transcend differences. To these commonalities, we *should* surrender. We all wish our lives to have meaning and purpose. Everyone wants to love and to feel loved. Everyone desires some level of financial success or independence. Everyone

---

75 I understand the prescribed approach will prove challenging when one of your teammates attempts violence or infringes upon your civil rights. I think we're capable of distinguishing those situations. Sometimes surrendering to our instincts makes perfect sense.

wants fair treatment. Everyone desires respect. We can understand that without purpose, life is more difficult to endure. Absence of love feels empty. Being treated unfairly or disrespected hurts and causes resentment and anger.

So what if our opinions differ? Our ability to disagree with one another in a civilized fashion is essential to our persistence. We must collaborate with people who think differently from us. Let's understand that seeing things differently makes us more formidable in total, so long as we maintain our pragmatic understanding of one another. Unifying fundamentals transcend our differences, and our differences contribute to team strength.

Empathetic understanding of differences we're programmed through evolution to perceive as potentially threatening is challenging. It's a struggle with our innate disposition for rational control over ourselves. Permitting oneself to be understood is even more challenging, by orders of magnitude. It's scary. It requires courage, as does progress.

—21—

Tribalism

People are wonderful. I love individuals. I hate groups of people. I hate a group of people with a "common purpose." 'Cause pretty soon they have little hats, and armbands, and fight songs, and a list of people they're going to visit at 3:00 a.m. So, I dislike and despise groups of people, but I love individuals. Every person you look at; you can see the universe in their eyes, if you're really looking.

—GEORGE CARLIN

The term "tribalism" as used in media will be familiar to those who follow politics on even a cursory level. In the context of hyperpartisanship, we're talking about the red and blue tribes. Tribal concerns not necessarily aligned with societal interests determine political positions and decisions. Tribal positioning can be interpreted as strategy to confound the other tribe.

Media commentators use the term as explanation. The explanation is tribalism. The reason so-and-so is taking that position or behaving that way is tribalism. If you follow politics, tribalism explains an awful lot.

However, there's little if any discussion of how partisan tribalism works. We live in a tribal world. That's just the way it is. But, if tribalism causes dysfunction, it should be rigorously explored. It shouldn't be accepted as premise and offered as explanation without investigation.

Ancestral Tribalism

Humans evolved in part under the social structure of tribes.[76] Tribes were small groups of extended kin with a common ancestor. Tribal life must have been adaptive. Living in a cooperative enhanced chances of survival. Evolution favors individuals adapted for the social requirements of life in small groups.

Good fortune aside, the more efficiently a tribe functioned, the more likely the tribe, along with its members, survived. Efficient functioning requires sensible decision-making. Decision-making can be authoritarian and spontaneous or democratic and deliberative. Authoritarian rulers in small groups can be open to suggestions or be bloody tyrants. Irrespective of decision-making processes, descendants of tribes that functioned efficiently walk the Earth today.

Implicit in tribal survival is acquiescence of individual members to tribal supremacy. Psychological effects, emotional responses, and observable behaviors provoked by the submission of individuals to the will of the group vary according to individual and group. Recorded history and fiction are replete with accounts of individuals who had a really hard time with the concept. The stories typically end tragically.

Tribes would have had to deal with such individuals. Some of them would have been smart enough, powerful enough, or fierce enough to take over the tribe. Others would have submitted to some form of tribal justice or bullying. Justice would have been a function of tribal character and/or the nature of the transgression. Regardless of sentencing, its consideration and imposition would've had an intimate quality. It would have been discussed, if at all, and carried out, face-to-face.

Partisan Tribes

If tribalism is as destructive as its media reputation suggests, examining the modern partisan tribe (PT) is compulsory. What exactly are *tribes* in the

76 Cory J. Clark, Brittany S. Liu, & Peter H. Ditto, "Tribalism Is Human Nature," *Sage Journals*, Aug. 20, 2019, https://journals.sagepub.com/doi/10.1177/0963721419862289.

context of hyperpartisanship? Do they truly exist? If so, what's their membership? How do they function? What is their function? Ironically, the last question might be easiest to answer, but we need to go through the exercise of answering, or at least outlining parameters by which we might answer the earlier questions to shed light on it.

I suggested we're talking about red and blue tribes. In other words, PTs are bound by partisan affiliation or political ideology rather than familial relation—partisanship, not kinship. But that doesn't define membership. For example, does the red tribe consist of all registered Republicans? Is it the Republican base? Is it exclusive to professionals and activists? How fluid is membership? Are independents who tend to vote Republican included?

No doubt PTs are substantially larger than ancestral tribes. Registered voters number in the tens of millions. If we just count professionals and activists, we're still talking tens of thousands. Think of how many people attend or take part in national conventions and campaigns. Regardless of inclusion parameters, size and geographic distribution matter.

I think of PT and party membership as aligning closely. But precise rank-and-file membership doesn't interest me. Who are the tribal leaders? How is tribal justice carried out? How do PTs function, and what's the relationship between PT function and societal dysfunction?

Group Dynamics

PTs are a type of group. Group dynamics have been studied extensively. It's well documented that in addition to quenching yearnings for identity and self-esteem, groups incubate bigotries.[77]

Prejudices are not benign, and the extent to which group members become invested in championing the group seems dystopian. One dynamic suggests groups prefer gaining relative advantage over other groups over obtaining a more substantial absolute gain for themselves.[78] Groups undermine the

---

77 For a synopsis, see Scott Plous, "The Psychology of Prejudice: An Overview," accessed Nov. 11, 2022, https://secure.understandingprejudice.org/apa/english/index.htm.

78 Plous, "Prejudice," p.7.

interests of other groups at the expense of their own advancement.

This may seem like cutting off one's nose to spite one's face. But from the perspective of ancestral tribalism, it's rational. If tribes in proximity compete for the same resources, hurting the other tribe at the expense of your own may prove beneficial in the long run. It may be possible to run the other tribe off, thereby securing a more promising future. War appears more desirable than peace. But surrendering to psychological predispositions evolved during our tribal existences without inspection undermines civilization.

Out-Group Homogeneity Effect

The "out-group homogeneity effect" (OHE) is so broadly relevant it must be considered before going ahead. OHE suggests people perceive members of their own groups as individuals and diverse, whereas members of other groups appear indistinguishable and homogenous. "As a result, out-group members are at risk of being seen as interchangeable or expendable, and they are more likely to be stereotyped."[79] OHE is strongest when groups are naturally occurring, enduring, and large.

Inferring that the intensity of group bigotries correlates with the extent to which members identify with the group and depend upon the group for self-esteem is reasonable. But it doesn't take much. Experiments show when complete strangers divide into groups based on trivial distinctions like a coin flip, group-related prejudices develop within minutes.[80]

Although the entire canon of group dynamics may apply, unique features of PTs focus our inquiry and illuminate hyperpartisan dynamics.

Partisan Tribalism

The breadth of PTs as well as processes for establishing PT orthodoxy and adjudicating PT law are of particular interest.

---

79 Plous, "Prejudice," p.6.

80 Plous, "Prejudice," p.7.

Size Matters

Large groups differ from small groups in at least two significant ways. Small groups foster intense relationships among group members but tend to be unstable.[81] As group size increases, the intensity of relationships between members decreases, but the groups become more durable. Less passionate relationships aren't as likely to detonate or devastate the entire group. Large groups aren't prone to single-point failure.

The size of PTs creates stability. If a tribal member becomes disillusioned and decides to move on, she might be missed by some, but the tribe will carry on without her. Untenable working relationships between tribal members may require restructuring or banishment, but the tribe will persist.

So, PTs are large and enduring. They're also naturally occurring. They're not decided by a coin flip in a laboratory experiment. That's three for three for qualities maximizing OHE. No wonder group bigotries shape our politics.

The size and breadth of PTs in conjunction with media evolution is transformative. Former Speaker of the House Tip O'Neill famously proclaimed, "all politics is local." The phrase seems quaint and vestigial. PTs are national, with international ideological underpinnings. Our politics are becoming less local and more national.

Nationalizing Politics via Partisan Tribalism Corrodes Society and Undermines Democracy by Transferring Power from People to PI

National and international tribes cannot deliberate intimately. Groups of that magnitude connect through media. Tribal dogma is established through media. Tribal law adjudicates through media. But media is fundamentally conflicted, and media access is not egalitarian.

We've discussed financial incentivization of conflict and extremism in Part I. Dramatic conflict sells. Extreme content amasses clicks. Influencers who understand the business hog media access.

---

81 "Group Dynamics and Behavior," University of Minnesota Libraries Publishing, accessed Nov. 26, 2022, https://open.lib.umn.edu/sociology/chapter/6-2-group-dynamics-and-behavior/.

Political influencers are financially incentivized toward partisanship. Tribal dogma is established through media outlets profiting from conflict. Financial inducements bias gatekeepers of tribal morality toward conflict and fundamentalism. Fundamentalism is a winner. Fundamentalist dogma precipitates conflict. The more power conferred upon fundamentally conflicted leaders, the more tribalism, partisan segregation, and hyperpartisanship.

Venues marketing extreme content adjudicate tribal law. Unforgiving decisions and punitive sentencing attract large crowds. Anonymity facilitates cruelty.

Anonymity Magnifies Conflict and Extremism

Anonymity provides the fabric for conversation and resolution on the internet. The consequences of anonymity in modern society are colossal.

Two layers of anonymity besiege PT dynamics. First, PTs are too large to know everyone. There's no intimacy. Everything is broadcast. Public excoriation and cancellation are in vogue for sentencing. You don't get to face your accuser.

Second, through the internet, tribes deliberate anonymously. Internet anonymity unleashes closeted repulsiveness. Trolls are not simple pranksters. They're serial stalkers of decency. They connect to annihilate. Their devastation goes unpunished because the formal legal framework doesn't recognize their pathology as criminal, and anonymity insulates them from informal community justice. Forget facing your accuser. You don't even get to know his name.

Tribal procedure and structure are obscured. Who are the chiefs? Are they political bosses, party leaders, or do they host websites and talk shows? What political system do PTs use? Is it authoritarian or democratic? Do twitterati (Xers?) fairly represent the tribal electorate? What is the decision-making process? What are the sentencing guidelines for violating tribal law, and what is the tribal law? Apparently, Democratic candidates using Republican talking points is disgraceful.

Does PT law serve tribal members or leaders? Does orthodoxy result from principle or product differentiation? What is the relationship between tribal law and the law of the land? Does PT law make treating with neighboring tribes easier, or does it demonize the other and entrench fiefdoms?

What is the point of public excoriation? Is it deterrent? Is it justice? Is it good for ratings? Does it advance a political agenda? Or is it about power?

Solidarity, i.e., In-Group Homogeneity

National tribalism not only precipitates OHE but also engenders actual in-group homogeneity of thought and opinion. Local politics ensure the survival of a heterogeneous patchwork of priorities. Within states and throughout the country, local differences plainly manifest in political parties. But local intra-party heterogeneity inconveniences national narratives, national media, and national tribal warfare, as well as fundraising based on national politics.

Enter tribal bullying. The right uses the acronym, RINO, standing for "Republican in name only." While the acronym has yet to manifest on the left, the sentiment exists. "Stop using Republican talking points" means "don't be a Democrat in name only (DINO)."

Tribal bullying is in-group coercion to conform. PT bullying establishes national orthodoxy. National standards for partisan dogma ensure greater product differentiation. Being more like members of your tribe means being less like members of the other tribe. "We all have to stick together," means we all must disconnect from the other tribe. Nationalized partisan dogma entrenches divides between tribes.

RINOs and DINOs are moderates or independent thinkers. They're people who share viewpoints with those outside their group. They're individuals who resist in-group coercion to conform. So, one goal of bullying by PT leaders is to eliminate or render impotent moderates and independent thinkers.

Eliminating moderates and independent thinkers in legislative bodies devastates democracy. Moderates and independent thinkers are bridge-builders. They're human expressions of common ground. They instinctively seek compromise.

Nationalizing Politics through PTs Benefits the National Business of Partisanship while Demeaning Local Politics

Top-down conforming tribalism builds resentment. In the political party chapter, I asked: "When you find yourself squeezed into a position not of your making, do you blame yourself, or does resentment kindle? How do you handle resentment? Do you identify its source? Are you more likely to blame your tribe for coercion or condemn the other?"

PPs inspire and manage resentment. They want you to blame the other.

Registering as Independent or Unaffiliated Is a Rational Response to National Partisan Tribalism

Unaffiliated voters are trending upward and, in some states, constitute the largest voting bloc, outnumbering registered Republicans or Democrats.[82] So, as moderates and independents disappear from Congress, political spending increases, and parties still control election processes, the electorate is unaffiliating. More money and more power are concentrating in entities that are becoming less representative. Will the trend continue unabated, or if enough of us unaffiliate can we achieve functional accord? My optimism is tempered by parties amassing more wealth despite the unaffiliating trend.

Individuality, Conformity, and Polarization

For perspective, I explore "team player." From the standpoint of PTs, RINOs and DINOs are not team players. They betray their teams, or at least the fundamentalist wings of their teams, to cut deals. You could say they put their individualism before their parties. They're sell-outs. They're splitters.

But from the perspective of the country as a whole, they're essential to the team. Progress depends on individuals who sell out their parties. So, while PI and PTs profit from in-group conformity, our country benefits from individuals who resist conforming pressures of partisan bullying. We need more RINOs and DINOs. Free and democratic societies benefit from independent thinkers. In other words, putting country before party requires putting individuality before party, or thinking for yourself. There's no "I" in team, but "democratic society" has a couple.

---

82 Rhonda Colvin, "Side effect of divisive politics? Unaffiliated voter numbers rise," *The Washington Post*, Oct. 24, 2022, https://www.washingtonpost.com/elections/2022/10/24/rise-of-independent-voters/.

Relationships among Individuality, Group Conformity, and Political Polarization Are Paradoxical

Group conformity worsens societal division by eliminating or shackling individuals who would bridge divides. Diversity of thinking by individuals and resistance to group-conforming pressures alleviate polarity. Organizing individuals into conforming groups provides polarizing structure for our differences. Structuring our differences inhibits collaboration. Group thought conformity is polarizing, whereas diversity of thinking is uniting.

Let's not forget ECs. OHE and in-group conformity blossom in such environments. Free from contrary opinion, ECs provide spaces where group orthodoxy and bigotries can safely incubate. ECs are simply a specific type of segregation. Segregation according to thought and opinion facilitates in-group conformity and exacerbates polarization.

Since freedom of thought is the most fundamental freedom, thinking for oneself is the most fundamental responsibility democracy requires. It's not voting. Voting is trivial compared with thinking. Responsible voting requires thinking.

Tribalism at its most fundamental subverts individuality of thought.

Tribal Culture and Cultural Tribalism

Putting the interests of small intimate groups such as family units before country is understandable. But at some point, as groups become larger and less intimate, tribal instinct loses utility and contributes to dysfunction. In other words, surrendering to psychological predispositions that evolved during our tribal existence without inspection in a modern society is lazy and undermines democracy.

Melting Pot versus Cultural Appropriation

Modern nations must transcend tribalism to succeed. America as a melting pot was an aspirational interpretation seeming to moderate cultural or ethnic tribalism. I say aspirational, because although there was some melting, there has also been a great deal of segregation.

More importantly, I used past tense. It's no longer clear that melting-pot paradigm is aspired to. The concept of "cultural appropriation" exemplifies an alternative aspiration that is, at least in its application, inapposite to melting pot. The alternative paradigm seeks to intensify ethnic or cultural tribalism.

First, cultural appropriation is popularly misunderstood. "Cultural appropriation takes place when members of a majority group adopt cultural elements of a minority group in an *exploitative, disrespectful,* or *stereotypical* way"[83] (emphasis added). However, from its popular application, cultural appropriation takes place any time members of a dominant group adopt cultural elements from a historically disenfranchised group, whether or not it's exploitative, disrespectful, or stereotypical.

The determination as to whether the adoption is exploitative, disrespectful, or stereotypical resides with members of the minority group or with a minority faction within the minority group. This raises a couple of issues.

First, minority groups aren't monolithic. Unanimity as to whether certain acts constitute cultural appropriation or whether cultural appropriation is something to be concerned about doesn't exist. This dynamic creates an opportunity for tribal bullies to exert coercive conforming pressures in the form of derisive labeling akin to RINOs and DINOS. The labels imply nonconforming members of an ethnic or cultural minority lose group status. They're sellouts. They're sucking up to the man.

A second issue involves good faith. This is the meta-discussion linking cultural tribalism with hyperpartisanship and a genuine desire for functional democracy. The following are good-faith premises for this good-faith exploration:

1. A genuine desire to reduce that which is exploitative, disrespectful, or engenders harmful stereotypes;
2. A genuine desire for equal treatment under the law and equal opportunity for all members of society, regardless of group or individual identity; and
3. A genuine desire for America to succeed.

83 The Editors of Encyclopaedia Britannica, "What is Cultural Appropriation," Britannica, accessed Dec. 2, 2022, https://www.britannica.com/story/what-is-cultural-appropriation.

I see no conflict between the premises. The question is: How do we get there? The sub-question is: What role does tribalism play in the pursuit of our mutual goals? Here, I use the concept of cultural appropriation to explore the relationship between cultural tribalism and the pursuit of our mutual goals. While none of us can identify with certainty the precise evolutionary pathway maximizing our chances for success, we can all take part in the discussion. That's democracy.

The concepts of integration and segregation are central. I've argued throughout that segregation undermines functionality. However, I should describe or contextualize integration.

I'll start with what I *don't* mean. I don't mean every single residential block, every single business, school, or government agency must precisely reflect demographic proportionality according to race, gender, sexual orientation, religious affiliation, partisan or ideological affiliation, ethnicity, or cultural or socioeconomic background of our nation as a whole or for an individual state or city. Even if integration with such precision is achievable, with every newborn, immigrant, and every religious, political, or ideological conversion, the equation would change. Precise proportional integration requires a continuous game of musical chairs. It's silly and unnecessary.

Also, precise proportional integration isn't possible without government enforcement. There are nuances. National service provides choice and transitory integrating opportunities. Understanding the pitfalls of government-enforced integration requires examining the purposes of integration in context of tribalism, group dynamics, and hyperpartisanship.

OHE suggests members of an insular group perceive out-group members as indistinguishable and homogenous, which engenders harmful stereotypes, setting the stage for exploitation and disrespect. Group insularity creates psychological barriers interfering with meaningful comprehension of out-group members.

The Goal of Integration Is to Dissolve Psychological Barriers to Permit Understanding Out-Group Members as Individuals

Forcing people hardens psychological barriers. Going through the motions of enforced integration while maintaining a private bigotry isn't helpful.

Without choice, individuals could double down on hateful psychology or segregate from reality.

We should mind our ambitions, both with respect to choice and result. Let's deal with result first. In the previous chapter, I raised the concept of functional or pragmatic understanding. I advocate for thinking similarly of integration. We need pragmatic integration—integration to an extent that helps us understand individual character is independent of group identity, i.e., character and group identity are independent traits.

Characters of individuals in any group exist on a continuum. I carve out exceptions for extremists and ideological or religious fundamentalists who may possess personality flaws, placing them on the fringes of the character continuum. We examined vulnerabilities to radicalization in the extremism chapter, and we'll explore ideological fundamentalism in the ensuing chapter.[84] Extremists and fundamentalists aside, functional or pragmatic integration facilitates understanding character cannot be divined from group identity.

Now let's revisit integration and choice. I have no idea where Goldilocks is on this one, but I know she is somewhere between strict enforcement and laissez-faire. I support national service programs, such as AmeriCorps, that encourage and provide opportunities for integration across tribal boundaries. But government can only do so much. Our culture must inspire functional integration. The message from popular culture must be that the character of an individual cannot be divined from group identity. I'm not sure we're hearing that at this time.

Let's get back to cultural appropriation.

Is Concern with Cultural Appropriation Functionally Integrating, or Does It Reinforce Tribal Boundaries That Interfere with Our Desire or Capacity to Understand That Group Identity Does Not Define Character?

Intuitively, obsessing on cultural appropriation seems segregating. On the other hand, using cultural elements of traditionally disenfranchised or his-

---

84 With respect to extremists and fundamentalists, I would bifurcate the analysis according to leaders and followers. The leaders are at the exploiter fringe of the continuum and the followers at the exploitable fringe.

torically subjugated groups in exploitative, disrespectful, or harmfully stereotypical ways alienates minority groups. So, it can be argued that either the act of cultural appropriation or obsessing over cultural appropriation is segregating.

Most of us who accept the stated good-faith premises believe voluntary sharing and mutual exchange between cultures is desirable. In other words, employing elements from any and all cultures in ways not exploitative, disrespectful, or harmfully stereotypical is integrating. However, in context of tribalism and group identity, even voluntary sharing and mutual exchange can be problematic.

This brings us back to our initial questions about establishment of tribal dogma and adjudication of tribal law. Who decides for an entire culture what is exploitative, disrespectful, or harmfully stereotypical? What is the decision-making process for a globe-spanning cultural tribe? How are differences among tribal members over sharing cultural elements resolved? Is unanimity required to endorse sharing? If a single cultural member feels disrespected, has cultural appropriation occurred?

In context of these unresolved questions, let's revisit adjudication through media. Which story is likely to garner more clicks and secure higher ratings: a piece alleging exploitation, or one concluding no harm was done? I acknowledge cultural appropriation. But we also must acknowledge accusation is financially incentivized for media. "There's nothing to see here," is not a good catchphrase for a business profiting from people coming to see something.

Nation-States as Tribes

Near the beginning of the previous section, I stated, "modern nations must transcend tribalism to succeed." But isn't an element of tribalism embedded within nation-states? Have you ever watched the Olympics or World Cup? Face-painting, flag-waving, and singing national songs seem tribal.

Many nation-states consist of people of similar cultures and ethnicities. Aren't Italian culture and the nation-state of Italy linked?

However, with globalization, most nations, like America, are becoming less ethnically homogeneous. The world *is* a melting pot.

Let's revisit our good-faith premises, but alter the last in favor of humanity rather than the nation-state of America:

1. A genuine desire to reduce that which is exploitative, disrespectful, or engenders harmful stereotypes;
2. A genuine desire for equal treatment under the law and equal opportunity for all members of society, regardless of group or individual identity; and
3. A genuine desire for humanity to succeed.

If nation-states are like tribes, then for humanity to succeed, the modern world must transcend nation-states. Intellectually, I could get behind that idea. Accounting for human suffering associated with genocides, war, and subjugation for profit unavoidably implicates nation-states.

Let's apply the same functional society logic to global humanity as we applied to America. I indicated support for government programs like AmeriCorps and a popular culture facilitating and encouraging functional integration across tribal boundaries.

But if the world map of nation-states delineates boundaries, don't tribes based on political ideology, culture, ethnicity, gender, or group identity integrate across those boundaries? Isn't the same tribalism destabilizing constitutionally democratic nation-states through segregation in some respects also integrating on a global scale? So, from the perspective of the nation-state, tribalism is segregating, but from a global perspective, tribalism seems to be integrating.

"End of days" mythology aside, I see value in aspiring to world government. Isolation from the vagaries of global ecology and economy is childish. Resources and systems that can either curtail or prolong humanity are global. Global governance seems harmonious with reality and human persistence.

But realizing aspirations requires more than aspiration. There's work to be done. Humanity isn't ready to abandon nation-states.

Time Frame Contextualization

Our earliest human relatives walked the Earth some six million years ago and we, *Homo sapiens*, emerged between 550,000 to 750,000 years ago.[85] Human agriculture began around 10,000 B.C.E.[86] and the first human civilizations appeared around 4,000 B.C.E.[87] Ancient Greeks created the first democracy around the fifth century B.C.E.,[88] and nation-states came into being some 300 years ago in medieval Europe.[89] So the combination of regional organizational units called "nation-states" and the political framework of self-governance occurred less than 300 years ago.

Consider the human time frame. If *Homo sapiens* came to be 550,000 years ago, 300 years represents .0005 or .05 percent of our existence. If the average human lifespan is seventy-five years, .05 percent is .04 years old. That's half a month or two weeks. A two-week old is considered newborn.

With respect to nation-state democracies, humanity is in the early stages of its infancy. Even if we consider the beginning of our transition away from ancestral tribalism to be at the dawn of agriculture or some 12,000 years ago, 98 percent of our existence and evolution occurred prior. We live in a constitutional republic, but our evolutionary wiring is tribal. However, surrendering to psychological predispositions evolved during our tribal

---

85 Brian Handwerk, "An Evolutionary Timeline of Homo Sapiens," *Smithsonian Magazine*, Feb. 2, 2021, https://www.smithsonianmag.com/science-nature/essential-timeline-understanding-evolution-homo-sapiens-180976807/.

86 National Geographic Society, "The Development of Agriculture," *National Geographic*, accessed Dec. 7, 2022, https://education.nationalgeographic.org/resource/development-agriculture.

87 Lesley Kennedy, "The 6 Earliest Human Civilizations," History, Aug. 9, 2022, https://www.history.com/news/first-earliest-human-civilizations.

88 National Geographic Society, "Democracy (Ancient Greece)," *National Geographic*, accessed Dec. 7, 2022, https://education.nationalgeographic.org/resource/democracy-ancient-greece#:~:text=The first known democracy in the world was, to take an active part in the government.

89 William R. Bowen, "The Rise of the Nation-State," Owlcation, Jul. 19, 2022, https://owlcation.com/humanities/nation-state.

existences without inspection is lazy and undermines constitutionally democratic nation-states.

We're born into a world dominated by nation-states with a biology preparing us for pre-nation-state, pre-democracy tribalism. Before writing this section, I took the nation-state for granted. Most of us do. It's just the way things are.

Persisting within Nation-State Democracies with Ancestral Tribalism Hardwired into Our Psychology

We should do a better job of preparing for life in the modern world. Functional or pragmatic understanding of the relationship between our biological evolution and our current existence within the social framework of constitutional democracy helps us prepare.

Elements of functional understanding include:

1. An understanding that our inherited tribal psychology results from the majority of our evolution occurring under ancestral tribal conditions;
2. A functional understanding of nation-states on a planet of eight billion people;
3. A pragmatic understanding of constitutional democracy; and
4. The relationships between hardwired tribal psychology, constitutional democracy, and nation-states.

Currently, I see no evidence of such understanding at the societal level, in media, among government or private sector leaders, or among even a small percentage of people. I'm pessimistic about the epoch of constitutionally democratic nation-states persisting without functional understanding.

Let's imagine abandoning nation-states and skipping to the next stage of human organization. We can attempt higher or lower levels of organization. The highest level is world government and the lowest is anarchy. I don't think anarchy enhances human survival or works on a planet of eight billion people.

If we're to abandon nation-states, the next logical step is world governance. Earlier, I indicated I see value in aspiring to a world government. First, I'm not interested in undemocratic world governance. If humanity adopts world governance, it must be constitutional democracy.

Second, local sovereignty must endure. Imagine each nation-state as a state within a global republic–a type of global federalism, i.e., a system of shared and exclusive powers between the central global government and individual nation-states. I can't help thinking like an American.

Whether or not every nation-state within a global government must themselves be constitutional democracies is an interesting question not requiring immediate resolution. Nonetheless, a global democratic republic containing autocratic theocracies and monarchies seems unworkable. I would insert a supremacy clause into a global constitution containing a global bill of rights with free speech, freedom of and from religion, due process, equal protection, etc.

The question, as always, is: How do we get there? I see two basic pathways. Either existing nation-states accede, or we first abolish nation-states to form a new world government.

Imagining global democracy will organically arise from the ashes of chaos caused by the collapse of nation-states is farfetched. On a planet of Earth's dimensions and population, dystopian anarchy would ensue. The idea of choosing provisional dystopia to achieve a superior type of humane organizational structure could inspire a fascinating academic discussion or might make for a compelling novel, but in reality, most humans would oppose such nonsense.

What does democracy mean without nation-states on a planet of eight billion people with Earth's dimensions? Is democracy without government workable in large societies? How is democracy without government enforced? Do you truly believe human exploitation will be reduced without nation-states? How about street justice? Can eight billion people be fed without a system? What system would you prefer to constitutional democracy?

At this point in time, our best chance of:

1. reducing exploitation, disrespect, and harmful stereotyping of the traditionally disenfranchised;
2. realizing equal treatment under the law and equal opportunity for all

members of society regardless of group or individual identity; and

3. giving humanity its best chance to succeed,

is through constitutionally democratic nation-states.

Succeeding constitutional democracies are in humanity's best interest. In other words, for sake of human rights and longevity, as well as some level of cultural persistence, America needs to succeed. Tribalism weakens constitutional democracies like America.

In sum, we increase the odds of constitutional democracies surviving in the context of modern tribalism by:

1. Achieving a functional understanding of the relationships between hardwired tribal psychology, constitutional democracy, and nation-states, which includes a pragmatic understanding of democracy;
2. Localizing politics to form a heterogeneous patchwork of priorities, thereby undermining conforming pressures associated with national and international partisan tribalism;
3. Functionally integrating across tribal boundaries to an extent that the notion that the character of an individual can be divined from group identity is taken as seriously as the notion that the world is flat;
4. Supporting government programs that encourage and provide opportunities for functional integration across tribal boundaries;
5. Glamorizing through pop culture that the character of an individual cannot be divined from group identity;
6. Glamorizing voluntary sharing and mutual exchange between cultures;
7. Glamorizing compromise; and
8. Cherishing and nurturing individual identity preferentially over group identity.

Wicked Intention and Bad Faith

The preceding list falls under the heading of enhancing viability of constitutional democracies. But the script could be flipped to provide a recipe for sabotage. I addressed this in Chapter 15, "Ancillary Beneficiaries to 'Dysfunctional' Hyperpartisanship." Our enemies understand tribalism as a weapon to be used against us. While most Americans enlisting in PTs do so without wicked intention, malicious manipulations by foreign hackers to exacerbate tribal conflict have been documented.[90]

But you can't assign the universe of malicious exploitation to foreigners. I'm sure basic human yearnings for identity and self-esteem drive substantial tribal membership. I'm certain some view PTs as organizational tools to achieve progress for their group. Even most sketchy tribal influencers using media to chase clicks or ratings do so to line their pockets rather than out of traitorous intent. However, those within our midst who aspire to undermine our constitutional democracy in pursuit of radical ambition understand the value of tribalism as profoundly as our foreign enemies. Not everyone promoting group identity as virtue does so in good faith.

Pragmatic Understanding of Democracy

Basically, TBD. We haven't figured it out yet. The honeymoon phase of democracy, if there ever was one, is over. But divorce is not an option. We have to figure it out.

I can tell you what it isn't. Self-government does not mean all people can have everything they want whenever they want it. Notice the vexing tautology. Because democracy implicates majority rule, all the people cannot get everything they want. That's why we vote.

Although any natural-born citizen can be president, everyone cannot. I'm sorry. Maybe your parents told you that you could be whatever you want if you put your mind to it. They wanted you to give it your best. They told you this because they loved you.

---

90 Lawrence Andrea, "Foreign actors seeking to sow divisions by targeting Native American populations, cyber intelligence firms says," *Milwaukee Journal Sentinel*, Aug. 27, 2020, https://www.jsonline.com/story/news/politics/elections/2020/08/27/election-trolls-targeting-native-populations-cyber-group-says/5481408002/?; Dan De Luce, "Counterintelligence chief warns of threat to democracy from foreign hackers, spies," NBC News, Feb. 10, 2020, https://www.nbcnews.com/politics/national-security/u-s-counterintel-chief-warns-threat-democracy-foreign-hackers-spies-n1134476; Steve Zurier, "Hackers, nation-states target US black community to commit fraud, sow division," SC Media, Mar. 3, 2021, https://www.scmagazine.com/news/cybercrime/hackers-nation-states-target-us-black-community-to-commit-fraud-sow-division.

Love has a place in a healthy society. Some would love to proclaim for all the world to hear that we should govern with love. Doesn't that sound divine? Oh, he's so wonderful for proclaiming we should govern with love.

Democracy is relational. You may love the person you are in a relationship with, but you don't get to have everything you want whenever you want it. You don't get to win every time, unless the relationship is unequal and abusive. Healthy relationships require compromise. Tribalism makes compromise more difficult. Relationships, including democracy, are hard work. Tribalism makes them harder.

George Carlin Epigraph

The epigraph beginning this chapter included a provocative and controversial sentiment: "I hate a group of people with a common purpose." The entire quote provides a fitting prelude for exploring partisan tribalism. But that single sentence is a little over the top.

Groups of people with common purposes have advanced human rights. Civil rights advocacy in the 1950s and '60s was conducted by groups of people with common purpose. I distinguish those activist groups from contemporary PTs.

First, differences aren't absolute. Historical civil rights advocacy included tribalistic individuals and contemporary partisan tribalism includes individuals motivated by a desire to make progress on specific issues or by a common purpose.

One way to distinguish is by evaluating "common purpose." What did it mean then, and what does it mean now? In context of contemporary tribalism, purpose seems to be group or tribal identity. The common purpose of contemporary tribalism is tribalism. Establishing group identity supersedes other purposes. The group is an end in and of itself, rather than a means to an end. Group identity is the common purpose.

Establishing group identity is unavoidably segregating. Within segregated groups, debilitating prejudices develop, interfering with intergroup cooperation, or worse, precipitating aggression toward other groups and individuals outside the group—OHE. Therefore, establishing groups based on identity can undercut democratic progress.

Progress in Democracy Requires Identity-Transcending Collaboration

A utilitarian basis or common purpose other than identity should precipitate organization. Organization should enjoy functional fluidity sanctioning the transitory. Individuals must be free to temporarily unite across every existing classification to solve problems. Identity groups interfere with utilitarian fluidity by alienating potential supporters lacking group-identity accreditation.

And here we are. Group identity has become synonymous with purpose, which in application results in group identity superseding purpose. The lines have been drawn. With each passing day, reaching out across those lines becomes more difficult. Our prescribed identities, or rather our identity groups, become more and more determinative of our purposes. Or rather, our purpose is our identity group and maintaining good standing within the group.

My Identity

In the RBCI Chapter, I chastised readers for wondering if this book's ideas benefit the red or blue team. In the introduction, I staked out a dispassionate vantage above the fray. Does that mean I'm on a fence? Does that mean I'm unmoved by issues? What is the author's tribe?

My ideology is pragmatism inoffensive to the Constitution. I support anything that works so long as it doesn't violate anyone's rights. In other words, not unbridled, but regulated pragmatism. Some may argue that is no ideology at all. So what? So be it. Who cares? With respect to political parties and religions, I am unaffiliated. My faith is uncertainty, and my ambition is evolution. My obsession is sustainability, and my cause is functional democracy. I practice yoga, and I'm a Mets fan. My complexion is fair and my features European, but I was adopted and am uncertain of my specific biological ethnicity. I won't submit a DNA sample to determine my precise ancestry. So what? So be it. Who cares? Evolutionary theory places human origins in Africa. From Africa, the diaspora. *Homo sapiens*, people. I am one of you.

What tribe would you have me in?

I'm an environmentalist. Ecology is my favorite subject. My father bequeathed to me his love for nature and the outdoors. He was a Republican.

I worked for an environmental organization for twelve years. I don't eat mammals, birds, reptiles, or amphibians, but I'm not a vegan. In addition to pasta, rice, beans, and vegetables, I eat cheese, eggs, fish, and shellfish, and I'm open minded about insects. I reserve my antipathy for the sanctimonious.

Before hearing of global warming or climate change,[91] I learned of the "greenhouse effect" in ninth-grade Earth science in the 1970s. My teacher sported a military-style buzzcut. He threw an eraser at me one time for yukking-it-up in the back of the class. I deserved it. The idea of snitching on him never crossed my mind.

I learned certain gases in Earth's atmosphere allow shortwave radiation from the sun to pass through to warm Earth. As Earth warms, it reradiates heat in the form of longwave infrared radiation, which is trapped by these same gases. I learned this "greenhouse effect" keeps Earth warm and facilitated the evolution of life.

When I first heard of global warming, it made perfect sense because of what I learned in Earth science. Adding more "greenhouse gases" to the atmosphere exacerbates the "greenhouse effect" and contributes to warming. It's undeniable. It's not rocket science. It's ninth-grade Earth science.

I am no longer a Democrat because of my environmentalism and my specific concerns with global warming. In the age of comic-book movies, this is my "unaffiliated origin story."

Unaffiliated Origin Story

I preface my story with a simple yet seemingly paradoxical argument containing a single premise and conclusion.

Premise: I am as ambitious as anyone with respect to combating global warming.

Conclusion: Therefore, the Democratic Party is too extreme on global warming.

Global warming isn't a hoax, and fossil fuel combustion substantially increasing atmospheric greenhouse gases is a primary cause. We should reduce

---

91 I tend to use the terms interchangeably. Although climate change is more fashionable, I prefer global warming because it's more fundamental. The climate is changing because the planet is warming.

greenhouse gas emissions. A global warming action plan (GWAP) includes at least four components:

1. Government policy;
2. Technological innovation;
3. Corporate responsibility and behavior; and
4. Individual responsibility and behavior.

Embedded within successful strategies are concepts of interconnectedness and synergism. This is especially true for the first three GWAP components. Passing appropriate legislation spurs technological innovation by regulating corporate behavior. However, I don't hear much talk these days on the fourth component from those publicly concerned with climate change.

Individual Responsibility versus Collective Action

I remember when environmental activists valued reducing their ecological footprints regardless of government or corporate policy. But leading by example on energy consumption is passé. Distinguishing logical explanation from dubious rationalization can be challenging.

First off, many environmentalists still take care to minimize negative impacts to our ecology. But POEP spends little time with consumer-choice environmentalism. Public discussion singularly focuses on passing legislation or policy change. This makes good business sense from the perspective of both PI subsectors for reasons previously discussed. Assigning too much responsibility to constituencies is a bummer. Plus, the big money, billions per year, is in campaign spending or partisan electoral strategy, not consumer activism.

Unfortunately, there's a recent trend among those fronting deep concern over global warming to disparage individual responsibility and behavior. It sounds something like: "We're never going to get individuals to sacrifice or change to an extent that will solve global warming, so only through collective action will we succeed." That statement is true if "collective action" means a substantial majority of individuals act collectively to reduce their carbon footprints. On the other hand, if collective action means simply passing laws, the statement is misleading and undercuts GWAP efficacy. Arguing for collective action is not an argument against accepting individual responsibility or changing individual behavior, but it's being used as rationalization for exactly that.

Energy is not like other issues. No magic law solves the problem without inconvenience or change. Barring a technological miracle, we're going to have to change the way we do things. If you think we can simply pass a law solving global warming without changing energy-consumptive behavior, you're participating in a lefty circle-jerk.

From a tactical perspective, putting all our eggs in the policy change basket while downplaying individual responsibility seems to make sense. The argument goes something like: The most important component of any GWAP is government policy. Passing comprehensive climate change legislation would broadly impact society. It takes advantage of interconnectedness, albeit, in one direction. Passing legislation changes government policy by regulating corporations and/or providing subsidies and/or implementing programs that spur technological innovation and facilitate collective action.

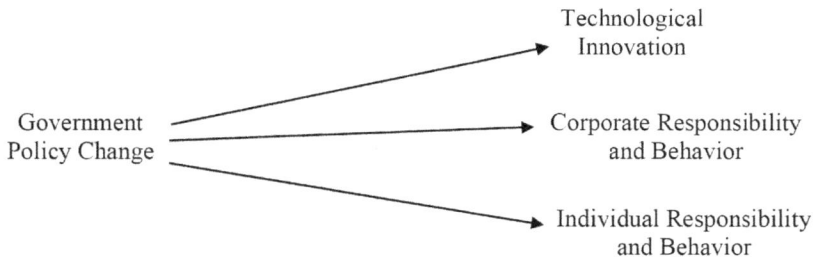

Figure 21.1: The Supremacy of Government Policy Change in an Unbalanced GWAP

For Democratic electoral politics, focusing on government is a no-brainer. All that's preventing progress on climate change is the Republican Party. All you must do to take action on global warming is vote Democrat. You're an environmentalist simply by voting Democrat. If rich people pay their fair share and corporations are aggressively regulated, you won't have to change a thing. It's all about passing the right law. Democrat = Environmentalist—PP holy grail.

I don't believe it. It abrades my understanding of the universe and mocks common sense. The idea that we've been living so fat for so long at the expense of global ecological balance and just signing a piece of paper allows us to

pursue convenience unabated while the magic law moves the invisible hand
to erase negative impact is a fairy tale. It's like saying we can have Medicare-
for-All without raising taxes. It's a lie.

Here's how I see it:

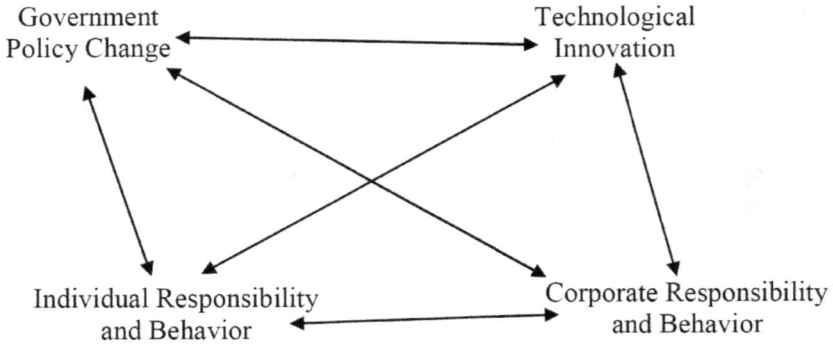

Government   Technological
Policy Change   Innovation

Individual Responsibility   Corporate Responsibility
and Behavior   and Behavior

Figure 21.2: Balanced GWAP

Interconnectivity isn't a one-way street. The more individuals change
behaviors to reduce their carbon footprints, the easier it will be to pass com-
plementary legislation. The more consumers exercise choice, the more likely
that corporations innovate to satisfy demand. In other words, you don't promote individual responsibility or stimulate consumer activism as detached
strategies to solve global warming. It's a means to an end. Working on all four
GWAP components enhances synergy and the likelihood of success on each
component, as well as overall success. Again, personal responsibility conflicts
with hyperpartisanship.

We're in the middle of my "unaffiliated origin story," and I've yet to make
my case. Next, I examine what taking constituencies for granted means in
application. It may not be what you think.

It begins with feeling your party doesn't push hard enough on your issue(s).
We're probably in agreement so far. As an environmentalist concerned with
global warming, I feel the Democratic Party has been taking me for granted.
They haven't been pushing hard enough on issues like global warming. That
sounds a little off, doesn't it? Aren't Democrats the ones who *are* pushing hard
on global warming?

Issue Subordination and Taking Constituents for Granted Are Two Sides of the Same Coin

This is the crux. It comes down to what "pushing hard" means in application and in the context of partisan politics.

I begin with examples of pushing hard and not pushing hard. In 2009 and 2010, President Obama and Speaker Nancy Pelosi really pushed hard to get ACA (Obamacare). I supported a public option and was disappointed it wasn't included in the version signed into law. Jettisoning the public option to get the bill passed is evidence of how hard the push was. They did their best and made progress on the issue. They did not take the health care constituency for granted. They got something.

If, on the other hand, Obama and Pelosi had proposed Medicare-for-All, they would have been taking their constituencies for granted. Medicare-for-All is an example of not pushing hard. It's counterintuitive. It comes down to this:

More Extreme Does Not Mean Trying Harder

Extreme, ambitious, and pushing harder all mean different things and measure different qualities. Medicare-for-All is a more extreme and ambitious legislative proposal, but it has no chance of passing because it lacks support from moderates and independents, not to mention all Republicans.

Introducing or claiming support for extremely ambitious proposals is not pushing hard. It's too easy for moderates and independents to reject without consequence. Pushing hard means introducing proposals that are difficult for moderates and independents to reject and engaging in relentless arm-twisting, like Obama and Pelosi did.

Now let's zero in on what it means to take constituencies for granted. Introducing extremely ambitious proposals with no chance of passing is part of it. The other part is convincing constituencies that by doing so, you're genuinely looking out for their best interests. Insinuating that more extreme equates to trying harder is the trick. Partisan media complicity takes the form of suggesting that moderates neglect constituencies or fail to excite the base.

But what of constituencies? What choice do we have? The other party has no interest in advancing our issues.

Here's why issue subordination and taking constituencies for granted are one and the same. Because one party has no interest in our issues, the other party can propose anything and receive issue credit, even if the proposal has zero chance of passing. From a partisan electoral strategy, the more extreme the proposal and the less chance it has of passing, the better, especially with media segregated along partisan lines. PPs create the impression that extreme zero-chance proposals are evidence the proposals' authors care more about their constituencies and are the ones pushing hard for them. In other words, using issues to advance partisan electoral pursuits rather than making progress on the issue appears righteous in partisan media.

As parties pull further apart, as product differentiation becomes more straightforward, as moderates in Congress are being pushed out, and our politics become more and more tribal, the con gets easier to pull off. Constituencies perceive zero-chance proposals as evidence of pushing hard and look at moderate proposals that can actually pass as evidence that they're being taken for granted. It's perverse.

I see things the other way around. I perceive zero-chance proposals as evidence I'm being taken for granted and see moderate proposals that can pass as evidence someone is looking out for me. I don't want my issues being used to gain partisan advantage. Constituencies are taken for granted by subordinating the particular nature of an issue for partisan advantage. Proposals like Medicare-for-All or a Green New Deal that give the appearance of heroic dedication are essentially shams.

Maybe sham is too strong, or perhaps I'm assigning cynical intent too casually. Let's look at issue subordination, or taking constituencies for granted, from one final perspective that's slightly more empathetic to the perpetrators.

Maybe overly zealous zero-chance proposals are nothing more than genuine, good-hearted efforts to achieve the best outcome or be something like perfect. To dissect this hypothesis, we'll explore the concept of intent in the context of democracy and function.

First, it's difficult to believe representatives who managed to get elected and experience even a single term don't understand the purpose of zero-chance proposals. The logic can be reduced to a simple conditional:

If: A legislative proposal has zero chance of passing, at least in the short term,

Then: It must have a purpose other than passing, at least in the short term.

Let's imagine the zero-chance proposal as an aspirational vehicle. In other words, although it has zero chance of passing in the short term, it could pass at some future time if:

1. The positions of representatives currently opposed to the zero-chance proposal change; or
2. We throw out representatives currently opposed and elect supportive representatives.

This implicates the electorate. In a democracy, compelling representatives to change positions or electing supportive representatives requires persuading voters. With democracy, we can:

1. Persuade people who disagree with us to change their positions;
2. Work with people who disagree with us; or
3. Some combination thereof.

Democracy is a grind.

Let's imagine as issue activists we would like to focus on number one. We want to change peoples' minds. How do we successfully persuade?

Let's start with how we fail, then look at a couple of success stories and see if we can frame our GWAP to enhance chances for success.

Weaponizing zero-chance proposals to publicly assign blame profits PI at the expense of issue progress. That's how we fail.

ACA and Same-Sex Marriage Are Success Stories

ACA is less ambitious than Medicare-for-All. It doesn't include a public option, but it's a starting point. Because of ACA, a pathway toward universal coverage with a public option is feasible. If Obama and Pelosi had proposed

Medicare-for-All, we wouldn't even be at the starting point. We would've achieved nothing.

The lesson gleaned from same-sex marriage concerns the power of private action. Government policy in the form of a SCOTUS decision was a de facto acknowledgement of what was already happening.

It wasn't just one thing. There was traditional policy activism involving speaking out and protesting. People were coming out. Couples were marrying regardless of state acknowledgement. Hollywood movies and TV shows humanized and mainstreamed same-sex relationships.

Most importantly, synergism transpired through implementation of various elements. Public protest made coming out easier. More people coming out made protests larger and more effective. More people coming out made it easier for TV and Hollywood. TV and Hollywood made it easier for people to come out, etc. Eventually, government followed suit.

Now let's revisit global warming and the notion of changing peoples' minds to achieve progress. Before beginning, I stipulate global warming is easily distinguishable from both health care and same-sex marriage. Same-sex marriage is a civil right, climate is not. Every person needs health care and has had intimately impactful experience with the health care system, global warming, not so much. Nonetheless, we can apply lessons learned.

Moderation Is a Reliable Pathway to Progress

In other words, more like ACA and less like Medicare-for-All or the Green New Deal proposed by Rep. Alexandria Ocasio-Cortez (D-NY), which calls for net zero greenhouse gas emissions and 100 percent renewable zero-emission energy sources by 2030.[92] The country is getting used to ACA. We've lived with Obamacare and the sky remains in the sky. Our worst fears have not come to pass. The scare tactics were a lie. Because of ACA, next steps will be easier to take.

Consider applying similar logic to global warming policy. Let's take a

---

92 Deborah D'Souza, "Understanding the Green New Deal and What's in the Climate Proposal," Investopedia, updated May 28, 2022, https://www.investopedia.com/the-green-new-deal-explained-4588463.

modest step we can live with to demonstrate that making reductions won't cause the sky to fall.

Pick the Low-Hanging Fruit

Disparaging the idea is fashionable, but leaving such bounty to rot on the vine is either negligence or professional incompetence. Harvesting what's in reach is common sense and efficient. Accessing the available may bring the loftier within reach–synergy. Attaching the accessible to the unobtainable for partisan advantage is malfeasance.

Some climate change fanatics will say that isn't enough. I understand. Please don't deliberately misunderstand me. All I have been hearing since the late 1990s is, if we don't take drastic steps by such and such a date, we'll reach a "tipping point" and all will be lost. As a result of continuously forsaking necessary drastic steps and missing deadlines, a lot of us are under the impression we've failed, and it's time to move on. Time for humanity to adjust to a warming planet. In other words, climate change scare tactics combined with focusing almost exclusively on government action has failed. Maybe we should try something new.

First, concede different levels of failure and success. Sea levels rising one foot is bad; three feet is worse. Modest steps are better than no steps. Modest progress begets more ambitious progress. We've been in this all-or-nothing paradigm resulting in nothing.

Devaluing Private Action in America Is Counterproductive

Second, while I acknowledge government action is important, in the current milieu of "dysfunctional" hyperpartisanship, investing more resources in the other three GWAP components makes sense, at least in the short term. I also recognize some people, institutions, and corporations are already investing in technological innovation and behavioral change, but such efforts are removed from the mainstream. As a result, we squander synergistic opportunity.

How Can We Help, Other than Sending Cash to the Democratic Party?

The question cuts straight to the heart. Do you see the problem? We need to enlist the entire human race in the battle. However, the impression I'm left with is we're just waiting for Congress to act. It's all up to them. There's nothing we can do other than voting Democrat. That's a lie, and that lie contributes to inaction.

Impacts of policy change on society will be less drastic on individuals the more individuals act on their own. Call it synergism or another positive feedback loop. Private action makes public action more palatable, and public action makes private action easier.

A popular aphorism of soundbite dimension repeated ad nauseam and without inspection goes: We know what the solutions are, all that's lacking is political will. The cliché is a malignancy because it subordinates the issue to partisan electoral strategy and places the entire burden on a dysfunctional sector of our society, but mostly because it deters private action and innovation.

It's *too clever by half.* If we know the solutions, there's no need to innovate. Discovery is pointless. In fact, it's likely the best solutions have yet to be discovered. Our slogans should encourage ingenuity. We need to unlink the issue from the politics. We need new knowledge and tools. Let's develop them.

The effort to combat global warming apart from government action should be featured more prominently and be better coordinated—not because we can solve global warming without government action, but because we can help mainstream the effort, making it easier for governments to follow suit. Let me be clear on this. Simply creating a list including things like switching from incandescent bulbs to LEDs is insufficient. I mean running campaigns marketing and inspiring consumer change. We need to aggressively promote and facilitate effective private action.

I can't watch commercial television without seeing advertising spots for animal shelters. I see PSAs all the time about driving while buzzed. Is getting people to take action on energy more challenging than tugging heart strings with images of neglected pets? Maybe. Are rising sea levels as immediately distressing as killing someone while driving under the influence? Probably not. But I'll bet there's a madman adman currently hawking sugar water on Madison

Avenue who has a pretty good idea about how to get it done. "Just do it."

Different Stories Appeal to Different People

Third, boiling the entire issue down to emissions and climate change is mono-chromatic and uninspired. Petroleum might be the most valuable substance on the planet. It's used to make fertilizers, plastics, synthetic fabrics like polyester and nylon, industrial solvents, detergents, pharmaceuticals, cosmetics, synthetic rubber, and more. Setting a match to it seems imprudent to say the least. We've forgotten conservation. I'm not claiming conservation is as compelling as the end of the world as we know it. But human psychology is diverse. Valid reasons apart from climate change exist for transitioning from fossil fuels. We shouldn't be afraid to include them in a comprehensive action plan.

Right Now, We Don't Have a Comprehensive Plan

We have "Congress needs to pass a law, and Republicans are in the way." Once again, I'm not claiming we can beat this without government action. But compelling reasons to broaden the effort exist. One of the most compelling is resource management. With government inaction due to "dysfunctional" hyperpartisanship, sending money that could be used to reduce greenhouse gas emissions to the Democratic Party wastes resources. If global warming is your issue, spend your money tightening up your home. Explore private sector avenues resulting in actual and immediate reductions.

The Democratic Party and "independent" not-for-profits—legally nonpartisan but functionally conjoined with the professional left—have mismanaged the issue. I know there are well-meaning people involved in partisan politics and environmental advocacy whose dedication to solving global warming is genuine. I've worked with some of them.

But let's not forget financial incentive, system hierarchy, and function. While singularly focusing on an all-or-nothing legislative proposal may have failed as an issue strategy, it works as a partisan electoral strategy. Money spent on consumer activism is money pinched from partisan campaigning. Energy expended on promoting behavioral change cannot be utilized for electoral advantage. Power accumulating beyond the influence of political parties threatens the game.

Imagine if the professional left put as much effort into a comprehensive GWAP as it does into prosecuting Trump. Imagine if media dedicated as much airtime to informing the public on how we can help as it does to informing us on Trump. By this point, you know the problem. If behavioral changes are part of a solution, then the way we currently behave is part of the problem. That inevitably leads to the forbidden zone of self-examination. For the business of partisanship, blaming the other side is cleaner. Implying your constituency is part of the problem is a loser.

Whether through intelligent design, natural selection, or some combination thereof, results for PI are glorious. Progress outside the electoral process on issues like climate change squanders valuable partisan chits. My fear is the particular nature of global warming as an issue has been corrupted beyond redemption. In other words, global warming has functioned primarily to energize partisanship for so long, its transformation back to an issue whose primary purpose is to advance through Congress via compromise and bipartisanship is no longer possible. That's a victory for partisanship and a defeat for issue advocacy.

So, my dispassionate vantage from which I choose to analyze hyperpartisanship is not a function of my detachment from issues. It's not that I don't have positions on issues; it's that partisan advantage subordinates issues I care about.

If one party attains exclusive dominion over your issue, you're screwed on that issue. Exclusive dominion means progress can only be achieved by voting out the other side. Exclusive dominion is accomplished by disdaining moderates, moderation, and private action.

Whether progress is more likely via tribal victory or by defeating tribalism is impossible to know. The most effective pathway to sustainability is uncertain. I choose to resist tribalism. My side opposes hyperpartisanship. What tribe does that put me in?

Self-Interested Patriot

To put my unaffiliated origin story to bed, I'll explore one more concept distinguishing issue advocacy from partisan campaigning. As an issue advocate,

I want to make the case that taking appropriate action is in your own best interest. For example, replacing burned out incandescent lightbulbs with LEDs is smart. While LEDs cost more, they reduce electric bills and last much longer. By switching to LEDs, you gain a financial advantage over competing businesses or for your family. Aren't smart investments better than stupid investments?

The same type of argument works on the national level. Countries with the most solar panels and wind turbines per capita gain a long-term competitive advantage over other nations. Up-front costs associated with wind and solar installations are recuperated by using free energy in the form of wind and sunlight.

Notice how I didn't mention saving the planet, or it's the right thing to do. Financial realities associated with energy are found in a ledger. Solar, wind, and LEDs are sound investments because of arithmetic. As for morality, freedom to decide one's faith complicates the equation. While solar, wind, and LEDs are cost effective because of math, whether such investments are "the right thing to do" depends on your brand of faith.

Using Right and Wrong Arguments Provokes Tribalism

As an issue advocate, I don't want to impose my morality on potential supporters or inject my theology into the reasoning. I want everyone to see the rationality of progress. I want people to appreciate that change is in their self-interest. I want potential supporters to understand that our nation and society will function more efficiently with their support. As an issue advocate, I don't want to divide people according to ideology.

But as a partisan, that's exactly what I want to do. I want to rub it in. I want to trumpet my righteousness at the opposition's expense. We're the good guys. You're the bad guys. I don't even want your support on my issues. I just want to beat you. I want you to go away.

When I hear right-and-wrong arguments, my partisanship radar activates. Advocacy based on morality provides a pulpit for evangelizing flimflammers. Moralizing is a wedge tactic. I detect issue subordination. I suspect I'm being taken for granted on my issues.

If right-and-wrong arguments are made, the Constitution should provide their basis, rather than tribal ideology. The First Amendment proscribes establishing state theology. The Constitution represents common morality.

Violating civil rights is illegal because the Constitution says so. Racial bias within the criminal justice system violates the constitutional guarantee of equal protection under the law.

However, national interest arguments work even for civil rights. The closer we get to a genuine merit-based system, the better society functions. Discrimination undermines efficacy.

Advocacy Approach

The reason we haven't taken more substantial actions to combat global warming is because Americans have not been sufficiently convinced it's in their individual self-interest or collective national interest to do so.

The reason universal health care proposals such as single-payer or Medicare-for-All have failed to gain traction is that the majority of Americans who already have health insurance haven't been convinced they'll be better off under a different system. Democracy is a grind.

I support renewable energy development, energy conservation, and equal treatment under the law, as well as equal opportunity for all people regardless of race, gender, sexual orientation, or national origin, as a self-interested patriot. What is my tribe?

Affiliation Options

My former party seems more interested in building broad coalitions for electoral advantage than advancing policy through collaboration and compromise. This trend isn't nascent. In the preface, I referred to observing corroborating data in the early to mid-1990s. But don't confuse my antipathy for the Democratic Party as affection for the Republican Party. I have never been a Republican, and I doubt I ever will be. At this point, the Republican Party platform reads: "against anything Democrat."

In truth, I am hybrid. I'm *trans*-partisan. I don't fit into the binary construct of a two-party system. As both parties trend toward extremity, they distance themselves from my natural identity.

So, what are my options? I could register with either party. As such I would be RINO or DINO. I would be partisan in name only (PINO). I could easily go through life as PINO as long as I kept my head down and mouth shut. But if I dared speak, it would be clear to all I'm not a real Democrat or real Republican.

I could conform or pretend to conform to a partisan ideal so whenever I spoke, I would sound like a real Democrat or real Republican. That's the hyperpartisan approach. It's trendy, but it's not for me. Squeezing myself into a partisan mold feels icky.

I choose to unaffiliate because:

1. It's my natural state;
2. I don't want either party to use my membership as endorsement of their shenanigans; and
3. I don't wish to patronize our disunion.

What is my tribe?

Tribal Psychology and Business Models Underwriting Partisanship Transcend Politics

Brace yourself for another sports metaphor. I occasionally listen to sports talk on WFAN in NY. The phrase "real fan" is pervasive. If you like the Jets but don't hate the Giants, you're not a real Jets fan. Rooting for a team is inadequate. You must hate the competition. Otherwise, you're not a real fan.

So, in addition to me not being a real Democrat or a real Republican, I guess I'm not a real sports fan either. I don't hate enough.

This isn't trivial. Entertainment talk, including sports talk, isn't disconnected from political talk. The psychology and profitability of tribalism and partisanship are deeper and broader than politics. Partisanship is financially, psychologically, and culturally incentivized.

Tribalism and Common Law

Stare Decisis

To stand by things decided. While in law school, I met an LLM (Master of Laws) student from China in the laundromat. We had a legal conversation lasting for the duration of our laundry. Her father is a judge in China.

She told me China prohibits judges from applying precedent to render verdicts. She described with a fair amount of pride how each case was as singular as the individual on trial, which made dependence on earlier decisions unseemly. Sagacious justices assimilate the unique circumstances encompassing the immediate case to craft decisions with appropriate particularity. Doesn't that sound celestial?

But there are some itty-bitty problems with that. First, it opens the door for bias. Disdaining precedent invites application of double standards. This is especially problematic under authoritarian regimes. Considering precedent interferes with the state's desire to discriminate between vocal critics and party suck-ups committing similar offenses. Political activism isn't the only rationale for judicial discrimination. Any group identity or tribal affiliation can provide a solid foundation for prejudicial judgmentalism absent a genuine respect for *stare decisis*.

Second, and more pertinent to tribalism, disdaining precedent creates uncertainty as to what the law is. Standing by previous decisions establishes reasonable expectations as to how the law applies and what the law is. This allows well-intentioned members of the public to plan and act accordingly and with confidence.

Confidence is fundamental. Disregarding precedent or enforcing precedent by group identity undermines confidence, because rules could either change at any moment or be applied inconsistently. On the other hand, uncertainty empowers authoritarian regimes. The message is clear. The law is whatever we say it is, whenever we say it. Watch your step.

Uncertainty as to the law creates anxiety and dependence. Engineering dependence is a marketing coup. PT influencers monetizing traffic benefit from plebeian anxiety. Tribal members must plug into appropriate ECs to remain contemporary.

Therefore, perpetually shifting tribal dogma is profitable. If doctrine is stable and adjudication of tribal law consistent, tuning in all the time isn't necessary.

Disregarding precedent shifts the balance of power from people to the authoritarian regime. The electorate becomes like children, dependent on adults to inform their values. It's about control. Disdaining precedent expedites authoritarianism and destabilizes democracy.

On the other hand, precedent is not my god. Laws of the land evolve with changing values and conditions. But statutes reflecting transformation are codified, and legislative processes are prescribed and recorded. Jurisprudence of common law lies bare in cases for all to inspect.

Not so with PT law. It's uncertain whether development of tribal canon is authoritarian, democratic, a product of social media populism, or some combination thereof. Regardless of the process, extreme doctrine that's continuously modified is financially incentivized while moderation and stability are deterred. A website featuring reasonable principles that rarely change isn't going to generate profitable traffic.

Ex Post Facto Judgmentalism

Two constitutional clauses prohibit retroactively criminalizing an act that was legal when committed. Article I, section 9, clause 3 prohibits Congress from passing any ex post facto law, and article I, section 10, clause 1 prohibits states from doing so. The fairness is plain.

No law prevents private citizens or media from perpetrating analogous injustices. Defiling the character or reputation of people for their antecedent actions or creations based on contemporary mores is considered good sport within certain tribes. Here, I'm not concerned with the fairness of such vulgarity or even that it's financially incentivized. Tearing people down for media content is as traditional as fireworks on the fourth of July. It predates the internet.

I'm more concerned with the psychology of ex post facto judgmentalism and its relationship to self-government. As a child, when I first became aware of the Holocaust, the idea that I could take part in such atrocity was inconceivable. Nazis were evil, and Germans that let it happen were weak or bad. I knew I was better than them.

But life teaches humility, or at least it should. At some point I wondered: As an adult German during the Nazi regime, would I have stood against the machine? Would I have been brave? Would I have developed sensibilities prompting defiance? What if I had a family? Would I have been willing to sacrifice my family for principle? Is sacrificing one's children brave or principled?

Does the equation become simpler or more complex for single adults? No family to worry about . . . or to use as an excuse. We all like to think well of ourselves. But if I am to be honest, at best, I'm uncertain.

It's the certainty of ex post facto judgmentalism I find disturbing. It's understandable in children or the unexperienced. But the pathway to adult responsibility is paved with self-examination with a modicum of self-awareness as its reward . . . or sentence. Ex post facto judgmentalism exposes a childish psychology bereft of self-awareness, and effective self-government requires at least a smidgen of self-awareness.

Believing we can simultaneously govern ourselves while deceiving ourselves into thinking we are superior in character to all who precede us by virtue of birthdate is ludicrous. Notice I said, "superior in character," rather than *morally* superior. By and large, society has evolved its moral sensibilities. Condemning cannibalism in twenty-first century America is not indicative of superior character. Refusing to take part in cannibalism in a tribe full of cannibals . . . that's character.

Nazi Germany is an extreme example. Even at the time of WWII, I think most people would have viewed both the ideology behind the Holocaust as well as its cold-blooded logistics as pure evil. Most of the fashionable ex post facto judgmentalism involves developing sensibilities around moral conundrums less severe than genocide. But self-examination should be universally incorporated into any method for understanding history. Using contemporary values to impugn past acts does not suggest superior character. It indicates unconsciousness.

Practicing ex post facto judgment interferes with absorbing essential lessons. Learning from history requires understanding that although we're living in a time of more refined sensibilities, our character for tribal conformity remains robust.

Believing strength of character evolves with refined morality is a tragic mistake. If we can subdue our judgmentalism, history provides glimpses of our nature. Even a hint of increased self-awareness gleaned through an unbiased appraisal of history may marginally moderate our susceptibility to psychological predispositions evolved during our primordial existences. Resistance to conforming tribal predispositions can help us dodge authoritarianism.

Constitutional democracy represents a profound understanding of human nature and history. Checks and balances evince self-awareness. It's why we have democracy and why we must take care to nurture and treasure it. Robust democratic institutions occupied with people of ordinary character and courage have the potential to thwart extreme terrors with extraordinary facility.

It has been said the price of liberty or democracy is eternal vigilance.[93] But the nature of the compulsory vigilance is rarely considered. I assumed it meant something like: Be a good citizen by paying attention to what's going on with our politics and actively participate by voting in every election. While that's true, it's inadequate.

Threats to freedom or democracy, within a democracy, may arise from the self-governed. Where now the vigilance? To be vigilant about structures and processes of democracy while ignoring the fundamental units is blindness. Vigilance applied to self-governance means self-awareness. Ex post facto judgmentalism results from, and contributes to, self-deception.

The time for acting against Nazis was before they took power. That's the lesson. That's when it was doable. That's when people of ordinary character and courage could have stood up without threat of mortal peril—while the institutions of democracy still held.

Through self-awareness, timely action becomes more likely. Imagining that strength of character correlates with recency of birth is self-delusion. It's a fatal flaw.

Sometimes omens of authoritarianism are plain. Sometimes they're more subtle. Disrespecting precedent is not obvious. A predilection for ex post facto judgmentalism cultivates hubris as to our contemporary character, making us more susceptible to social malfeasance and blind to our complicity. Tribalism exploits primordial instincts and identity insecurity to provide organizational structure for authoritarian movements.

Celebrity

Celebrities wield disproportionate tribal authority. Along with tribal culture and cultural tribalism, we have a culture of celebrity. The mélange spawns a

---

93 "Eternal vigilance is the price of liberty (Spurious Quotation)," Thomas Jefferson Foundation, accessed Jan. 1, 2023, https://www.monticello.org/research-education/thomas-jefferson-encyclopedia/eternal-vigilance-price-liberty-spurious-quotation/.

culture of tribal celebrity.

It's popular to declare that celebrities who publicly signal their political preferences are making responsible use of their platforms or are using their voice responsibly. Occasionally that's true, but more often not.

My analysis implicates ubiquitous concepts of media segregation and self-awareness.

Celebrities, in terms of democracy or "one person, one vote," have disproportionate media access and therefore disproportionate influence. Celebrity endorsement works.

So, by virtue of success in the entertainment industry, celebrities are granted disproportionate weight in political and public policy discussions.

Let's begin with self-awareness. If you combine average or mediocre insight into society with disproportionate influence, maybe the responsible thing is showing a little restraint. Aren't restraint and responsibility compatible? Do you honestly believe the problem with society is that too many people, especially celebrities, exercise too much restraint? Is that our problem? Are we restraining ourselves too much?

Celebrities *can* have unique perspective or insight into specific issues. Insight can be peculiar to celebrity status or through experience outside the entertainment industry. By all means, make responsible use of platform.

More typically, it's chasing likes or applause, which is fine. Celebrities have the same First Amendment rights as the rest of us. Expecting entertainers to eschew ovations is like asking new leaves to turn from sunlight. But manufacturing praise isn't a responsible use of platform.

Enter media segregation with self-awareness still in play.

"Responsible use of platform" by "speaking out" implies putting something on the line. During the 1950s, when Senator Joseph McCarthy used his office for an anti-communist witch hunt, Hollywood celebrities who spoke out were blacklisted. They paid a serious price for "speaking out."

But with media and audiences segregated according to partisan affiliation, including late-night shows featuring celebrity interviews, the risk of speaking out is adoration and applause. Celebrities have every right to engage in virtue signaling to receive accolades from desired constituencies, but don't pretend it's responsible use of platform.

Celebrities could use their platforms to speak for comity. They could endorse compromise and inspire aggressive pursuit of common ground. But that wouldn't garner the same applause with segregated audiences. Few venues reward celebrities who advocate for civility, moderation, and accord.

Many of us remember entertaining family and friends as children and how good it felt to make people smile and laugh. Professional entertainers chase that feeling their entire lives. Pursuing adoration for cash is fine, but that's what it is.

Here, this business of celebrity is in context of tribalism. Once again, the process for deciding orthodoxy and adjudicating PT law is opaque. We know extremism is financially incentivized. We also know insecure personalities chasing applause have disproportionate influence and leadership roles. PTs dominating our politics is insane.

Eyes On/Off the Prize

I want to examine the concept of "speaking out" irrespective of celebrity.

The act of speaking out has been whittled down through repurposing. Its primary function is content. I call it *contentification*. It's broader than speaking out or hyperpartisanship. The apprehension in a media-dominated society is everything functions primarily as content. The concept is so broad it sounds like a motif for generic satire.

Relevant parts of the equation include media evolution and individual exposure. Media has evolved to infiltrate our lives more fully. With mobile internet devices, we're never completely removed. As individuals, we're overexposed.

As an overexposed individual, maybe it's just me. Through habituation, my brain processes input as media content. On some level, cooking shows or sporting events are not so different from activists speaking out on injustices. I'm just watching TV. I'm consuming content.

Another part of the equation is the speaker. It appears as performance art. Even people in the street seem to be playing their parts by repeating popularized catchphrases.

Volume or quantity is also relevant. Recognizing speaking out as viable content must be partly responsible for its fecundity. But volume has ironically contributed to its diminishment. I say ironically because as an activist, I want increased visibility and participation.

Content Profiling

There's something rotten in the volume—contentification. To a certain extent, we can discern purpose. To a certain extent, we can tell the difference between genuine and clickbait. But oversaturation with clickbait conceals the genuine. It's like RBCI/RBAF. Our brains are content profiling, thereby impairing cognition. This is especially true through flat screens, which cue us for content.

Within ECs, speaking out is simply another manifestation of affirming identity righteousness, which is another form of contentification.

All I know for certain is when I hear people speaking out, most of the time, something is off. It sounds contrived. It comes off as performance. It's just content for content's sake.

Contentification as Escapism

With mobile internet devices, opportunity to connect is eternal. But the same device used for legal or scientific research connects us to word games and pornography. When scanning news headlines, are we educating ourselves or just killing time? When amusement park fuses with academic institution, which element dominates?

America excels at marketing escape. On the other hand, dealing with psychological predispositions that evolved during our tribal existences requires consciousness achieved through presence. With ubiquitous media through mobile internet devices, we're never fully present. We're eternally processing content that affirms the righteousness of our identities within ECs, inhibiting self-evaluation and personal evolution, or content that lays trails to increasingly extreme philosophies that nurture division and conflict.

The Prize Is Content

Contentification also raises efficacy concerns like the HM effect on issue advocacy as depicted in figure 5.2, i.e., *too clever by half*. Does ubiquitous "activist" content lead to increased progress? Fanatically presenting radical content could be interpreted as evidence progressives have taken their eyes off the prize. I disagree. The prize isn't progress. It's content.

Conclusions

While certain human predispositions developed during our tribal existences appear vestigial or counter-evolutionary, they act to support a highly adaptive sociological phenomenon, hyperpartisanship, which is blooming out of control due to changing cultural factors such as partisan media segregation and industrial political spending.

Aspects of human psychology that provided great utility when we lived in tribes on a planet of less than one million people aren't serving us as well on a planet of nation-states with a population over eight billion. If our populous nation-state existence endures for hundreds of millennia, we could biologically evolve commensurate psychology. In the meantime, we need to come to grips with disparities between our evolutionary environment and the one in which we exist. Our wiring for sparsely populated tribal existence isn't up to code.

But surrendering to psychological predispositions evolved during our tribal existence without inspection is lazy. Understanding the relationship between our primitive and more evolved selves is part of the job of *Homo sapiens*, and I consider it a duty for fundamental units of democracy.

Sustaining Democracy Requires Vigilant Self-Awareness

We need to discuss it. We need to deal with it as an issue in and of itself. We need to treat it as seriously as we treat crime, education, health care, immigration, and democracy. It's an issue of democracy. Perhaps if we better understood the relationship between our psychological evolution, the ecological conditions under which that evolution occurred, and the utility of our ancestral psychology in the modern world, our densely populated, constitutionally democratic nation-states would work better—perhaps. It's worth a try. Simply writing off democratic dysfunction as tribalism isn't cutting it. Tribalism cannot serve as both premise and explanation without examination. We can do better.

Cultural and Technological Evolution Outpace Biological Evolution

With each passing moment, we move further from environments in which our inherited psychology evolved. Biological evolution requires thousands of generations, whereas the internet took a few decades. We can't go back.

Since we can't de-evolve our culture or technology and we can't evolve our biology fast enough to catch up, solutions must exist within an evolving culture. The first step is global acknowledgement that:

> When the rate of cultural and technological evolution is several orders of magnitude greater than the rate of biological evolution, anomalies emerge. Inherited human psychology is disjointed from contemporary reality by hundreds of millennia.

With Respect to Tribalism, Segregation Is Unquestionably Relevant

Familial relation, geography, and space segregated ancestral tribes. Is segregation an artifact of tribalism, or is there an independent drive to segregate? Within the modern world, absent abundant space, cubicles formed of building material, internet protocol, ideology, and group identity segregate our existences.

We recognize each other's humanity through functional integration involving substantial contacts across tribal boundaries. Substantial contacts provide meaningful data points of interaction, allowing us to see through group identity to the individual. As meaningful data points of interaction across tribal boundaries increase, epiphanies that group identity doesn't determine character become more likely.

Lateral Expansion and Cultural Fluidity

The answer to whether our constitutional republic can survive tribal politics transcends the constitutional framework. Checks and balances within our guiding document seem inadequate. Tribal politics subsidized by an unholy trinity of tribal journalism, tribal academia, and tribal science are roadblocks to our persistence.

I doubt constitutionally democratic nation-states can survive tribal politics along with tribalism-saturated culture. The good news is culture is fluid. But advocating for change in some cultures and preservation in others is not advocacy for cultural evolution. It's tribalism. It's hyperpartisanship.

Evolving Culture

Consider evolving culture as a form of AI or just intelligence for that matter. Culture runs permutations for solving its evolution through incalculable interactions between humans within all their systems.

This is not to say culture is sentient. (Or if it is, evidence of its consciousness is conveyed through its instrumentalities or ongoing permutations.) No single site directly links to a singular entity called "culture," though the incalculable interactions determining cultural evolution are increasingly virtual.

Intuitively, intelligence implies intelligent. But permutations must be on point, and some are. Financial incentivization factors in determining the variety and concentration of the incalculable human interactions that evolve culture. Factors guiding permutations determine the distribution of cultural intelligence. For example, our culture is at the savant level in its ability to market trifles.

On the other hand, our cultural aptitude for functional democracy is unsatisfactory. This book identifies factors, including tribal psychology, that guide cultural permutations toward evolving democratic dysfunction.

We must evolve a nontribal culture, and we must make a point of doing so. Without being too prescriptive, such as suggesting that within such a nontribal human culture, self-serving affectations like virtue-signaling would be considered gauche, I propose a foundational framework.

The framework's premise is: Existential threats are uniting. The ideal approach to crises requires uniting, and common purpose forges alliance. What is our common purpose?

The Purpose of Humanity Is Survival

Purpose beyond survival can only be carried out through survival. To do better than *just* survive, we must survive.

Threats to survival come from within and without. As humans possessed by ancestral psychology institutionalize conflict, machinations of the universe conspire with inevitability to impel occasional celestial projectiles toward our home. We await their arrival. Are we prepared? Observe the moon's surface. Its impact craters indicate our natural history. Is it our fate?

On our planet of eight billion people, constitutional democracies offer the best chance of solving problems that allow us to sustain our existence without compromising individual rights. We must work on our survival. Though tribalism was integral to our primordial subsistence, it now interferes.

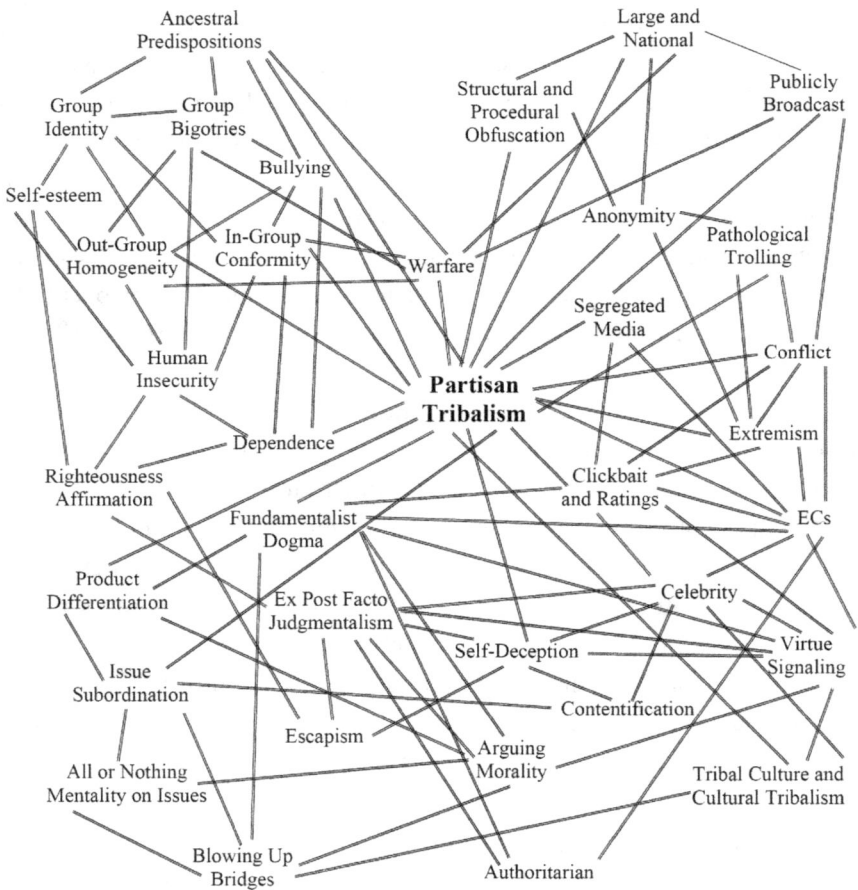

Figure 21.3: The Partisan Tribalism Sub-web

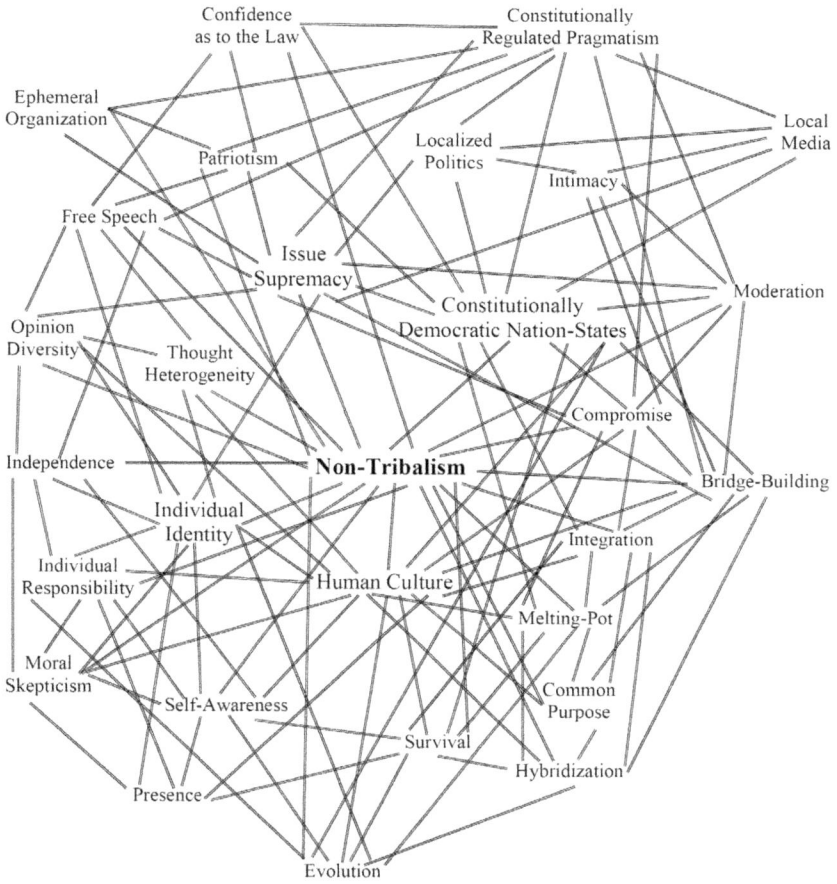

Figure 21.4: Non-Tribalism Web

Weight of Religion and Dominion of Faith

If the path before you is clear, you're probably on someone else's.
—CARL GUSTAV JUNG

I doubt we're conscious of the extent to which human existence entwines with religion. Factors discussed below scaffold the hyperpartisanship web and implicate religion and faith. Whether these factors are begotten of organized religion or simply seem religious is academic. I justify their inclusion with: *So it is written.*

Religion, along with its deities, was and is a placeholder for that which humans can't explain. At one time, lightning was thought to emanate from an angry god's fingertips. Now we understand electrical discharge. The quantity of material within the placeholder continuously diminishes, at an accelerating pace.

This is another instance of cultural evolution outpacing biological evolution. It's tempting to consider both science and religion as cultural phenomena and that science is simply replacing religion. But that doesn't explain ideological faith, or just faith, for that matter.

Faith Seems Biological

The concept of supreme beings has been with us for a long time. For it to suffice as explanation for elemental occurrences such as seasons or meteorological wonders requires faith. Those with faith are less troubled by invisible gods as cause or reason.

Without faith, imperceptible divine entities fall short of quenching fear of or answering the unfathomable. Those troubled by such things could upset tribal harmony and/or be trouble to themselves. I see faith as a biological adaptation allowing *Homo sapiens* to make peace with the mystifying.

Faith ameliorates anxiety over what is beyond our control or understanding. The ability to ameliorate anxiety is adaptive. Individuals who manifested faith enjoyed prehistoric advantage over those frustrated by the concept of invisible immortals. Those with faith were more likely to survive and pass the trait to their offspring. To manage the inexplicable, we evolved a need to believe.

Science offers explanation but fails to satiate our need to believe. We are left unfulfilled. Faith's role as a placeholder diminishes, but the underlying biological drive continues unabated.

As membership in organized religion in America declines,[94] political ideology and party membership gain prominence as indices of self-identification.[95] Causality is difficult to prove, but I'm suspicious. Pure coincidence seems miraculous. The part of our brains organized through evolutionary millennia to nurture and warehouse faith-based thinking craves a fix. Exorcising religion from our minds creates a ravenous void.

 But what is religion? I have reviewed numerous definitions. Some include the idea of a supreme being and some don't. All include some form of the word "belief." We're back to faith. But what is faith and what do we need to believe?

For faith, I accept: A "firm belief in something for which there is no proof."[96]

So, my thesis amounts to: Humans evolved a biological need to believe in

---

94 Jeffrey M. Jones, "U.S. Church Membership Falls Below Majority for First Time," Gallup, Mar. 29, 2021, https://news.gallup.com/poll/341963/church-membership-falls-below-majority-first-time.aspx#:~:text=The.

95 Milenko Martinovich, "Americans' partisan identities are stronger than race and ethnicity, Stanford scholar finds," *Stanford Report*, Aug. 31, 2017, https://news.stanford.edu/2017/08/31/political-party-identities-stronger-race-religion/.

96 "faith," Merriam-Webster Dictionary, accessed Jan. 16, 2023, https://www.merriam-webster.com/dictionary/faith.

something(s) for which no proof exists. While belief in deities satiates, other unprovable fascinations, such as religious or ideological dogma, may suffice.

Dogma seems fundamental—even more fundamental than divine super-beings. The idea that some set of universal precepts is correct or true is irresistible. By irresistible, I mean on a level similar to the need to procreate. That's why I suspect biology. Infusing cerebral folds with political ideology may be an attempt to quench a biological urge. But surrendering to primitive urges without inspection is lazy and undermines democracy.

Political Ideology

The *divine being* and *soul* are extraordinary concepts. Both are difficult to fathom or describe using either conventional or scientific terminology. Is the supreme being made of matter or pure energy? Where do our souls reside? We cannot measure nor infer their existence through observation as we infer gravity from planets' motions. Through faith we acquiesce.

That leap of faith precipitates a cascade. If precepts of religion truly come from a deity, then allowing those precepts to permeate the core of our being without filtration or inspection is understandable. Dogmatic adherence seems reasonable. Zealous implementation develops as a logical consequence to faith in the divine. Results flowing from such blind faith may not be desirable or excusable, but they're understandable.

For political ideology or party platforms, acquiescence by faith is indefensible. No supreme being is involved. Ideologies and party platforms descend from mortals. Though humans are capable of astonishing utility, we're flawed. We make mistakes. We engage in self-serving behavior while feigning selflessness. We cheat. We lie. We steal. We also create beauty. We're complex.

Ideas must be critically examined, especially for integration of those ideas into an individual's core analytical framework. There's no good reason to upload an ideology or platform in its entirety into your brain's hard drive without rigorous scrutiny.

However, there are some really bad reasons. For one thing, it's lazy. Specialization is efficacious. Division of labor is indicative of highly evolved social organization. But one thing we *must* do for ourselves. We have to think.

Subbing out our thinking, especially to people with a partisan agenda, is a bad idea.

Our positions on specific issues should not be decided via ideological consultation. Self-government implies thinking for oneself. If public policy is determined by consulting ideological precepts, we've abandoned democracy for the ideological equivalent of theocracy.

More importantly, we become tools. We become useful things to a thing like a political party. Political parties and PACs are like churches passing around the hat. People make donations commensurate with their faith—faith that a particular party is the best hope for representative democracy, faith that issues aren't subordinated for partisan advantage, or faith that hard-earned money isn't for product differentiation or manufacturing division. That faith is misplaced and abused. Faith allows political parties to take constituencies for granted.

In political context, "you gotta go on faith" is prelude to a con. If an invisible deity is involved, faith is your only option. But representative democracy requires reason, scrutiny, and skepticism. Faith interferes with reason, sabotages scrutiny, and is inapposite to skepticism.

Religion versus Political Ideology

As to the malignity of crippling division, whether religion or ideology has the upper hand isn't clear. Historically, religion is the clear winner. But ideology gains ground as more people transpose their faith.

Both religion and political ideology indulge fanaticism. Both have been used to justify violence. Both have scholars tacitly validating zealotry and condoning abomination. Both have sheep to be herded and sheared.

The concept of invisible deities tips the scale toward religion. Going into battle with omnipotent immortals on your side sounds fantastic!

On the other hand, religious creeds include constraints. Admonishments against judgmentalism persist. Concepts such as forgiveness and redemption are embraced. "Hate the sin not the sinner."

I'm not hearing a great deal of "love your neighbor" from political ideologues. Hating "sinners" and judging them to be deplorable without possibility of redemption is in vogue. Forgiveness is either weakness or sin.

There aren't any "constraints on the expression of hostility toward people who adhere to opposing political ideologies."[97]

Faith versus Scientific Method

The competition between science and religion is a distraction. It's a red herring. Methodology or process is material to democracy.

The scientific method is a process for acquiring knowledge and describing reality. On the other hand, just as hope is not a strategy, faith is not a process. Faith is belief without proof, which results in decisions without process.

Science replacing religion is ancillary to scientific method replacing faith. Scientific method is more fundamental than science. The path to scientific knowledge is through its method. The way to religion is through faith.

The way to democracy is through dialogue, deliberation, and voting—the democratic process. Decision-making or policy in democracy is through democratic processes. *Democracy demands process.* Faith is decision-making without proof or process and is therefore inapposite to democracy.

Scientific method evolves our understanding of reality. Democratic process evolves the guiding principles and legal framework of society. Faith inhibits the evolution of cultural intelligence.

Faith and Intransigence

There's commonality between religion and ideology, implicating segregated media and public discourse dysfunction. Conscious beings may suffer experiences conflicting with their worldview. Reason demands adjusting one's worldview to resemble reality more closely—a process or methodology. Even without religion, people cling to worldviews the way Linus clings to his blanket. In the eternal competition between reality and worldview, I put my money on worldview.

Implicit in the evolution of worldview is an acknowledgement of error and even fault. We've been wrong about some things. But it's not just that. Worldview is a tool for navigating life. We become accustomed to tools that fit

---

97 Martinovich, "Americans' partisan identities."

comfortably. The longer we stick with a specific worldview, the more difficult it is to let it go in favor of one that works more reliably.

I'm describing a brand of intransigence particularly problematic for democracy:

Ideological Consistency Is the Hobgoblin of Hyperpartisan Minds[98]

It's foolish. It has no inherent value. It's made up. As a value, it's bankrupt. It's make-believe. It's imaginary. It's mythical.

Ideologies should be like tools in a toolbox. Pick the right one for the moment. There's no going to hell for picking the right tool for the job.

If you don't like the tool metaphor, consider worldviews or ideologies as problem-solving frameworks. No single ideology explains everything or holds all truth. Elements of truth are scattered throughout human philosophies. No philosopher has been right about everything, i.e., ideological purity = stupidity.

It's not only RBAF. Rigidly adhering to *any* analytical framework impairs cognition. Using a single political ideology to appraise every situation is a handicap. Competency in a free and democratic society demands either flexible or hybrid analyses. Developing ideological ruts dulls problem-solving. You don't use grammar rules to solve physics problems. Approaching every single problem with the same problem-solving framework doesn't make sense. Using the same political ideology to understand every single issue facing society is insane.

But when you add the ingredient of faith, ideological intransigence becomes consecrated. Combining a compulsion to believe with human, i.e., flawed worldviews beatifies ideological consistency and sanctifies belligerence.

Although we're in a different part of the book, let's not forget financial incentive. Cultivating an audience or constituency by promoting a specific worldview financially incentivizes intransigence with respect to that worldview.

---

98 "A foolish consistency is the hobgoblin of little minds, adored by little statesmen and philosophers and divines." Ralph Waldo Emerson, Self-Reliance, from Essays: First Series (1841), EmersonCentral.com, accessed March 9, 2024, https://emersoncentral.com/ebook/Self-Reliance.pdf.

Entrenched constituency + faith + financial incentive → dysfunctional ideological intransigence

No single ideology solves all problems. Faith in ideology is tragically misplaced. With public policy, we must be pragmatists, and guiding principles of the Constitution must regulate our pragmatism. Whatever works, so long as it doesn't violate civil rights. Whatever improves the situation, so long as it doesn't offend the Constitution. Stuff all your ideologies.

Separation of Faith and Policy

We need to engage a different part of the brain for our politics. A U.S. founding principle is separation of church and state. We need to do that with our brains. Deliberating public policy with the part of our brain warehousing faith in supreme beings or consecrating ideologies is dysfunctional. Functional democracy requires flexibility and compromise, not the intransigence of faith-based inventions. Religious reckoning or faith is antithetical to democratic process. Only conscious reason penetrates faith-based authority.

Judgmentalism, Purity, and Cancellation

> Thinking is difficult, that's why most people judge.
> —CARL GUSTAV JUNG

All three concepts deserve their own sections or even chapters, but in diabolical synergy they advance hyperpartisanship. With religious association suggested and sinister collaboration foreshadowed, I discuss each individually.

Judgmentalism

We have a penchant for judgment. I'm willing to bet it's an evolutionary adaptation. Tribal existence required dealing with members whose behavior threatened survival. Prompt adjudication minimizes threats. We're quick to judge. But surrendering to psychological predispositions that evolved during our tribal existence without inspection is lazy and inhibits productive thinking.

Watching sprinters break the tape is gratifying. Results are unequivocal. Yet the Olympic sports garnering the most attention are figure skating and gymnastics. Maybe it's aesthetics. It couldn't be judging. We complain and criticize the judging if our favorites don't come out on top. But perhaps we protest too much, or rather, protesting is the thing.

When a sport, or anything for that matter, includes judging, audiences get to play along. We are elevated above mere spectators. We're involved at a higher level. Judging has become a recreational activity.

Its breadth is sweeping and its magnitude industrial. Reality TV in all its manifestations features judgment. Whether it's half- or fully naked adults stabbing each other in the back on jungle islands or children baking cookies, the dramatic climax features a final judgment. It's a pastime.

Judgmentalism establishes inescapable hierarchy. Judge assumes superior position to judged. If I judge you, *I* am the subject, and *you* are the object.

Functional democracy requires judgment as well. We cast votes and render verdicts.

The problem is our responsibility as self-governing citizens commingles with for-profit recreational activity. Judging red or blue team members means ratings and clickbait. Tickling the irresistible impulse to judge in conjunction with partisan political content that exploits psychological need for identity validation is a ratings winner. One set of human beings tunes in to see another set of human beings pronounce judgment on a third set of human beings. Yay!

Judgment in anticipation of suitable punishment is more profitable than forgiveness. Executions draw crowds. Watch as villagers amass in bloodthirsty frenzy with pitchforks and torches to banish the monster . . . following the next commercial break.

Social media threads are, by and large, judgment threads. Judging the other side is sport. If you're hosting the website, good for you. You're making a pretty penny off alleged political discourse as entertainment. You're the beneficiary. Congratulations!

Purity

Not all types are objectionable. I'll start with science and work toward partisanship.

Within a chemistry lab, chasing purity makes sense. Purest reagents, including distilled water, produce the best results, even when you're breaking bad.

On the other hand, a pond of pure distilled water is not as biologically productive as one soiled with nutrients. Sterility constrains life.

Evolution favors heterozygosity. Purebreds are impoverished in survivability. As a biological trait, purity is useless.

Consider systems and ideologies. "Pure" seems incongruous with natural systems. Nature has ecosystems, star systems, galaxies, and the universe. Is our solar system a pure star system? It is what it is. It's our solar system.

Nation-states like America are hybrid systems. America operates with a mixture of regulated capitalism and government-run programs like public education. I support hybrid systems. We could argue over optimal mix, and we do. Determining the relative roles of government and private sector is fundamental to policy debate. But when the dust settles, if America persists, it will be hybrid.

With respect to ideology, pure means it belongs to someone else. It means you're on someone else's path. You're covering someone else's tune without making it your own. If you make it your own, it's not pure. To say someone's ideology is pure is logically equivalent to saying he doesn't think for himself. Ideological purity is lazy or incompetent.

Pursuing partisan purity wastes time and resources, or worse. As to human systems and ideologies, pursuing purity seems religious. I wished to say, "in other words, it's without reason." Though faith is implicated, reason is also on the table.

Purity aids the partisan war effort. Remember "RINOs" and "stop using Republican talking points." How shall we understand partisan purification?

First, it's clearly bullying. Although linguistic demeanor suits squabbling adolescents, insults enjoy religious authority. High inquisitors of ideological purity persecute heretics.

Impurity is uniting. Partisan heretics are uniters. They're hybrids. They have both conservative and liberal elements. They are moderates and independents. They're bridge-builders. In other words, they get in the way of financially incentivized product differentiation and are inconvenient to partisan warfare.

They must conform or be shunned.

Cancellation

Cancellation implicates another type of impurity or more precisely, imperfection. People get canceled for committing some form of sin. The transgression exposes human shortcomings. It can be moral turpitude or corruption associated with abuse of power, or it can be ignorance or stupidity or some combination thereof.

It usually does not rise to the level of felonious criminality or incarceration, but it's not necessarily victimless. When a societal member acts hurtfully, it is right for society to respond, especially absent formal prosecution. The issue is whether tribal banishment or religious excommunication, or cancellation in modern parlance, is appropriate.

In pursuit of the partisan angle, I frame the discussion according to classic parameters as well as modern concerns about our justice system. In other words, what is the utility of cancellation? Will it rehabilitate the perpetrator? Is it a useful deterrent, or is it punishment plain and simple? Or is there some purpose outside the classical framework? Thinking of cancellation as deterrent is fashionable.

As far as modern concerns about criminal justice, our society is moving toward progressive reform, especially for nonviolent offenders.

In sum, what is the utility of cancellation, and should there be cancellation reform for nonviolent offenders? Before answering, I embark upon an outrageous non sequitur.

When contemplating the attitude and behavior of congressional representatives, especially PWs, humility isn't the first word that comes to mind. It's easier to visualize finger-pointing politicians holding forth at the expense of the other side of the aisle. While style might vary from red-faced bombast to stiletto erudition, uncompromised champions pontificate from a pillar of sanctimony. Made-for-TV performances titillate and revolt appropriate partisan viewers while eliciting praise or condemnation from corresponding PPs. These types of recitals are essential for ambitious full-fledged PWs conducting all-out partisan war.

On the other hand, legislating effectively, or democracy for that matter, involves cultivating relationships and building bridges across ideological gorges. It requires continuous reasonable dialogue with political adversaries to diligently and sincerely identify common ground. It implies genuine disposition toward compromise. Legislating successfully means playing the blame game infrequently and with great reservation. A dash of humility facilitates legislating. Sanctimonious displays at the expense of colleagues frustrate functional democracy. Unfortunately, Congress appears deficient in humility, while arrogance and sanctimony abound.

The preceding two paragraphs apply just as well to media, especially PPs. Sanctimony is at a premium, whereas humility is in short supply. While humility enhances empathetic understanding and information sharing, i.e., journalism, it interferes with judgmentalism. Humility is bad for the partisanship business.

Let's get back to examining the utility of cancellation. It comes down to whether individuals can evolve. Is rehabilitation possible? A school of thought asserts, "people don't change." If you attend that school, are you the same person you were at fifteen? (Unless you are fifteen, in which case, are you the same person you were at eight, or something like that?)

I know I have changed. I'm sober. Aptitude for rehabilitation exists on a continuum. At one end are people whose capacity for change is extremely limited and at the other end are people who exhibit a rare talent. Most of us are somewhere between.

Cancellation Is Regressive Justice Squandering Opportunity for Growth or Rehabilitation

Exposing our sins and imperfections for public examination can be quite embarrassing or even humiliating. Our capacity for sanctimony naturally deflates. From a human resource management perspective, society is presented with an incredible opportunity.

In the wake of exposure of our foibles, our capacity for self-examination, humility, and evolution is at its apogee. Conversely, we can point to examples where people respond to unflattering revelations with sanctimonious stubbornness. Whether the accused doubles down on his own righteousness or shows humility is a function of both the persuasiveness of incriminating evidence as well as the character of the accused.

Throwing people away when the probability of humility and epiphanies of self-awareness are at their highest wastes human resources. This is especially true for legislators and media members. Finger-pointing and for-profit judgmentalism are harder when your imperfections are on public display.

From PI's perspective, the utility of cancellation is to remove from public position those whose capacity for judgmentalism has been handicapped. Infusing humility into legislators or media members is unsuitable to the PI business model. Humility is de-escalating. If you can't ride in on your high horse and with unblemished sanctimony condemn the actions or philosophies of the other side, your PW utility has been blunted. Time to go to pasture.

Cancellation reform for nonviolent offenders is progressive. Simply offending contemporary mores or violating some tribal credo shouldn't result in permanent residence in the garbage heap. Not because offensive actions are excusable, but because we can't afford to squander opportunities or waste human resources.

I don't think a person is fully realized or competent without suffering an epiphany of humility. Please don't misunderstand. I do not seek to encourage public offense or preferentially promote the pathologically flawed. We're all flawed. Revelations of deficiency do not impart defect.

But revelation provides an opening for redress and growth. Discuss it publicly. Permit alleged perpetrators and victims to have their say. Encourage humility and suggest a pathway for redemption. Marginalize or cut the sanctimonious from the conversation. Don't squander opportunities for transforming full-fledged PWs disguised as legislators into legislators and PPs disguised as analysts and journalists into analysts and journalists.

Progressives believe in reform and the possibility of rehabilitation. Is rehabilitation guaranteed? Of course not. Do we get it wrong sometimes? Of course. That's the nature of any justice system. Sometimes innocents get punished, and sometimes the guilty get away. Some people game the system, which can include feigning humility or pretending to change. But social utility diminishes without the possibility for redemption, and a society that doesn't value forgiveness is bankrupt.

Cancellation Is Corporate

Cancellation is *not* the progressive way. It's the corporate way. Just get rid of them. It's cleaner. No PR problems. Just move on. It's good business.

Cancellation is financially incentivized, like for-profit prisons. It's private sector, for-profit punishment for sport.

But keeping nonviolent offenders in prison reduces GDP. It's inefficient. Reform is pragmatic.

Coming clean should result in reduced sentencing. Avoiding trial conserves resources. But TV has different priorities. TV doesn't want to get robbed of programming opportunities.

Being flawed is being perfectly human. We are united through our flaws. Our alleged enemies seem less threatening when we recognize the commonality of our frailties. Awareness of our imperfection elicits mercy.

The affectation of purity cultivates intolerance, and every time you judge someone you become a little more segregated from your humanity.

Cancellation is heartless and regressive. It rewards judgmentalism, promotes the merry chase of purity, and contributes to hyperpartisanship and democratic dysfunction.

Apocalypse Always

I get the impression through media and casual conversation that a portion of the electorate doesn't consider hyperpartisanship problematic. The problem for those people is their side has thus far been unable to annihilate the enemy. In other words, partisanship is problematic because opposition endures. War is fine. It's only problematic if the enemy can't be vanquished. The other side won't give up or die voluntarily. That's a problem.

Contrasting substance with procedure illustrates cognitive disconnect. Understanding hyperpartisanship as a problem of substantive disagreement between factions is misconstruction. When I hear media analysts incessantly proclaim, "there are real substantive differences out there," or "the divisions are real," I want to pull out my hair because they're missing the point.

Democracy is a system for peacefully resolving substantive differences. Because we can't all agree on substance, we vote. If no substantive differences existed, the vote, and perhaps democracy itself, would be superfluous. Democracy, along with the vote, implies substantive differences. Right to vote implies right to substantively disagree. Voting rights implies substantive disagreement rights.

Hyperpartisanship sabotages the process by which substantive differences resolve. Hyperpartisanship undermines democratic processes. This book examines factors contributing to hyperpartisanship. That process continues.

Good versus Evil

In the final battle, good triumphs. The religious archetype is pregnant with pretense.

Debate over whether good and evil exist in a religious sense is not lucrative. The idea that human capacity for good or bad blends in a continuum inconveniences storytelling.

Hollywood shoot-'em-up movies predicate bad guys being so bad they deserve to be killed in cold blood. Satisfied audiences exit theaters untroubled by the absence of due process. The nuance of continuum spoils the genre.

I confess vulnerability to the bloody gratification. As I imagine myself the single-minded hero, critical introspection and uncertainty melt into spectacular flow of relentless motion and sanctified violence.

Democracy, on the other hand, is the antithesis of the final battle. Perpetuating democracy requires perpetuating disputes. Disagreement is the lifeforce of democracy. Without disagreement, what is the reason for voting?

We must disagree with one another. We must argue. That doesn't mean screaming and yelling with popping neck veins. That's fighting, not arguing. It doesn't mean throwing stones. It means rational public debate.

Progress within democracy arises from dialectics and is therefore incompatible with a final-battle mentality. Vanquishing the enemy is both senseless and counterproductive. It's senseless because people we disagree with aren't our enemies, and it's counterproductive because vanquishing debate opponents terminates dialectics. Terminating opposition extinguishes democracy.

We must respect debate opponents—not because they are necessarily worthy of our respect—but because we need them. How about another sports analogy? I'm channeling Lakers/Celtics. A childish vision of rivalry might involve annihilating the competition.

But as we mature, appreciation for rivalry itself evolves. Through honest and open competition and according to rules, something magnificent emerges from the most intense of struggles—something unattainable to individual protagonists. Competition tests theories of the game and verifies measures of productivity. As we experience beauty tempered with heartbreak, the game evolves.

A Singular Vision in Democracy Is as Useful as a Singular Protagonist in Sport

Evolution dies.

People we disagree with are necessary rivals. Maybe "rivals" is too harsh. We're all partners in the same league. We're in league with one another. *We're in league with people we disagree with.* Survival of that league requires us to conduct a respectful, honest, and open competition of ideas.

Unfortunately, media segregated according to ideological vision undermines the type of respectful, open, and honest competition of ideas necessary for progress within constitutional democracy. Clicker determines debate winner.

Imagine if you could guarantee victory for your favorite sports team by simply choosing the right channel to watch the game. At first, it might seem as though you discovered something marvelous. It would feel like a cozy dream. But that type of gratification is ephemeral. Eventually, dissatisfaction would creep in. You crave something real.

Yet for political debate, portions of the public never tire of orchestrated conquest. They keep tuning in. They keep clicking to guaranteed outcome.

If we take a step back, there's an objectivity breathing within us. We've been wrong before. We've been wrong about so many things. Occasionally we remember specific instances. We don't like to, but occasionally we do. Then we get to relive the emotion. Our faces burn. We blush anew. Best not to dwell on it. Let's move on.

How could we believe a political team is permanently correct? It defies logic. Why is sports different than politics in this regard? Why would we eventually become bored with a channel guaranteeing victory for our sports team, but never tire of hearing that our political team is eternally righteous?

Because POEP has nothing to do with winning. I've been comparing apples with oranges. Being eternally righteous is different than winning all the time. But how?

Rationally, being right all the time is as ludicrous as winning all the time. Yet there's a difference. Winning is about who scores the most points or who gets the most votes. It's like sprinters breaking the tape. Results are unequivocal.

But being right, unless it's something like an arithmetic problem, is often a matter of opinion. Faith is the secret ingredient whereby righteousness becomes indelible. The apocalypse is not a contest between competing ideas. It's the final battle between good and evil.

Democracy, on the other hand, is for peacefully settling legal and policy disputes. Constitutionally democratic nation-states aren't purposed for resolving the apocalypse. The legislature isn't the proper venue for the final battle between good and evil.

In some sense, elections don't matter. It's more about finding the church that affirms preexisting beliefs or the preacher whose sermons make you feel right about yourself. Regardless of election outcome, ideological evangelicals can be summoned with a click to provide reveries of the promised land located on the other side of some impending ultimate victory. We may have lost the election, but we were *right*, and while our final victory did not come today, it's inevitable because we're good and the other side is evil. *That's not democracy.*

Religious Apocalyptic Psychology Undermines Democracy

Final-battle psychology coupled with ideologically segregated media makes for a toxic brew. If your eternally righteous political views are eventually rewarded at the apocalypse, why compromise? What's the point of seeking common ground other than postponing the final battle? It's sinful procrastination.

Democracy is premised on division, differences, and disagreement. We must disagree with each other. But we need to get better at it. We need to improve the skills essential to democracy.

Integral to improving any skill is approaching the challenge with facilitating psychology. Ask any coach or teacher. The bellicosity of apocalyptic psychology impairs the peaceful resolution of inevitable disagreement through democratic processes.

PPs characterize every disagreement as threat. Disagreements are not threats. They're opportunities to realize democracy. Realizing democracy means resolving differences through process, which is inapposite to achieving ultimate victory in the final battle.

The war to end all wars is a lie. Final-battle psychology poisons democracy. There's no ultimate victory. It's not good versus evil. There's no partisan exceptionalism. We must live and work with each other or abandon democracy.

Evolution

This section is premised on the desirability of evolution and implicates a hodgepodge of factors with religious undertones impeding societal evolution. If "evolution" makes you uncomfortable, think of it as progress. We must progress. Adapt or die. Maintaining status quo, i.e., stagnation, is ultimately expiring.

We know a little bit about evolution and extinction. Analogies between the biological concepts and arcs of human civilizations abound. Both science and history, minus ex post facto judgmentalism, instruct.

Science Informs That Evolution Results from Trial and Error

There's a psychological relationship between trial and error. Fear of making a mistake may prevent us from trying. For some, it's debilitating. Others keep trying. They don't give up. They persist through mistakes and succeed.

If we're to be a society that persists, we must not permit fear of error to subordinate experimentation. High inquisitors of religious and ideological dogma threaten progress with incapacitating fear.

Censorship Is Counter-Evolutionary

Its approach is religious. Eliminating sinful utterances, or sin by word, may reduce or eliminate sinful thoughts. The logic of mindfulness imbues the process. We *should* think about what we say before we say it. And if we think about what we say or what we're going to say, we inevitably think about what we're thinking. Thinking about what we're thinking portends self-awareness, which is integral to self-government.

But teaching mindfulness is different than censorship. Censorship is punitive and relies on fear. The use of fear circumvents introspective or educational processes. It reduces speech without increasing self-awareness. If you express what you think is true, you might offend someone's religious or ideological dogma. If you commit the sin of offense by word, you will be punished. Like a mugshot on an FBI most-wanted poster, permanent unflattering captions will forever tarnish your image. Best to keep head down and mouth shut.

Tribalism and HM are implicated. Procedures establishing tribal orthodoxy aren't democratic. Continuously changing the law creates dependence and is financially incentivized. In other words, with tribal dogma, yesterday's virtue is today's sin. Combining threat of punishment with constantly shifting doctrine incentivizes silence. Leave public speaking to administrators of tribal canon. Let ideological priests do all the talking.

Censorship, along with corresponding punitive measures like cancellation, supported by financially incentivized judgmentalism, stymie evolution because they discourage trial and error, which inhibits problem-solving. Saying the wrong thing aloud is part of the process of getting to the right thing, and we should treat it that way. Any good teacher knows anxiety interferes with learning.

Democracy withers and dies if censorship subordinates experimentation through speech. Free speech is the antidote to both religious and ideological dogma. Open expression and debate of ideas facilitates both individual and societal erudition. Free speech is evolutionary because it stimulates trial and error.

Hybridization

In addition to trial and error, evolution employs hybridization. Purity is antithetical to hybridization, and segregation inhibits hybridization.

The realization of purity as a mainstream political and ideological virtue in America is fascinating. To me, purity is un-American. I'm aware of ignorant and malignant crusades of racial purity exemplified by Nazis and the KKK. Foundational to racism, including American racism, are unscientific notions of racial purity. I've discussed how partisan purification abets financially incentivized product differentiation. But we've gotten to the point where mainstream political analysis infuses partisan purity with value, without proper scrutiny.

Each time partisan purity is endorsed as virtue through language like "RINO" or "stop using Republican talking points," analysis and commentary around the suitability of purity in context of American ideals and its relevance to governing within a constitutional democracy should ensue.

Evolution, including American evolution in both private and public sectors, employs hybridization. We take the best ideas from everywhere and blend them. The best leaders know good ideas can come from anywhere. Evolution is nonjudgmental as to source. All that matters is whether it works. The Constitution and our laws prescribe caveats to efficacy. Partisan and ideological purity are irrelevant to effective governance and interfere with societal evolution.

Diversity

Another way of evaluating the evolutionary consequences of purity is by understanding its relationship with diversity. Purity reduces diversity. Before outlining how, although it seems plain, I need to discuss a hidden premise. If purity is virtuous, some common understanding of what purity means must exist. With a substance like water, understanding is uncomplicated. For partisan ideals, however, the calculus isn't straightforward. We've examined problems surrounding establishing PT dogma. The process is inscrutable and dominated by those with disproportionate media access. It financially incentivizes extremism, and ideals to be aspired to constantly shift.

But let's put that aside. Imagine widespread agreement as to the meaning of partisan or ideological purity. Assume purity in that sense is virtuous. Pressure to conform to virtue is eternal. The greater the conformity to the virtue of ideological purity, the less diverse our society becomes in thought and opinion. As diversity wanes, evolutionary possibilities decrease. As evolutionary possibilities decrease, persistence becomes less likely. Purity annihilates exceptionalism.

Segregation

Segregating ideas, philosophies, and principles also impedes hybridization. Synthesizing different elements is difficult if they're kept apart. Partisan or ideological segregation inhibits hybridization in many ways. We've exhaustively discussed separate media outlets for distinct political views. Only listening to people you agree with is the functional equivalent of not listening to anyone. Hybridization cannot result from masturbation.

Extremism reduces hybridization. Extremism is segregating. As people migrate to outer extremes of the partisan spectrum, chances of getting together for a mutual exchange of ideas decrease. Conceptual hybridization is difficult without conversation.

That's why censorship impedes hybridization. No conversation means no exchange of ideas. Censorship is also segregating. Fear of speaking in the public square drives people to ECs. ECs are sterile vacuums segregated according to ideology or opinion, inhibiting free exchange of the diverse ideas essential for hybridization. Think of ECs as cages separating life by ideological classification. Wild ecosystems provide greater opportunity for hybridization.

Hyperpartisan Marriage

Politically homogenous marriages are both symptomatic and contributory. I grew up in a bipartisan household. My father was a Republican and my mother a Democrat. The heterogeneous household hybridized my ideological development.

What are the evolutionary implications of mate selection based on partisanship? Does political ideology correlate with capacity for love? Will homogeneity of political views within a household enhance offspring viability? Evolution favors heterozygosity.

Marriages trending toward partisan homogeneity alter the ecosystem. I predict the children of such unions will statistically be more likely to consider ideological purity virtuous. They'll be less likely to tolerate or genuinely consider contrary opinions. In other words, as marriages trend toward partisan homogeneity, their offspring will be increasingly hyperpartisan. Do you recognize the positive feedback?

Intolerance

Consider these counter-evolutionary concepts as of, or relating to, plain old human intolerance. Partisan purification is intolerance. We're simply not going to tolerate people who don't conform. PINOs not welcomed. Purity as virtue provides another reason or excuse to be intolerant. Intolerance inhibits hybridization. "Stop using Republican talking points."

The hybridization analysis reveals another counter-evolutionary feedback loop. Purity as virtue contributes to intolerance, which is segregating. Segregation facilitates purification and increased intolerance. Greater intolerance for that which does not conform to insular concepts of purity drives further segregation, etc.

There's not only beauty in imperfection and richness in impurity, but reason, efficacy, and evolution as well. Diversity implies imperfection. Perfection is singular. If evolution discovers perfection, the need for diversity is obviated. That which eternally evolves is never perfect.

Embracing purity as virtue is equally absurd. Strictly clinging to partisan dogma deters hybridization. Evolution flourishes where life integrates.

Selfless Mythology and Dysfunction

Whether or not acts of pure selflessness exist or it's possible to be purely selfless has been debated and is open to debate, but can't be proved. Resolving that debate isn't presently necessary, but it merits some consideration in the context of hyperpartisanship within a chapter on religion and faith.

I initiate analysis with non-dispositive anecdotes. They merely set the stage, and since it's my play, I set the stage as I see fit.

First, if you do an internet search, the majority of results either take the concept of selflessness for granted or hawk it like a cure-all. In other words, it's a popular notion with market value.

Second, as part of my undergraduate curriculum, I took an elective in early to medieval Christianity. I remember reading an excerpt from the writings of one of the saints. He spent his life engaged in saintly activities with the hope of spending the eternity of his afterlife in the loving embrace of the Almighty.

Performing saintly acts to enhance one's chances of going to heaven cannot be fairly characterized as purely selfless. The acts may appear selfless, but if we consider psychological motivation, denying an element of selfishness is difficult.

Here's the point we'll revisit relentlessly: The fact that saintly acts aren't purely selfless doesn't mean they aren't divine. Good doesn't mean selfless and selfish doesn't mean bad. Conflating or equating good with selfless and bad with selfish needlessly encumbers individual psychology and democracy.

Third, I also took an introductory psychology course. I remember my professor telling us of instances where people made the "ultimate sacrifice" for loved ones. Is anything more purely selfless than a parent dying to save a child or a soldier dying to save a brother- or sister-in-arms?

Occasionally, however, the hero lives through the experience. Testimony from survivors muddies the waters of pure selflessness. Survivors assert that living with failure to save a loved one would be worse than dying. Avoiding that failure was better than living. They would rather die than live with that failure. Notice in these iterations, the welfare or feelings of those needing saving are irrelevant. Deciding to act was based on what was more psychologically palatable to the savior. That doesn't make it less noble, but it isn't purely selfless.

That analysis is going to bother those who need to believe in the concept of selflessness and that an act isn't truly good unless it's purely selfless. Where does that come from? From the perspective of survival of a species, a certain amount of altruism is adaptive. But submitting to a biological imperative cannot be fairly characterized as selfless.

A desire to feel good or alleviate guilt can motivate altruistic behavior. Some gift-giving places others in one's debt. Some "charitable" contributions are tax deductible. Sometimes the net effect is good. Sometimes it's not. But obsessing on whether an act is purely selfless is, at best, off the mark. Compassion doesn't require selflessness.

Utility

The most compelling argument for helping others is that in doing so, we help ourselves. In that sense, acts of pure selflessness have inferior utility. They help fewer people. They don't help the helper.

That's why conflating "good" with "selfless" is harmful. We reduce the amount of good we can do. Pragmatically, good doesn't mean selfless. By doing the right thing, we better ourselves. As a result, helping others isn't some ethereal act dependent upon dubious psychology.

As a matter of psychological health and energy conservation, we should get comfortable with the selfishness of helping others. There's nothing wrong with it. If you help others because it makes you feel good, great! Psychological gymnastics needed to convince yourself or others you're engaging in acts of pure selflessness is a waste of time and psychological energy. It's debilitating.

Likewise with public policy. Infecting public policy debate with religious, ideological, or mythological concepts of selflessness sabotages democratic processes.

On January 20, 1961, President John F. Kennedy said: "And so, my fellow Americans, ask not what your country can do for you, ask what you can do for your country."[99] I support that sentiment wholeheartedly as enlightened selfishness. By helping our country, we help ourselves. Helping our fellow Americans enriches our own lives on a personal level and improves the society to which we belong, which can result in more tangible benefits. We get a return on our investment.

I don't mean that in an esoteric way. I'm talking social utility signified in measurables like GDP. If you can't convince the electorate a proposed policy will either benefit individuals from whom you seek support, raise overall social utility, or make America stronger as a nation, then you've failed to make your case.

Advocacy

Arguing something is "the right thing to do" or expecting the electorate to act selflessly is at best a failure of advocacy, or worse, weaponizing psychological vulnerabilities for partisan advantage. Conflating "good" with "selfless" is politically expedient. It's devious. When I hear people pushing those buttons, I grow suspicious. The tactics befit a proselytizing scoundrel with one hand on the Bible and the other in the collection basket.

---

99 "Ask Not What Your Country Can Do For You," US history.org., accessed December 19, 2024, hMps://www.ushistory.org/documents/ask-not.htm.

Expecting people to support policies not in their own self-interest evinces disconnected privilege. Privileged people can afford to parade selflessness. Those less privileged cannot.

Promoting the idea that public policy can be justified solely based on self-lessness is a con. Don't make yourself an easy mark. Do you believe candidates and politicians beckoning selflessness from the electorate aren't acting in their own self-interest? Do you believe TV personalities making six-, seven-, or eight-figure salaries *selflessly* hawk selflessness?

The guilt trip is a manipulative weapon that should be restricted to the pulpit and nuclear family or banished altogether. Guilt-tripping for policy in a democratic and free society joins church with state. Changing policy according to some religious or ideological tenet offends constitutional democracy.

Much worse than being inappropriate, it's ineffective advocacy. It only works to divide people into the eternally sanctimonious who have deluded themselves into believing in their superior capacity for selflessness and those who resent having guilt trips laid on them. On a personal level, partisan guilt-tripping helped cement my unaffiliated status.

Identifying and inspiring behaviors that reward individuals while providing social utility yields progress. A utilitarian objective for government or public policy is to incentivize individuals to do that which benefits society. Conversely, a dogmatic regulatory framework discouraging or preempting the type of selfish behavior that provides social utility, such as installing solar panels, is dysfunctional. In other words, transforming social utility into acts of pure selflessness is government failure.

Cultivating enlightened selfishness is more likely to succeed than guilt-tripping. It's a pragmatic approach independent of either theological or ideological dogma. Elaborate or debilitating psychological gymnastics aren't needed. It depends upon neither chicanery nor self-deception.

Most importantly, the burden shifts from partisan morality to persuasive argument. Petitioning morality incites sectarianism. It creates a venue for an Olympiad in moral superiority. It provokes judgmentalism and finger-pointing. It divides us. It emboldens proselytizing scoundrels. It favors demagogues, and it makes for great TV.

Convincing the electorate that something is in their best interest is a better *issue* strategy than decreeing it's the right thing to do. Conflating good with selflessness makes sense if you're marketing either your own or your tribe's sanctimony.

Cultivating enlightened selfishness doesn't require demagoguery. I'm not advocating for unprincipled lawmaking. Rational persuasion must be regulated by the Constitution, which represents our common principles and articulates our civil rights. Oaths of office are to the Constitution. The process of rational persuasion regulated by common principles respecting civil rights is uniting.

Separating Wheat from Chaff

Ancient religious texts have not aged well. To understand the Bible as something other than an endorsement of slavery requires spectacular contortionism. Yet portions, like the Golden Rule (GR), transcend millennia to endure as wisdom.

Here, I briefly examine the process for separating wheat from chaff.

The notion that societal morality evolves toward greater enlightenment is irresistible. It's one I subscribe to, although there's a self-serving and tautological element in the reasoning. The society we currently occupy is governed by different laws and guided by different principles than previous iterations. As members of the current society, we can choose to view those differences as superior, inferior, or neutral. If we are evolving toward greater enlightenment, then because we have succeeded previous generations, it follows we must be more enlightened morally.

Slavery is obviously wrong. Yet there's no mathematical proof. If I were to make an argument, I would invoke GR. Because I do not wish to be enslaved, enslaving others is wrong. GR is wheat. Biblical rules prescribing proper slave management are chaff.

But here, the arc of moral evolution is premise. We're examining process. Why does humanity evolve toward greater moral enlightenment? Enter the tautology. What does it mean to evolve? We are more evolved because we succeed what precedes us. Therefore, our morality is more evolved.

Let's distinguish results from cause. What causes us to evolve toward greater moral enlightenment? Maybe it's a cultural/intellectual process. As humans, we discuss right and wrong ad nauseam, both formally and informally, eternally, and throughout history. Our case law, the Congressional

Record, historical documents, and discussions in bars and cafeterias evince our proclivity. As a result of rigorous debate, the best ideas rise to the top and maintain their perch until greater ideas supersede. In other words, moral evolution results from a dialectic. The intellectual process takes place. But whether moral evolution *results* from that process is impossible to prove.

Evolution of Virtue

It's also true GR has social utility.[100] Principles embodying empathy may facilitate the cooperation necessary for the evolution of complex and populous societies. Therefore, evolving morality endures because it is adaptive for increasing complexity of human civilization.

As an intellectual exercise, or perhaps an exercise in humility, consider an alternative hypothesis. GR can be regarded as adaptive in the more traditional evolutionary sense. It is biologically adaptive for individuals.

Adhering to GR enhances individual survivability. If I treat others the way I wish to be treated, I'm less likely to be killed and more likely to survive. I'm aware of ruthless individuals who treated others with contempt and were highly successful from an evolutionary perspective. History tells of merciless rulers whose mates outnumber our acquaintances and whose progeny could populate small cities. But they are exceptions. They represent a small percentage of humanity. Most of us have to get along without an army or gang.

Even those who flout GR for their own short-term benefit may eventually receive a comeuppance. Following GR reduces the likelihood of incarceration or getting popped. It's not foolproof. People who treat others with respect can be murdered. But from a statistical perspective, over tens of thousands of generations, which is the way evolution works, GR is adaptive.

It's possible the inclination to treat others according to GR has existed as a trait in a percentage of the human population since our inception. The inclination might predate our species. Formalization in the New Testament may have resulted from enlightened introspection as well as an epiphany

---

100 Nathan Cofnas, "The Golden Rule: A Naturalistic Perspective," *Utilitas*, Cambridge University Press, April 7, 2022, https://www.cambridge.org/core/journals/utilitas/article/golden-rule-a-naturalistic-perspective/23D7AAC2FCA9B09DD64F267994F0722A.

of utility. Civilizations incorporating GR into their core principles enhance their evolutionary potential. In other words, humanity has a better chance of persisting under the auspices of GR. It saves us.

So, it's possible to understand evolving morality as:

1. The result of a dialectic;
2. A pragmatic adaptation of social utility facilitating the evolution of complex civilization;
3. Biologically adaptive;
4. Some combination thereof; or
5. Something else.

The point of this exercise is threefold. First, as civilization evolves, we must discard outdated moral chaff. Second, we should be careful of patting ourselves on the back for our moral evolution. When we simultaneously accept the roles of both scientist and subject, we are conflicted and vulnerable to self-serving subjectivity. Humility abets objectivity.

Finally, we should be mindful of both cause and utility when we endeavor to evolve morally. For example, are new "virtues" in service to the utility of society and persistence of human civilization, or do they serve as profitable media content, or both? Or worse, is their primary purpose partisan advantage? In free societies, discussing the utility of evolving morality is appropriate and essential.

Analyzing Virtue Utility Is Complex and Contextual

Here, I briefly explore the virtue of humility. We've seen how humility can serve as both asset and liability depending on objective. For legislating, humility is an asset because it permits compromise. Humility provides a mental framework amenable to recognizing common ground.

On the other hand, competition for limelight requires aggression, which is hindered by humility. The media gives lip-service to humility and airtime to arrogance. Yet humility perseveres as virtue.

The concept of perseverance provides a clue. Humility perseveres because it contributes to perseverance.

The utility of a virtue like humility can be time frame–dependent. Just as humility can be an asset or liability depending on objective, it can be an asset or liability depending on time frame. Humility's value increases with duration. Arrogance or vanity provide immediate advantage, but perseverance requires humility.

Consider the advantages and disadvantages of arrogance and humility in the short and long run for human relationships as well as the arc of civilizations or nation-states. In the short run, arrogance can have great utility in both individual relationships and in ascendency of civilizations and nation-states. A certain amount of arrogance and vanity may win a mate. But the persistence of healthy relationships where partners share equal bargaining power requires humility.

Likewise with civilizations. Human history over the last 5,000 years can be conceptualized as studying the duration of various civilizations. Investigating civilization collapse is a robust academic field.[101] Specifics aren't presently relevant. The general issue is whether qualities useful in conquest and expansion elicit longevity. I'm suggesting that as the arc of a civilization progresses, the utility of arrogance wanes and the pragmatism of humility waxes. The hypothesis is impossible to prove, but the discussion explores complexities involved with assessing utility of specific virtues. I conclude virtue's utility is contextual.

Exceptionalism versus Humility

The more immediate concern is the sustainability of constitutionally democratic nation-states like America. This brings us back to faith.

I agree with President Biden that America is a nation uniquely based on ideas including liberty, equality, and democracy, rather than geography or ethnicity.[102] But what is the utility of exceptionalism with respect to our sustainability? Ideas may persist but resources are finite. Noble ideas predicating our exceptionalism can't turn garbage dumps into wetlands, carbon dioxide

---

101 Rosamond Hutt, "Why do civilizations collapse?" World Economic Forum, Mar. 17, 2016, https://www.weforum.org/agenda/2016/03/why-do-civilizations-collapse; Ian Morris, "Incredible Archaeological Discoveries," World Economic Forum, Feb. 19, 2016, 11:17, https://www.youtube.com/watch?v=oxieVARtZ7c.

102 President Joe Biden, "State of the Union Address," The White House, Feb. 7, 2023, https://www.whitehouse.gov/state-of-the-union-2023/.

into oxygen, or badlands into farmland any more than they can turn water into wine.

Faith that our exceptionalism inoculates us against "uncontrollable population movements; new epidemic diseases; failing states leading to increased warfare; collapse of trade routes leading to famine; and climate change,"[103] is vanity. Faith in our exceptionalism has no place in crafting public policy for enhancing our longevity.

Humility reduces the likelihood of making the worst mistakes. One way to understand civilization collapse is as humility deficiency. Arrogant overreaching inevitably becomes a liability even for the most powerful.

Humility can be considered an evolutionary adaptation sustaining egalitarian relationships and prolonging civilization. Or, as virtue, it is vestigial and will fade to oblivion. I think it more likely its fate will depend on utility than morality. Its utility for individuals is more discernible than for complex systems or entities transcending human lifetimes such as civilizations or nation-states. What we know is that previous iterations of civilization ended. America, some humility, please!

Academia

The concern is institutionalizing binary ideological catechisms according to partisan, red-state/blue-state dominion. There are at least two negative consequences. First, it embeds elements of hyperpartisanship at early stages of human development. Formalizing ideological division through education entrenches polarity more deeply into the developing psyche, and as a result, our society.

Second, as ideology gains prominence in shaping curriculum, the determinative status of other factors, like academic rigor, diminishes.

In law school, I realized the purpose wasn't to learn the compendium of law, which is impossible. The goal was to learn how to *figure out* the law for any potential case and make persuasive arguments based on legal principles, precedent, evolving societal norms, and logic.

Before suggesting parameters for an academic curriculum to reduce hyperpartisanship and improve democracy, I would like to impart an aphorism,

---

103 Hutt, ""Why do civilizations collapse?"

which combined with my law school example, provides philosophical under-pinnings for my recommendations.

If you give someone a fish, he eats for a day; if you teach him to fish, he eats for a lifetime.

Logic

First and foremost, we should teach children how to reason, not what to think. In addition to emphasizing mathematics, we should teach logic. Both mathematics and logic are more about the how than the what. I'm not suggesting we force preschoolers to work with if/then clauses. All curricula should be age appropriate—but the sooner, the better.

Second, we should learn about ourselves. It's said that ignorance is bliss. The most fundamental iteration is self-ignorance. I argue throughout that self-awareness for the fundamental units of democracy is integral to the vigilance required to sustain democracy. To bolster that concept, I embark on a brief excursion back to my law school experience.

Levels of Intent

The law considers different levels of intent. I discuss two to illustrate. The highest level is "specific intent." It's the one we're most familiar with. For example, I could blow up a plane with the specific intent of killing passengers. That would make me guilty of murder.

I could also blow up a plane with the specific intent of destroying documents containing dispositive evidence that I committed a felony. Although my specific intent wasn't to kill passengers, I knew with substantial certainty everyone on board would die. I'm still guilty of murder. Knowledge satisfies intent requirements. Knowledge = Intent.

Now let's get out of law school and substitute awareness for knowledge. An adult conception of intent incorporates awareness. I'm sure some of you have been injured, inconvenienced, or disrespected in some way and the perpetrator claimed, "well, at least my intentions were good." Maybe the perp's intentions weren't malevolent, but a deficiency of knowledge or awareness was operating. Do you see how unconsciousness is psychologically incentivized? By maintaining a convenient lack of awareness, one can reliably claim good intent. Ignorance is bliss.

Awareness disclosure: Although my specific intent is to explore hyperpartisanship, I'm aware some of what I've written is liable to upset or offend some people. Some may think, "well, if you know some of your ideas are going to offend some people, then you should keep them to yourself." Wrong!

Both law and life compel balancing. Here, I weigh the utility of exploration against the impropriety of offense. Equations vary according to circumstance and individuality. The struggle to understand and resolve such balancing equations defines human adult responsibility. Freethinking guarantees diversity of resolution. Sometimes we must risk offense, and sometimes discretion is the better part of honesty. Occasional offense and self-censorship are both features of free, diverse, and democratic societies. Orthodoxy of "always" and "never" is for little children.

Here, I resolve the equation in favor of exploration. I'm aware my resolution is self-serving. I hope my exploration provides democratic utility. Regardless, my actions are deliberate and conscious, as is democracy.

Self-Awareness

I don't remember taking a psychology course until college. We should start earlier—not to indoctrinate children into specific psychological dogma, but to prepare them for life.

Human psychology exists. Our decisions and actions are in part a function of our inherited psychology. The preponderance of our psychology evolved during an existence more primitive than modern society. Our primitive psychology makes us vulnerable to manipulation. Marketing employs psychological manipulation. Peer pressure is a form of psychological manipulation.

Teaching self-awareness is not esoteric. It's pragmatic and responsible instruction. Once again, all curricula should be age appropriate, but psychological awareness education should begin before college. I would title the curriculum: "Psychology of Freedom and Democracy." Hint: it emphasizes individual responsibility.

Citizenship

Third, learning about ourselves means learning about our society, especially our form of government, our rights and responsibilities under that government, and especially the dynamic relationship between people and democratic government. Consciousness within free and democratic societies forces us to concede we are diverse, not solely in appearance, but in thought and opinion as well. Freethinking is the most fundamental freedom. Democracy provides peaceful means to exist in cooperative freedom and diversity of thought.

Public school curricula should include citizenship, or democracy practice. An integral component of democracy practice is learning how to disagree with one another or learning how to argue. Teaching disagreement, or the art of argument, is essential to a liberal education within constitutional democracies. Without being overly prescriptive, here are a few recommendations.

Focus on civility. Disagreement training concerns reasoning and formulating persuasive arguments without temper tantrums. Teaching anger to children is vile.

Likewise, labeling or name-calling breaks the rules. A child can't be correct simply because she belongs to group X or wrong because she belongs to group Y. Teaching otherwise is child abuse.

It's also professional incompetence. Imagine arguing before SCOTUS that justices should rule in your favor simply because you are a member of group X, and your adversary is a member of group Y. I graduated law school. That argument won't cut it. Teaching children you win debates by categorizing your opponent sets them up to fail. It also cultivates a citizenry incapable of managing dialectics. In other words, it contributes to dysfunction.

History

Fourth, learning about us means learning about how we got here. We must teach our history. History is *thorny*. Many of you may be nodding "yes" to yourselves, and I agree with you that history should be accurate and comprehensive or inclusive, but I mean "thorny" in a different way.

Revisiting our opening aphorism, history seems more like providing fish than teaching how to fish. It's more like a "what" than a "how." But it doesn't have to be.

The first step in a more enlightened approach to history is emphasizing history is about *us*. I mean "us" today, not "us" in the past. Human history isn't about a bygone species. When I studied history, that point was not stressed enough. I got the impression I was learning of people who were fundamentally different from me. That is false. We are not inherently different from historical figures.

Recorded history is less than 6,000 years old.[104] Significant biological evolution for complex organisms takes much longer. Inherently, we're the same people we study in history. We are *Homo sapiens*.

I want to drive that point home by using the specific example of Nazi Germany. Nazis came to power through a series of political manipulations eviscerating and eventually eliminating democratic institutions capable of restraining authoritarianism.[105]

Since that occurred less than 100 years ago, evolutionary biology cannot separate us from Nazis. Our form of government and democratic institutions distinguish us. Notice how I didn't say, "our values." True, most of us don't have Nazi values. But many Germans in the 1930s, perhaps a majority, shared democratic values.

However, democratic values without the support of democratic institutions don't have much value. Don't get me wrong. They're nice. It's nice to have democratic values. But against a gang of armed thugs, your values are gonna get you beaten or killed. Bringing democratic values not backed by formidable institutions to a struggle against authoritarianism is like bringing a peashooter to a tank battle. You're gonna lose. Don't get too enamored with your superior values.

That's why ex post facto judgmentalism poses such a threat. Imagining we're inherently superior to recent ancestors, and by recent, I mean the last

104 "Recorded History," Wikipedia, accessed Feb. 11, 2023, https://en.wikipedia.org/wiki/Recorded_history.

105 "Third Reich," Britannica, accessed Feb. 12, 2023, https://www.britannica.com/place/Third-Reich/The-Enabling-Act-and-the-Nazi-revolution.

6,000 years or so, conjures an insidious lullaby dulling the eternal vigilance required to maintain democratic institutions that guard against authoritarianism. If we stroke ourselves into thinking we're inherently superior to those who have preceded us, our vigilance deviates.

I'm deeply suspicious of those promoting the concept that we're inherently superior to our ancestors. At best, it reveals an ignorance of evolutionary biology. At worst, it's a tactic for dulling our vigilance. History should be taught without ex post facto judgmentalism.

Two Schools

Most of us want our laws and democratic institutions to prevail. There are two schools of thought in this regard. The first encourages the idea we are inherently better than those who have preceded us as aspirational strategy. In other words, if we believe we're better, we'll behave like we're better. Through faith in our ascendency, actual advancement transpires.

I'm of the other school. Teaching history by stressing we're fundamentally the same as our ancestors gives us a better chance. We're capable of making the same mistakes. We're capable of brutality and compassion. We're capable of repression and creativity. We must remain vigilant to our capacities.

If we fail to understand genocides and subjugations and other abominable forms of injustices were committed by people genetically indistinguishable from us as a species, we fail to be enlightened by history. History becomes a series of names who aren't us and dates before our time. Consequently, we graduate students with a creel full of fish but without the ingenuity to fish for themselves.

One final thought on academia. I would also teach reading, writing, and science, especially evolutionary biology.

Conclusion

"Congress shall make no law respecting an establishment of religion . . ."

Separation of church and state is a foundational principle of our democratic republic, formalized in the First Amendment's Establishment Clause. From my twenty-first century perch, religion or church seem symptomatic of something deeper. On an intellectual level, we understand the value of separating religion from public policy, but *faith* subverts our unconscious.

Different religions along with different ideologies represent different brands of faith. The first functional element of the first sentence of our Bill of Rights admonishes against establishing specific brands of faith. The Framers put that atop the list. Faith frustrates reason and cloaks bad ideas in costumes of wisdom. Through faith, moral certainty sanctions extremism and spits on compromise. Discretion is never the better part of valor for the exponentially sanctimonious.

Faith-based proselytizing, whether religious or ideological, corrupts public policy debate. Though the Constitution is specifically apprehensive about religion, we should be equally wary of ideological establishment. Establishing a particular brand of faith mocks freedom and violates democracy.

Neither religion nor ideology should provide exclusive justification for policy. Allowing philosophies of adaptive pragmatism to influence deliberation is OK, but we should excise from policy debate the sanctimony accompanying blind faith in either a supreme being or political ideology.

—23—

PP Tools of the Trade

B efore enumerating specific tactics, I'll make some general observations. First, I'll confess my bigotry. I don't care for paid professionals on the right or left making profitable sport out of partisanship. Overall, I don't like these people. They are financial beneficiaries of our disunion. Skewing public discussion for partisan advantage by media, public officials, or paid analysts is a professional breach. It's like embezzling by an accountant.

Second, I have asserted ad nauseam that surrendering to psychological predispositions that evolved during our primordial existence without inspection is lazy and undermines civilization. In general, PPs want us to submit to the primitive mindset. Taking advantage of our encrypted psychology to market partisan division disturbs me. Infiltrating the subconscious to peddle underwear or shampoo is one thing, but public policy discussion should be deliberate.

Last, PPs are evolving the language of public discourse toward bellicosity, making democracy more challenging.

Emotional Display and Provocation

> The opinions that are held with passion are always those for which no good ground exists; indeed, the passion is the measure of the holder's lack of rational conviction. Opinions in politics and religion are almost always held passionately.
> —BERTRAND RUSSELL, *Sceptical Essays*

With PPs, passion or emotion mostly means anger. So, let's deal with anger first. Activists like to proclaim, "if you're not angry, you're not paying attention." I used to consider that pithy. Now I understand it as pathological.

Anger frustrates the ability to pay attention. Have you ever tried to solve a math problem while you were angry? How about reading a novel? You read the same sentence over and over or you just pretend to read until you calm down. Anger impairs cognition. It interferes with problem-solving.

Permitting anger to have undue influence corrupts both the internal dialectic of individuals and societal dialectics. In other words, anger impedes personal growth and cultural evolution.

Anger does have its place, but that place occupies a smaller space than you might think. During the pregame show for the College Football National Championship between Georgia and TCU on January 9, 2023, ESPN analyst and Alabama head football coach Nick Saban indicated he was always concerned before a big game that his players would initially play with too much emotion. "Emotional people make bad decisions," he said.

Anger doesn't serve you. It serves them. PPs create an ambiance encouraging outrage and absolving anger. POEP creates safe spaces for negative emotion.

That's part of the allure. They let you have your cake and eat it too. PPs encourage you to simultaneously blame others for your anger and take credit for its righteousness. The cause of your negative emotion belongs to someone else, but its virtue belongs to you.

Anger Mismanagement

Adult temper tantrums are endorsed as proper emotional response. "You shouldn't be ashamed of showing emotion. We're not going to judge you for that. This is a judgment-free zone for negative emotional responses if you share our opinions. As long as you share our opinions, there's no such thing as negative emotional response. Adult temper tantrums are spot-on if you share our opinions. You have a right to be angry. Your anger is justified. It's righteous. You *should* be angry." Whether or not there's some cathartic value is beyond the scope of this book, but I have my doubts.

Angry mobs serve mob leaders. Tribal leaders promote the notion that anger serves you. They're lying and you know it. Acting and speaking out of anger reliably leads to regret.

Anger Subordinates Reason

Therefore, inciting anger is a subordinating tactic. The angry mob relinquishes reason. Anger interferes with autonomous thinking. Anger rots autonomy. It makes you a tool.

Characterizing tantrums as proper shows of emotion is PP euphemistic propaganda. Joy, surprise, trust, and love are emotions non grata. PPs cultivate negative emotions of anger, contempt, and fear, all of which nurture division and frustrate democracy.

We're a nation of convenience. We consume what's easy to consume. For someone who is angry, consuming anger-sanctifying content is easy. On the other hand, content suggesting anger creates impediments to cognition and success will be difficult to swallow. Public policy by tantrum doesn't work, but content by tantrum does.

Passion Is a Red Herring

Don't we want passionate leaders? I have three points on passion. First, passion is not evidence of correctness. People passionate about Earth being flat are flat-out wrong. It doesn't matter how passionate they are. Passion is a red herring regarding correctness.

Second, passionate displays are not evidence of truth. Liars can speak with great passion.

Last, passionate displays are not proof of commitment. Passionate displays evince talent for displays of passion. Posturing is adaptive behavior to gain advantage while reducing risk. Male gorillas engage in posturing contests to prove dominance without injury or death. Saying someone speaks with great passion or someone is passionate based on TV appearances is really saying someone has great posturing talent.

Overvaluing posturing unhinges public discussion from reason. Functional democracy should not depend on delivery. Passion of delivery is independent of veracity or substance. If passionate displays control us, we relinquish democracy to the best actors. If you're taken with delivery, you're an easy mark.

What do the emotional protagonists mean absent their histrionics?

Difficult to execute in real time. On the other hand, maybe you just like entertaining TV.

Categories Are Tricky

> The human mind must think with the aid of categories. Once formed, categories are the basis for normal prejudgment. We cannot possibly avoid this process. Orderly living depends upon it.
> —GORDON W. ALLPORT, *The Nature of Prejudice*

PPs love hanging labels on the opposition. But let's face it, labels are impossible to avoid. PP is a label I'm hanging on a group of people, and by so doing, I'm undeniably trying to prejudice the reader. Rather than distinguishing myself from PPs in vain attempt at absolution, I stipulate my guilt. We're all a little guilty in this regard. Let's challenge ourselves to understand the dynamics of putting people into categories so we might mitigate negative consequences, or as penance for our sniping.

I begin by articulating two intertwining concepts providing foundation for this exploration. First is acknowledging the similarity between insults and labels considered accurately descriptive, e.g., "jerk" and "Democrat."

The second concept involves balancing a label's utility for stimulating understanding versus its capacity for inducing prejudice. The apprehension is that a label's communicative value might be substantially outweighed by its capacity to fuel prejudice. Referring to someone as a "jerk" does more to fuel prejudice than to convey substantive information. But less facially abusive labels like "Democrat" or "Republican" can also be highly prejudicial without conveying anything useful.

Context is eternally relevant. Are you looking for a poll watcher or carpenter? But as PI lateral expansion continues unabated and the ecosystem becomes more hyperpartisan, decision-making paradigms can shift to allow partisan stereotypes to obfuscate character and competence regardless of context.

With PPs, I'm simply encouraging an awareness of the dynamic. Examine the utility of the label and its emotional effect. How did it make you feel?

The Primary Concern Is Substituting Categories and Labeling for Rational Argument

"She's wrong because she's a stupid jerk," is not valid argument. Unfortunately, that basic template with a couple of flimsy modifications passes for persuasion in segregated partisan media.

The first type of insubstantial adjustment is to the label itself. We need to do better than "jerk." An illusion of hierarchy deceives us as to the validity of categories as argument. We assign greater or argument-level value to certain labels. To see what I mean, consider the following:

> stupid, ignorant, moron, racist, misogynist, conservative, liberal, radical, extremist, RINOs, DINOs, Marxist, white people, whites, Asians, Latinos, Latinas, Latinx, blacks, African Americans, men, women, white man, old white man, Karen, woke, snowflake, nerd, socialist, fascist, communist, white supremacist, narcissist, bigot, Republican, Democrat, racialist, xenophobe, homophobe, transphobe, coward, jerk, stupid jerk, big fat stupid jerk, body-shamer, juvenile, philistine, liar, etc.

The list isn't exhaustive, and the categories aren't all facially insulting. But no matter how sophisticated or multisyllabic the labels, they're not lines of reasoning. Cheering audiences moving their heads up and down like submissive little bobbleheads in response to clever labels hurled at the other is not evidence of valid argument. It means partisan manipulation succeeded. By the way, "submissive little bobbleheads" was clearly pejorative labeling on my part. It's hard to avoid sometimes. You gotta try.

Insulting labels are mostly subcategories of jerk. Declaring an argument is specious because its protagonist is a "misogynistic philistine" has equal validity to "she's wrong because she's a stupid jerk."

The phenomenon can be analyzed using a substance versus process framework. As adults, we learn bigger words. The substance of our insults becomes more impressive. But the process of categorizing people to win arguments remains childish regardless of erudition.

Attacking the Messenger

The second type of insubstantial adjustment to the invalid template concerns form. No one says, "she's wrong because she's a stupid jerk." Instead, it's statements like:

"That's coming from a Republican," or

"That's because she's a socialist," or

"He's made racist comments in the past," or

"We have to consider the source."

Appraising an argument based upon its source is symptomatic of tribalism.

Attacking the messenger violates egalitarianism. Democracy demands understanding that insight on any topic can come from any place or anyone regardless of any category the person belongs to, even the category of "big fat jerks." Even a big fat jerk can make a valid argument, have a good idea, or have insight about people outside the group of big fat jerks to which he belongs.

The merit of an idea is independent of source. Either the force acting on a body is equal to its mass times its acceleration ($F = ma$), or it's not. The fact that idea came from Sir Isaac Newton isn't relevant when planning a trip to the moon. The equation, i.e., the message, must be verified. Supremacy of message over messenger is a guiding principle of meritocracy.

The tactic is employed to distract audiences from the message itself, either because the message is valid or because media analysts lack competency to identify or articulate invalidities in real time. Other times, it conceals laziness. Regardless of motivation, the tactic derails the rigorous inquiry meritocracy requires.

Capable leaders understand this. Whether in a public official or corporate officer, competency demands attention to the message itself. In a meritocracy, the ability to acknowledge and objectively evaluate ideas from unpopular sources is essential. That talent provides a competitive advantage. Inability to do so is a handicap.

Fixating on the messenger's group identity devalues the message. When identity subordinates the acts or words of an individual, tribalism subordinates democracy. As identity increases in value relative to ideas, an idiocracy ensues.

Sometimes, instead of either attacking the messenger or undermining a message with persuasive reasoning, PPs will simply label the argument. "The argument is specious," which is the slightly more sophisticated version of "that's stupid."

That's not good enough. Advocates or analysts must show how or why an argument is flawed. "That's a bad idea," or "that doesn't make sense and *here's why*." Maybe the argument is specious because it relies on a false premise or utilizes a straw man. But stating that isn't enough. Why is the premise false and how is the straw man used? Otherwise, the most essential element of the dialectic is absent.

Identifying argument flaws can be difficult. You might intuitively feel an argument is specious, but the why is difficult to articulate. But that's the analyst's job!

On the other hand, if it's so stupid the audience doesn't need it explained, why mention it except for partisan advantage? That's not news analysis. That's partisan advocacy.

Either explain the stupidity or don't bring it up. Don't pretend it's a time-management issue. You've got 24/7 to cover a handful of stories. Take time to properly analyze arguments to productively advance the dialectic.

We need to up our game. Upping our game doesn't mean using more sophisticated insults. Keeping "arguments" on the level of labeling perpetuates the war and terminates the dialectic. Identifying and articulating argument flaws informs the electorate, creates good habits, and perpetuates the dialectic, which helps sustain functional democracy.

Putting people into categories isn't intelligent, at least not in the sense of problem-solving. On the other hand, if your business model relies on identity validation, pejorative labeling is cleverly expedient or just lazy.

I was going to say, if you want to substitute labels for reasoning with your acquaintances, that's fine, but for public discourse, we need rational argument. However, I'm going to walk that sentiment back. "We need to up our game" begins with us. Self-government means governing ourselves. We need to consciously practice civility in our private lives. Expecting media discussion to be rational while we label each other is both hypocritical and counterproductive.

The hypocrisy is plain. It's counterproductive in at least two ways. First, we accustom ourselves to unproductive discourse. POEP reinforces the bad habit, and the bad habit finds refuge in POEP. Second, public figures weren't always so. They come from us. *We* need to up our game.

Putting People into Categories Is a Subordinating Tactic

The scientist labels the moth beneath the glass, not the other way around. If I categorize you, I seize a position superior to yours. It's condescension.

Labeling can be a punch to the stomach. Responding intelligently to labeling is difficult. What are you gonna say? "No, I'm not." Or "Yeah, so what?" What about, "I know you are but what am I?" It stops intelligent discourse. I think that's its main purpose. If a PP perceives danger of finding common ground with the enemy, hanging a well-timed label is like throwing a hand grenade. Peace talks are over.

Categories and labels implicate the balance between elucidation and something else. If I were marketing categories, I would focus on elucidation. But usually, it's something else, like possession or power—putting someone in your collection like the entomologist with the moth.

Unfortunately, hanging labels is fashionable across the political spectrum, perhaps because identity politics depend on stereotyping. Categories provide generalities about groups, but for an individual, those same categories often lead us astray.

Understanding individuals requires us to understand how labels and categories function. If our interest in understanding an individual is genuine, we must try to perceive the individual through the obfuscation of generality. In other words, to be understood simply as Democrat or Republican is to be barely understood, if at all, or worse, to be misunderstood.

We've come full circle. Labeling induces prejudice or prejudgment. Categories provide templates for discrimination and division. They're segregating. Putting people into categories is inherent to OHE. Out-group members are more likely to be perceived as interchangeable or expendable.

Both espousing group identity and assigning group identity through labeling erode individuality and support hyperpartisanship. Labels distract us from perceiving the individual. Out-group homogeneity is fundamental to partisan marketing and product differentiation. *Democrats are like this, and Republicans are like that.* Categories are fundamental to stereotyping, and stereotyping is fundamental to hyperpartisanship.

Social Media Induces Labeling

Making cogent arguments or engaging in substantive lines of reasoning with information platforms that require sound-bite length communication is challenging. For character assassination and name-calling, restrictive length is auspicious.

Language and Manner of Disagreement

I have a neighbor with whom I occasionally discuss politics. Sometimes we agree, and sometimes we don't. When we disagree, he has a habit of beginning his argument with phrases like, "what you don't understand is . . .," or "what they don't understand . . . ." In other words, all disagreement stems from someone else's lack of understanding. If everyone had his profound understanding, everyone would always agree with him. It couldn't possibly be that people who disagree are suitably informed but nonetheless disagree.

Democracy is premised on disagreement. Functional democracy requires effective disagreement. Effective disagreement means advancing the dialectic.

Contextualizing the Vote

Not every disagreement can be effectively resolved through compromise or dialectics. That's why we vote. Here, I examine the relationship between the way we conduct public disagreement and voting, as well as the role PPs play in that relationship.

In general, PPs want to use the vote to resolve all disagreement. This is just another formulation of issue subordination, which is part of "The Eternal Game" discussed in Chapter 14. Disagreements, like issues, are chits in the partisan game. Resolving disagreement before Election Day is throwing away chits that can be used to gain or maintain electoral advantage. From an electoral perspective, there's little incentive to resolve disagreement through compromise or by advancing the dialectic.

For functional democracy, using Election Day to resolve *all* disagreement is incompetence. It's like bringing every suit to trial without reaching a settlement. It's like using nuclear weapons to resolve treaty disputes.

Society would function better by managing public disagreement as if we didn't have the vote. Please don't misunderstand. The vote is essential. Every citizen should vote, and voting shouldn't be frustrated. But to resolve differences, voting should be the last resort. If all our disagreements are in anticipation of Election Day, partisan advantage will supersede good-faith argument.

PPs could care less about advancing the dialectic. It's apocalypse always. It's election mode on tilt. All disagreement results from the opposition's deficiency. People who disagree with us lack our superior understanding. Our only chance at salvation is Election Day.

I Have a Problem With . . .

PPs excel at derailing productive discourse. Forget settling; let's go to trial. Provoking anger and hanging labels on the opposition reduces the likelihood of achieving resolution absent a partisan verdict.

But some tactics are more subtle. We take language for granted. Its evolution, to our detriment, largely goes unnoticed. Relationships between our chosen words, emotional state, psychology, and ability to solve problems or resolve differences are not properly elucidated. Without being exhaustive, I provide some examples.

PPs regularly have a problem with people or ideas they disagree with. Rather than, "I disagree with such and such and here's why," it's "I have a problem with such and such." Divas have a problem with anyone who would dare to disagree with them, and divas don't compromise.

Putting the diva thing aside, there's a partisan purity angle. It's as if the person who takes offense most often or is offended by the most things is the purest and best partisan. The offended display problems with out-group ideas and members like honor badges of bling.

It's dystopian. People with the most problems aren't the most virtuous; they're the most maladjusted. We could attribute dysfunctional democracy to mismanagement of public discourse by the maladjusted.

Choosing "I have a problem with" instead of "I disagree with" is more than a language choice. It's an outcome choice. Disagreements can be resolved through discussion or compromise, or they can be put aside.

Problems, on the other hand, are more problematic and therefore more useful to PPs. We don't simply disagree with one another. Your position on the issue causes me to have a problem. *My* problem is *your* fault, as if your position on an issue could provide grounds for a lawsuit. You are liable for my problem. Disagreeing with me means you're guilty of something. You're a bad person for having a different opinion from mine. Therefore, you must change your position. It's not the language of diplomacy. It's not helpful to the dialectic.

I'm Offended By . . .

Sometimes political discussion sounds more like a combination of self-help, reality TV, and group therapy. Even without a partisan angle, the desirability of such a format as a media business model is plain.

The group session is conducted by people upset with contrary opinion. The session kicks off with comments such as, "It upsets me that blah blah blah," or "I resent that so and so said such and such," or "I can't stand it when . . .," or "I'm so sick of so and so claiming blah blah blah," or "it offends me that . . .," etc.

What relevance does the resentment of a "journalist" or "independent analyst" have to a policy issue? As a matter of public policy, what offends you has no bearing. What upsets you holds no interest. Emotional states of PPs cannot be a factor in deciding national policy in a constitutional democracy. Stick to the facts; make your case; and spare us emotional manipulations.

My disagreement with the tactic of using the language of emotional manipulation isn't a function of my lack of understanding. I understand why people, people whose group identity differs from my own, would be upset, resent, hate, or be sick of certain policies, opinions, or people, people like me for instance. I disagree with the tactic because it doesn't work.

Efficacy

I need to qualify that last sentence and in doing so echo previous analysis. It doesn't work for advancing narrowly tailored solutions to specific policy issues, because it focuses discussions on disaffected feelings of protagonists, and groups of people being blamed, instead of on problem-solving. Focusing on disaffection and blame, rather than specific approaches to improve the situation, works as either a partisan electoral strategy or as provocation for radical change, i.e., "we need to get rid of the people at fault in the next election, or we need to change the whole system, and don't bother us with your silly little ideas for incremental change."

Emotional manipulation also works as content for segregated audiences. I've discussed ad nauseam the concept of righteousness affirmation. Let's add the notions of group therapy and self-help. POEP reminds me of afternoon therapy shows like Dr. Phil, except the therapy is in bad faith.

Imagine going to a therapist because you have a hard time getting along with people, so you've isolated yourself. After describing several incidents precipitating your seclusion, the therapist responds, "I conclude you have nothing to work through. All your problems can be blamed on others. You're perfect as you are. See me once a week to get things off your chest. Whenever you find yourself in disagreeable circumstances from exposure to iniquities of others, hunker down in the comfort of your rightness until the situation passes, and you can look forward to telling me about it in our next session. Leave your payment with my assistant on your way out."

They say if you smell body odor all the time, it's probably coming from you. Alternatively, it could be because you're eternally surrounded by people who stink. I'll leave it to you to determine the statistical probabilities of the two scenarios.

Complaining Is Not Activism

In addition to being ineffective at solving problems, resentment or partisan grievance programming misleads, creates bad habits, and ultimately serves PI. Expressing resentment is not activism. Activism is working for political or social change. Defining the problem is part of it. But the process also includes proposing specific solutions and convincing either government or private sector elements to pursue those solutions.

This is one of those moments in which my take has evolved contemporaneously with my consideration of the topic. As a result of the popularity of grievance programming, supported by human psychological needs along the lines of "misery loves company," coupled with universal access to social media, a substantial portion of our electorate behaves as if complaining publicly is activism. So, the bad habit is already ensconced into the collective psyche: activism is complaining.

How democratic. Anyone can complain about anything. Internet egalitarianism ennobles maladjusted whiners.

In a sense, we're revisiting the concept of decentralized movements discussed in Chapter 6, except this is decentralization in extremis. Everyone with a platform, which is everyone, is part of a decentralized movement of general dissatisfaction. Anyone publicly complaining or expressing resentment over anything is an activist of disaffection.

The problem is this "activism" is long on expressions of disaffection and short on solutions. Enter professionals. Mass disaffection at the fingertips of hardened professionals compels me to imagine an enterprising Casanova in a palace of virgins. While possibilities are as numerous as the pages of the *Kama Sutra*, I only want to mention a few, all of which have been previously suggested.

The first is ratings, clicks, and subscriptions for partisan group-therapy programming. This is identity validation or righteousness affirmation plus misery loves company. Gather round the flat screen with people who are upset with, sick of, can't stand, resent, or have a problem with the same stuff. There's gold in them thar disaffections.

The second and third result from organizing around general disaffection rather than specific policies. There are only two ways to go. Get rid of the other tribe in the next election or change the whole system. Whether marketing partisanship or revolution, widespread expressions of disaffection work.

In sum, widespread expressions of disaffection can be effectively harnessed for ratings, exploited for partisan advantage, or used to market revolution, as opposed to working within the system to advance specific policies through collaboration.

Let's combine this point with one made earlier. Like substituting labeling for argument, substituting resentment for activism also facilitates partisanship. Both are PP tools of the trade.

The Same with Judging

Judging others isn't activism. The psychology is akin to labeling—condescending self-aggrandizement. A judge occupies a superior position to one being judged.

Judgmentalism isn't a duty. There's no incessant moral imperative to judge. Whether the compulsion is biological, religious, tribal, or an affectation of an entertainment-dominated society, is impossible to say. But surrendering to the inclination to judge without inspection undermines democracy and is mostly unnecessary.

It's cancerous to the dialectic. Debating someone who has prejudged you to be malicious or debilitated through unsuitable identity frustrates utility. There's no need to try an idea or line of reasoning with the verdict already in. On the other hand, substituting judgmentalism for activism is easy or lazy and makes for great TV.

"Not-So-Royal We"

The percentage of monolithic communities is *zero.* Therefore, use of first-person-plural pronouns such as "we" or "us" by a singular person is reliably inappropriate. In other words, individuals should use singular pronouns when referring to their opinions or positions.

The plural incentive is obvious. The speaker gives the impression of speaking for many others, even an entire "community." But the percentage of monolithic communities is zero.

Here's where news programming hosts or anchors drop the ball. Clarifying who the speaker is speaking for, or represents, is a journalistic duty. For example:

Guest or Interviewee: "We think x, y, z."

Anchor or Interviewer: "Who's *we?*"

Guest or Interviewee:	"My community (or party or group)."
Anchor or Interviewer:	"Does everyone in your community think the same way you do?"
Guest or Interviewee:	"Maybe not everyone, but most people do."
Anchor or Interviewer:	"How do you know most people have the same opinion as you? Did you conduct a poll or a survey?"
Guest or Interviewee:	"No, but I know most people think the way I do because I talk to people in my community."
Anchor or Interviewer:	"So anecdotally, based on your personal contacts, you feel most people—but not everyone—in your community, have the same opinion as you on this issue. OK, continue."

Two major problems confound this level of accountability and precision. First, it's cumbersome. Just getting through preliminaries devours considerable airtime. Guess what—democracy is a grind. But in a contest between the precision needed for functional democracy and entertainment value, precision is gonna have to take a dive, maybe. If journalists and anchors were routinely precise, frequent guests, held accountable, might be less prone to personal plurals. Maybe PPs can be trained to speak for themselves. Hah.

The second major problem implicates the relationship between anchors and frequent guests, which was briefly discussed in Chapter 5. POEP hosts introduce and/or treat certain guests as "friends" of the show. Accountability could spoil those relationships. Sustaining a righteousness-affirming ambiance under the rigor of scrupulous journalism is difficult. Pronoun exactitude interferes with successful programming formulae. Forcing guests to continuously explain "we" not only disrupts show flow, but also spoils cordiality between hosts and guests. Good! Eliminating partisan-driven conviviality dispenses with a journalistic conflict of interest.

There are discernable instances where use of "we" is proper, e.g., if someone speaks for an organization with an organizational position, or if someone reports results from a poll or study conducted by a group of people to which the reporter belongs.

Notice how decentralization should preclude use of "not-so-royal we." No individual can speak for an entire decentralized movement. The "defund the police" fiasco made that plain. As previously stated, attempting to appreciate a decentralized movement under a single narrative is nonsensical, and a decentralized movement is better understood as a collection of movements.[106] Use of "not-so-royal we" implies centralized authority or unanimity of opinion, thereby obfuscating decentralization realities.

Having said that, plural pronouns such as "not-so-royal we" enjoy a decentralizing aspect. A singular pronoun is unequivocally centered on a specific individual. Plural pronouns disperse focus and responsibility.

When we combine the decentralizing aspect of "not-so-royal we" with its incompatibility with decentralized movements, a delightfully vexing dynamic arises. The media spins like out-of-control carnival rides in vain attempts to impose centrality of purpose or singular narrative on decentralized crowds. Reticence to understand and articulate implications of decentralization isn't born of journalistic principle.

Nonetheless, we understand what "not so royal we" means. "We" means everyone who has the exact same opinion as me or everyone who thinks like I do. Therefore, because at least one other person always shares our opinions, we can say *we* all the time.

"We think we need to get rid of capitalism."

"Who's we?"

"Everyone who thinks we need to get rid of capitalism."

"We believe that to address this issue we need to change the whole system."

"Who's we?"

"Everyone who believes that to address this issue, we need to change the whole system."

"We think the world is flat."

---

106 For a more thorough analysis of decentralized movements, see Chapter 6, section titled: "Relationship between Decentralized Movements, Extremism, and Hyperpartisanship."

You get the point. *We* think democracy is a grind. *We* think the tedium of democracy done correctly doesn't make for great TV most of the time. *We* think giving PPs a pass on their use of "not so royal we" is some sleazy bullshit.

We also think use of "not so royal we" is a conforming bullying tactic. No community above a certain number can speak with one voice on any single issue. Monolithic opinion within a large group evinces coercion or subjugation as well as absence of democracy. When a prominent member of a group you identify with uses "not so royal we," the message is clear. If you wish to be in good standing with our group, this is how we think, and this is how we speak. *We* don't use Republican talking points.

Incorporation

Incorporation in this context means using inherently nonpartisan or bipartisan issues, like COVID, for partisan advantage or product differentiation. Theoretically nonpartisan issues are incorporated into the partisan war and become partisan.

Imagine the world divided into fiefdoms according to genre. Consider the TV channel guide a fiefdom menu. Partisanship occupies a growing space. I refer to this throughout as PI lateral expansion. Incorporation facilitates and/or is a form of lateral expansion.

Incorporation and/or lateral expansion means more revenue opportunity and power. If I work for PI, I want everything to be partisan. I want sports to be partisan. I want food to be partisan. I want partisan comedy, partisan drama, partisan clothing, partisan science, partisan education, partisan shelter, and I want disease to be partisan. My relative prominence, along with absolute revenue, increases as partisanship incorporates more issues and genres. The more that's partisan, the larger my fiefdom.

It doesn't require PI personnel to figure out how to make each and every thing partisan. Natural selection is the methodology. Selective pressures are ratings, clicks, subscriptions, and perhaps votes. Polarized biota naturally seek partisan advantage, and whether that advantage comes from economic policy or a pandemic is irrelevant. Segregated audiences conditioned to partisan content are receptive to incorporation, to the benefit of PI and PPs.

Evolutionary Adaptation

Imagine policy issues as living organisms struggling for survival with media attention as their sustenance. HM/POEP are more likely to cover issues with a partisan angle. If an issue can transform itself from nonpartisan to partisan, it enhances its chances for survival. From the perspective of the issue itself, incorporation is adaptive mutation.

Notice how issue survival and issue progress are at odds. Bipartisanship makes legislative progress more likely. But achieving legislative victory, especially one that's bipartisan, may result in the issue vanishing from public airways. Bipartisan progress may result in the extinction of a partisan issue.

Aggressive Partisan Humor

> It is a curious fact that people are never so trivial
> as when they take themselves seriously.
> —Oscar Wilde

Humor has many purposes. Yet to say that is slightly misleading because the statement creates separation. The hammer in the toolbox has many purposes, but it isn't us.

The ubiquity of humor implicates biology. It must be adaptive.[107] Humor can reduce the temperature of heated disputes. Laughter is pleasurable and therefore reinforceable and may boost immunity. Humor aids courtship. In other words, a good sense of humor can help secure a mate, thereby increasing viability.

Regardless of its evolutionary origins, humor permeates our cognition. It is a measure of intelligence. It assists reasoning. Through humor, we receive insight into ourselves, which is the presently relevant quality.

Cognizance of our flaws and iniquities becomes more palatable with a dose of laughter, like a spoonful of sugar helping the medicine go down. Humor

---

107 For an exploration of the evolutionary basis for humor, see: J. Polimeni and J.P. Reiss, "The First Joke: Exploring the Evolutionary Origins of Humor," *Evolutionary Psychology*, 4(1), (2006), https://doi.org/10.1177/147470490600400129.

makes scrutinizing ourselves easier. It facilitates introspection.

Comedians who help us laugh at ourselves not only have a special talent, but they also provide a public service. Through laughter, they help us acknowledge our imperfections and transgressions. They hold us accountable, or rather, they help us to hold ourselves accountable.

In addition to accountability, laughing at ourselves is uniting. We are united through our shortcomings. When within ourselves we recognize the same frailties imputed to our alleged enemies, they seem less threatening. Awareness of our own flaws engenders mercy toward others. Imperfection is common ground for all humanity. To find it, we need to look within. Humor aids that endeavor.

Aggressive partisan humor impedes finding common ground. Instead of laughing at ourselves, we laugh at *them*. Aggressive partisan humor reinforces the unconscious barrier to introspection. Aggressive partisan humor and POEP are simpatico.

Aggressive partisan humor analogizes to HM accountability. As discussed in Chapter 5, media segregated along partisan lines makes self-policing impotent. Instead, accountability becomes a ruse incorporated into partisan warfare when media personalities on the left and right point fingers at one another. Likewise, aggressive partisan humor undermines the utility of comedy by transforming it from a tool of self-knowledge into a weapon of division. Aggressive partisan humor is another means for emphasizing our differences.

Balancing Partisanship

Begin by thinking of the fox guarding the henhouse. It's tricky business for the fox to stay employed. Balancing appetite with job security is beyond even the cleverest of foxes.

Getting a system employing beneficiaries of dysfunction, i.e., PPs, to accurately diagnose the phenomenon and faithfully convey the diagnosis to their benefactors, i.e., the audience, without any legal responsibility to do so is similarly tricky. Whether individual human beneficiaries possess the requisite cleverness or systems employing them incorporate balance through evolution is beyond deduction. Here, I simply admire the balancing act.

Before exploring the logistics and implications of balancing, let's spend some time on necessity. Is balance necessary? A die-hard partisan would probably answer: "Hell no!"

However, venues for these high-wire acts are media, and particularly news outlets. Although we're in an era of segregation according to partisan viewpoint, the media in general, and news media in particular, likes to operate under the rubric of balance.

Or perhaps not. Maybe balance isn't the right word. If one side is clearly wrong, isn't saying so fair? Maybe fairness is a better word. Balance is a bit passé. Nonetheless, not everyone is fashionable. See if you can amalgamate concepts of balance and fairness for this analysis.

I also evoke the continuum. At one end, news programming appears deeply concerned with balance and fairness, and at the other end, not so much. The professionalism of PPs, as measured by their talent for contorting themselves to fit various venues within the continuum of balance, is remarkable. I once saw the same (based on physical appearance) analyst on MSNBC in the afternoon materialize later that day on the PBS News Hour to discuss the same issue. The contrasting performances were so frightening, I straightaway considered alien possession to be a real thing.

But all kidding aside, for covering hyperpartisanship, is balance and/or fairness necessary? Before continuing this analysis, let's revisit our definitions of partisanship and hyperpartisanship.

Partisanship: prejudicial allegiance or opposition to a political party, faction, group, tribe, person, ideology, or cause.

Hyperpartisanship: prejudicial allegiance or opposition to a political party, faction, group, tribe, person, ideology, or cause, to an extent that substantially alters or determines the opinions, beliefs, ideals, principles, behavior, or personality of those so aligned.

News outlets, journalists, and "independent" analysts don't wish to appear prejudicially aligned, or opposed, at least not always. For extreme exceptions, I like to use Nazis. Hardly anyone will get out of sorts over news outlets signaling prejudice against Nazis. (As an aside, notice again how extremism facilitates partisanship, this time by authorizing bias.)

Dealing with partisanship or hyperpartisanship, *as issues*, while appearing fair and/or balanced, or at least nonprejudicial, by PPs or partisan news outlets is tricky. The heart of the problem is, as issues, partisanship and hyperpartisanship are *not partisan*. Both sides of the aisle acknowledge that hyperpartisanship damages our republic.

Hyperpartisanship Presents a Structural Dilemma to Unilateral Culpability

Wait. Didn't I just contradict myself? How is appearing fair and/or balanced or nonprejudicial on a nonpartisan issue tricky? That one should be easy. Where's the trickiness?

I touched on this in the media chapter in the section titled: "Treat It as a Real Issue." The problem isn't appearing fair or balanced. The problem with bipartisan agreement on issues like hyperpartisanship, with media outlets whose business model depends on partisan segregation and validation, is identifying and articulating partisan advantage or a partisan angle.

With most issues, it's not an issue. Democrats and Republicans stake out opposing positions that are optimally mutually exclusive. But with hyperpartisanship, that's impossible. The opposing and mutually exclusive position to: "Hyperpartisanship is a problem," is: "Hyperpartisanship *isn't* a problem." Do you see how awkward this issue is for PI?

Another way to go is to acknowledge hyperpartisanship as a real problem, but lay fault exclusively on the other side. So far, no one has pulled that off. It's like placing blame for static electrical discharges between charged opposites exclusively on positive charges while exonerating negatives. It doesn't make sense.

For hyperpartisanship as an issue, unilateral culpability, i.e., partisanship, doesn't make sense, but dichotomy of coverage by news outlets is blatantly partisan.

The Other Side's Worse

I'll state several relevant and noncontroversial concepts apparently at odds with one another. I will then balance the equation.

1. A press free from prejudicial allegiances is fundamental to functional democracy;

2. Prejudicial allegiance is human nature; and
3. Even prejudicially aligned individuals, by and large, recognize that a press free from prejudicial allegiances is fundamental to functional democracy, and that the press is not free from such allegiances.

I now derive the universal partisan balancing equation by moving from the specific to the abstract. Start with something like: Our side's press might be partisan, but not as partisan as their side's. Through a series of scientifically and mathematically valid transpositions we arrive at:

Our actions may not be defensible on principle, but at least we're not as bad as them.

Variants include: "you can't compare," or "but they do it too, and when they do it, it's worse than when we do it," or my personal favorite, "we may be f***d up, but we're not as f***d up as them."

As premise to further analysis, I stipulate degrees of bad or worse exist. In general, our society suffers from a reticence to acknowledge degree. Demeaning someone with language is different than stabbing them in the abdomen, and referring to both as violence regresses communication.

But dynamics specific to hyperpartisanship discussed throughout make me want to hit pause when tempted to parse the subject matter with philosophy of degree. The justification is pragmatism and progress, with segregation and accountability implicated.

The Logic of Triage

Regardless of your affiliation, let's assume the other side is worse. After all, they are, aren't they? And addressing what's worse, first, makes sense. The toothache can wait while we stop the arterial bleeding. Let's focus on the other team, because they present the bigger problem and pose the bigger threat. The reasoning is plain.

But segregated media focusing on the other team's problems, even if the other team's problems are worse, comes off as media bias. This has been discussed at length and isn't the main concern here. The media business model is what it is. Here, I address consumers of partisan content and the trap we set for ourselves when we focus on degree in association with hyperpartisanship as an issue.

In a Culture Segregated along Partisan Lines, Trying to Fix Their Problems or Change Them Is Resource Mismanagement

The philosophy of, "we may have some problems, but nothing compared with them," provides pervasive rationale to excuse or deflect and disincentivizes personal growth.

Instead, let's work on fixing or improving that over which we have some level of control—ourselves and the groups, organizations, and communities we belong to—unless you're already perfect, in which case, bully for you. If the groups, organizations, or communities you belong to singularly focus on accusing and blaming other groups, organizations, or communities, that's a problem worth fixing, or a reason for joining with others.

On Election Day, degree or the lesser of two evils matters. Most who vote spend fifteen minutes or so in the election booth per year. For the rest of the 365 days, let's not be overly concerned about who's worse. Continuously working under the principle of, "we're bad, but they're worse" inhibits problem-solving. Let's spend time and energy working on what we can effectively influence.

Compromise Conundrum

Democracy aside, simple arithmetic and physical reality prescribe compromise. Our country of more than 300 million people and our planet of more than eight billion are of finite dimensions with finite resources. Resolving distribution involves compromise. Could distribution be more egalitarian? Of course. But in a finite system, everyone can't have everything they want, whenever they want it.

Compromise is essential. Implying otherwise lays the ground for belligerence and conflict. Tell the people compromise is unnecessary and observe them at each other's throats over finite resources. Get your popcorn.

Let's make this more intimate. Four acquaintances are stuck with each other in a small rental car for a ten-hour trip. One prefers country music, one hip-hop, one classical, and one jazz. Can you find a solution not involving compromise? Where does your mind go? Take a moment to reflect. Treat this as an opportunity for introspection.

We can go in many directions. Some involve changing parameters of the dilemma. For instance, you might think traveling with people of disparate musical tastes is a bad idea. We should segregate and only get into vehicles for extended periods with people who like the same music.

But let's not avoid the dilemma. Maybe there's an opportunity for unilateral triumph. Popular culture promotes *uncompromising hero* mythology, which reckons self-righteous indignation admirable. He refused to compromise. What a hero! What would an uncompromising hero do?

Uncompromising hero has a real problem with other genres. Through vilification of alternatives, our hero can come out on top. Uncompromising hero claims, it's not simply that he doesn't care for other genres, other genres make him suffer. He can't stand listening to other genres and resents being put in a position where he's forced to listen to music he's sick of. Listening to other genres will result in psychological trauma and emotional pain. He's so clever!

Maybe music is a bad idea altogether. How about talk radio? Sports talk or political talk? Uh-oh. Maybe conversation instead. What should we talk about? Uh-oh. When all is said and done, maybe sitting in silence is the way to go—not an option for Congress. We need to promote compromise as a democratic value. Or maybe we just give in to the PPs and uncompromising heroes holding us hostage.

You say you're tired of compromise. First, in my experience, people who declare they're tired of compromise lack practice. Second, maybe democracy isn't your cup of tea. I have news for you. Longevity, even for authoritarian dictators, involves compromise.

Language Redux

The opposition perpetually presents existential threat. I endeavor to pose one to PPs with this book—sounds megalomaniacal.

"In Trouble with" versus Courageous

Someone associated with a particular group publicly expressing opinions discordant with the majority is fairly common in politics and life. It's not a big deal. We need more of it.

Enter PPs fortified with political expedience. If minority opinion jibes with partisan advantage, then the holder and speaker of the minority opinion is courageous. On the other hand, if minority opinion is inconvenient, the holder and speaker of that opinion is in trouble with someone. He got himself into trouble.

Publicly expressing opinions a PP agrees with is courageous, whereas publicly expressing discordant opinions means you're in trouble.

Mistake versus Political Miscalculation versus Poor Judgment versus Corruption

Imagine you have a child who gets caught cheating on a test. When his teacher calls, you say, "Oh, he just made a mistake." Turning left when you're supposed to turn right is a mistake. Cheating isn't a mistake. It's deliberate. Thinking he could get away with it was a mistake or a miscalculation or poor judgment, but the act was corrupt.

While a parent characterizing a child's delinquency as a mistake is understandable, such characterization has no place in political analysis. When politicians, public figures, or anyone, for that matter, gets caught lying, misleading, cheating, stealing, or engaging in any form of corruption, please don't refer to it as a mistake. The only mistake was thinking they could get away with it.

That doesn't mean that, depending on circumstances, opportunities for redemption and forgiveness should be repressed. But redemption and forgiveness aren't required for honest mistakes. PPs habitually refer to wrongdoings by members of their own team as mistakes. That type of patronization facilitated by partisan segregation frustrates growth or evolution.

Reading between the Lines: Hyperpartisan Translation

Apparently, nothing can be taken at face value, and PPs possess secret de-coder rings allowing them to translate or "unpack" statements that should be treated with great skepticism. How marvelous. Every public statement requires some form of translation. Talk about job security! Thank goodness the electorate needs every single public statement translated. Where would this country be if we didn't have so many qualified professionals to translate English into English? When you imagine what blank spaces between the lines say, you can translate any statement into one discovering partisan advantage.

Hyperpartisan translation is used for offense and defense. Reading between the lines usually indicates a less-than-flattering interpretation of an opponent's utterances. When PPs read between the lines, they're on offense.

Defensive translation manifests in statements like: "That's not what she actually meant." Pronouns aside, we heard plenty of that from Trump sup-porters. For instance, whether Trump *actually* meant injecting bleach was a prudent methodology for combating coronavirus provided excellent POEP content. PPs on the left spent significant airtime struggling to convince the public "defund the police" doesn't really mean defund the police. Defensive translation is akin to characterizing malfeasance or incompetence as mistake.

Contrived Heroism

Occasionally PPs laud ideological comrades with statements along the lines of ". . . and he's not afraid to state his political beliefs." Wow, what a hero. Are you kidding me? POEP ratings depend upon such declarations. I'm not say-ing people should keep their political beliefs to themselves. But PPs making POEP-worthy pronouncements aren't heroic. It's the job description.

The same can be said for having the "temerity" to criticize the opposition. You don't deserve to be decorated for "calling out" the opposition. You deserve to cash your paycheck. With media segregated along partisan lines, PPs form a daisy chain of caller-outers. This one calls that one out and that one calls this one out, and all that's accomplished is members of the calling-out industry, i.e., PI, cash their checks.

Using Unsubstantiated Conclusions as Premises and Stating Opinion as Fact

It happens all the time. PPs want their opinions to carry the weight of fact for obvious reasons. I'll use an extreme example that will piss off many. "Donald Trump is a racist. That's a *fact*." Actually, because it's an evaluation of a person, it's *opinion*.

After a white supremacist rally in Charlottesville, Virginia, Trump declared, "But you also had people that were very fine people, on both sides."[108] That's a fact. It happened. Trump kicked off his 2016 presidential bid with the following comments about Mexican immigrants: "They're bringing drugs. They're bringing crime. They're rapists. And some, I assume, are good people."[109] He said that. It's a fact that he said that.

Combining those facts, what he truly said or what really occurred, one may have the opinion or conclude Donald Trump is a racist. Trump's statements inform the opinion he's a racist. Facts are like evidence introduced at trial, and opinions are like judgments, verdicts, or conclusions based on facts or evidence. I don't know if they teach this stuff in schools, but having a job in network TV should require knowing fact from opinion and operating accordingly.

Stating opinion as fact or using unsubstantiated conclusions as premises isn't trivial. It degrades communication. Or should I say, "I conclude it degrades communication." I say this because conveying facts and opinions is accomplished through communication. Common understanding of concepts, and the meaning of words representing those concepts, helps communication. Using words that don't stand for the concepts we're trying to convey is miscommunication. Whether miscommunication by PPs is deliberate or incompetent depends on speaker and situation.

Degrading communication degrades democracy. This opinion is widely held, and I won't go through the reasoning. However, regardless of how widely

---

108 Rick Klein, "Trump said 'blame on both sides' in Charlottesville, now the anniversary puts him on the spot," ABC News, April 12, 2018, https://abcnews.go.com/Politics/trump-blame-sides-charlottesville-now-anniversary-puts-spot/story?id=57141612.

109 Katie Reilly, "Here Are All the Times Donald Trump Insulted Mexico," *TIME*, Aug. 31, 2016, https://time.com/4473972/donald-trump-mexico-meeting-insult/.

held an opinion is, it's not fact.

Sometimes an opinion is so widely and persistently held it's treated as fact. We should be cautious of building structures, systems, or a future on such opinions. Identifying and analyzing such widely and persistently held opinions so foundational to society they're accepted as fact could be a life's pursuit, and a noble one at that.

Partisan Expedience, Respect, and Evolution

Rather than exhaustively enumerating the litany of underhanded tools utilized by PPs and before concluding with some remedial philosophy, I'll make some general observations echoing or supporting introductory sentiments of this chapter.

First, the guiding principle is partisan expedience. Public discourse can be a vehicle for achieving higher levels of understanding or for promoting misunderstanding. Nothing is off the table. We can follow the science, or we can question it. Psychological and emotional manipulations, especially those associated with tribalism, are accepted industry practices.

Admit Everything Relevant

More subtle and more effective is selectivity concerning facts and particulars. To illustrate the targeted concept, I'll share some anecdotal wisdom from my law school experience. Evidence was a required course, as well it should be. Federal and state rules guide admission and exclusion of evidence at trial. For example, hearsay is inadmissible.[110] However, exceptions to the hearsay rule are substantial.

According to my professor, evidence rules show a bias toward admissibility rather than exclusion. The guiding philosophy is: *The jury can figure it out.* We should be extremely reticent to exclude relevant evidence from the jury. The law gives juries credit for their ability to discern. Respect!

---

110 Rule 802—The Rule Against Hearsay, Federal Rules of Evidence 2023 Edition, accessed April 9, 2023, https://www.rulesofevidence.org/article-viii/rule-802/.

Don't Exclude Relevant Evidence Out of Fear of Prejudice

The other relevant bit I would like to share from my evidence course concerns prejudice. From legal dramas, non-lawyers can get the impression prejudicial evidence is excluded out of hand. This is categorically false. Lawyers on both sides must seek to introduce prejudicial evidence on behalf of their clients. If evidence doesn't prejudice the jury one way or the other, there's a good chance it's not relevant and therefore inadmissible.

Rule 403 states: "The court *may* [not shall] exclude relevant evidence if its probative value is *substantially outweighed* by a danger of . . . *unfair* prejudice . . ." (emphasis and bracketed content added).[111] A video recording of a defendant repeatedly stabbing the victim is highly prejudicial to the defendant but should not be excluded because its probative value—its tendency to prove or show truth—is so high it cannot be substantially outweighed by a danger of unfair prejudice.

Relevant information, whether in court or the media, includes prejudicial or persuasive information. Getting media to communicate information that persuades or prejudices the public toward a particular viewpoint is the job of the advocate.

Editorializing in favor of a particular viewpoint is perfectly appropriate journalism. However, allowing an editorial viewpoint to decide what information is relevant is a digression into dodgy advocacy or intellectual dishonesty.

Notice the analogy between partisanship and editorializing as well as hyperpartisanship and partisan news. Editorializing is aligning with a particular viewpoint. It's partisanship. But when that viewpoint substantially alters or determines the information conveyed to audiences, that's hyperpartisanship.

It disrespects the audience. Present all relevant information. Let the audience figure it out. Give them credit. Treat them like discerning adults. To do otherwise degrades the electorate by teaching deceit and training oversimplification.

---

111 Rule 403 —Excluding Relevant Evidence for Prejudice, Confusion, Waste of Time, or Other Reasons, Federal Rules of Evidence 2023 Edition, accessed April 9, 2023, https://www.rulesofevidence.org/article-iv/rule-403/.

Advocacy Journalism Is Patronizing

Another law professor said questions too difficult for lawyers or judges are left to the jury. So it is with democracy and the citizenry. The vote should be a verdict based on all relevant evidence. Allowing editorial positions to determine the relevancy of facts is advocacy under the banner of journalism. Restricting relevant information because it might prejudice audiences away from a news outlet's consensus opinion is disgustingly patronizing. Show respect.

A lamentation of disrespect accompanies hyperpartisan refrains. While choruses of professionals proudly proclaim we shouldn't underestimate the American public, PPs manipulate audiences segregated according to partisan identity through validating narrative that represses ideological deviation. Partisan sources dole out information as if there's a danger that truth may compromise loyalty, affection, or faith. In other words, PPs treat the electorate like children.

It's comforting. We enjoy the coziness of our positions.

Evolution, on the other hand, requires discomfort. Why change if we're comfortable? From whence does our discomfort arise? Not from ECs. ECs don't impede evolution exclusively by making us comfortable. They also delegate our discomfort to outside sources.

System and Fundamental Unit Integration

Within concepts of respect and evolution, responsibility or basis substantially diverge. At the heart of this discrepancy is our understanding of the relationship between the systems within which we exist and ourselves. They're not separate. Our facility to segregate ourselves from that which we are, factors in the hyperpartisan dilemma. It's easy for us. We're good at it.

The notion that change is necessary premises the following analysis. A philosophy or strategy focusing exclusively on changing policies, principles, procedure, and/or institutions of society is not fully developed. Within self-government through constitutional democracy, agencies and structures of society are of us. We are fundamental units of both intransigence and change.

The relationship between people and agencies of society is dynamic.

Agencies affect people and people affect agencies. Evolving ourselves is part of the equation.

Activists organize to change the system. Even activists who would acknowledge the need to change hearts and minds of people tend to look outward at others. When I say, "we need to evolve," I don't mean people who think differently than I do need to change their thinking to come into compliance with my philosophy. Evolution of opinion or political position is a red herring. Those who agree with my political positions are not more evolved. No! I mean all of us, me included, and it has nothing to do with our substantive political positions. It's about process.

We need to work on ourselves. We need to be activists of our personal evolution. Evolving democratic society demands personal growth by its fundamental units. You can't change the picture without changing the pixels. Examine the psychology sustaining the notion of "we need to change the whole system." It's childish. The entire system needs to change to follow the ideology of a handful, or perhaps a single person. I don't have to move. Everything and everyone else must change because of *my* moral certainty. If I'm feeling out of balance with the system, the entire system needs to change, not me.

Don't misunderstand. I'm not advocating for individuals to conform themselves to corruption. I'm suggesting we consider the relationship between systems and their fundamental units to be dynamic. As a tactic for positively changing systems, we may work on ourselves because we compose systems. If you can't effect positive change within yourself, how likely is it you can change a system made up of several hundred million people?

Consider resource management. It's possible that, after 6,000 years of "civilization" and several hundred years of constitutionally democratic nation-states, we're receiving diminishing returns from tinkering with "the system." Maybe at this particular time we get a bigger bang for our buck by working on ourselves to improve the system.

Free Will, Quantum Theory, and Remedy

> Things without all remedy
> Should be without regard
> —WILLIAM SHAKESPEARE, *Macbeth*

The following consideration was inspired by a debate between Sam Harris and Daniel Dennett on free will.[112] I don't intend to persuade on the issue of free will. I subscribe to naturalism, which is to say we are entirely of the natural world and "there is nothing supernatural about us."[113] I also subscribe to causal determinism—everything that happens flows from prior conditions according to laws of nature. Whether or not free will is compatible with causal determinism is philosophically fascinating,[114] but not necessary to resolve to suggest remedial measures for combatting hyperpartisanship.

Let's assume our thoughts and actions result from our wiring as determined by biology and experience. While reading this, thoughts occurring to you result from your inherited biological systems coupled with your life experiences. Harris suggests, "if you rewound the universe to precisely its prior state, with all relevant variables intact," the exact same thoughts would occur to you each and every time. I use the notion as a starting point without taking sides in the free-will debate.

The precise location and trajectory of quantum particles are indeterminate.[115] Even if it were possible to know the exact location of every bit of matter in the universe, we couldn't predict the future because at the quantum level, trajectory would be indeterminate.

---

112 Scott Smith75. "Sam Harris vs. Daniel Dennett. Free Will Debate," YouTube, February 22, 2022, https://www.youtube.com/watch?v=_J_9DKIAn48.

113 For a synopsis of naturalism and free will, see Tom Clark, "Naturalism, Choice, and Creativity: Transcending Free Will," Naturalism, Feb. 24, 2004, https://www.naturalism.org/resources/talks/naturalism-choice-and-creativity-transcending-free-will.

114 For a synopsis on compatibilism, see Michael McKenna and D. Justin Coates, "Compatibilism," *Stanford Encyclopedia of Philosophy, revised Nov. 26, 2019,* https://plato.stanford.edu/entries/compatibilism/.

115 Norton, "Quantum Theory."

Consider the indeterminate nature of quantum particles in conjunction with causal determinism. It's not a refutation. Everything that will happen flows from the universe's current state as you read this sentence according to laws of nature. But laws of nature, at the quantum level, include indefiniteness. The future unfolds as the universe of quantum particles realizes their trajectories.

So it is with human thoughts and actions. Our neural network operates electrochemically. Conscious thought is in part a function of quantum particle trajectories like electrons across neural synapses in the brain.

Now let's revisit Harris's hypothetical. I stipulate that "if you rewound the universe to precisely its prior state, with all relevant variables intact," the exact same thoughts would occur to you each and every time you read this sentence because in the hypothetical rewind, all relevant variables include the locations and trajectories of all quantum particles, including relevant electrons associated with cerebral neurons.

On the other hand, if you read the same sentence *for the first time* just one moment later, the exact same thoughts might not transpire because location and trajectories of quantum particles in your brain would be different. Different synapses might fire, triggering different thoughts.

Yet, in either case, you would recognize your thinking as yours. Quantum fluctuations would not change you into an entirely different person. In fact, there is an element of predictability.

This is also like quantum particles. Electrons surrounding the nucleus of an atom, for example, may be represented by clouds whose densities correspond to location probabilities. While odds of predicting a precise location of an electron would be magnificently long, expecting an electron to manifest in a certain region within the atom is reasonable.

Thought/Action Probability Equation (TAPE)

Like density clouds representing location probabilities for electrons, similar probability patterns could represent our potential thoughts and actions given specific circumstances. In other words, although we couldn't predict with 100-percent certainty the thoughts and actions of any human, we could formulate outcome probabilities. Like fingerprints, each human has a distinct TAPE.

I'm suggesting we cultivate our TAPEs. Although our biological inheritance is fixed, we can choose experience, which means we can change our wiring and affect our TAPEs. We are what we consume, which includes what we choose to experience, such as media content.

In sum, phenomena like hyperpartisanship undermine democratic systems and institutions. Democratic systems and institutions are of, from, and by *us*. Relationships between people and their systems and institutions are dynamic.

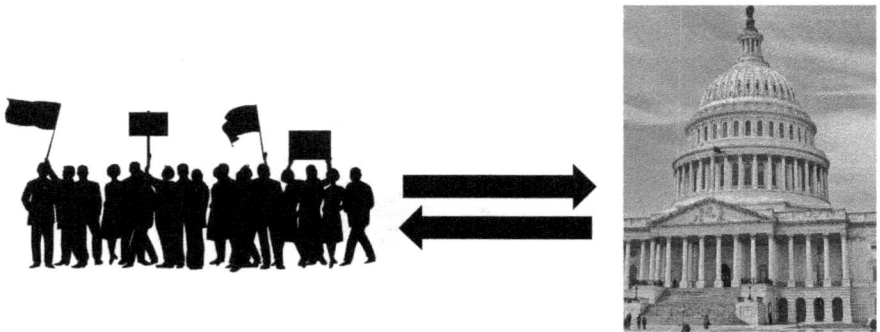

Figure 23.1: Dynamic Relationship between People
and Democratic Systems and Institutions

We're part of the equation! In dynamic relationships, working on either side of the equation affects both sides.

We can improve our systems and institutions through individual experiences that dissipate the hyperpartisan mindset and nurture democracy consciousness.

Also, notice that systems designed to micromanage our lives disincentivize personal growth. What's the goal here?

Developing your TAPE-enriching curriculum is up to you. It's like diet. You know what's best for you. Fewer empty calories, less junk food, fewer snacks between meals. Those aren't just metaphors for less POEP. Our biological systems integrate mind and body. Physical health impacts brain function.[116]

---

116 "Working out boosts brain health," American Psychological Association, Mar. 4, 2020, https://www.apa.org/topics/exercise-fitness/stress.

But since we're in a PP tactics chapter within a hyperpartisanship book, I'll suggest some factors relevant to TAPE enrichment in consideration of democracy consciousness. It begins with genuine desire. Next is introspection, or becoming conscious of our experiential diet, including media consumption. Next is: What do you need to change? You know the answer to that.

For consuming partisan media, I'll sparingly reiterate some concepts scattered throughout. Consuming media that stokes outrage and resentment toward other groups wires you for intransigence. If you recognize the seduction of righteousness affirmation, quickly stick a finger down your throat. You're ingesting a drug of appeasement that wires you for a matrix of homogenous thinking that impedes personal growth. If consumption requires homogenous thinking, abort. Your faith-based wiring is being hacked and reinforced to establish ideology.

Democracy Technique: Emphasizing Fundamentals

I've played a lot of sports and consumed tons of sports programming. As a result, I'm wired for sports metaphors. Here's another.

When teams underperform for extended periods, as remedy, coaches will emphasize fundamentals or getting back to basics. Intricate, complex, and time-consuming plays can't be carried out if the team cannot effectively block, dribble, pass, or catch, depending on the sport.

In general, players want to run complex plays or scrimmage during practice. Drilling fundamentals for extended periods is a drag. Players typically lack patience and consider repetitive drilling on fundamentals to be punishment. It can be, but it's more.

Think of music if you prefer. Working on a single song over and over results in single-song competence. But practicing scales, chords, and arpeggios develops technique and understanding that transfer to all songs. Mastering fundamentals provides foundation for musical improvisation. It means we can play jazz together!

But hyperpartisanship obscures or distracts us from fundamentals.

As a self-appointed democracy coach, I recommend working on fundamentals to develop democracy consciousness. We could argue about what the fundamentals of democracy are, and that would be a useful argument to have. I simply suggest a rudimentary framework.

For democracy, fundamentals involve process more than substance, i.e., how a bill gets passed rather than what's in the bill. It begins, as discussed throughout, with how we conduct the public discussion.

Emphasizing identity, tribal affiliation, party, faith, ideology, or religion of the messenger over the message itself is poor democracy technique. Manipulating emotions rather than appealing to reason is fundamentally unsound.

Process Is Fundamental

Stating opinions or conclusions isn't as essential as discussing parameters for establishing opinions or conclusions. In democracy, "cutting to the chase" skips a crucial part of the discussion.

The idea that we can skip to the finish line doesn't get us closer to the finish line. It sets us back. We must grind it out—the democratic process. I counsel process not as an obsessive process nit who isn't concerned with results, but as a pragmatist. Going through the process is more likely to result in lasting progress.

We place too much value on having people simply state their conclusions. POEP shows assemble panels of experts and hurriedly move around the circle to parrot talking points. POEP hosts pressure guests from the other team to state their opinions without contextualization. "Yes or no. It was a yes or no question. Just answer." Insistence on definitive conclusions without exploring parameters reduces the utility of interactions to a judgment as to whether the guest is one of us or them. A more fruitful public discussion articulates relevant factors for decision-making and leaves the audiences or electorate to reach their own conclusions. Forming your own opinions is fundamentally sound.

The other fundamental I would work on is the fundamental unit. The idea that through legislation, constitutional amendment, economic theory, or cultural systems, we can institutionalize a utopia not requiring individuals to compromise or find common ground with intellectual opponents is absurd. Can we improve the system or make systemic progress? Of course. In 1787, the U.S. Constitution was an example of systemic progress. Can we do better? Of course. But institutions of any system we create will be peopled.

Developing a more utilitarian democracy consciousness among a relevant portion of the electorate is no small task. It's like promoting herd immunity to hyperpartisanship, but there is no vaccine to provide a quick fix. Democracy is a grind.

Impatience Corrupts Process, Thereby Subordinating Democracy

Therein lies the rub. Perhaps the greatest weapon in the PP arsenal is our impatience. Players want to run a quadruple reverse flea-flicker in tomorrow's game, but they can't hold their blocks long enough to pull it off. Bandmembers want to play improvisational jazz in tonight's gig, but they don't know their scales well enough to make it swing. The electorate wants Congress to pass legislation solving all their problems in the current session, but their incompetence in the language of diplomacy and process of collaboration frustrates their ambitions.

Convenience culture exacerbates the infirmity. You can get pizza delivered in twenty minutes, but there's no app for political progress. There's no refund if your version of democracy doesn't promptly arrive. Democracy is process. Getting back to basics isn't going to play well on TV. Practicing fundamentals is for off-hour infomercials. If we don't pass a 10,000-page bill in the current session of Congress, the world will end. That's prime time!

I'm not diminishing the scale of problems we face. I'm suggesting the most efficient pathway toward ambitious endeavors is, at least initially, through more modest efforts. To use another sports analogy, for the time being, we need to play "small ball." We're in a pattern, or slump, of swinging for the fences on every pitch and striking out a lot.

In conspicuous dissonance, PP refrains of, "there's no time," or "I'm tired of waiting," play incessantly like bubblegum-pop tunes in teenage coming-of-age movies. The refrains make perfect sense but are beside the point. Rushing to build a resplendent roof before laying the foundation and framing the structure is pointless. All the speed in the world can't make a roof right without suitable support. The fastest way to create a magnificent superstructure is by taking the necessary time to lay a solid foundation.

The Constitution was a good start, but its preamble begins with "We the people . . ." *We* are not just the beneficiaries of its purpose but its instrumentalities as well. Through our thoughtful actions, we receive its benefits. By more fully developing democracy consciousness, we'll be more efficient instruments of our Constitution's aspirations. Developing greater democracy consciousness results in greater democracy. Improving ourselves improves our systems. Cultivating our TAPEs is part of the vigilance functional democracy requires.

Whether the choice to become a conscious caretaker of your TAPE is of free will or an inevitable consequence of your wiring, which this book is now a part of, is without regard.

24

The Partisan Warrior

Bronzed and glistening, like an adolescent Achilles, PW strikes a pose al fresco, simultaneously resplendent and auspicious in reverence of, or entitlement to the sun's regard, and in consideration of the spectators' vantage. Pristine, newly minted by the gods, and therefore at the prime of her political acumen, PW contemplates her radiance. His aspect is beyond capture by mere mortals. But I shall try.

She understands the wisdom of "trust your feelings" with impeccable clarity because she always feels she is always right about everything.

His moral certainty obviates self-evaluation.

She can't imagine a commodity more valuable than her righteousness, although her sanctimony dwarfs her imagination.

His résumé is as pristine as his background. He's never done anything wrong, because he's never done anything.

Her empathy for people willing to walk in her shoes is infinite.

His tolerance for people of similar identity is exemplary.

She knows sticking together means sticking with her. Groupthink is solidarity.

His position on speech is: Your freedom to agree with him is absolute. "We all have to agree," is edict. Disagreement is prima facie evidence of stupidity, craziness, or malice.

The consecrated nature of her EC is presumed. Therefore, integrating across tribal boundaries is corruption.

He views moderates and independents as contamination personified. They disgust him.

She appreciates tribalism as an organizational paradigm permitting application of double standards, which is essential for prosecuting sanctimonious warfare. Moral equivalence is heresy. The universe of similarities is eternally distinguishable by virtue of identity. Intention is of parochial relevance.

He considers himself under a moral imperative to extinguish dissent.

The virtue of her ideology serves as premise, reason, and conclusion.

He understands meritocracy as a system financially incentivizing his sanctimony.

Common ground is the area of her pedestal.

He collaborates with his reflection.

She thinks of science as commodity and the scientific method as nuisance.

He recognizes the dialectic as the greatest existential threat. Antithesis to his faith is conspiracy.

She interprets her righteousness as a mandate for sanctimony.

He speaks for everyone whether they appreciate it or not.

They understand patience as opposition and democratic process as stonewalling.

They see compromise as conflict of interest.

They apprehend a bipartisan bill as a Trojan horse.

They find pragmatism most unsettling.

Within their ECs, likes and applause are dispositive.

They define progress as absolute victory. They are PWs.

25

America the Beautiful Hybrid

> By the collision of different sentiments, sparks of truth
> are struck, and political light is obtained.
> —BENJAMIN FRANKLIN

Quest for purity is worse than quixotic. It corrodes the foundations of our republic with dogma and infects our national spirit with distraction. America is a hybrid nation. Our political system is not pure democracy. Our economic system is not pure capitalism. Our people are ethnically diverse. Our culture is an amalgam, and our ideas on national character naturally cross. Deal with it!

The promise of America appearing in any single, uncontaminated vision is mirage. One such vision is equal treatment under the law—the idea that a peasant and an aristocrat are both entitled to the same legal protections and processes, and both are equally accountable. Another vision is driven by opportunity for economic advancement—the idea that one born to peasantry, through hard work, skill, and creativity, can rise above his or her inherited station to afford the advantages of an aristocrat. Perhaps one of those ideas is more likely to manifest in your vision of America. Maybe one rubs you the wrong way. But like it or not, both visions are a part of our history and national character, and both subsume fairness. They are valid, and in a sense, intertwined, but neither, by itself, adequately realizes America. The promise of America exists in the tensions between. Disparaging either vision intensifies division while diminishing our capacity.

Likewise, our systems integrate the socialism of public education and highway construction with incentive-driven free markets for goods and services. If tensions between our competing philosophies dissipate via total victory of one vision over another, America will be left in total defeat. I am not privy to where the sweet spot within the tensions is precisely located. But I know it moves to and fro with the times and is approximated through pragmatism.

The thematic content of stories permeating our consciousness includes the desolate perseverance of stubborn individualism and the rewards of camaraderie. The composition of our teams includes collaborations of all-stars like the 1992 Olympic "Dream Team," as well as assortments of unlikely protagonists like the 1980 Olympics' "Miracle on Ice." Some Americans feel right when results confirm chalk. The rest prefer upsets by dogs. Whether outcomes flow from superior talent, hard work, or some combination thereof, almost all of us desire a system rewarding merit.

Tensions between American freedoms and responsibility contribute to the dialectic. Freedom to achieve financial enrichment grinds against responsibility to manage resources. Freedom to maximize utility in the present challenges sustainability. Our entire legal system can be understood as a codification of tensions between rights and responsibilities.

Even freedom of speech should be tempered with mindfulness and carries potential for defamatory liability. Our most cherished rights spoil when subjected to purification rituals or absolutist dogma. Absolute freedom and absolute equality are mutually exclusive. Through a fellowship of pragmatic understanding, we may integrate our values and balance our ambitions.

Tensions between Competing Visions, Ideals, and Aspirations Are Constitutional Democracies' Greatest Resources

To begin, competing viewpoints is an attribute of democracy. Authoritarianism quashes ideas that challenge authority. Crucial tensions are repressed.

I beseech an understanding of these tensions as more than a mere feature of democracy. They are its lifeblood. Tensions between competing visions are the *most essential* feature of a free and democratic society. Pragmatism roots my activism for this understanding.

I launch my advocacy by interpreting democracy as a human organizational system. You could substitute "form of government" for "human organizational system," but governments are organizational systems, and here I emphasize system functionality over academic classification. According to dictionaries, democracy is "government by the people,"[117] and government is "the political system by which a country or community is administered and regulated."[118]

For this discussion, I define democracy as:

> An organizational system permitting human diversities, including thought diversity, and resolving conflicts arising from such diversities through peaceful means and processes administered by the people or their elected representatives.

"Peaceful" seems a bit aspirational at this point, but that's OK. I want to focus on something else. A hidden premise within the definition requires exposition. Why do we or should we permit diversity, especially thought diversity?

Democratic, i.e., Pragmatic Justification for Diversity

There are at least two correct answers. The first is more familiar and relies on the moral underpinnings of democracy. We have the right to "Life, Liberty and the pursuit of Happiness."[119] The first answer has to do with our rights. Democratic rights permit diversity of thought, vision, ideals, and aspirations.

While I agree democratic rights permit diversity, fixating exclusively on rights stifles more practical explorations. Relying on moral underpinnings introduces an element of dogma sustained by faith, interfering with intellectual investigation. I believe I have the right and that's that.

Also, focusing on rights contributes to a dynamic by which contrary human

117 "democracy," Merriam-Webster, accessed May 20, 2023, https://www.merriam-webster.com/dictionary/democracy.

118 Hugh Brogan, "government," Britannica, accessed May 20, 2023, https://www.britannica.com/topic/government.

119 "Declaration of Independence: A Transcription," National Archives, accessed May 20, 2023, https://www.archives.gov/founding-docs/declaration-transcript.

expression is analyzed as potential danger. In other words, anyone exercising rights to challenge my opinions, vision, ideology, or aspirations threatens my rights. PPs are adept at organizing analytical paradigms pitting one group's rights against another's.

Finally, obsessing on rights can create an ambiance of patronizing self-aggrandizement. In other words, "your opinions are downright stupid, but because we live in a democracy and because I believe in democracy and because I am such a good democratic citizen, I acknowledge your right to your stupid opinions and I'm willing to tolerate your stupid opinions, which is a demonstration of my superior conception of democracy." Therefore, we should attend more scrupulously to the second answer.

Progress Requires Thought Diversity

So rather than an entitlement to diversity or right to our opinions, I want to focus on the functionality of diversity of thought, vision, ideals, and aspirations. I'm making a policy argument. As a matter of public policy, we should give greater consideration to the utility of diversity rather than dwell exclusively on its morality.

Tensions between our competing thoughts and visions should be understood as a means to progress. The tensions propel the dialectic. Therefore, absolute partisan victory, or even aspiring to such a thing, corrupts democracy.

Our perseverance demands not consenting to belligerence. Hyperpartisanship is counterproductive, except for PI profit. Understanding all political opposition as existential threat is unexceptional.

Instead, we must cultivate and nurture a democratic mindset. Tensions between our competing visions should be managed as a resource. Harvesting the fruits of these tensions is the utility of a free and democratic society. Understanding ourselves as both a source and beneficiary of these tensions lights a pathway toward exceptionalism. It is the citizenship of democracy.

Evolution Smiles on Hybridization

Contriving purity offends life. No single person or group gets to make America in their image. The effort to do so is narcissism. America isn't one idea.

Realizing we need people who think differently than we do for our own persistence undermines both hyperpartisanship and bigotry.

America doesn't need pure little liberal Democrats or pure little conservative Republicans. But PI craves clear choices. Candidates reflecting the hybrid nature of America are more difficult to distinguish and therefore problematic products to market. Don't let PPs establish purity limitations on your philosophy. Don't let PI establish permanent bifurcation. Become a beautiful American hybrid. We waste too much time and energy on ideological purification. Quest for purity is a fool's errand. Leave it!

Conclusions

The greatest and most important problems of life . . .
can never be solved but only outgrown.
—C.G. JUNG

How can we outgrow hyperpartisanship? What does it mean to outgrow something? Reflect upon what you have outgrown. Understanding correlates with maturation.

Hyperpartisanship

Hyperpartisanship is an adaptive phenomenon thriving in segregated environments. Our media and political systems financially incentivize partisan segregation and differentiation. The two-party system provides polarizing structure for disagreement and division. Human psychological predispositions evolved during our tribal existences make us vulnerable to manipulations associated with group identity. Groups exert conforming pressures, subordinating individual identity. Individual identity transcends groupings. The natural condition of free individuals and democratic systems is hybrid.

Segregation

Our understanding of the universe is predicated and confounded by segregation. Paradoxes associated with categorical separation challenge our conceptual framework. We differentiate between "here on Earth" and "out in space," yet Earth exists within space. We say, "mind and body," yet our biological systems fully integrate brain and body in a dynamic relationship. We envision our political systems and institutions as features apart from us to be tinkered with.

Democracy

When government is of, by, and for the people, government dysfunction is symptomatic of human dysfunction. Choosing to write off anyone who disagrees with us as stupid, crazy, or evil is dysfunctional. When a substantial portion of the population chooses dysfunction, societal dysfunction ensues. We are trending toward dysfunction. No legislative package can remedy a mindset dissonant with democracy. Where is the consent of the governed on the psychology of collaboration?

Faith

Faith in religions or ideologies that disdain compromise or shun common ground is antithetical to democratic process. Establishing singular ideology sabotages democracy. The persistence of constitutional democracy requires hybridization.

Perpetuating the Cycle

Segregation, tribal psychology, and ideological faith, along with economics of escalation, work in adaptive synergy to nourish hyperpartisanship. Segregated media, political parties, and PPs are financially incentivized to perpetuate the cycle. While hyperpartisanship functions to enrich PI, its effect on other parts of society, including legislative processes, is dysfunctional. "Dysfunctional" hyperpartisanship allows PPs on both sides to make the case to segregated constituencies that the system is broken, and it's the other side's fault. Legislative dysfunction sustains hyperpartisanship, and hyperpartisanship sabotages legislating. The positive feedback loop provides job security for PPs and persists through our patronage and consent.

Segregated Media

Conflict of interest contaminates public discourse, which is democracy's heart and fundamental to progress and remedy. Intentions aside, those who frame and mediate our national conversations profit from polarization. It persists through our patronage and consent.

Eternal Vigilance

To sustain democracy, we should familiarize ourselves with the price of its sustenance. The requisite vigilance has not been adequately described.

To be vigilant is to be "alertly watchful, especially to avoid danger."[120] It means paying attention. Before focusing that attention, let's consider vigilance in the context of democracy.

First off, vigilance is not a right. It's a responsibility. Formal education, along with popular discourse concerning the framework and advantages of constitutional democracies, tends to emphasize rights over responsibilities. When the subject of responsibility is broached, it usually involves government or our representatives. In other words, *people* have rights, and *government* is responsible for ensuring those rights.

Thinking rights come without responsibility is childish. Balance requires rights and responsibilities to accrue conjointly. Vigilance is a responsibility eternally accruing to the fundamental units of democracy. Understanding democracy solely as a bonanza of rights is not just childish, but also bankrupt. Bankrupt understanding of democracy contributes to dysfunction.

Instead of exclusively emphasizing rights, understanding democracy as a mandate for individual responsibility would serve us better. Undertaking responsibility demands evolution. It makes us stretch. It's uniting. It means we're part of a team. We're all pitching in. Responsibility is shared. Sharing interferes with blaming the other. In other words, emphasizing responsibility to parochial constituencies inconveniences PI's business model.

But at least we have a slogan involving responsibility for vigilance. Let's

---

120 "vigilant," Merriam-Webster, accessed Aug. 1, 2023, https://www.merriam-webster.com/dictionary/vigilant.

build on that. In all its iterations, the slogan's vigilance is correctly understood to mean keeping a watchful eye on government machinations. Eternal vigilance is intended as a prophylactic against losing our republic to monarchy or other forms of authoritarianism.

That's about as far as the slogan has taken us. Let's take it further. Our resolve to do so crashes into our determination to segregate. Understanding government as a thing apart from ourselves renders vigilance impotent.

Democracy Consciousness

The primary responsibility or vigilance self-government demands is *self-awareness*. With democracy, government is not separate from people. Therefore, we must be vigilant in our understanding of the dynamic relationship between government, i.e., institutions of democracy, and the fundamental units. The vigilance required of people is to develop an awareness of the dynamic nature of that relationship. In other words, we must evolve our democracy consciousness.

Briefly, I revisit substance versus process. The substance of democracy consciousness or prescription for its perfection is unknown, and most likely varies according to the individual and times. We desire evolution and evolution is process. Eternally evolving consciousness is never perfect. Having said that, I conclude by reiterating what I consider essential.

Evolutionary Rates

Government progression, cultural development, and technological innovation all occur at rates that make biological evolution appear static. We inherit a psychological template predating mass media and constitutional democracy by hundreds of millennia.

Democracy Requires Disagreement

Understanding disagreement as a means to progress facilitates democracy. Funneling disagreement into a binary or polarizing structure is financially incentivized and supported by primitive tribal psychology but sabotages the productive potential of our disagreements.

Vigilance Demands Ascertaining Complicity

The hyperpartisan system profits from unconscious participation. Evolving democracy consciousness requires us to think about things we don't wish to think about, such as the fact that our insecurities provide the basis for addiction to identity validation. Or that by subbing out our vigilance by writing a check to a political party, we're financially complicit in institutionalizing polarization. Or that consuming media content according to partisan desires patronizes segregation, incapacitating productive disagreement.

Evolving Culture

We don't have time to wait for biology to catch up with our circumstances. Therefore, we must evolve culture to enhance the productivity of our disagreements to the benefit of constitutional democracy. That type of cultural evolution requires conscious effort. Although our psychological template is anachronistic, awareness is the first step to liberation. By simply surrendering to primitive psychology, we surrender democracy.

Breaking the Cycle

Breaking violent and destructive cycles requires courage bolstered by understanding. If we refuse to integrate across boundaries of our own making, like political parties, or of our own imagination, like race, we will fail. When our identities become inexorably linked to tribal hostility, functional accord can be perceived as existential threat to self. If we are first and foremost partisans in a partisan war, we subordinate our status as citizen colleagues.

Integration Is an Act of Realization

If we can realize we depend upon those with whom we disagree so our ideas are subjected to the crucible of argument, then the synthesis of our dialectics will be a product of reason rather than faith, and a treaty of pragmatism among the citizenry becomes feasible. Democracy demands sharing power even with those who wish to diminish us.

American exceptionalism, or the endurance of constitutional democracy, as well as integration itself, requires us to realize we are integrated.

One Last Thing

Thank you for reading this book. If you enjoyed it, please visit the online store where you made your purchase and leave a review. Even just a few sentences will help potential readers make informed decisions.

Appendix A

Feedback Loops

Positive

1. More partisan content in the media nurtures societal partisanship, and as societal partisanship grows, the financial incentive to provide partisan content grows. As more and more fragmented partisan content is provided, more and more people migrate toward a fragment, and so on.

2. Internet algorithms learn user preferences for extreme content and present and expose users to a more extreme internet environment, which affects the users' worldview toward extremism, which affects the users' preferences toward extremism, which refines algorithms toward presenting more extreme content, etc.

3. Hyperpartisanship impedes legislative functionality, which leads to public finger-pointing and blame, which escalates partisanship, which further impedes legislative functionality, etc. Legislative dysfunction sustains hyperpartisanship, and hyperpartisanship sabotages legislative functioning.

4. The perception of deteriorating conditions, dysfunctional systems, and untrustworthy institutions bolsters justification for extremism. Engaging in procedural extremism heightens perception of deteriorating conditions, dysfunctional systems, and untrustworthy institutions.

5. As POEP hosts, analysts, and guests develop expertise in partisan analysis, incentive to cover stories that can be used for partisan advantage increases. And as incentive to cover stories that can be used for partisan

advantage increases, incentive to staff media with experts in partisan analysis increases, and so on.

6. Media discussions about hyperpartisanship that resolve with comments reinforcing the notion that "dysfunctional" hyperpartisanship is unsolvable disincentivize productive thinking, discussion, and action, reducing the likelihood of solving hyperpartisanship.

7. We are environmental factors within our environment. Likewise, our behavior is influenced by our environment. Our nature, developed through evolution within environments carrying selective factors, drives our actions. Our actions modify the landscape, and so on.

8. Barriers to understanding segregate, and segregation creates barriers to understanding. Communication between segregated populations becomes more challenging as the depth and duration of segregation increases. As communication degenerates, understanding becomes more difficult. As barriers to understanding grow, segregation becomes more entrenched, and so on.

9. As marriages trend toward partisan homogeneity, offspring will be increasingly hyperpartisan. Hyperpartisan offspring will be more likely to pursue ideologically similar mates, and so on.

10. Purity as a virtue contributes to intolerance, which is segregating. Segregation facilitates purification and increases intolerance. Greater intolerance for that which does not conform to insular concepts of purity drives further segregation, etc.

11. As more resources are dedicated to radical change, opportunities for modest progress within the system diminish, and as opportunities for modest progress diminish, the argument for radical change increases, and so on.

Negative

1. A reduction in faith in free press dampens the effect of increased presence of activist content. As free press becomes hyperpartisan and certain issues are more likely to be championed, public faith in free press for objective journalism decreases. As public faith in free press for objective journalism decreases, efficacy of using free press for advocacy also decreases.

Appendix B

Hypothesized Rules and Relationships

1. If a *persistent* phenomenon *persistently* prevents a subsystem from functioning properly, then that subsystem is inferior or subordinate to the (sub)system(s) where that same phenomenon supports function.

2. The incentive, ability, and opportunity to defragment, or integrate with those outside your fragment, diminish as connections within your fragment become more substantial.

3. As the pool of money used to distinguish partisan adversaries increases, financial incentives for polarization and adversarial behavior increase accordingly.

4. Partisan gamesmanship within traditionally nonpartisan institutions contributes to declining faith in democratic institutions.

5. As media hyperpartisanship increases, faith in the institution of the free press decreases.

6. As media segregates according to ideology and partisan affiliation, credibility to broader audiences diminishes.

7. Advocacy journalism strengthens connections to narrow, ideologically aligned audiences, while undermining credibility to broader audiences.

8. PI lateral expansion facilitates a deeper identification with partisanship.

9. Media fragmentation opens the door for the fringe to enter the mainstream.

10. Moral certainty expedites extremism and healthy uncertainty restrains it.

11. The more extreme both sides become, the less likely functional accord can be achieved.

12. As the time an individual spends within ECs increases, his or her desire and ability to conduct civil discourse decreases, and as the time humanity spends within ECs increases, the desire and ability of humanity to conduct civil discourse decreases.

13. As the importance of party affiliation for an individual increases for self-identification or self-worth, the sway a party holds over that individual increases.

14. As a person derives an increasing share of individual identity from a group, psychological pressure to conform to group identity increases.

15. The probability a person will derive an increasing share of individual identity from a group increases with segregation.

16. As segregation according to partisan affiliation or political ideology within society increases, the probability of "dysfunctional" hyperpartisanship also increases.

17. Leading a political party conflicts with leading a nation.

18. As PI's entertainment subsector expands, partisan identification strengthens.

19. As revenue for the campaign subsector increases through increased political spending, spending on differentiating candidates, politicians,

and ideology of parties increases.

20. As wealth of partisan entities or groups such as political parties or PACs increases, their influence over individual identity within partisan groups strengthens.

21. As partisan or ideological segregation increases, so does extremism.

22. Fortifying the independent viability of ideological or partisan fragments within society obscures the urgency of interdependence and strengthens division.

23. The longer and more completely an issue serves primarily as a wedge, as part of a partisan electoral scheme, or as a fundraising vehicle for political parties, the more difficult is its transformation back to an issue whose primary purpose is to advance itself through the legislature via compromise and bipartisanship.

24. If one party attains exclusive dominion over your issue, you're screwed on that issue. Exclusive dominion means progress can only be achieved by voting out the other side. Exclusive dominion is accomplished by disdaining moderates, moderation, and private action.

25. As the identities of more individuals become entangled with partisan entities, more issues will exist primarily to advance partisan interests.

26. As the proportion of issues used primarily to advance partisan interests increases, legislative functionality decreases, and PI functionality increases.

27. Moderate progress dampens oscillation.

28. Paying for bipartisan influence bankrolls partisan warfare.

29. More extreme or ambitious does not mean pushing harder.

30. That which eternally evolves can never be perfect.

31. As partisan affiliation becomes a more conspicuous component of identity, media content affirming the righteousness of the audience's partisanship becomes more desirable.

32. We can improve our systems and institutions through individual experiences that dissipate the hyperpartisan mindset and nurture democracy consciousness.

33. Emphasizing the identity, tribal affiliation, party, faith, ideology, or religion of the messenger over the message itself is poor democracy technique. Manipulating emotions rather than appealing to reason is fundamentally unsound.

34. Vigilance applied to self-government means self-awareness.

References

Oregon State University. (2011, August 22). *Lasting evolutionary change takes about one million years* . Retrieved October 22, 2023, from Oregon State University: https://today.oregonstate.edu/archives/2011/aug/lasting-evolutionary-change-takes-about-one-million-years

Thomas Jefferson Encyclopedia . (n.d.). *Eternal vigilance is the price of liberty (Spurious Quotation)*. Retrieved January 1, 2023, from The Jefferson Monticello: https://www.monticello.org/research-education/thomas-jefferson-encyclopedia/eternal-vigilance-price-liberty-spurious-quotation/

American Psychological Association. (2020, March 4). *Working out boosts brain health*. Retrieved October 7, 2023, from American Psychological Association: https://www.apa.org/topics/exercise-fitness/stress

Andrea, L. (2020, August 27). *Foreign actors seeking to sow divisions by targeting Native American populations, cyber intelligence firms says*. Retrieved October 6, 2023, from milwaukee journal sentinel: https://www.jsonline.com/story/news/politics/elections/2020/08/27/election-trolls-targeting-native-populations-cyber-group-says/5481408002/?

Ask Not What Your Country Can Do For You. (n.d.). Retrieved December 19, 2024, from US history.org: https://www.ushistory.org/documents/ask-not.htm

Bailey, R. (2019, October 26). *6 Things You Should Know About Biological Evolution*. Retrieved October 22, 2023, from ThoughtCo.: https://www.thoughtco.com/biological-evolution-373416

Barbuscia, D. (2023, August 2). *Fitch cuts US credit rating to AA+; Treasury calls it 'arbitrary'*. Retrieved October 5, 2023, from REUTERS: https://www.reuters.com/markets/us/fitch-cuts-us-governments-aaa-credit-rating-by-one-notch-2023-08-01/

Barras, C. (2017, October 12). *Gene study shows human skin tone has varied for 900,000 years*. Retrieved October 6, 2023, from NewScientist: https://www.newscientist.com/article/2150253-gene-study-shows-human-skin-tone-has-varied-for-900000-years/

Biden, J. U. (2023, February 7). *State of the Union Address*. Retrieved October 6, 2023, from The White House: https://www.whitehouse.gov/state-of-the-union-2023/

Bontemps, T. (2020, May 4). *Michael Jordan stands firm on 'Republicans buy sneakers, too' quote, says it was made in jest*. Retrieved October 5, 2023, from ESPN: https://www.espn.com/nba/story/_/id/29130478/michael-jordan-stands-firm-republicans-buy-sneakers-too-quote-says-was-made-jest

Bowen, W. R. (2022, July 19). *The Rise of the Nation-State*. Retrieved October 6, 2023, from Owlcation: https://owlcation.com/humanities/nation-state

Breech, J. (2020, February 5). *2020 Super Bowl ratings revealed: Chiefs-49ers ranks as the 11th most-watched show in TV history*. Retrieved Jauary 10, 2021, from CBS.com: https://www.cbssports.com/nfl/news/2020-super-bowl-ratings-revealed-chiefs-49ers-ranks-as-the-11th-most-watched-show-in-tv-history/

Bregman, M. (Producer), Stone, O. (Writer), & Palma, B. D. (Director). (1983). *Scarface* [Motion Picture]. Universal Pictures.

Britannica Encyclopaedia, T. E. (n.d.). *What Is Cultural Appropriation?* Retrieved December 2, 2022, from Britannica: https://www. britannica.com/story/what-is-cultural-appropriation

Britannica. (n.d.). *political machine*. Retrieved August 11, 2022, from Britannica: https://www.britannica.com/topic/political-machine

Britannica. (n.d.). *Third Reich*. Retrieved February 12, 2023, from Britannica: https://www.britannica.com/place/Third-Reich/ The-Enabling-Act-and-the-Nazi-revolution

Brogan, H. (n.d.). *government*. Retrieved May 20, 2023, from Britannica: https://www.britannica.com/topic/government

Brooks, J. (2017, April 10). *Identity Politics: A Lesson for Brands*. Retrieved October 5, 2023, from LRW: https://lrwonline.com/perspective/ identity-politics-lesson-brands/

Burns, K. (2020, April 14). The Gene: An Intimate History. Part 2: Revolution in the Treatment of Disease. PBS.

Cáceres, I. B. (2019, June 25). *Advocacy Journalism*. Retrieved January 18, 2024, from Oxford Research Encyclopedias: https://oxfordre.com/communication/display/10.1093/ acrefore/9780190228613.001.0001/acrefore-9780190228613-e-776

Campaign Zero. (n.d.). *About*. Retrieved October 4, 2023, from Campaign Zero: https://campaignzero.org/about/what-we-do/

Capra, F. (Producer), Buchman, S. a. (Writer), & Capra, F. (Director). (1939). *Mr. Smith Goes to Washington* [Motion Picture]. Columbia Pictures.

Caruso, H. G. (Producer), Chayefsky, P. (Writer), & Lumet, S. (Director). (1976). *Network* [Motion Picture]. United Artists.

Castrovince, A. (2023, February 1). *Pitch timer, shift restrictions among announced rule changes for '23.* Retrieved March 1, 2023, from mlb.com: https://www.mlb.com/news/ mlb-2023-rule-changes-pitch-timer-larger-bases-shifts

Cherry, K. M. (2023, February 22). *What is Empathy?* Retrieved October 6, 2023, from verywellmind: https://www.verywellmind.com/ what-is-empathy-2795562

CITIZENS UNITED v. FEDERAL ELECTION COMMISSION, 558 (U.S. Supreme Court 2010). Retrieved October 5, 2023, from https://tile.loc.gov/storage-services/service/ll/usrep/usrep558/ usrep558310/usrep558310.pdf

Clark, T. (2004, February 24). *Naturalism, Choice, and Creativity: Transcending Free Will.* Retrieved October 7, 2023, from Naturalism: https://www.naturalism.org/resources/talks/ naturalism-choice-and-creativity-transcending-free-will

Cofnas, N. (2022, April 7). *The Golden Rule: A Naturalistic Perspective.* Retrieved October 6, 2023, from Cambridge University Press: https://www.cambridge.org/core/journals/utilitas/article/ golden-rule-a-naturalistic-perspective/23D7AAC2FCA9B09DD 64F267994F0722A

Colleen Carey, E. M. (n.d.). *Drug Firms' Payments and Physicians' Prescribing Behavior in Medicare Part D.* National Bureau of Economic Research. Retrieved August 17, 2024, from https:// www.nber.org/system/files/working_papers/w26751/w26751.pdf

Colvin, R. (2022, October 24). *Side effect of divisive politics? Unaffiliated voter numbers rise.* Retrieved October 6, 2023, from The Washington Post: https://www.washingtonpost.com/elections/2022/10/24/rise-of-independent-voters/

Cory J. Clark, B. S. (2019, August 20). *Tribalism Is Human Nature.* Retrieved August 17, 2024, from Sage Journales: https://journals.sagepub.com/doi/10.1177/0963721419862289

De Luce, D. (2020, February 10). *Counterintelligence chief warns of threat to democracy from foreign hackers, spies.* Retrieved October 6, 2023, from NBC News: https://www.nbcnews.com/politics/national-security/u-s-counterintel-chief-warns-threat-democracy-foreign-hackers-spies-n1134476

Declaration of Independence: A Transcription. (n.d.). Retrieved May 20, 2023, from National Archives: https://www.archives.gov/founding-docs/declaration-transcript

Dictionary.com. (2023). *speciation.* Retrieved October 4, 2023, from Dictionary.com: https://www.dictionary.com/browse/speciation

D'Souza, D. (2022, May 28). *Understanding the Green New Deal & What's in the Climate Proposal.* Retrieved October 6, 2023, from Investopedia: https://www.investopedia.com/the-green-new-deal-explained-4588463

Duello, T. M. (2021, June 15). Race and genetics versus 'race' in genetics: A systematic review of the use of African ancestry in genetic studies. *Evolution, Medicine, & Public Health, 9,* 232–245. Retrieved October 23, 2023, from https://academic.oup.com/emph/article/9/1/232/6299389#eoab018-BOX1

Duverger, M. (n.d.). *political party.* Retrieved June 14, 2023, from Britannica: https://www.britannica.com/topic/political-party

Editors, B. (2017, April 28). *Mutualism.* Retrieved March 14, 2024, from biology dictionary: https://biologydictionary.net/mutualism/

Emerson, R. W. (1996-2019). *Self-Reliance.* Retrieved March 9, 2024, from EmersonCentral.com: https://emersoncentral.com/ebook/Self-Reliance.pdf

Fair Vote. (2013, November). *The Polarization Crisis in Congress: The Decline of Crossover Representatives and Crossover Voting in the U.S. House.* Retrieved October 4, 2023, from Crossover_Voting_2014.pdf: https://fairvote.app.box.com/v/mp14-crossover-voting

Federal Election Commission. (n.d.). *Making electioneering communications.* Retrieved October 5, 2023, from Federal Election Commission: https://www.fec.gov/help-candidates-and-committees/other-filers/making-electioneering-communications/

Fuchs, E. (2014, June 27). *6 Constitutional Amendments That Could Dramatically Improve America.* Retrieved October 5, 2023, from Insider: https://www.businessinsider.com/john-paul-stevens-six-amendments-2014-6

Galston, W. A. (2021, October 1). *For COVID-19 vaccinations, party affiliation matters more than race and ethnicity.* Retrieved October 5, 2023, from Brookings: https://www.brookings.edu/articles/for-covid-19-vaccinations-party-affiliation-matters-more-than-race-and-ethnicity/

Giorno, T. a. (2022, November 3). *Total cost of 2022 state and federal elections projected to exceed $16.7 billion.* Retrieved from Open Secrets: https://www.opensecrets.org/news/2022/11/total-cost-of-2022-state-and-federal-elections-projected-to-exceed-16-7-billion/

Handley, L. (2019, February 1). *The Super Bowl is worth billions each year — Here's who makes what.* Retrieved January 10, 2020, from CNBC: https://www.cnbc.com/2019/02/01/the-super-bowl-is-worth-billions-each-year--heres-who-makes-what.html

Handwerk, B. (2021, February 2). An Evolutionary Timeline of Homo Sapiens. *Smithsonian Magazine.* Retrieved October 6, 2023, from https://www.smithsonianmag.com/science-nature/essential-timeline-understanding-evolution-homo-sapiens-180976807/

Helderman, R. S. (2022, February 9). *All the ways Trump tried to overturn the election — and how it could happen again.* Retrieved October 5, 2023, from The Washington Post: https://www.washingtonpost.com/politics/interactive/2022/election-overturn-plans/

Hutt, R. (2016, March 17). *Why do civilizations collapse?* Retrieved October 6, 2023, from World Economic Forum: https://www.weforum.org/agenda/2016/03/why-do-civilizations-collapse

Jones, J. M. (2021, March 29). *U.S. Church Membership Falls Below Majority for First Time.* Retrieved October 6, 2023, from Gallup: https://news.gallup.com/poll/341963/church-membership-falls-below-majority-first-time.aspx#:~:text=The

Kennedy, L. (2022, August 9). *6 Early Human Civilizations.* Retrieved October 6, 2023, from History: https://www.history.com/news/first-earliest-human-civilizations

Klein, R. (2018, August 12). *Trump said 'blame on both sides' in Charlottesville, now the anniversary puts him on the spot.* Retrieved October 6, 2023, from abcNEWS: https://abcnews.go.com/Politics/trump-blame-sides-charlottesville-now-anniversary-puts-spot/story?id=57141612

Krulwich, R. (2012, October 22). *How Human Beings Almost Vanished From Earth In 70,000 B.C.* Retrieved August 10, 2024, from npr: https://www.npr.org/sections/krulwich/2012/10/22/163397584/ how-human-beings-almost-vanished-from-earth-in-70-000-b-c

Kubrick, S. (Producer), Kubrick, S. (Writer), & Kubrick, S. (Director). (1964). *Dr. Strangelove or: How I Learned to Stop Worrying and Love the Bomb* [Motion Picture]. United Kingdom & United States: Columbia Pictures.

Martinovich, M. (2017, August 31). *Americans' partisan identities are stronger than race and ethnicity, Stanford scholar finds.* Retrieved October 6, 2023, from Stanford: https://news.stanford. edu/2017/08/31/political-party-identities-stronger-race-religion/

McKenna, M. &. (2021). *Compatibilism.* (E. N. Zalta, Editor) Retrieved October 7, 2023, from The Stanford Encyclopedia of Philosophy : https://plato.stanford.edu/entries/compatibilism/

Merriam-Webster. (n.d.). *boondoggle.* Retrieved February 6, 2024, from Merriam-Webster: https://www.merriam-webster.com/ dictionary/boondoggle

Merriam-Webster. (n.d.). *democracy.* Retrieved May 20, 2023, from Merriam-Webster: https://www.merriam-webster.com/ dictionary/democracy

Merriam-Webster. (n.d.). *empathy.* Retrieved October 6, 2023, from Merriam-Webster: https://www.merriam-webster.com/ dictionary/empathy

Merriam-Webster. (n.d.). *faith.* Retrieved January 16, 2023, from Merriam-Webster: https://www.merriam-webster.com/ dictionary/faith

Merriam-Webster. (n.d.). *vigilant.* Retrieved August 1, 2023, from Merriam-Webster: https://www.merriam-webster.com/dictionary/vigilant

Monty Python's Flying Circus . (n.d.). *Me Doctor.* Retrieved August 12, 2023, from https://www.youtube.com/watch?v=BQSbKBTuQBc&ab_channel=rylxyc

Morris, I. (2016, Feruary 19). *Incredible Archaeological Discoveries.* Retrieved August 17, 2024, from YouTube: https://www.youtube.com/watch?v=oxieVARtZ7c

Murse, T. (2019, July 3). *How Political Parties Work in the United States.* Retrieved October 5, 2023, from ThoughtCo.: https://www.thoughtco.com/political-party-definition-4285031

National Constitution Center. (2017, January 23). *Executive Orders 101: What are they and how do Presidents use them?* Retrieved October 5, 2023, from National Constitution Center: https://constitutioncenter.org/blog/executive-orders-101-what-are-they-and-how-do-presidents-use-them

National Court Rules Committee. (n.d.). Rule 403 – Excluding Relevant Evidence for Prejudice, Confusion, Waste of Time, or Other Reasons. *Federal Rules of Evidence*(2023). Retrieved April 9, 2023, from https://www.rulesofevidence.org/article-iv/rule-403/

National Court Rules Committee. (n.d.). Rule 802 – The Rule Against Hearsay. *Federal Rules of Evidence*(2023). Retrieved April 9, 2023, from https://www.rulesofevidence.org/article-viii/rule-802/

National Geographic Society. (n.d.). *Democracy (Ancient Greece)*. Retrieved Decmber 7, 2022, from National Geographic: https://education.nationalgeographic.org/resource/democracy-ancient-greece#:~:text=The first known democracy in the world was,to take an active part in the government

National Geographic Society. (n.d.). *The Development of Agriculture*. Retrieved December 7, 2022, from National Geographic: https://education.nationalgeographic.org/resource/development-agriculture

NJ. (2024, June 9). *How Many Websites Are There in the World?* Retrieved August 12, 2024, from siteefy: https://siteefy.com/how-many-websites-are-there/

Nolan, J. &. (2016-2022). Westworld. *Westworld*. United States: HBO.

Norton, J. D. (2022, February 6). *The Quantum Theory of Waves and Particles*. Retrieved October 5, 2023, from pitt.edu: https://sites.pitt.edu/~jdnorton/teaching/HPS_0410/chapters/quantum_theory_waves/index.html

Obama, B. (2018, September 7). Full speech: Obama brands trump as 'symptom not the cause of division'. (N. NEWS, Compiler) Retrieved October 7, 2023, from https://www.nbcnews.com/video/full-speech-obama-brands-trump-as-symptom-not-the-cause-of-division-1315294787749?v=railb&

Office of Management and Budget. (2024). *Budget of the U.S. Gov't Fiscal Year 2024*. The White House, Office of Management and Budget. Office of Management and Budget. Retrieved October 5, 2023, from https://www.govinfo.gov/content/pkg/BUDGET-2024-BUD/pdf/BUDGET-2024-BUD.pdf

Open Secrets. (n.d.). *Cost of Election*. Retrieved October 4, 2023, from
     Open Secrets: https://www.opensecrets.org/elections-overview/
     cost-of-election

Open Secrets. (n.d.). *Expenditures*. Retrieved July 5, 2023,
     from Open Secrets: https://www.opensecrets.org/
     campaign-expenditures?cycle=2020

PBS (Producer), & Burns, K. (Director). (2020). *The Gene: An Intimate
     History. Part 1: Dawn of the Modern Age of Genetics* [Motion
     Picture].

Pew Research Center. (2012, June 4). *Partisan Polarization Surges in
     Bush, Obama Years*. Retrieved October 4, 2023, from Pew
     Research Center: https://www.people-press.org/2012/06/04/
     partisan-polarization-surges-in-bush-obama-years/

Pew Research Center. (2019, December 17). *In a Politically Polarized Era,
     Sharp Divides in Both Partisan Coalitions*. Retrieved October 4,
     2023, from Pew Research Center: https://www.pewresearch.org/
     politics/2019/12/17/in-a-politically-polarized-era-sharp-divides-
     in-both-partisan-coalitions/

Plous, S. (n.d.). *The Psychology of Prejudice: An Overview*. Retrieved
     November 11, 2022, from Understanding Prejudice: https://
     secure.understandingprejudice.org/apa/english/index.htm

Polimeni, J. &. (2006). The First Joke: Exploring the Evolutionary
     Origins of Humor. *Evolutionary Psychology, 4*(1). Retrieved from
     https://doi.org/10.1177/147470490600400129

Psychology Today. (n.d.). *Evolutionary Psychology*. Retrieved October 22,
     2023, from Psychology Today: https://www.psychologytoday.
     com/us/basics/evolutionary-psychology

Reilly, K. (2016, August 31). *Here Are All the Times Donald Trump Insulted Mexico*. Retrieved October 6, 2023, from TIME: https://time.com/4473972/donald-trump-mexico-meeting-insult/

Reilly, K. (2016, September 10). Read Hillary Clinton's 'Basket of Deplorables' Remarks About Donald Trump Supporters. *TIME*. Retrieved from https://time.com/4486502/hillary-clinton-basket-of-deplorables-transcript/

Richard Lardner, J. M. (2023, June 12). *The Great Grift: How billions in COVID-19 relief aid was stolen or wasted*. Retrieved October 5, 2023, from AP: https://apnews.com/article/pandemic-fraud-waste-billions-small-business-labor-fb1d9a9eb24857efbe4611344311ae78

Ridley Scott, G. F. (Producer), Landesman, P. (Writer), & Landesman, P. (Director). (2015). *Concussion* [Motion Picture]. Sony Pictures Releasing.

Robins-Early, N. (2019, November 19). *These Key Witnesses Won't Appear At The Impeachment Hearings*. Retrieved October 5, 2023, from HUFFPOST: https://www.huffpost.com/entry/impeachment-hearings-bolton-mulvaney-trump_n_5dd4691be4b0fc53f20a529b

Sam Harris vs. Daniel Dennett. Free Will Debate. (2022, February 22). (S. Smith75, Compiler) Retrieved October 7, 2023, from https://www.youtube.com/watch?v=_J_9DKIAn48

Schwartz, M. L. (2011, March 7). Why Is It So Important to Be Right? *Psychology Today*. Retrieved October 4, 2023, from https://www.psychologytoday.com/intl/blog/shift-mind/201103/why-is-it-so-important-be-right

The American Heritage Dictionary . (2022). *wedge issue*. Retrieved October 5, 2023, from The American Heritage Dictionary: https://www.ahdictionary.com/word/search.html?q=wedge+issue

The Naked City. (1958-1963). *The Naked City*. ABC Television.

Therborn, G. (2020, October 28). *States, Nations, and Civilizations* . Retrieved October 6, 2023, from SpringerLink: https://link. springer.com/article/10.1007/s40647-020-00307-1#Sec9

Transformation Marketing Admin. (2016, January 25). *Politics, Ideology and Identity in Marketing*. Retrieved October 5, 2023, from transformation marketing : https://www.transformationmarketing.com/ politics-ideology-and-identity-in-marketing/

Turley, J. (2020, February 1). *How the House lost the witness battle along with impeachment*. Retrieved October 5, 2023, from THE HILL: https://thehill.com/opinion/judiciary/481015-how-the-house-lost-the-witness-battle-along-with-impeachment/

University of Minnesota. (n.d.). *Group Dynamics and Behavior*. Retrieved November 26, 2022, from University of Minnesota Libraries: https://open.lib.umn.edu/sociology/ chapter/6-2-group-dynamics-and-behavior/

Waxman, O. B. (2017, May 18). *Before Fox News, Roger Ailes Helped Get Richard Nixon Elected*. Retrieved August 17, 2024, from TIME: https://time.com/4784104/roger-ailes-richard-nixon/

Welch, A. (2015, December 24). *The real doctors behind "Concussion" movie speak out*. Retrieved October 5, 2023, from CBS News: https://www.cbsnews.com/news/ concussion-movie-doctors-speak-out-nfl-cte/

Wikipedia. (2024, March 8). *Decentralization*. Retrieved March 20, 2024, from Wikipedia: https://en.wikipedia.org/wiki/Decentralization

Wikipedia. (n.d.). *Black Lives Matter*. Retrieved October 5, 2023, from Wikipedia: https://en.wikipedia.org/wiki/Black_Lives_Matter

Wikipedia. (n.d.). *Diversity of tactics*. Retrieved October 5, 2023, from Wikipedia: https://en.wikipedia.org/wiki/Diversity_of_tactics

Wikipedia. (n.d.). *Echo chamber (media)*. Retrieved October 16, 2023, from Wikipedia: https://en.wikipedia.org/wiki/Echo_chamber_(media)

Wikipedia. (n.d.). *Impeachment inquiry against Donald Trump*. Retrieved October 5, 2023, from Wikipedia: https://en.wikipedia.org/wiki/Impeachment_inquiry_against_Donald_Trump

Wikipedia. (n.d.). *Recorded history*. Retrieved February 11, 2023, from Wikipedia: https://en.wikipedia.org/wiki/Recorded_history

Wikipedia. (n.d.). *Roger Ailes*. Retrieved October 4, 2023, from Wikipedia: https://en.wikipedia.org/wiki/Roger_Ailes

Williams, J. (2021, March 5). *Poll: Number who think George Floyd's death was murder down more than 20 percent*. Retrieved May 19, 2024, from THE HILL: https://thehill.com/blogs/blog-briefing-room/news/541788-percentage-that-thinks-george-floyd-death-was-murder-down-more/

Winkler, A. (2019). Corporate Person-hood and Constitutional Rights for Corporations. *New England Law Review, 54*(23). Retrieved October 5, 2023.

Zurier, S. (2021, March 3). *Hackers, nation-states target US black community to commit fraud, sow division.* Retrieved October 6, 2023, from SCMEDIA: https://www.scmagazine.com/news/cybercrime/hackers-nation-states-target-us-black-community-to-commit-fraud-sow-division

Glossary

Boondoggle: a wasteful or impractical project, often involving graft.[121]

Contentification: repurposing political speech and advocacy for media content.

Decentralized Movements: movements without centralized organization or authority where planning and decision-making is distributed to dispersed factions.[122]

Democracy: an organizational system permitting human diversities, including thought diversity, and resolving conflicts arising from such diversities through peaceful means and processes administered by the people or their elected representatives.

Dysfunctional Hyperpartisanship: promotion of or opposition to the particular interests of a political party, faction, group, tribe, person, ideology, or cause to an extent that communication or cooperation with those not similarly aligned is unworkable except in crises, where, nonetheless, collaboration may be impaired to an extent that undermines crisis management.

Echo Chamber: an environment or ecosystem in which participants encounter beliefs amplifying or reinforcing preexisting beliefs by communication and repetition inside a closed system insulated from rebuttal; or

---

121 "boondoggle," Merriam-Webster, accessed Feb. 6, 2024, https://www.merriam-webster.com/dictionary/boondoggle.

122 "Decentralization," Wikipedia, accessed Mar. 20, 2024, https://en.wikipedia.org/wiki/Decentralization.

a media construct designed to ensnare the public to prey and profit from insecurity by providing escape through the narcotic of self-induced affirmation. Sequestration from reality through intoxication by self-induced affirmation may reduce civility, cause radicalization, extremism, stagnation, or some combination thereof, depending on the personality or character of the ensnared.

Empathy: the action of understanding, being aware of, being sensitive to, and vicariously experiencing the feelings, thoughts, and experience of another of either the past or present without having the feelings, thoughts, and experience fully communicated in an objectively explicit manner, or:

the ability to emotionally understand what other people feel, see things from their point of view, and imagine yourself in their place. It's putting yourself in someone else's position and feeling what they're feeling.

Ex Post Facto Judgmentalism: judging people for their antecedent actions or creations based on contemporary mores.

Feedback: outputs of a system become future inputs to the same system.

Fundamental Unit: the fundamental unit of democracy is a person.

Hyperpartisanship: prejudicial allegiance or opposition to a political party, faction, group, tribe, person, ideology, or cause to an extent that substantially alters or determines the opinions, beliefs, ideals, principles, behavior, or personality of those so aligned.

Incorporation: using inherently nonpartisan or bipartisan issues, such as COVID, for partisan advantage or product differentiation.

Issue Subordination: using an issue to advance a partisan or revolutionary agenda instead of advancing the issue itself through collaboration and compromise.

Lateral Expansion: infiltration of partisanship and partisan content into traditionally nonpolitical sectors of society, increasing niches available to PPs.

Mutualism: interactions between organisms of two different species, in which each organism benefits from the interaction in some way.

Out-Group Homogeneity Effect: a bias of group dynamics causing people to perceive members of their own groups as individuals and diverse and members of other groups as indistinguishable and homogenous. Out-group members are seen as interchangeable or expendable and more likely to be stereotyped.

Partisanship: prejudicial allegiance or opposition to a political party, faction, group, tribe, person, ideology, or cause.

Partisan Warrior: intensely partisan legislator or government official.

Political Parties: conduits for cash flow between the private sector and political campaigns that institutionalize polarity and diminish individuality by restricting ideological freedom and diversity for the financial benefit of PI.

Procedural Extremism: using extreme methods such as destructive acts, violence, or terrorism to advocate for political change.

Professional Partisan: someone profiting from the presentation of partisan content or getting paid to create or ascertain partisan advantage. PPs work for the private sector.

Substantive Extremism: advocating for change including substantive policy that is extreme on its face, extreme in quantity, or extreme by time frame.

Wedge Issue: a sharply divisive political issue, especially one raised by a candidate or party in hopes of attracting or disaffecting a portion of an opponent's customary supporters.

Index

— O —

— P —

About the Author

ROBERT L. FOSTER has been a U.S. citizen and member of American society since 1962. His attention to the present subject matter developed subsequently. He believes those qualifications provide sufficient standing for authorship.

He worked for twelve years at a not-for-profit environmental organization where he collaborated with community groups, managed government relations and communications, and directed program activities. He regularly met with government officials and their staff at the local, state, and federal levels to advocate for reasonable policy change.

Nonetheless, Rob believes his four-year stint as a construction laborer provided the most solid foundation for egalitarian comprehension. He also worked as a courier and kitchen staff.

He studied environmental science as an undergraduate, earned a B.S. in Interdisciplinary Studies, and graduated law school *magna cum laude*. He practices Iyengar yoga and is currently working on his third book.

Contact Rob by visiting: https://robertlfosterauthor.wordpress.com.